This book contains a selection of Andy Goldsworthy's works which represent his art as a whole. The pieces range from his early works to the most recent, and from many locations around the world. Some of Goldsworthy's sculptures can be viewed in public spaces, and many are private commissions.

CONTEMPORARY ART

FROM CRESCENT MOON PUBLISHING

The Art of Andy Goldsworthy: Complete Works: Special Edition
by William Malpas

The Art of Andy Goldsworthy
by William Malpas

Andy Goldsworthy: Touching Nature
by William Malpas

Andy Goldsworthy In America
by William Malpas

Richard Long: The Art of Walking
by William Malpas

The Art of Richard Long: Complete Works: Special Edition
by William Malpas

Constantin Brancusi: Sculpting the Essence of Things
by James Pearson

Alison Wilding: The Embrace of Sculpture
by Susan Quinnell

Eric Gill: Nuptials of God
by Anthony Hoyland

*The Erotic Object: Sexuality in Sculpture
From Prehistory to the Present Day*
by Susan Quinnell

Minimal Art and Artists in the 1960s and After
by Laura Garrard

Land Art, Earthworks, Installations, Environments, Sculpture
by William Malpas

*Land Art: A Complete Guide to Landscape, Environmental,
Earthworks, Nature, Sculpture and Installation Art*
by William Malpas

Richard Long In Close-Up
by William Malpas

Land Art In Close-Up
by William Malpas

*Colourfield Painting: Minimal, Cool, Hard Edge, Serial
and Post-Painterly Abstract Art From the Sixties to the Present*
by Laura Garrard

Mark Rothko: The Art of Transcendence
by Julia Davis

Jasper Johns: Painting By Numbers
by L.M.. Poole

Brice Marden
by Laura Garrard

Frank Stella: American Abstract Artist: Special Edition
by James Pearson

Maurice Sendak and the Art of Children's Book Illustration
byL.M. Poole

The Erotic Object In Close-Up: Sexuality in Sculpture
From Prehistory to the Present Day
By Susan Quinnell

Sacred Gardens: The Garden in Myth, Religion and Art
by Jeremy Mark Robinson

Sex in Art: Pornography and Pleasure in Painting and Sculpture
by Cassidy Hughes

Postwar Art
by George Knighton

Andy Goldsworthy In Close-Up

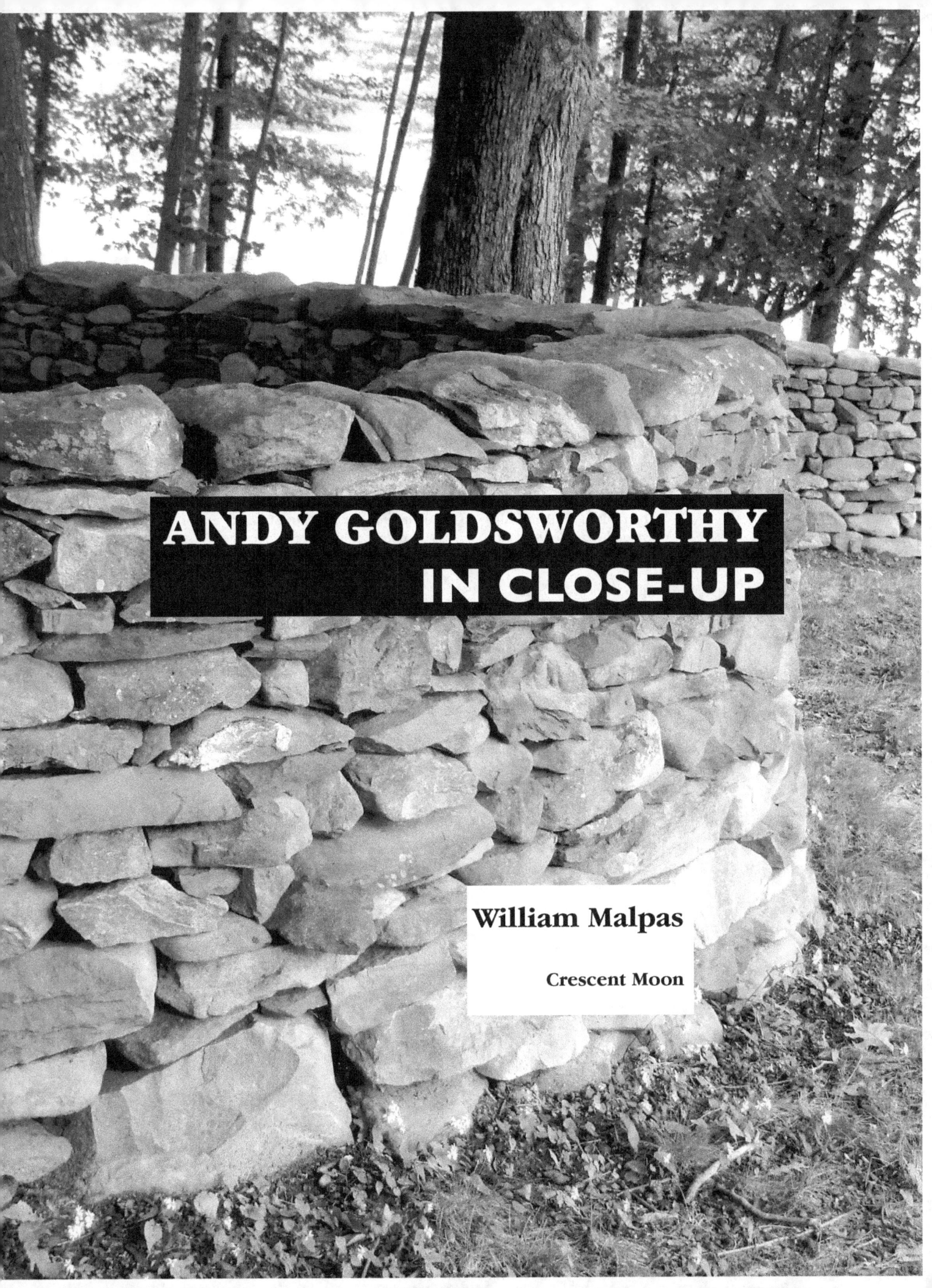

ANDY GOLDSWORTHY IN CLOSE-UP

William Malpas

Crescent Moon

CRESCENT MOON PUBLISHING
P.O. Box 393
Maidstone
Kent, ME14 5XU
United Kingdom

First published 2001. Second edition 2006. Third edition 2006.
Fourth edition 2010.
© William Malpas 2001, 2006, 2010.

Printed and bound in the U.S.A.
Set in Garamond Book 9 on 14pt.
Designed by Radiance Graphics.

British Library Cataloguing in Publication data

Malpas, William
Andy Goldsworthy In Close-Up - 3rd ed. - (Sculptors Series)
1. Goldsworthy, Andy, 1956 – Criticism and interpretation
2. Outdoor sculpture – Great Britain
I. Title

730. 9'2

ISBN-13 9781861712936 (Pbk)

Contents

Acknowledgements

Thanks to Andy Goldsworthy; Ellie Hall; Viking Press, London; Penguin, London; Thames & Hudson, London; Cameron Books, Moffat; Harry N. Abrams, New York; Richard Long; Michael Hue-Williams Gallery/ Albion, London; Anthony d'Offay Gallery, London; Henry Moore Centre for Sculpture, Leeds; Storm King Art Center, New York; Old Museum of Transport, Glasgow; Common Ground, London; Fabian Carlsson, London; Galerie Lelong, New York; Galerie S65, Aalst; Galerie Aline Vidal, Paris; Haines Gallery, San Francisco; the British Museum, London.

Thanks to the authors quoted and their publishers.

Illustrations by Andy Goldsworthy © Andy Goldsworthy.

Thanks to the copyright holders of the illustrations:
Musée d'Art Moderne de la Ville de Paris. Tate Modern, London. Royal Mail Group. John Weber Gallery, New York. Harry N. Abrams, New York. Michael Hue-Williams Gallery/ Albion, London. Henry Moore Centre for Sculpture, Leeds. Old Museum of Transport, Glasgow. Thames & Hudson, London. Harry N. Abrams, New York.

Andy Goldsworthy's art dealers: Fabian Carlsson, London; Galerie Lelong, New York; Galerie S65, Aalst; Haines Gallery, San Francisco; Springer und Winckler, Berlin; and Michael Hue-Williams Gallery/ Albion, London.

Abbreviations

ANDY GOLDSWORTHY

S   *Andy Goldsworthy: Stone*
AG   *Andy Goldsworthy,* 1990
HE   *Hand to Earth: Andy Goldsworthy, Sculpture, 1976-1990*
SS   *Snowballs in Summer Installation*
RSS   *Rain sun snow hail mist calm*
WH   *Winter Harvest*
MC   *Mountains and Coast, Autumn into Winter*
Sh   *Sheepfolds*
W   *Wood*
BS   *Black Stones*
TM   *Time Machine*
Wall   *Wall*
A   *Arch*
MS   *Midsummer Snowballs*
T   *Time*
RA   *Réfuges d'Art*
P   *Passage*
E   *Enclosure*

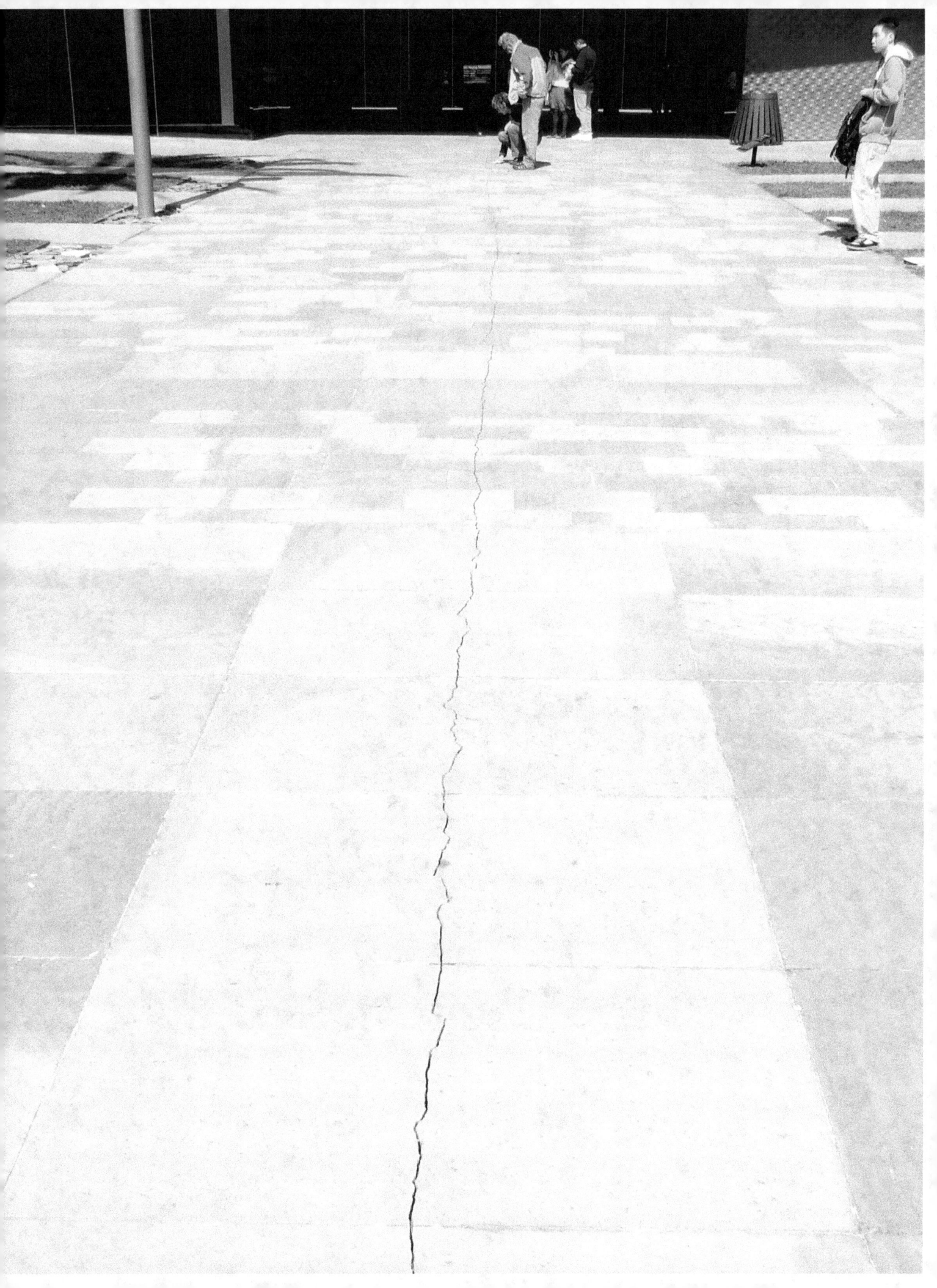

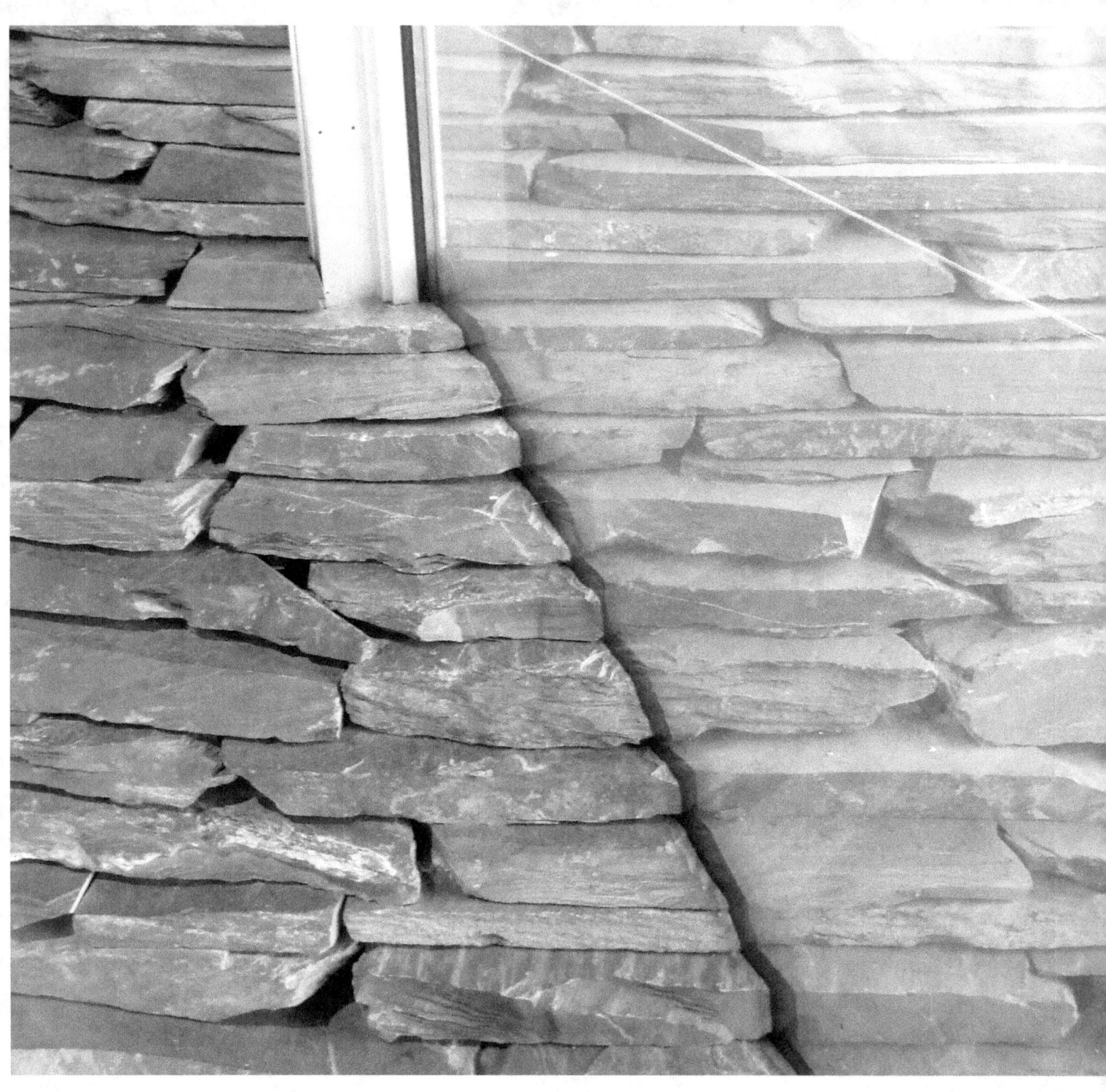

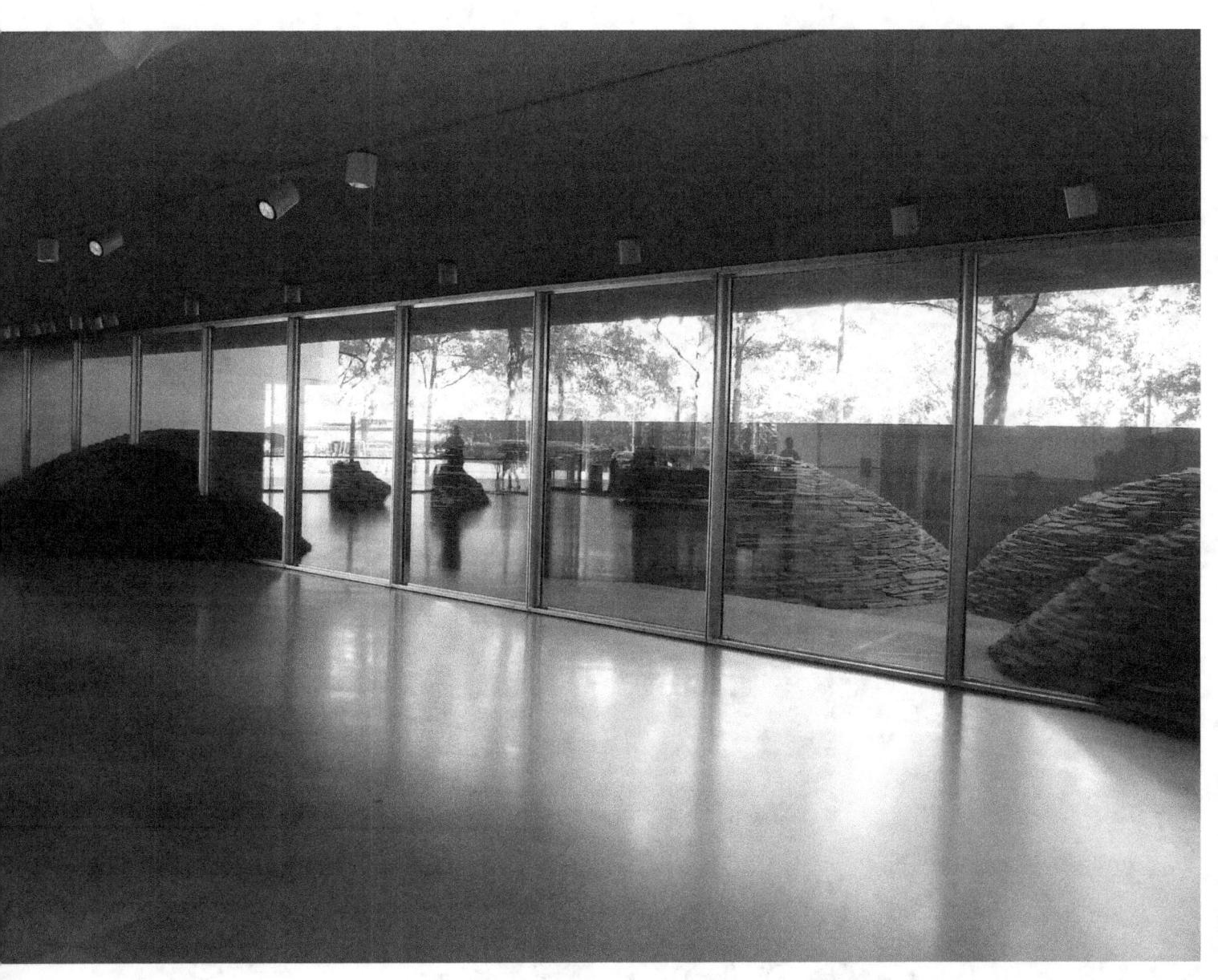

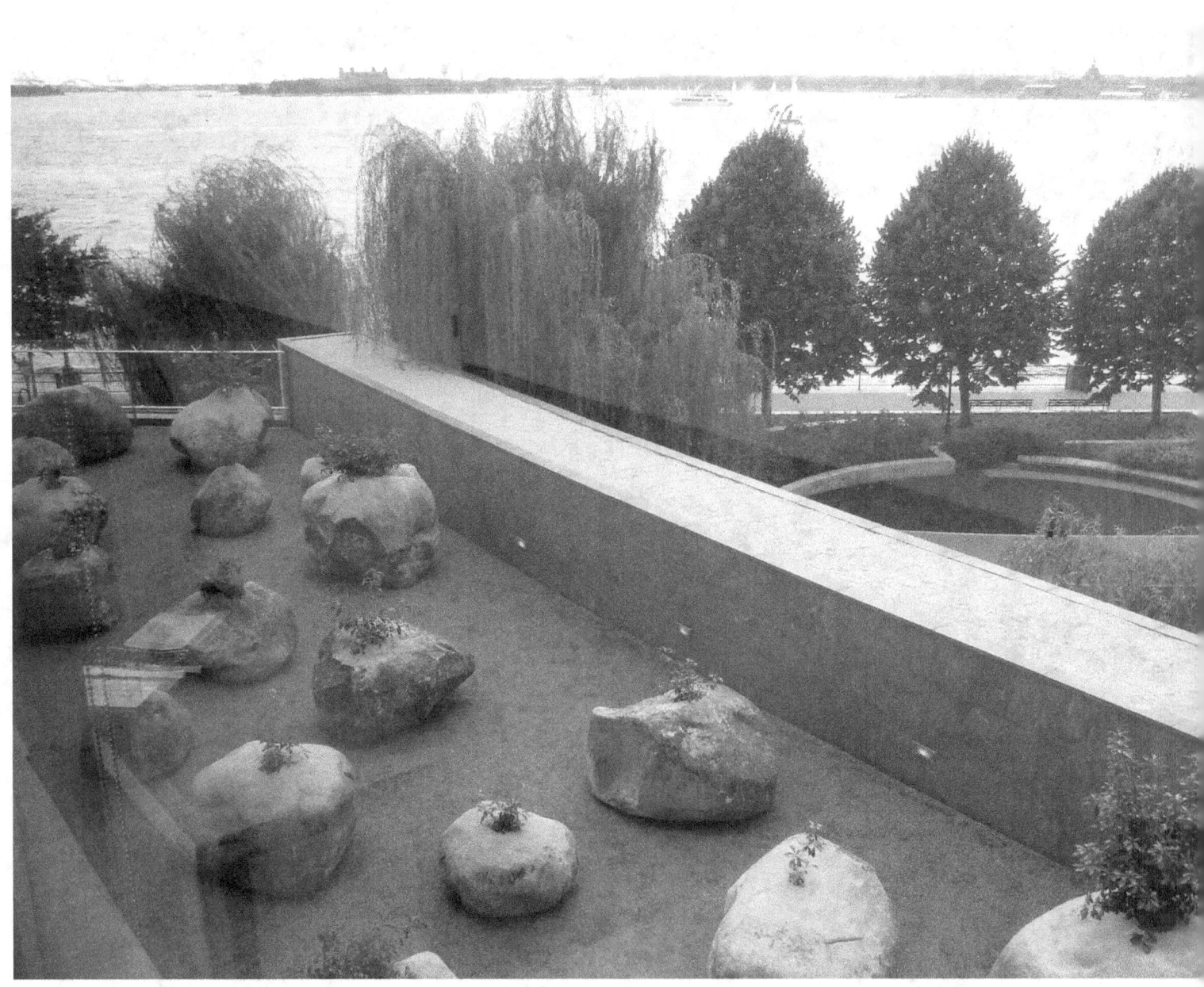

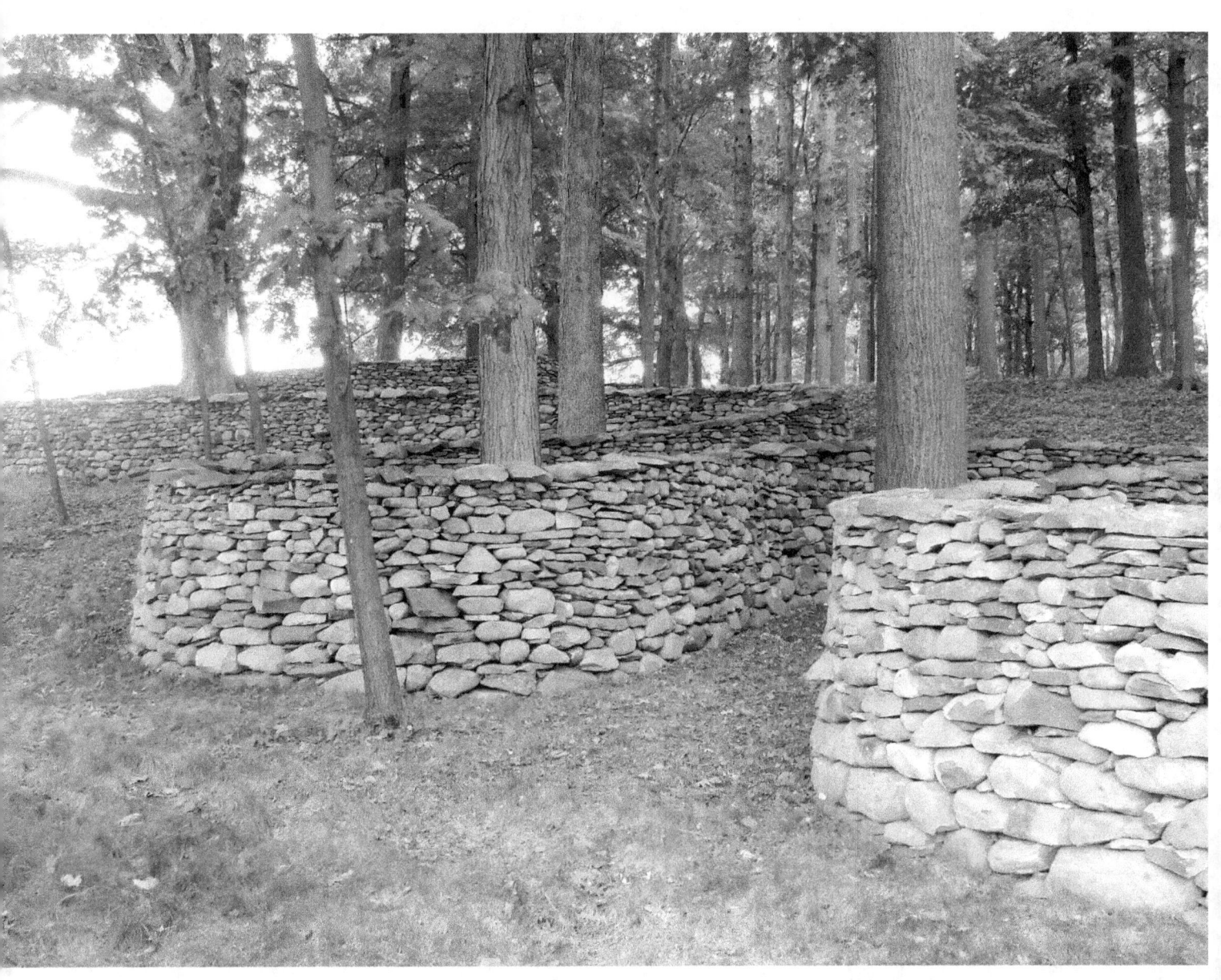

Introduction

Andy Goldsworthy was born in Cheshire in 1956. He studied at Harrogate High School, Bradford College of Art and Preston Polytechnic, where he took the BA Fine Art course, graduating in 1978. It was a regular art school education, where the art school ethics of liberalism, experimentation, art history lectures and the embrace of *avant garde* art prevailed.

Andrew Charles Goldsworthy has lived mainly in the North of the UK: Bentham and Illkley (Yorkshire), Brough (Cumbria) and Penpont (Dumfriesshire). Cumbria was 'very important for me during the two years I lived there' Goldsworthy said (*Sheepfolds,* 11). Many of Goldsworthy's site-specific works and commissions have been in the North: the giant maze and Lambton Earthwork (at County Durham, 1988-89), the Grizedale Forest site works (1984 onwards), residencies at Yorkshire Sculpture Park (1987-88), the Lake District National Park (1988), St Louis Arts Festival (1986); Quay Arts Centre, Isle of Wight (1987), and so on. Large Northern commissions included *Sidewinder* (1985) and *Seven Spires* (1984), *The Wall That Went For a Walk* (1991) at Grizedale, Cumbria, *Steel Cone* at Gateshead (1991), *Lambton Earthwork* and *Maze* in Durham (1988), *Stone Gathering* at Northumberland (1993) and *Enclosure* in Edinburgh (1990).

Andy Goldsworthy has created land art in Grise Fiord, the North Pole, in Japan, upstate New York, California, the US Mid-West, Castres, Digne, La Rochelle and Sidobre in France, the Australian outback, and in Haarlem,

Holland. The first work that Andy Goldsworthy sold was a bunch of photographs to the Arts Council (via Andrew Causey at North West Arts).

Andy Goldsworthy has had one-man shows in France, Japan, Holland, the US and the UK, and participated in groups shows in Italy, Germany, and the US. Among Goldsworthy's one-man exhibitions are the Serpentine Gallery (1981); *Evidence* (Coracle Press Gallery, 1985); *Rain sun snow hail mist calm* (1985, Henry Moore Centre for the Study of Sculpture, and touring); Kendall, Cumbria (1985); Lincoln (1986); Fabian Carlsson Gallery, London (1987); *Winter Harvest* (Scottish Arts Council, 1987); Gallery Takagi, Nagoya, Japan (1988); Yurakucho Asahi Gallery, Tokyo (1988); *Distant Thunder* (Liverpool, 1988); *Mountain and Coast, Autumn Into Winter* (Fabian Carlsson Gallery, 1988); *Touching North* (Edinburgh, 1989); *Black in Black* (1989); *Snowballs in Summer* (Glasgow, 1989); Ayr (1989); *Leaves* (Natural History Museum, 1989); *Garden Mountain* (Paris, 1990); *Photography as Sculpture* (Cardiff, 1990); *Drawings* (Paris, 1990); *Leaves* (1990-91); *Sand Leaves* (Chicago Arts Club, 1991); *Attitudes to Nature* (Ile de Vassivière, 1991); *Mid Winter Muster* (Adelaide, 1992); *Lowther Snowballs* (Aaslt, Belgium, 1992); *Stone Sky* (Belgium, 1992); *Snow and Ice Drawings and Throws* (Edinburgh and Paris, 1992); *Flow of Earth* (1992); *Hard Earth* (London, 1992); *California Project* (San Francisco, 1992); *Morecambe Bay Works* (Lancaster, 1993); *Wood Land* (Galerie Lelong, New York, 1993); *Two Autumns* (Japan, 1993); *Stone* (London, Paris, Cardiff, St Louis, San Francisco); *Breath of Earth* (San Jose Museum of Art, 1995); *Four Stones* (Aasalt, Belgium, 1995); *Black Stones, Red Pools* (New York, 1995); *Earth Memory* (Musée de Digne les Baines, 1995); *For the Night* (Green on Red Gallery, Dublin, 1995); *Sheepfolds* (Carlisle and St Albans, 1996); *Wood* (London, New York, San Francisco, 1996); *Sheepfolds* (Cumbria, 1997); *Cairns* (Digne, 1997-98); *Sheepfolds Drawings* (Cumbria, 1998); *Arche* (Montréal, 1998); *Être Nature* (Paris, 1998); *Installation und Photographer* (Berlin, 1998); photographs (Michael Hue-Williams, London, 1999-2000); *Two Rivers* (Santa Fe, New Mexico, 2000); *Digne Works* (2000); an important show at Storm King in upstate New York and Galerie Lelong (2000); *Fall Creek* (Cornell University, 2000); Austin Museum of Art (2003); *Stone Houses* (New York, 2004); *Roof* (National Gallery of Art, Washington, DC, 2005); *Stone Light Drawings* (Haines Gallery, San Francisco); *Arches* at the Frederick Meijer Sculpture Garden, Grand Rapids (MI); *Two Creeks – Andy Goldsworthy: Ephemeral Works in the Roaring Fork Valley* and *Stone River* in Aspen, Colorado (2006);

Yorkshire Sculpture Park (2007); *White Walls*, Galerie Lelong, New York (2007), and *Spire* (San Francisco, 2008-09).

A major retrospective, *Hand to Earth: Andy Goldsworthy: Sculpture: 1976-1990*, was held at the Henry Moore Centre for the Study of Sculpture, Leeds City Art Gallery: the show also travelled to the Royal Botanic Gardens in Edinburgh, Stedelijke Musea, Gouda and Centre Regional d'Art Contemporain Midi-Pyrenees in Toulouse. This show also produced the most useful and detailed publication to date on Goldsworthy's art (*Hand to Earth* – see bibliography). In 2000 Goldsworthy had a major show at London's Barbican Centre, with a book, *Time*, to coincide with the event.

Goldsworthy's work has appeared on TV in, as expected, Channel Four documentaries (*Alter Image,* 1987; *A Prospect of Rivers,* 1988; *Grizedale,* 1989); BBC 2's *The Late Show* (*Touching North,* 1989); an Arts Council film (*Two Autumns*); regional current affairs programmes (*London Plus* in 1986; Tokai TV and NHK TV in 1988; Tyne Tees TV in 1989), as well as a couple of Japanese broadcasts); also the ubiquitous appearances on Radio 4's dull arts show *Kaleidoscope* and Radio 3's arts interview slot, *Third Ear.* A half-hour BBC TV programme on Goldsworthy's *Sheepfolds* project was aired in 1997; short BBC films were shown in 1998; the *Rivers and Tides* documentary (2001); there was also a *Sheepfolds* exhibition at Michael Hue-Williams Gallery in London. Goldsworthy was shown driving around the North of England in overalls, building stone walls and discoursing to the camera on art and the landscape.

In the 1990s, Goldsworthy's art began to rise in popularity: the glossy coffee table book *Stone* became a bestseller (bear in mind it was priced at 35 UK pounds). In 1994 Goldsworthy took over some West End galleries with a large one-man show (*Herd of Arches,* also made for the Hathill Sculpture Foundation at Goodwood in Sussex). In 1995 he took part in an intriguing group show, *Time Machine,* at the British Museum and Museo Egizio, Turin, creating sculptures, along with Richard Deacon, Peter Randall-Page and others, in amongst the monumental statuary of the famous Egyptian Hall. Also in 1995, Goldsworthy designed a set of Royal Mail stamps (and later, in 2000).

Other Goldsworthy shows and projects of the 1990s and after included *Mid Winter Muster* in Australia (1991), sand and mulga branchworks; *Seven Holes* (for Greenpeace, 1991); *Black Spring* in Adelaide (1992); a large gateway at Hooke Park in Dorset (1987); various wall commissions (such as in New York, 1993, 1996 and 1997); various *Cones* (New York and Oxford, 1995); *Four Corner Stones* (Nice, 1993); *Rockfold* (Northumberland, 1993); *Fieldgate* (New York, 1993); clay holes and throws at Runnymede Sculpture Farm, California (1992); *Two Autumns* in Japan (1994); *Breath of Earth* at San Jose Museum of Art (1995); a clay installation (a hole) in L.A. (at the Getty Center for the Arts, 1997; later destroyed by a burst pipe); 'ice houses' and stick lines made in Alaska (1995); a slate cone and chamber for British Airways at their West Drayton HQ in 1998; cairns and 'refuges' at Digne les Bains in 1998; new groups of work at the National Museum of Scotland in Edinburgh (1998); the new *Wall* at Storm King (1998); another wall at Storm King (*Folded Wall*, 1999); a large stone arch in Montréal (1998); *Snowballs in Summer* in London (2000); *Three Cairns* (Des Moines Art Center, Iowa, 2002); *Night Path* and *Chalk Stones Trail*, installed in Sussex in 2002-03; *Garden of Stone*, a memorial for victims and survivors of the Holocaust, sited in Manhattan (2003); the *Stones House*s exhibited at Gotham's Met in 2004; London installations in 2005; and the slate domes (*Roof*) in the US capital in 2005.

Andy Goldsworthy's presence in America grew steadily with a series of exhibitions beginning with the Storm King *Wall* and show at the end of the millennium: Cornell University in 2000; the *Three Cairns* show and installations in 2002-03; Austin Museum in 2003; the *Garden of Stone* and *Stone Houses* in New York City in 2003-04; *Roof* in Washington in 2005; and a group show at the Yale Center for British Art in 2006. Goldsworthy continues to work in countries such as Japan, Australia, Canada and North America, France, but his home ground of Dumfriesshire in Scotland remains (at) the heart of his work.

Goldsworthy's private commission clients tend to opt for stone cairns/ cones, stone walls and stone arches. Goldsworthy has undertaken private commissions for clients such as British Airways, Royal Mail, Cirque du Soleil, Parnham Trust, Greenpeace, Coracle Press, and many private houses and collectors (many of the commissions are for outdoor works – in Penpont, Oxford, Lancashire, Cumbria, Wiltshire, Nice, New York state, California, etc). While many public museums and galleries around the globe have bought and exhibited Andy Goldsworthy's work, in his home country, the premier public art gallery, the Tate Gallery, has tended to avoid it (up until 2005). While many Young British Artists have exhibited at the Tate, as well as most of Goldsworthy's contemporaries (Nash, Long, Cragg, Gormley, Flanagan, Fulton *et al*), Goldsworthy has not. (However, Goldsworthy has had exhibitions at prestigious public sites such as the British Museum, the Barbican, the V & A, the Yorkshire Sculpture Park, and the Henry Moore Centre).

Goldsworthy's publications often favour stark (one-word) titles: *Rain sun snow hail mist calm, Hand to Earth, Wood, Stone, Garden Mountain, Time, Wall* and *Sheepfolds. Wood* is divided into chapters with single-word titles: "Earth", "Seed", "Leaf" and so on. These titles came from *Végétal*, the dance Goldsworthy collaborated on in 1995. The title, *Wood*, continued Goldsworthy's preference for single-word titles, begun in *Stone*. However, *Wood*, like *Time*, might as easily be called *Snow* or *Ice* or, again, *Stone*, because there are many works based mainly on those elements.

As a young student Goldsworthy spent much of his time outside college, working on the beaches at Morecambe and Heysham. Goldsworthy would go into college for one or two days a week, for the art history classes. This was not enough for the lecturers, who suggested that he spend more time in college, including attending life drawing classes. Little did Goldsworthy's lecturers know – that their errant student, who spent hours clambering around the muddy reaches of Heysham Head and Morecambe Bay instead of dutifully attending college classes, would one day become an artist of international renown, with exhibitions and commissions around the world. At the time (*circa* mid-1970s), Goldsworthy must have seemed just another crazy art student, pursuing his own wacky ideas. Hearing of his activities on the beach, Goldsworthy's tutors must have sighed heavily and put another stroke through the 'absent' column on his attendance record. Amazing to think that this artist-in-the-making would one day be exhibiting at the one of the most prestigious museums in the world (the British Museum) and designing Royal Mail stamps.

Andy Goldsworthy's wife, Judith Gregson, was a ceramics teacher (she studied at Ilkley Teacher Training College in Yorkshire, and later taught at St Aidan's, Carlisle, Cumbria. Her father, Barry Gregson, ran the Lunesdale Pottery, which Goldsworthy used to make art). Goldsworthy met her at Ilkley in late 1979; they were married on July 17, 1982 (at Caton, Lancashire). Goldsworthy has four children are Holly, Anna, Thomas and Jamie. Goldsworthy's wife Judith occasionally accompanied the artist on his art-making trips into the wilds (though not as often as his assistants). Sometimes his children would come too (as in New Mexico in 1999), but one would expect that children would eventually get bored if their dad spent hours constructing ridges with sand or pinning leaves together. Later, Goldsworthy lived with Tina Fiske, an art historian who came to Goldsworthy's studio to help catalogue his work. Goldsworthy's wife moved out with the children in 2004, and a divorce followed.

Judith Gregson's influence on Goldsworthy's art would probably include his use of ceramics (such as working with clay), and various collaborations. Judith Gregson has probably had all manner of influences on the artist difficult to estimate exactly (partners and spouses have an immense influence on many artists, but credit is seldom accorded. There are many famous cases, of course, of husbands, wives and lovers collaborating with their artist partners. I'd guess that Gregson's influence is substantial in many areas).

Goldsworthy's sculpture grew out of modernism and, in particular, 1960s art, the era of late Henry Moore, Robert Morris, Robert Smithson, Yves Klein, Michael Heizer, Anthony Caro, William Tucker, Tony Smith and Phillip King. It was the 1970s era of what Rosalind Krauss called 'expanded field' sculpture (Krauss, 1979). Krauss's 'expanded field' sculptors included Robert Irwin, Michael Heizer, Richard Serra, Walter de Maria, Sol LeWitt, Bruce Nauman, Alice Aycock, Mary Miss, Dennis Oppenheim, Nancy Holt, George Trakis, Richard Long, Hamish Fulton, Christo and Joel Shapiro.

There's not a lot of anger, or angst, or suffering, or self-doubt, or lust, or violence, or propaganda, or neurosis, or disturbance in Andy Goldsworthy's art. He's definitely not a haunted, tormented artist like Vincent van Gogh, or an aggressive, flamboyant self-publicist like Salvador Dali or Andy Warhol, or an ironic, fey commentator on the postmodern condition, like Jeff Koons or Robert Rauschenberg, or a stridently ideological combatant like Ana Mendieta or Karen Finley, or an in-your-face performance artist like Stuart Brisley or Annie Sprinkle, or a darling of the *avant garde* scene, like Yoko Ono or Matthew Barney. Goldsworthy is a much more modest artist, at least in his public persona, which may be one reason why he hasn't been fêted by the popular media in Britain like the YBAs (although he's had plenty of media exposure: there are now hundreds of articles and reviews of his work).

Andy Goldsworthy seems to be a somewhat gentle and sensitive artist: he stitches together leaves to form lines, often placed in water, or makes circular slabs of snow, or entwines twigs in an arc. He creates a delicate spiral of chestnut leaves, called *Autumn Horn*; he pins bright yellow dandelions on willowherb stalks in a circle, on bluebells; he builds lines and cairns of pebbles; he fashions hollow, circular structures, like igloos, from slate, leaves, driftwood and bracken; he makes long wavy ridges in Arizonan desert sand; he makes arches, globes, hollow spheres, slabs, spires, spirals and star-shapes out of snow and ice. Very impressive it all is. The sculptures made of sticks, for instance, stuck together in an arch, or a line, reflected in the mirror-like water of Derwent Water in Cumbria, are indeed wonderful. The sculptures exude tranquillity, an early morning calm (quite the opposite of another water work, Klaus Rinke's *Water Sculpture*, where a water canon blasted water over visitors as they approached the gallery). Or the globe made from oak leaves in various states of autumnal decay, superb (Dumfriesshire, 1985). Or the globe of sticks made in Fairfax, California (1995), set next to a sheltering tree. Or the globe made out of snow, and perched amidst some young trees, or the slabs of snow, set up in a line with slits cut in them. Goldsworthy says: 'I want an intimate physical involvement with the earth. I must touch' (in A. Causey, 1980). Touching is 'deeply important' (in *Aspects*, 1986). Only touching gives the artist the deep understanding of his materials and nature, he says.[1]

Andy Goldsworthy always speaks of the significance of the surrounding environment in his works. His 'sculptures' are as much about the surroundings in which they are situated, as about the 'sculptures' themselves. An exhibition indoors, in a gallery, is always going to be a problem, then. For the contemporary gallery, with its sparse settings, white-washed walls and trendy magazines and postcards, is a powerfully cultural environment. The contemporary gallery is not 'natural', it is not 'nature', it is not a place of mist, wind, skies and soil. No wonder, then, that earth artists such as Walter de Maria wanted to fill a whole gallery with dark soil, to bring nature into the contemporary gallery in a big way. Goldsworthy's shows are something of a disappointment, in one way, because the works have to breathe without their usual natural surroundings.

Andy Goldsworthy's writings are sometimes simple, matter-of-fact, and sometimes blunt – in a stubborn, Northern fashion. Goldsworthy comes across a rugged man of the wild, a 'whole earth man', ecologically sensitive, someone 'in touch' with nature, working with his bare hands, in boots and an anorak, often in Winter. There is a macho posturing to this (no doubt unintentional) in which the relationship with nature is 'funda-mental', 'raw', 'violent', 'intense'. Goldsworthy sees working in the hard conditions of Winter a challenge, a 'test of my commitment to the landscape'.[2] Goldsworthy speaks about being 'shocked' by small-scale natural events, about work suddenly becoming 'intense', about the 'raw energy' of colours. Goldsworthy's writings are marked by words such as 'powerful', 'wildness', 'deeper', 'rooted', 'flesh and bone', 'feeling', 'essential', 'sense', 'energy', 'touching' and 'essence' (these words are taken from one page of Goldsworthyan philosophy, in *Stone*, 6). All this talk of raw, powerful essence in nature recalls one poet in particular – Ted Hughes, the stolid Yorkshireman whose books (*River, Hawk in the Rain, Lupercal, Wodwo, Elmet*) are full of post-Hopkinsian evocations of wild shingle beaches, desolate moorland, ancient forests and craggy heights. If ever there a poetic equivalent of Goldsworthy's boulders, melting snowballs, slate cairns and red mud 'throws', it is Ted Hughes' verse. Another link is nature-man Mellors in *Lady Chatterley's Lover*, the no-nonsense outdoor man who is in fact a New Man, painfully sensitive and alive. The D.H. Lawrence connection with Andy Goldsworthy is emphasized by Goldsworthy himself: in *Stone* he quotes from Lawrence's *The Rainbow,* one of those euphoric, ithyphallic passages about the ecstasy of consummation in an arch. Lawrence's intensely poetic novel about three generations of a Midland family (his 'Brangwen-saga') is a strident inrush of energy into Goldsworthy's otherwise pedestrian prose in *Stone*. Goldsworthy might do better to simply use quotes from write like Locke and Lawrence, as he does in *Stone*.

Goldsworthy has written two short statements on the relation between photography and his sculpture (both entitled "The Photograph" [in *Hand to Earth*, 9, and *Stone*, 120]). Both mini-essays reveal a confusion and ambiguity regarding photography and art. Firstly, Goldsworthy states that the photograph simply records the work, in a direct, clear, routine fashion. His idea is to capture the work of art, which may change at every minute or moment. The photograph, Goldsworthy says, is the outcome of his art, not the initial reason for it. He quoted Yves Klein on his mono-chrome pictures. The photograph is necessary because it brings an outdoor experience into the context of the indoor gallery. The photo-graph, Goldsworthy says, is needed to communicate something of the outdoor work in an indoor context, even though '[m]uch of the energy is lost' (*Hand to Earth*, 9). This is all very well, this view of Goldsworthy's of the photograph as a necessary record of the outdoor work. In *Stone*'s "The Photograph" essay, the urge to 'capture' the sculpture out of doors becomes much more anxious. For example, if the film goes wrong, Goldsworthy feels disappointed – the photograph is needed to 'confirm the success or failure' of the work. Goldsworthy acknowledged in *Wood* that in making balanced columns of stones there were 'inevitably more failures than successes' (23). Throughout his career Goldsworthy must have known hundreds of failed artworks, and must have photographs of sculptures that didn't work. If the film doesn't come out, then the sculpture becomes 'dislocated – like a half-forgotten memory'. This statement shows just how important photography is for Goldsworthy. He is not only a sculptor or land/ earth artist: he is also very much a photographer. The photograph is needed by Goldsworthy to keep the work alive – for himself, in his memory: it 'completes' the work, rounds it off. And, crucially, photography shows the work to others. Photography is Goldsworthy's main means of displaying his outdoor work. Rarely are the general public invited to see Goldsworthy making a work of art: 'I am not a performer' he says (*Stone*, 120). The ephemeral, outdoor sculpture 'lies at the core of my art and its making must be kept private' (ib.).

Goldsworthy's photographs, too, are carefully framed so that they miss out the electricity pylons, the trash heaps, the kicked-in fences, the smashed bottles, the abandoned cars, the supermarket trolleys, that are a feature of every landscape everywhere in the British Isles, no matter how far from the throbbing centres of humanity. No matter where one goes, one confronts the marks of humans. Go wandering in the wildernesses of central Wales, one of the least densely populated places in the British Isles, and one'll find litter. One may be able to purchase a few miles between oneself and the nearest road, so that the sound of cars will fade into the susurrus of the wind. But the marks of humanity are never far away.

Goldsworthy's photographs present an idealized world, veritably the pastoral world of ancient times. Goldsworthy's Arcadia, though, is definitely a Northern European pastoral realm, not the Southern, Mediterranean paradise of satyrs, shepherdesses, gods and wild animals. Goldsworthy's 'pastoral sublime', to use the phrase applied to a category of J.M.W. Turner's works, is a Northern European realm, very much in the tradition of Turner's paintings of the Alps, with lowering, gloomy skies, raging wind, snow-capped mountains and mossy river-banks. John Martin, Thomas Girtin, John Sell Cotman, John Constable and J.M.W. Turner made many paintings of the landscapes Goldsworthy's works in. Apart from Australia and Japan, Goldsworthy's art centres around cold, rain-sodden, Northern landscapes. True, there is much sunlight in his photographs of Australia, photographs that evoke the colonial view of the outback as a rugged, inhospitable place where the white people sit around camp fires. Goldsworthy's Japan is a more sublime, rarefied place, though it is still rough and distinctly non-human. He photographs his sculptures often looking down on them, so the surrounding landscape is not seen. He edits out unsightly buildings or roads, but art always has involved much more editing than many artists would admit. Goldsworthy knows that what one leaves out of a work is as important as what one puts in.

Much of Andy Goldsworthy's art is about and made from ice and snow. Goldsworthy is distinctly a 'Northern' artist, who makes work in landscapes that come out of the 'Celtic fringe', out of the sort of landscapes that Celtic culture exalts: misty, rocky hillscapes; sodden Autumnal forest floors knee-deep with leaves; wild snowscapes; cold, clear streams banked with large mossy boulders; still lakes at dawn. Goldsworthy's landscapes could have the Lady of Shallot, Lancelot or King Arthur riding through them without altering anything. They are the landscapes of Merlin, Taleissin and Morgan Le Fay, of Welsh legends such as *The Mabinogion*, of historical events shrouded in mists, of historical figures such as Robert the Bruce, Owen Glendower, King Edward, Macbeth, Boadiccea. The places associated with Goldsworthy – his studio at Penpont, near Scaur Water in Dumfriesshire, Carlisle, Yorkshire Sculpture Park, Grizedale in Cumbria, Leeds, Leadgate in Durham – are all Northern British sites. And the stereotypes of Britain's North – grimy towns, rain, bleak moors, gloomy skies, grim humour, down to Earth and no-nonsense attitudes – all chime with Goldsworthy's sculpture.

The biting cold maybe gives him a sense of heroism, for suffering invariably enhances a work (as in, 'this work was difficult, made under adverse conditions'). After all, Goldsworthy is not an artist who makes work in the 'comfort' of a home or studio. No: he goes out into the wilderness, where it can be uncomfortable and difficult. He claims to know the landscape around his studio in Penpont, Scotland, very well, so that the snow does not hide the world: 'I know what lies under the snow – I know the earth beneath' (*Hand to Earth*). Always Goldsworthy stresses the intimate relationship he has with nature. Part of this intimacy comes from returning to the same patch of land again and again. Through successive visits, layers of touch and meaning in the landscape are uncovered by the artist. The artist returning to the same space always works in time as well as space, for s/he creates a personal history of that place. S/he works with her former selves, as well as in the present – with the artist and ideas she had two years ago, ten years ago, twenty years ago.

Some places I return to over and over again, going deeper – a relationship, made in layers over a long time. (*Andy Goldsworthy*)

The personal dimension is important in Goldsworthy's work. His work is not 'impersonal' in the sense that it could be made 'anywhere'. It is, like most land art, always a product of a relationship between an artist and a particular place. Making the art itself, the doing of it, is important for Goldsworthy. So that when people ask the eternal question, but is it art?, he retorts, well, he doesn't know and doesn't care, but 'it is important and necessary for me as a person.'[3]

Sceptics can claim that many of Goldsworthy's sculptures gain much of their fire from their situation in wilderness landscapes. They would be right. Although Goldsworthy states that many of his sculptures are made in built-up areas, areas of dense population and human activity, a glance through any Goldsworthy book or a visit to a Goldsworthy show will reveal the large proportion of wilderness or rural landscapes in his art. He expunges all the litter, houses, telegraph poles, tower blocks, cars and roads from his photographs, and presents lush streams, moorland, forests and hillsides. There are no people at all in his art, except Goldsworthy himself, who is sometimes seen, with his beard, sweater and jeans, making a piece of art. In this sense, Goldsworthy's work is not at all figurative – but neither is it 'abstract', in the Mark Rothko or Piet Mondrian sense, for real, recognisable objects appear in his work. This is one of the reasons for the growing popularity of his work: apart from the Eighties ecological/ Green movement, and the accessible, decorative quality of his work, it is thoroughly countrified and rural, quite in keeping with primæval desires for escape into the country, that nostalgia for nature that lies behind the pastoral and landscape tradition in Britain.

Goldsworthy speaks as poets do of the spirit of place, where the place itself becomes as important as the object: 'the work is the place', Goldsworthy says (*Stone*, 6). Any number of artworks gain much from their setting, from Greek temples to a Caravaggio discovered in a dark, incense-smoky church in a back-street in Rome. For the land or earth artist, of course the place becomes (identical with) the work. In the typical Goldsworthy work, though, there is usually some object at the centre of the landscape or the photograph. There is usually a rock covered in leaves, a red pool, a slate cairn in the centre. At first glance, the object seems to be the subject of the artwork and the focus for the eye. Not so: the surroundings are just as important, and these pastoral landscapes help to sell Goldsworthy's art just as much as the woven grass stalks or the sticks wrapped around a boulder. Goldsworthy's skill is not just to 'touch nature' (whatever that means) but to touch the chords of desire for nature in people. Goldsworthy's art is popular partly because of this powerful desire among Western audiences for contact with the natural world, an appetite which is manifested in natural history programmes on television, in jaunts to zoos, gardens, windswept hillside car lots, in Constable, van Gogh and Monet posters and prints, in gardening magazines and gardening centres and plants in the house, in the popularity of rural novels by George Eliot, Thomas Hardy and Emily Brontë. The eco/ Green movement (and its associated movements in pagan/ New Age/ road and animal activism) taps into this nostalgic love of an urban-centred culture for all things 'natural'.[4] The natural world seems to be green and life-giving and untarnished by the complexities of modern life. The natural world, which is Goldsworthy's world, is a place of leaves, rivers, animals and stones, a place seemingly devoid of people, the ones who fuck things up, who complicate things, who introduce the concepts and realities of neurosis, confusion, waste, violence, consumption and politics into the 'pure' natural world.[5] It's not like that at all, but these eco/ Green/ pastoral feelings are powerful. Goldsworthy's art, like the pastoral novels of Eliot and Hardy, like Green politics or the money-spinning popularity of van Gogh and Monet, trades on the desires for an earlier, ancient Paradise, a time when things were simpler, richer, deeper. This is the 'green world' of childhood, a time of playfulness and living close to the Earth, enjoying the seasons passionately but also freely, in a relaxed manner. In mythology, it is the 'Golden Age', *il illo tempore, ab origine*, in the Creation era, at the origin of the world, before the Fall of Adam and Eve into sin, a time before oedipal anxiety and patriarchal psychosis, a Gaia time, a whole earth time, all 'natural' and recycled and vegetarian, a holistic time, a time of social unity, when everyone felt as one in communities and loved each other, a time of maternal bliss, when women were nurturing Mother Goddesses and men could be sweetly dreaming babies without feeling embarrassed. Goldsworthy's art books, commissions and shows trade on this pastoral imagery and desire: they allow stressed, confused, overworked and neurotic city dwellers time out from staring at the control screens (TV, computers, phones) of the megavisual world, encouraging a little day-dreaming into the soft greens and greys of wild moorlands. Goldsworthy's art may be increasingly successful because it reminds people that, yes, one does love nature after all: one came from it, one'll go back into it, in the end, in death.

One of the problems Goldsworthy's art addresses head on is the age-old relation between the 'real world' and art, between objects as they are in the everyday world, and objects as they are represented in art. Goldsworthy makes the viewer look again at nature: not just at the beauty of it, but at the multitudinous variety of forms in nature. His sculpture is a poetry of natural forms, in which notions of 'representation' are side-stepped, because he uses things 'as themselves' (the use of photography, though, sees a swift return of confusions over the politics of representation). The snowball in *Snowballs in Summer* (1989 and 2000) is not plastic masquerading as a snowball, but a real snowball. Similarly, the twigs and stalks and needles and pebbles folded into the snowballs are real. What's amazing is the actuality of nature: the variety of forms, the way the branches twist, for instance. Goldsworthy would have the viewer look closely at nature again. By using 'real' objects, Goldsworthy aims to demolish notions of representation and mediation. Instead of a picture of snow, one has in Goldsworthy's art snow itself; rather than paint pebbles, or sculpt them in bronze, Goldsworthy uses real pebbles.

Of course, there are problems with using objects as objects – Marcel Duchamp with his readymades confronted this problem. The problem is partly one of context: for, placed in a museum, so obviously as items to be studied, the natural forms become art. The snowballs may not be on pedestals, but they are perceived as art objects. The leaf sculptures are more obviously works of art, set on shelves, or photographed against paper backdrops, as bottles of perfume or Swiss watches are photographed for adverts. If one is looking at a Goldsworthy sculpture in a book or a gallery, one is already anchored in a gallery/ art/ æsthetic mode of viewing. If Goldsworthy's sculptures are in a gallery, one sees them as art (and a particular kind of Western, bourgeois art, the sort of art that is exhibited in Western, bourgeois galleries).

Carl Andre explored the relation between real and represented objects with his controversial pile of bricks. The sculpture was 'controversial' because the general public (whoever they are) perceived, via the media, that Andre had simply stuck some bricks into a gallery. Or rather, that taxpayer's money had been used to purchase Andre's bricks. A pile of bricks on a building site is... a pile of bricks. A pile of bricks in an art gallery is... sculpture. Context is everything here. This is what Carl Andre explored, whether consciously or not: the *response*, affected by so much of culture, socialization, physical context, education, and so on, makes objects sculptures. People make art. A leaf simply exists, but if someone puts it in a gallery or an art book, it becomes art (as well as remaining a leaf). If people think something is art, then it's art, as Donald Judd said.

Land artists such as Andy Goldsworthy use their hands, primarily, as their means of making art. Goldsworthy does not go out into the landscape with anything, except a knife.[6] Perhaps he should, to be really purist, make do without even a knife? Anyway, he *does* really go out into the landscape with 'tools' – the camera not least among them (also spare film too, maybe an extra lens filter or two, and a tripod). Without that camera, the viewer wouldn't know about many of his works. Ditto with all land artists. Without the camera, their work is 'lost'. That is, not really 'lost', but the camera means the viewer too can share in the work. Without the camera, the viewer would have to rely on written texts, perhaps, as a means of 'recording' artworks. Photography is also 'a way of communicating' Goldsworthy told an interviewer, 'and we wouldn't be sitting here if I didn't take the photographs.'[7] Here Goldsworthy admits that without the photographs there would be not much communicating going on with his art: it needs photography to work. But, as one can see, Goldsworthy and other land artists are not writers. Indeed, their writings are, well, often in note form, designed as a 'record' for themselves, or as notes towards some artwork. While there have been any number of painters and sculptors who were also good writers who provided many insights – Leonardo da Vinci, Ad Reinhardt, Vincent van Gogh, Donald Judd – Goldsworthy is not among them. So, relying on photographs, the viewer gets to find out about many works of land art that might otherwise have never known. The camera is thus an essential 'tool' for the land artist. Goldsworthy also goes out with many other invisible tools of his craft – his awareness of land art, his education, his knowledge of other sculptors and art history, his memory of previous works, and so on. No artist works alone, culturally. Goldsworthy's art, like all land art, works within a culture and tradition and history of postwar art. Tracing the links with Minimalism and Conceptualism, for instance, is only one way of looking at Goldsworthy's art.

Intensity is not perhaps a word one would apply to Goldsworthy's sculpture. His art seems so soft, so tenderly in tune with nature, so ecologically driven. Those delicate leafworks, they are not 'intense', surely? Yet the very nature of Goldsworthy's methodology, the way he goes out into the wilderness, to be alone, to work from dawn to dusk, speaks of an intense, creative personality. Further, those towers and arches which collapse are in fact very intense works. As Goldsworthy says, he likes to draw things out to an extreme point. In this he is intense, and is an archetypal Romantic modernist, someone who, like Rothko or Pollock, knew one has to go to extremes, artistically, to get results. It's not the same way of working for everybody. But for some artists, this aspect of intensity is crucial, and is bound up with the utter importance of solitude, concentration, purity and depth of feeling.

Snowballs in Summer [wrote Goldsworthy in the catalogue] is an exploration of snow and an expression of my understanding and feelings gathered over the years I have worked with it. It will bring together qualities of time, space, movement, noise, colour and texture forming often the unpredictable that makes up the character of snow.[8]

Andy Goldsworthy tries different methods of actualizing or exploring the space around and within stones, the light and weather around, the 'window' that's opened into their secret nature (*Hand to Earth*, 167). Sometimes he covers a boulder completely in bark, or branches (as at Lake Tahoe, 1992 [*Stone*, 7-9]). A boulder wrapped in small sheets of ice becomes a kinetic sculpture as the ice melts and slips off (*Stone*, 13). 'A good work is the result of being in the right place at the right time with the right material' said Goldsworthy.[9]

Time was central to Goldsworthy's dance collaboration. In 1995 the Ballet Atlantique-Regine Chopinot company put on a performance called *Végétal* at La Rochelle. *Végétal* consisted of five sections: earth, seed, root, branch and leaf. For the backdrop Goldsworthy made a wall drawing from ferns and bracken stuck on with rabbit skin glue in serpentine patterns. The ballet featured Goldsworthy's installations, which included sculptures (using stones, sticks, leaves and earth) that were built and taken down by the dancers. Goldsworthy explained that collaborating on a dance work was quite natural for him, because the body plays such a large part in making sculpture: 'the body as the sculpture. I've always seen myself as an object in the work; that I'm nature too' (*Wood*, 7). Goldsworthy had already used the body in many works – the various 'throws', for example, or the works made by lying on the ground during rain or snow. *Végétal* evoked the standard Goldsworthyan themes of growth and decay, of change and cycles, of time, of boundaries and breathing. Régine Chopinot danced around the circumference of the stage, suggesting the passage of time. *Végétal* began with a black hole and red earth spread on the stage. The dancers next built a single stone column. The combination of column and hole inevitably has sexual connections: phallus and vagina, masculine and feminine, *yang* and *yin*, and so on. The context of the phallic column and womb-like hole in a dance all about growth and cycles enhances the eroticism, as does having the dancers interact with each other in a 'germination dance'. This part of the dance is entitled 'Seed'. Goldsworthy spoke of stones and seeds in terms of phallic tumescence and orgasmic release: 'I found an energy in stone that can best be described as a seed that becomes taut as it ripens – often needing only the slightest of touch to make it explode and scatter its parts' (*Wood,* 23). Feminists might criticize the insistence on heterosexual relationships and gender stereotypes in *Végétal,* the way the dancers, for example, are often put together in male and female couples. *Végétal* continued in the 'Branch' section with ten dancers moving in circles around two dancers in the centre building a stick dome. This was then dismantled and the dancers made a large ring with the sticks. In the last part, 'Leaf', the dancers act like leaves, spinning and falling. 'The tree is bare, loses its foliage, turns back within itself. Full cycle' wrote Goldsworthy (*Wood,* 11). A mound of leaves was placed centre-stage. The dancers performed 'leaf throws'.

The selection of Andy Goldsworthy's works included here are fairly representative of his art as a whole. The pieces range from his early works to the most recent, and from many locations around the world. Some of Goldsworthy's sculptures can be viewed in public spaces (some of them have decayed or collapsed, however – *The wall that went for a walk* and *Seven Spires,* for example).

This paperback edition has updated the text of the hardback edition.

Notes

1. Goldsworthy, *The Third Ear*, June, 1989, *Hand to Earth*, 165.
2. Goldsworthy, interview with T. Friedman, *Third Ear*, 1989 in *Hand to Earth*, 166.
3. Goldsworthy, interview, 9 December 1987, in *Hand to Earth*, 163.
4. 'Urban living has always tended to produce a sentimental view of nature' wrote John Berger (*The White Bird: Writings by John Berger*, London, 1988, 7).
5. 'Nature for me is the clearest path to discover – *uncluttered by personalities* or associations – *it just is*' says Goldsworthy in a telling statement (my emphasis, sketch-book no., 19, 1988, *Hand to Earth*, 150).
6. Andrew Causey, "Environmental Sculptures", in *Hand to Earth*, 128.
7. Goldsworthy, *Third Ear*, BBC Radio 3, 30 June, 1989, in *Hand to Earth*, 168.
8. *Snowballs in Summer Installation*, Glasgow District Council Festivals Office, 1989.
9. J. Beardsley, 1984, 134.

Andy Goldsworthy In Close-Up

Leafworks (1989)

It is the leafworks that are the most colourful of Andy Goldsworthy's sculptures. What the leaf sculptures show is how beautiful the colours of nature are: Goldsworthy shows the viewer these subtle colours by contrasting one leaf with another. *Maple patch* grouped the red/ orange/ yellow of Japanese maple leaves together; *Poppy leave*s contrasted the red poppy leaves against the mid-green of an elderberry bush; a Stone Wood sculpture of 1992 consisted of poppy leaves wrapped around a hazel branch, the red constrasting vividly with the wet green leaves; *Dock Leaves* interwove red leaves in green grass stalks. Two sycamore leafworks of 1980 and 1981 are very simple: a leaf black from cow shit is placed against pale Autumn leaves; another leaf, bleached white, is set down on a bed of dark leaves. He pins together two colours of sycamore leaves (sycamore is a favourite Goldsworthy medium) in *Sycamore leaf sections* (1988), and hangs the line of leaves from a tree. Shot with the sun behind them, the photograph of the leaves shows them glowing green and gold, the two classic colours of poetry and alchemy. The Autumnal colours of course connote nostalgia, decadence, sensuality, Romanticism, time passing, the decay of the year, and so on, all those things John Keats wrote about in his 'Ode: To Autumn', and in a billion other poets. Goldsworthy's aim in the leaf pieces, though, draws attention to the fragility and delicacy of leaves, as well as their strength and function. A leaf, after all, is a complex biological factory, so the natural scientists say. 'There is a whole world in a single leaf' says Goldsworthy.[1] Goldsworthy's leafworks do not have a scientific agenda. Rather, they celebrate the presence of leaves, the being-in-the-world of leaves, so to speak.

1. Goldsworthy, quoted in Paul Nesbit: "Leafworks", in *Hand to Earth*, 108.

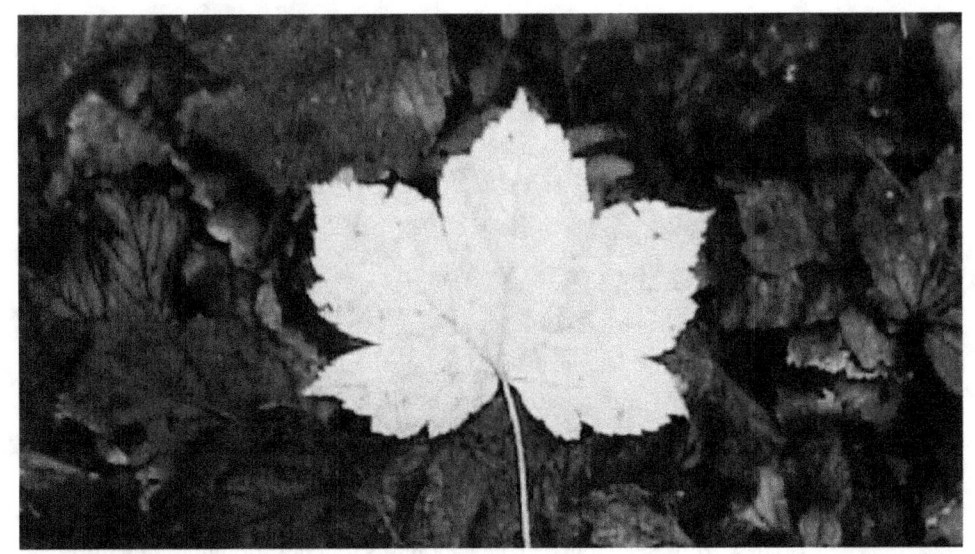

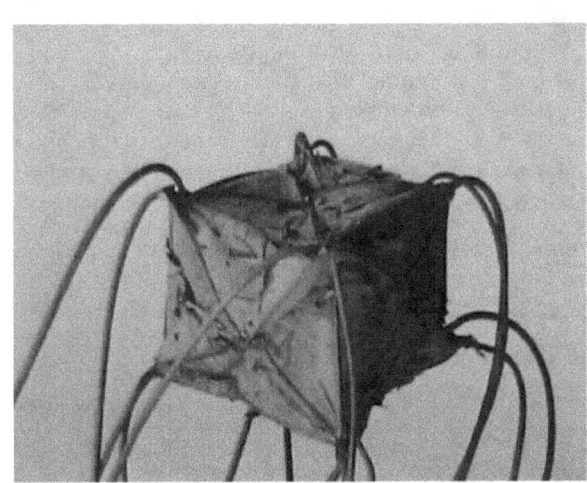

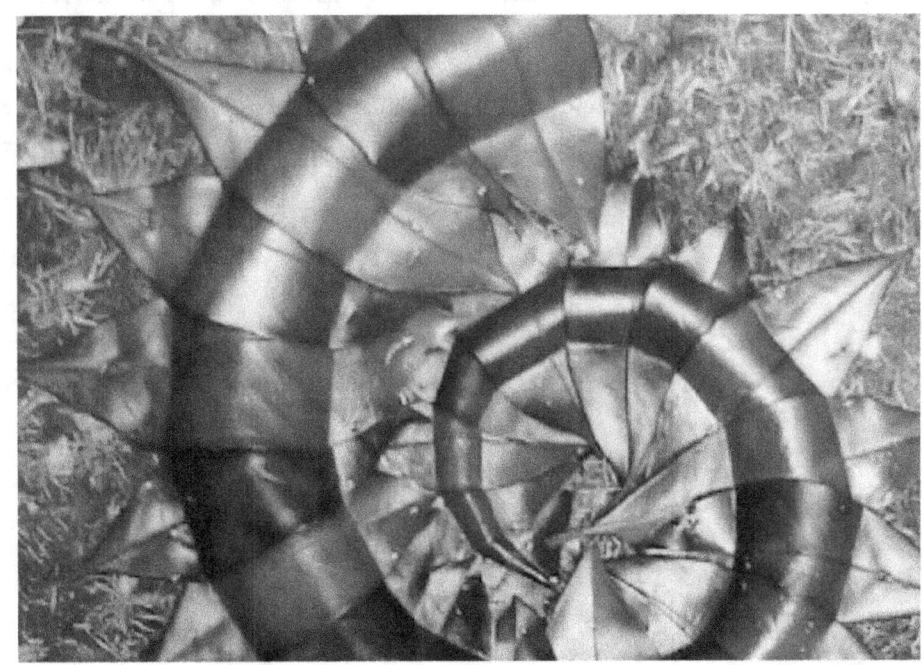

Lake Pieces (1988)

Andy Goldsworthy says he is not against long-term art: '[t]hat art should be permanent or impermanent is not the issue. Transience in my work reflects what I find in nature and should not be confused with an attitude towards art generally. I have never been against the well-made or long-lasting.' Domination and penetration. These are familiar terms describing patriarchal actions or constructions or ideologies used by feminists. Is Goldsworthy, seemingly so delicate in his touches, dominating nature? He says he isn't:

> By working large, I am not trying to dominate nature. If people feel small in relation to a work, they should not assume that there is an intention to make nature itself small. (*Andy Goldsworthy*)

Yet, clearly, Goldsworthy, and the American land artists (Heizer, de Maria, Smithson, Simonds, Aycock), do dominate nature. James Turrell's *Roden Crater* or Heizer's gigantic *Double Negative* will clearly be around for a long time, unless someone or something destroys them. Goldsworthy's stone pieces, too, may indeed stay around for a while. There is a sense of gloating when Goldsworthy says '[f]ourteen years ago I made a line of stones in Morecambe Bay. It is still there, buried under the sand, unseen. All my work still exists, in some form.'

Daring not to change or affect nature, land artists do just that, all the time. They 'interact' with nature, but their 'interactions', however small scale, can't help changing nature. 'I like the idea of using the land without possessing it' says Richard Long, ever the idealist.[1] Goldsworthy's aim is to 'touch' something in nature, the essence of nature itself, and the identification of himself within nature.[2] Thus, about the 'lake pieces', the stick/ stalk sculptures he was commissioned to do in the Lake District, he says: 'I felt I really got through in the lake pieces. I had touched it, and understood it' (B. Redhead, 19).

1. Richard Long, in *Words After the Fact*, in Fuchs, 236.
2. 'Goldsworthy's pieces dig at the roots of our relationship with nature, he is conducting an interrogative process with the fundamentals of our world - water, stone, earth, growing things and - latterly, in his work with volcanic rock and 'fired' stones - fire.' Peter Whitaker, "Andy Goldsworthy", *London Magazine*, January, 1995, 34, 10, 109.

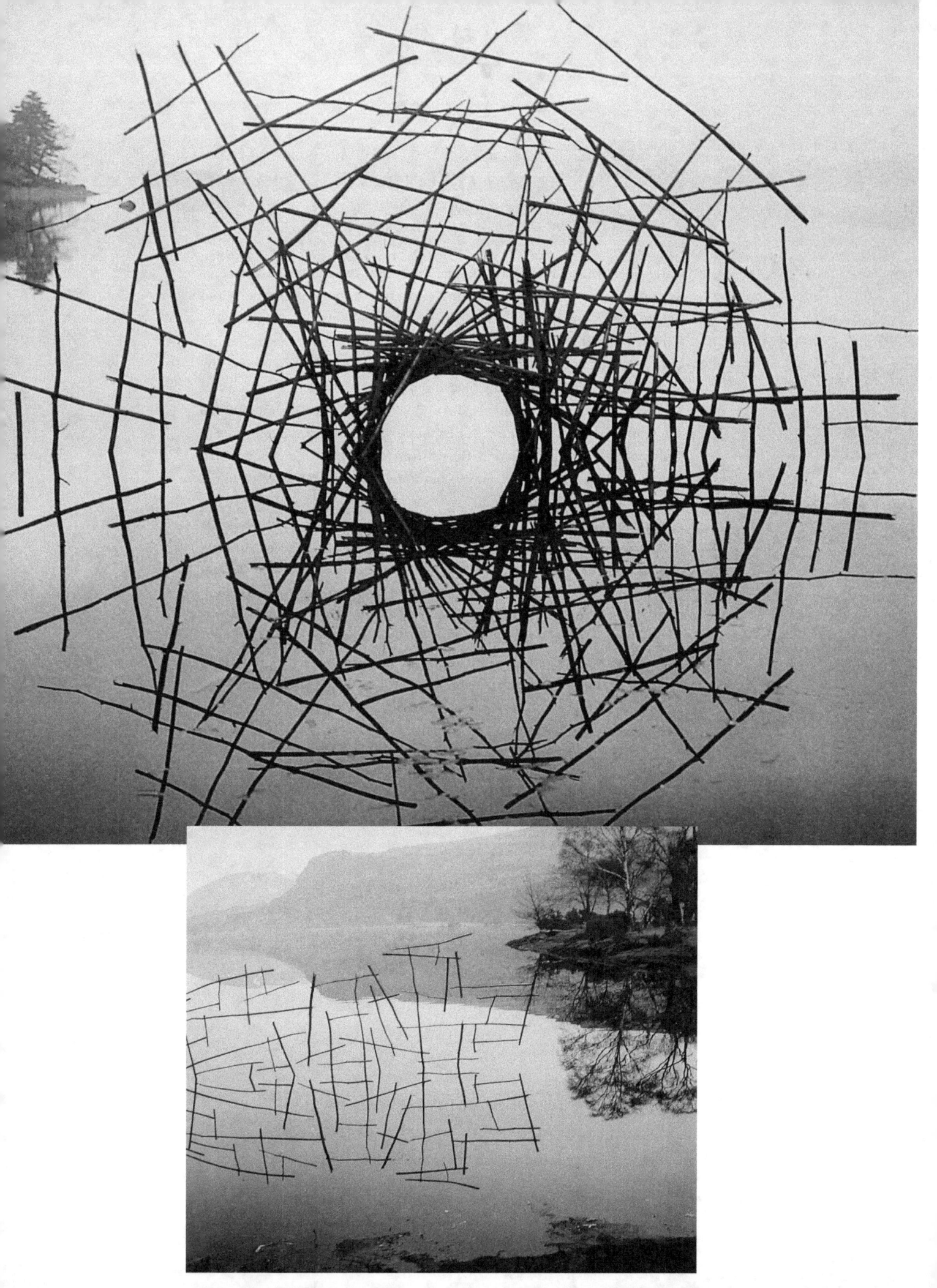

Leaf Line (1985)

Andy Goldsworthy is 'decorative', definitely, but the colours and patterns are taken from nature: the seemingly 'pretty' colours of bluebells and dandelions, of maple leaves and the Australian outback, are colours already present in nature: they've been there for millions of years. Rather than finding colour 'decorative', for Goldsworthy it is 'raw with energy' (*Stone,* 6). When Goldsworthy placed red Japanese maple leaves in water their colour 'becomes so intense' he said.[1] Many of his works are built on the 'patterns' found in nature. For example, there are many sculptures of Goldsworthy's which create patterns from leaves or stones which have changed colour. He makes lines of bramble leaves which have changed colour, becoming yellowed and browned (1985, *Andy Goldsworthy*). He aligns the coloured sections of the leaves together. There are lines made of cherry leaves, poplar leaves and rosebay willowherb leaves (1981-86, reproduced in *Andy Goldsworthy*). The colours of the *Cherry Leaves* (Cumbria, 1984) turn from green through yellow to red then brown. Some lines fuse different coloured pebbles together (*Line,* at St Abbs, 1985), going from grey through yellow to white to red. These are Autumnal works, rejoicing in the incredible colours of the season. Even in clogged-up, foggy cities the changing colours of Autumnal leaves may be noticed. In the countryside settings of (most of) Goldsworthy's sculpture, the colours are really rich. They really stand out, when the viewer is undistracted by the noise of the city.

1. A. Goldsworthy, *Mountains and Coast, Autumn into Winter*, 1988, HE, 163.

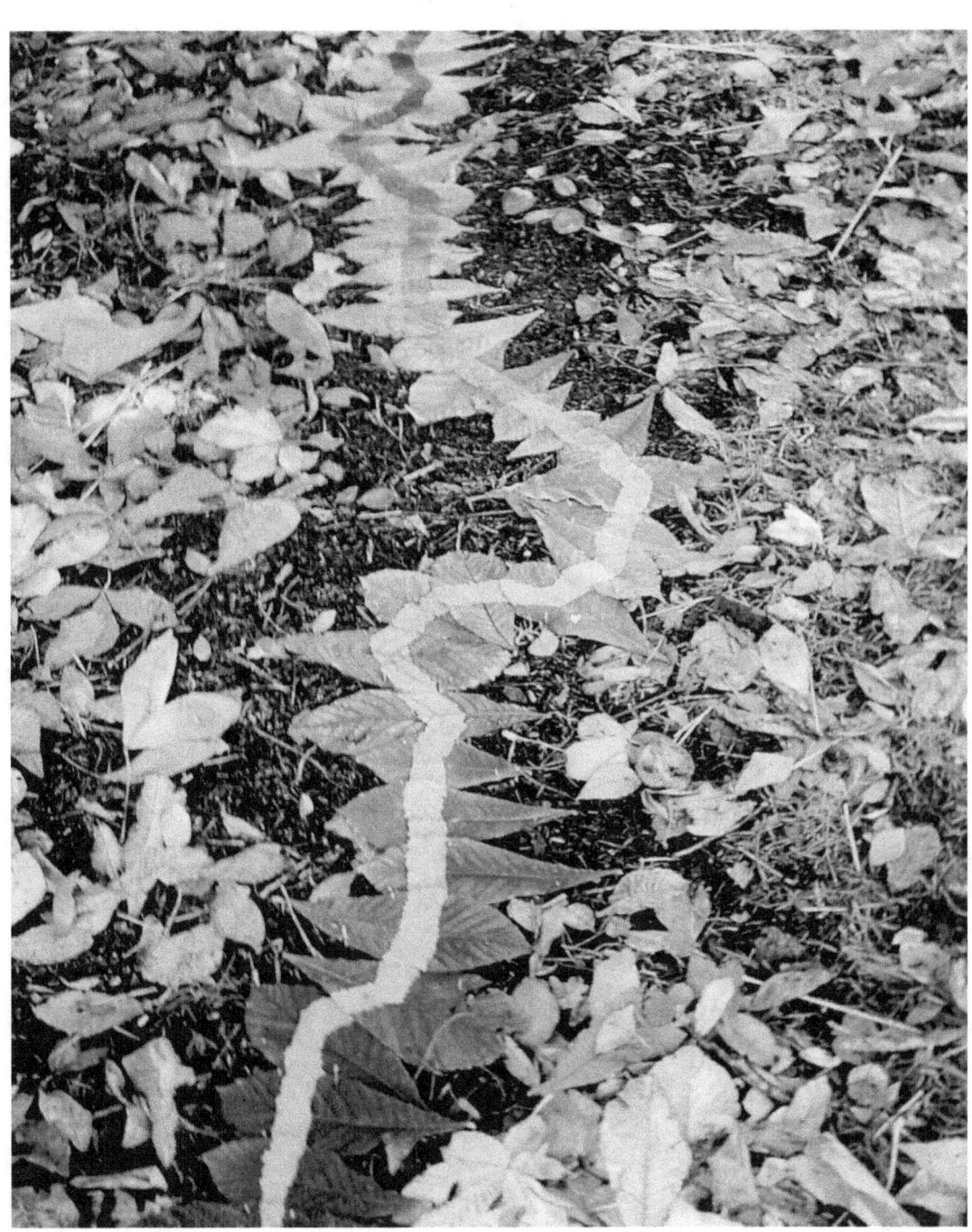

Leafworks

In his sketchbook of August 17, 1984, Andy Goldsworthy wrote:

I am beginning to get more structure into leaf work – forced to find structure in leaves – No rocks or branches. The key is in the leaf veins – The leaf architecture. Amazing how geometric the structure is. (HE, 100)

Goldsworthy's leaf sculptures are, like all land art, specific to particular places. The brilliant oranges and reds and yellows in *Maple patch* (1987) or *Line to explore colours in leaves, calm, overcast* (1987) could only occur in Japan, it seems. Place and work are one for Goldsworthy: he does not distinguish between elements in a work: '[l]ooking, touching, material, place, making the form and resulting work are totally integral'.[1]

1. Quoted in P. Nesbitt, "Leafworks", in HE, 108.

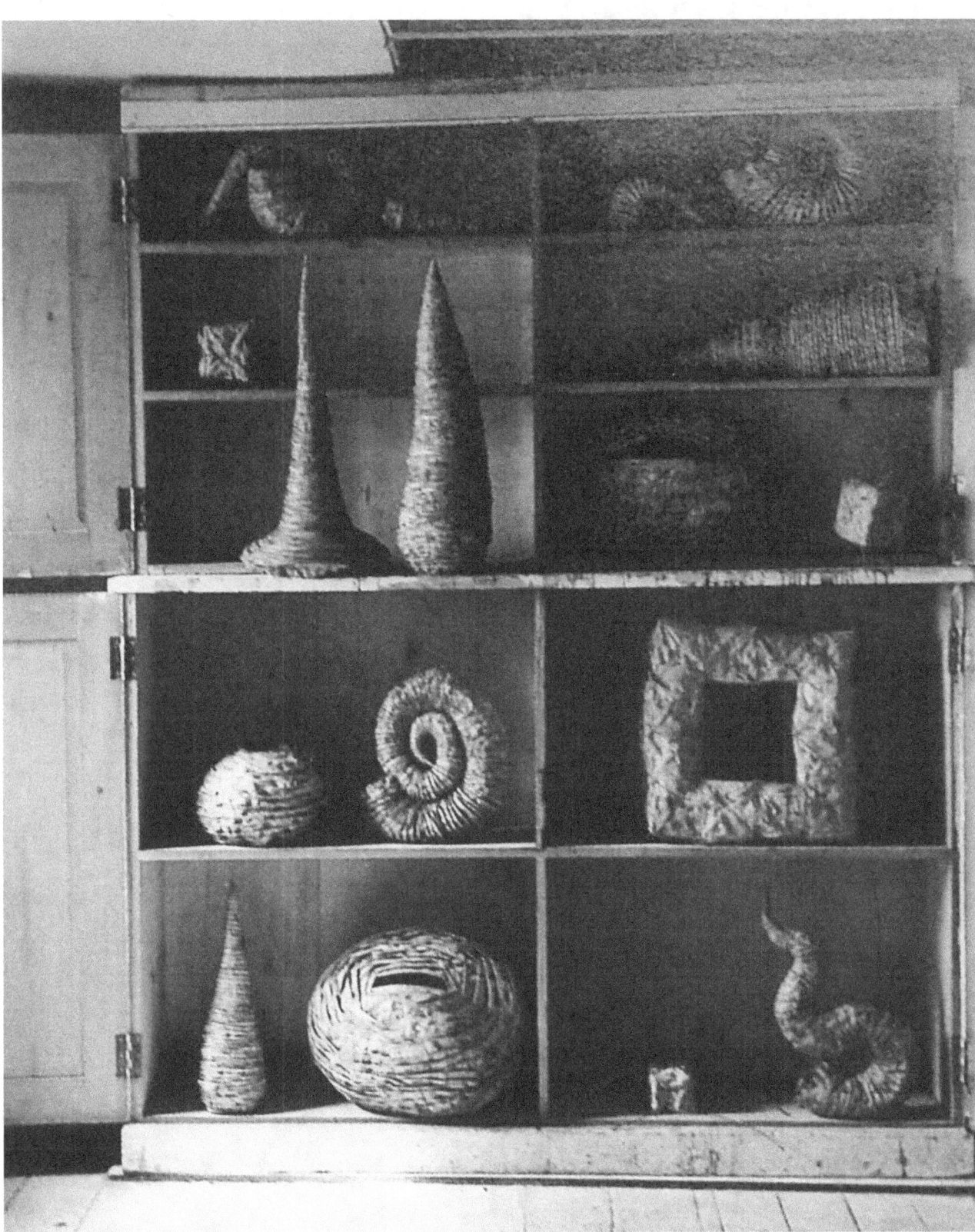

Dandelions (1987)

Andy Goldsworthy's flower pieces are inevitably 'pretty'. It's difficult to use flowers, in poetry, sculpture, painting or performance, without appearing 'pretty' (Goldsworthy realizes this [*Stone*, 6]). Think of Rainer Maria Rilke's many flower poems (to roses, irises, lilies), or the beautiful, sonorous flower watercolours of the German Expressionist Emil Nolde. Like Nolde's radiant flower-pieces, like the flowerpieces of Flemish and Dutch art, Goldsworthy's flower sculptures are luminous. The dandelion piece (April 28, 1987), which is a spread of flowers making a hole in the middle, is powerful not because of the shape the artist's made, but because of the vibrant yellow of the flowers. Flowers are amazing, some of the most exquisite creations on Earth. All Goldsworthy has to do is to arrange them in a simple structure and the beauty of the flowers does the rest. What's also noteworthy about *Dandelions newly flowered* is that the sculpture is set on 'a grass verge between dual carriageways', so the title informs us. If this is so, then this sculpture/ photograph is very noisy: there will be cars roaring up and down the roads on either side of the sculpture. Goldsworthy's art reveals, as good poetry does, the incredible beauty of nature, even amongst the horrible, stinking, grey environment of a major trunk road. Even at the verges of roads, in hedges beside hideous A-roads, on empty roundabouts, there are amazing things growing. Sometimes Goldsworthy goes too far in evoking the beauty of nature. In another dandelion piece, *Dandelion flowers pinned with thorns to wind-bent willowherb stalks laid in a ring held above bluebells with forked sticks* (May 1, 1987), Goldsworthy makes a large open circle of dandelions and ranges them above a fields of bluebells (*Stone,* 11). But it's too much: the incandescent yellow of the dandelions set against the equally rich blue of the bluebells. One doesn't need to do anything to bluebells in a wood to make them look beautiful. Thus, *Dandelion flowers* (May 1, 1987) is a powerful image, but does nothing to explore nature, Goldsworthy's avowed artistic aim.

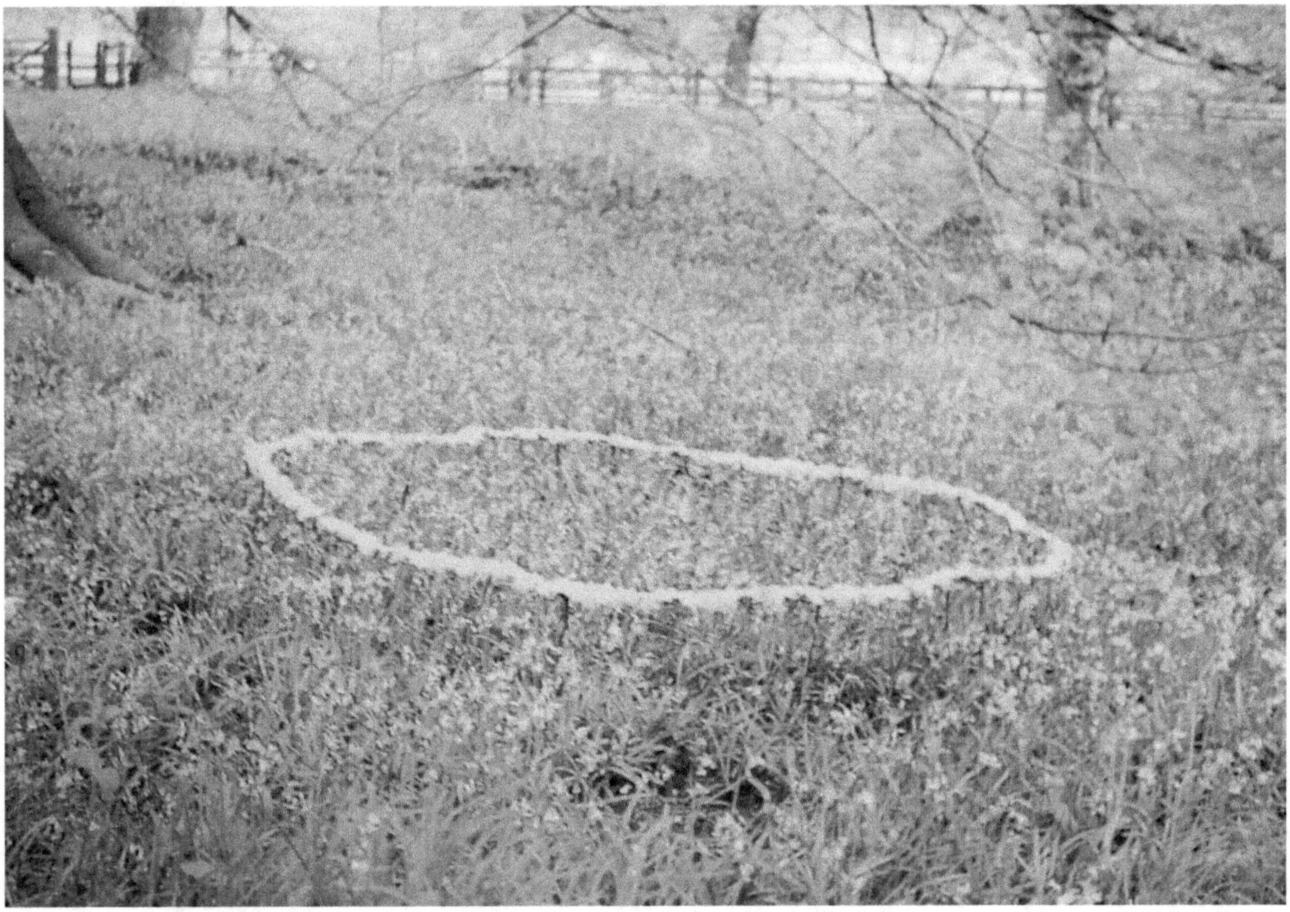

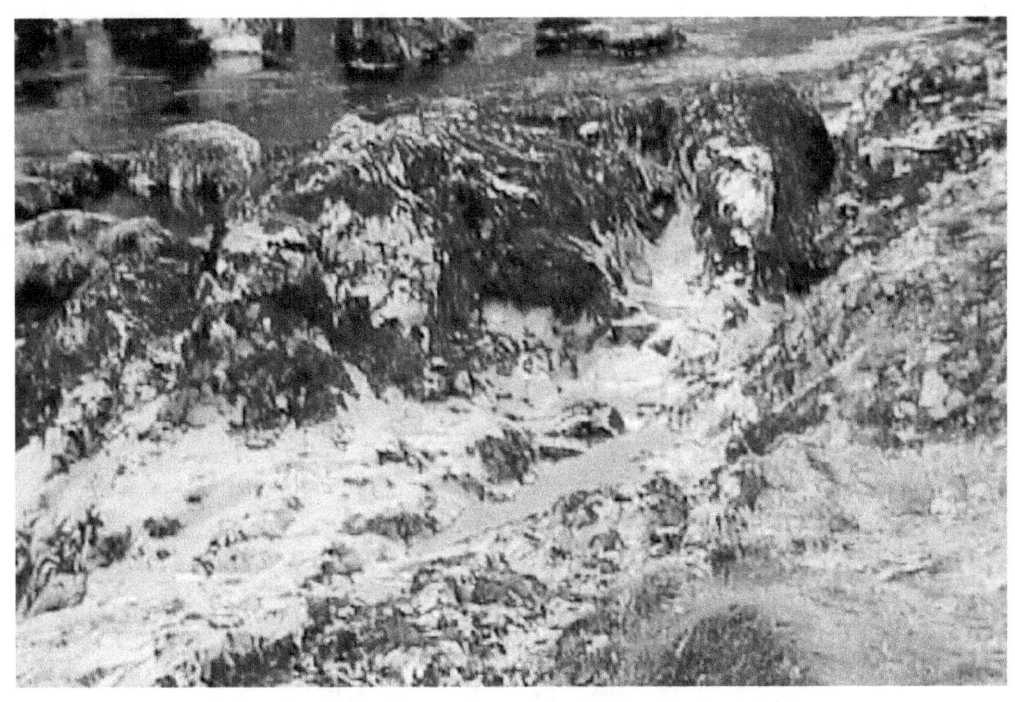

Dandelions

Andy Goldsworthy's art is 'decorative', definitely, but the colours and patterns are taken from nature: the seemingly 'pretty' colours of bluebells and dandelions, of maple leaves and the Australian outback, are colours already present in the natural world: they've been there for millions of years. Rather than finding colour 'decorative', for Goldsworthy it is 'raw with energy' (S, 6). The published books might have contributed towards the impression of the artist as decorative, Goldsworthy admitted, but he would carry on using colour anyway, because it was part of the natural world (P, 61).

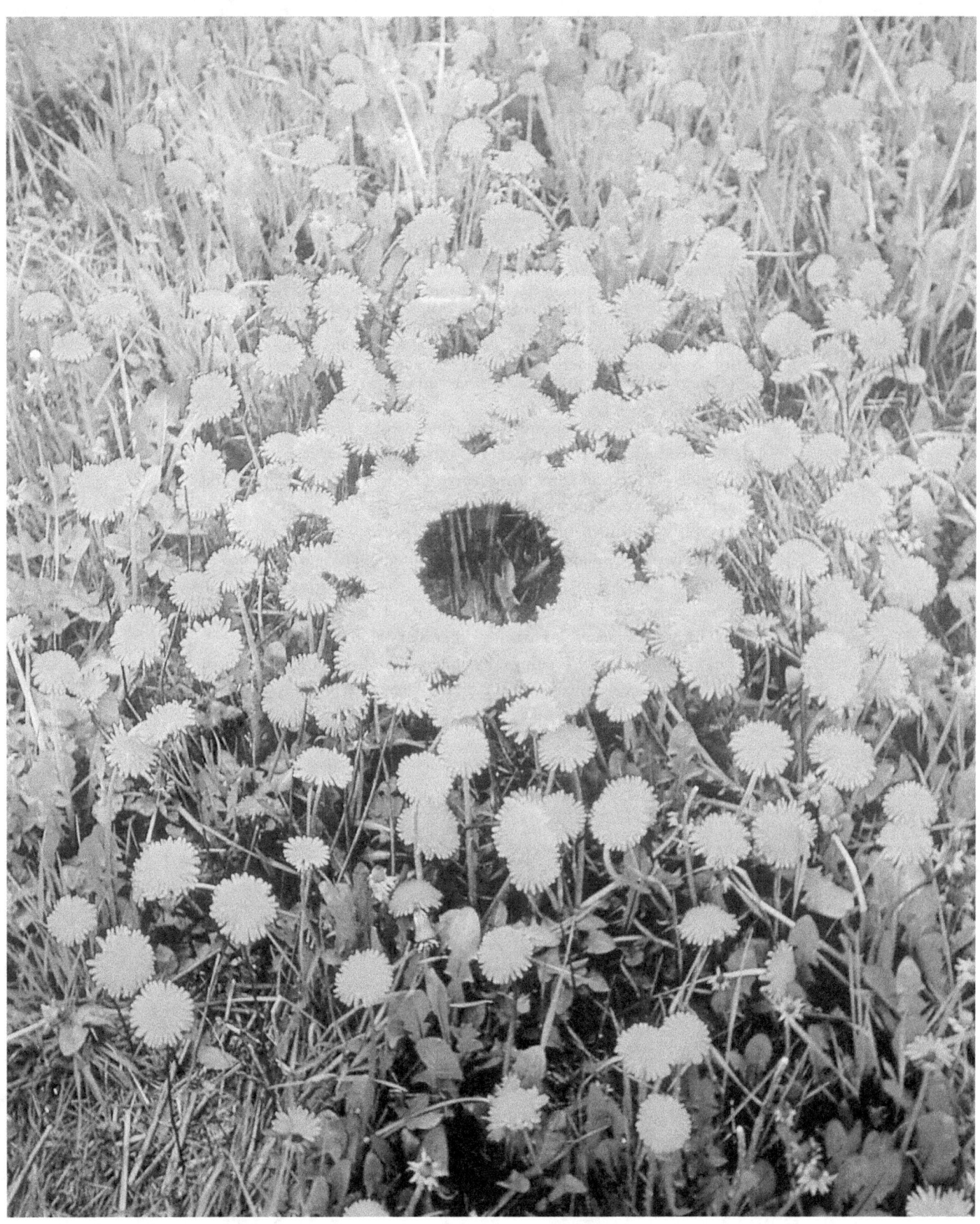

Sweet Chestnut Autumn Horn (1986)

Paul Nesbitt wrote of Andy Goldsworthy's art:

> Throughout these works the dominant theme is one of working with nature, to reveal nature itself – physical, chemical and biological. Goldsworthy uses nature's materials – rock, water (snow and ice, rain and mist), earth and the plants and animals which inhabit these; he uses nature's properties – structure, shape, form and colour; he uses nature's forces which together create, alter and animate those materials and properties – forces of light, heat, wind and gravity.[1]

What happens to a sculpture is determined largely by factors outside of itself. The fact of its being thought of as a sculpture is more critical to its existence, its life, than any other facts about it. This is a fundamental distinction between objects and sculpture.[2]

Obviously, Goldsworthy's leafworks – the sycamore boxes, the sweet chestnut horns, the maple circles – are sculptures, seen and described as sculptures. That's easy, to see the leafworks as sculptures. The petal-covered rocks, those too, are clearly sculptures. There is no mistaking the carefully crafted pieces as anything other than 'high art'. Every artwork creates a multitude of readings, but one of the dominant readings of Goldsworthy's 'real' objects is that they are 'high art' sculptures.

1. Paul Nesbitt, "A Landscape Touched by Gold", in Graham Hughes, *Arts Review: Yearbook 1990*, Arts Review Magazine 1990, 49.
2. Garth Evans, "Sculpture and Reality", *Studio International*, vol. 177, no. 908, February 1969, 62.

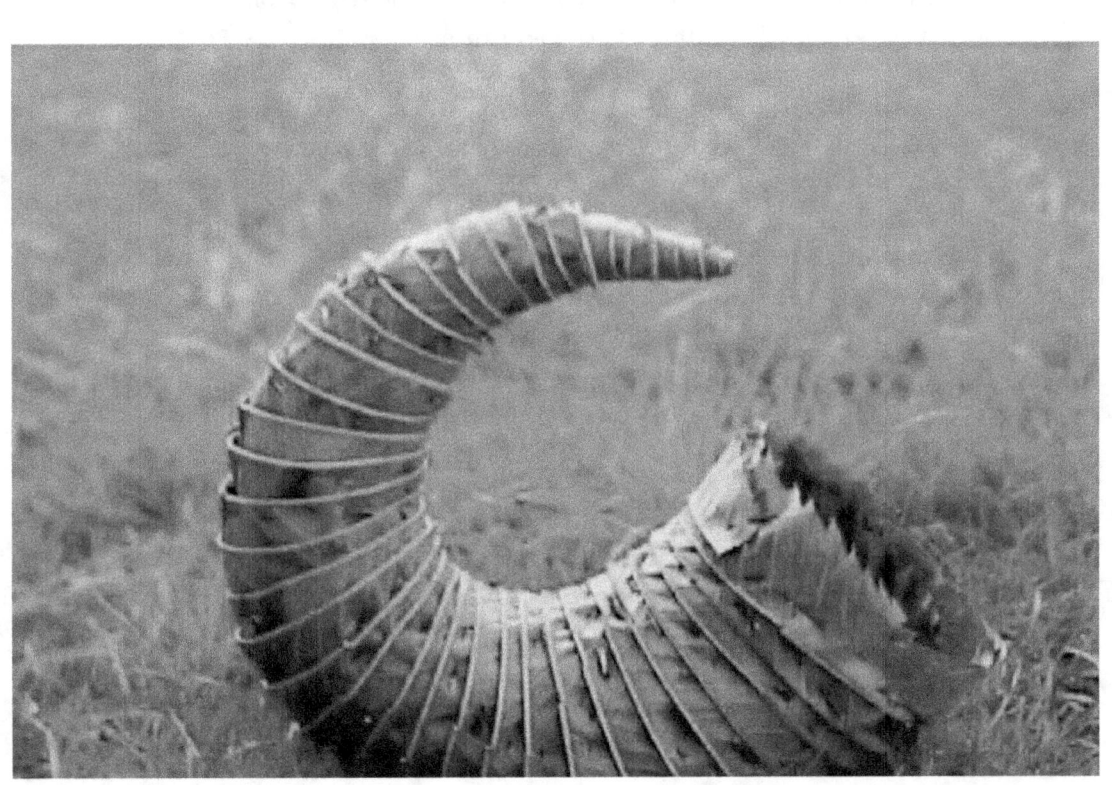

Rosebay Willowherb (1990)

One of the most beautiful of Andy Goldsworthy's works is *Rosebay willowherb* (1990), a web of willowherb stalks woven together into a circle. At the centre is an open circle made by the stalks: Goldsworthy weaves the stalks together so that they expand in gentle curves. Related to *Rosebay willowherb* is *Woven silver birch* (made at Langholm in Dumfriesshire, 1986): again the sticks are woven together to form an open circle at the centre. On the outside of the sculpture, the sticks move off in every direction. It looks like a Catherine Wheel, with the sparks frozen in the air.

Goldsworthy has produced a few of these 'drawings in air', free-standing sculptures which are practically two-dimensional. They are drawings in space, where Goldsworthy employs the fine bendy stalks to make elegant curves in the air. These works – *Knotwood stalks* (Holbeck Triangle, 1986), *Rosebay willowherb* and the stalks stuck in the lake bottom in the Lake District – are wholly dependent on Renaissance notions of space and illusion. They are flat works, best seen from one particular direction, and preferably with contrasting lighting, set against a sky, for instance. One or two stick works, though, break out in all directions, such as *Hazel sticks* (1980), made in Cumbria, where a group of straight sticks, some six or more feet long, are bound together on a pole.

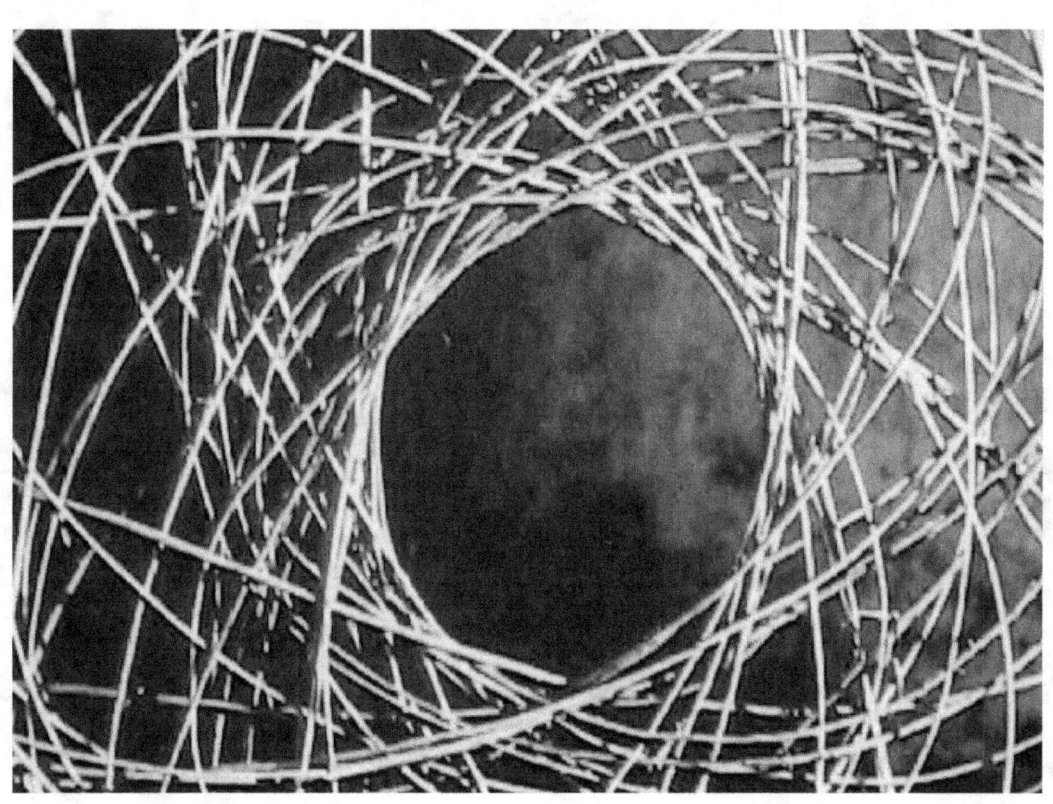

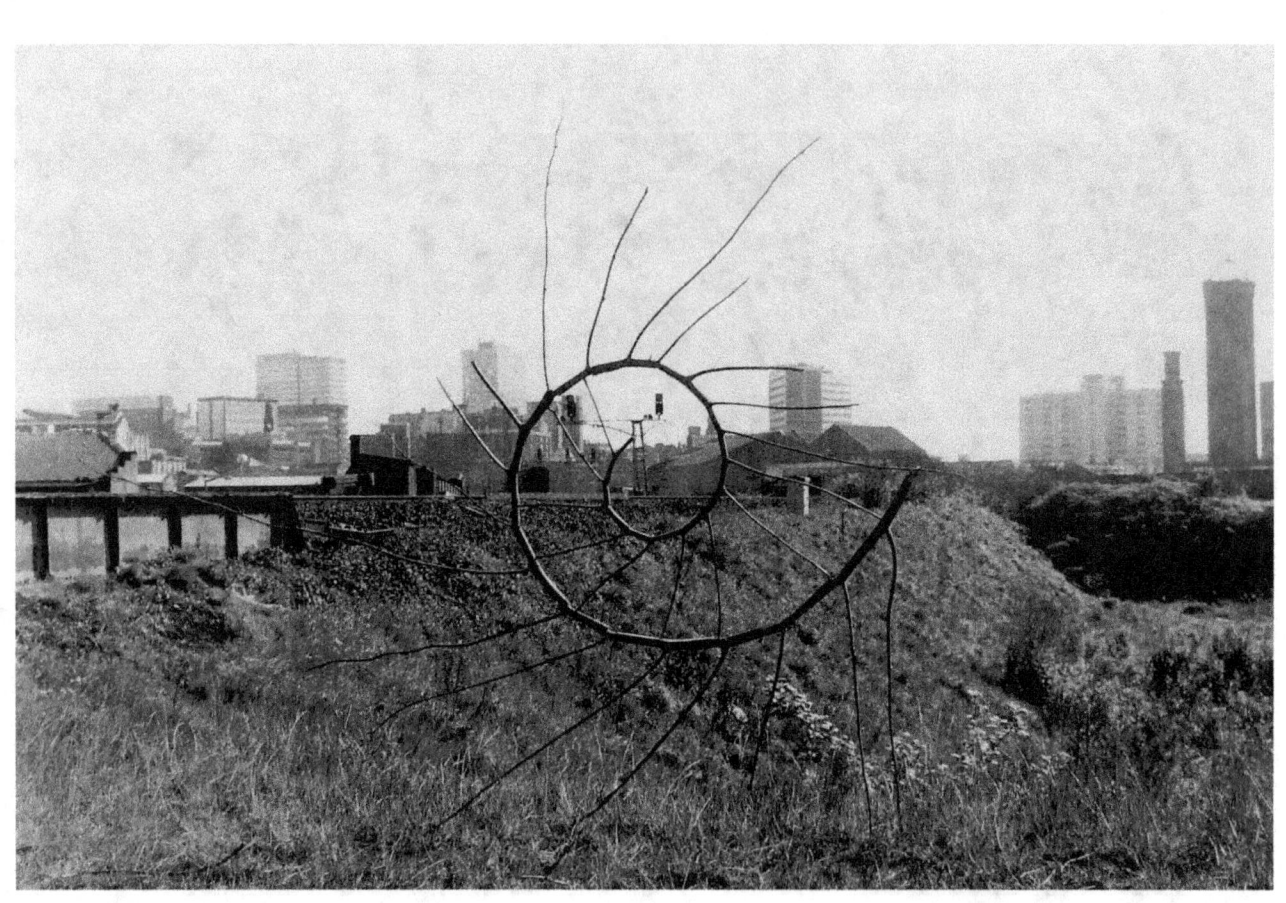

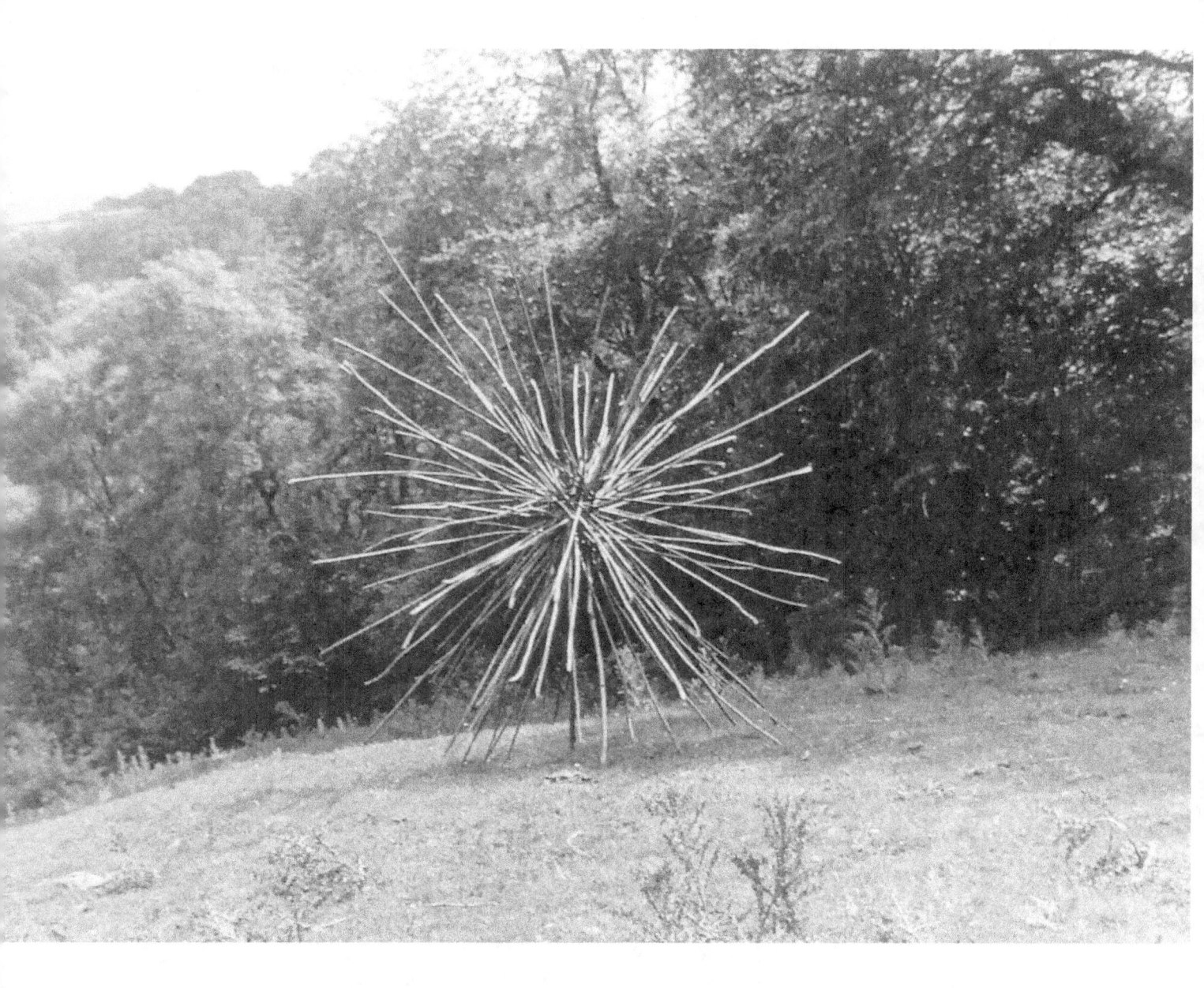

Lambton Earthwork (1988)

Commissioned by Sustrans and Northern Arts, *Lambton Earthwork* (1988) is a quarter-mile long bank which coils along the ground near Chester-le-Street in County Durham. The site was associated with railways and industry, but Goldsworthy turned it into something wholly concerned with æsthetic and religious themes. The long spiralling banks of earth clearly derived from the earthwork sculptures of Robert Smithson and American land art (Goldsworthy says he is wary of using the 'overblown spiral', the too-obvious spiral as a shape [*Hand to Earth*, 163]). Goldsworthy spoke of the serpentine shape as being like a river winding through a valley, or the root of a tree. *Lambton Earthwork* was seen by the artist as a 'river of earth', a response to the natural energies of the place (recall how Goldsworthy spoke of black holes and the energy in the Earth erupting from underneath). Certainly *Lambton Earthwork* was not about industrial archæology or nostalgic reminiscences of the bygone railway era: it was a piece of land art which had powerful mythic overtones. For example, Lambton on the River Wear in Durham is associated with one of the great dragon legends of Britain: the Loathly Worm of Lambton.[1] Andy Goldsworthy has thus created a dragon – or a quarter-mile earthwork which corresponds with the Loathly Worm of Lambton.[2]

1. Janet & Colin Bord, *Mysterious Britain*, Paladin, 1974, 240-1.
2. Goldsworthy says he heard about the dragon legend after he had made *Lambton Earthwork* (*Hand to Earth*, 135).

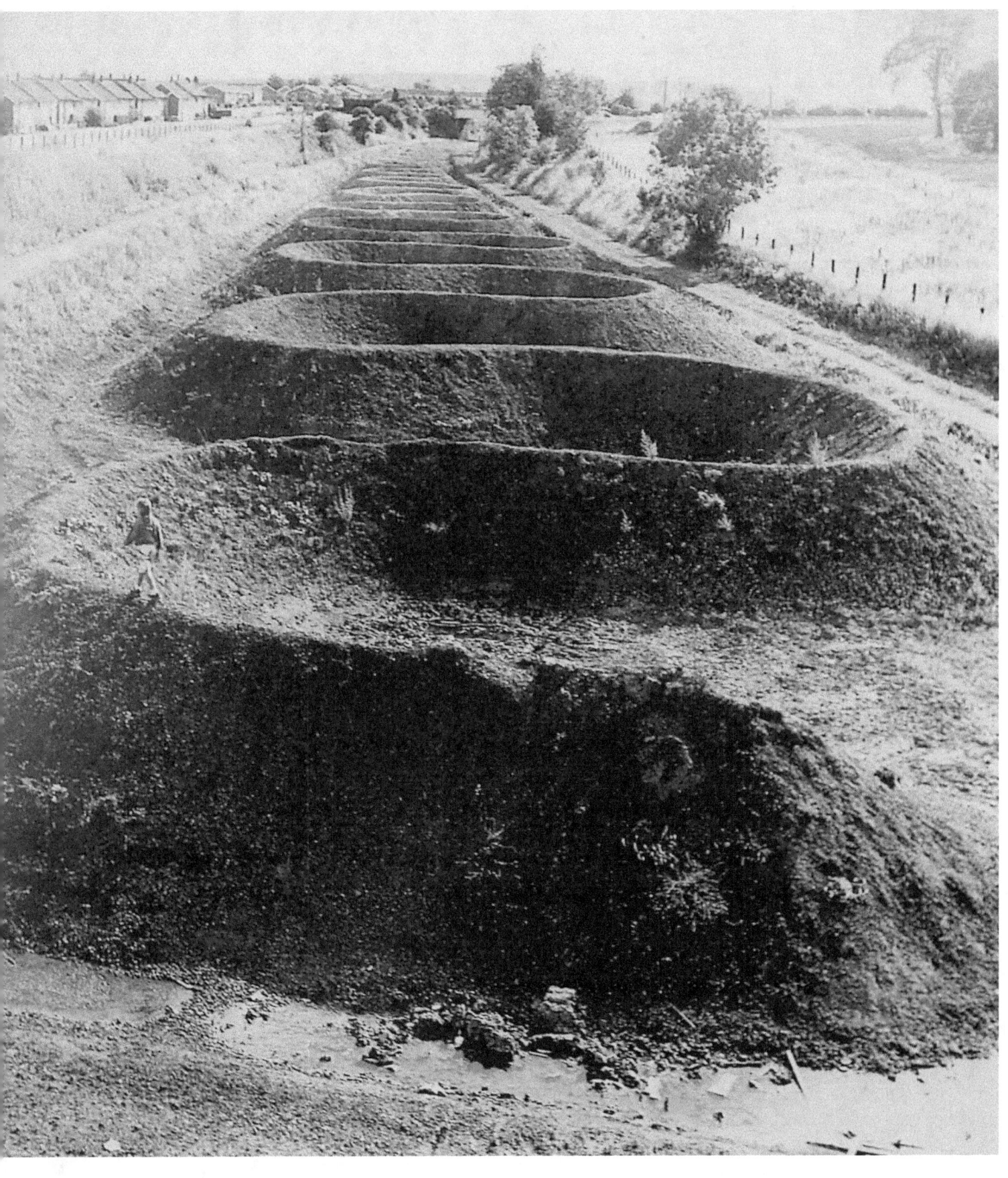

Maze (1989)

The other Durham earthwork (*Maze,* 1989, at Leadgate) also used ancient mythology and symbolism, this time the labyrinth (again, Robert Smithson had created large earthwork mazes in the late 1960s/ early 1970s). Andy Goldsworthy also designed an earthwork which was a curving ramp, exactly like *Armarillo Ramp*, though on a much smaller scale. Goldsworthy's *Maze* can be seen as a part of the resurgence of interest in mazes which occurred in the 1980s (aligned, as ever, with green/ ecological/ occult/ New Age trends). Mazes were commissioned for country houses and (theme) parks. 1991 was 'The Year of the Maze' (largely orchestrated by maze designer Adrian Fisher of Minotaur Designs).

The maze is a very satisfying motif or design: it is self-contained, like other geometric patterns; it can use almost any perimeter shape, from circles and squares to 'organic' shapes; it offers opportunities for games and play; it can be a visual device, for decorating floors or walls, or one of the main features of a garden; and it carries a sizeable slice of symbolism, religion, paganism and history. The symbolism and history of the labyrinth can be happily ignored in favour of simply enjoying solving a maze. Unlike sacred sites such as churches and stone circles, which are loaded with religious significance, and generally demand some religious or intellectual response from the visitor, the maze can be consumed simply as an interesting structure. One doesn't need to know about mythology (such as Theseus and the Minotaur) or religion (such as the ritual aspect in Christianity of walking a maze) to appreciate a maze. Like *Lambton Earthwork* (but unlike most of Goldsworthy's works), *Maze* was intended to be used by the general public. Both *Maze* and *Lambton Earthwork* were about responses to the energies in nature – thus the public was invited to explore similar things as they physically walked around the earthworks. The usual experiences of the maze were apparent in Goldsworthy's *Maze* – not being able to see the whole plan from above; being enclosed by high banks; a bewildering series of turns and paths. The interwoven series of embankments also recalled Iron Age forts (of which there are many in Britain), such as the complex (and enormous) array of defences at Maiden Castle in Dorset.

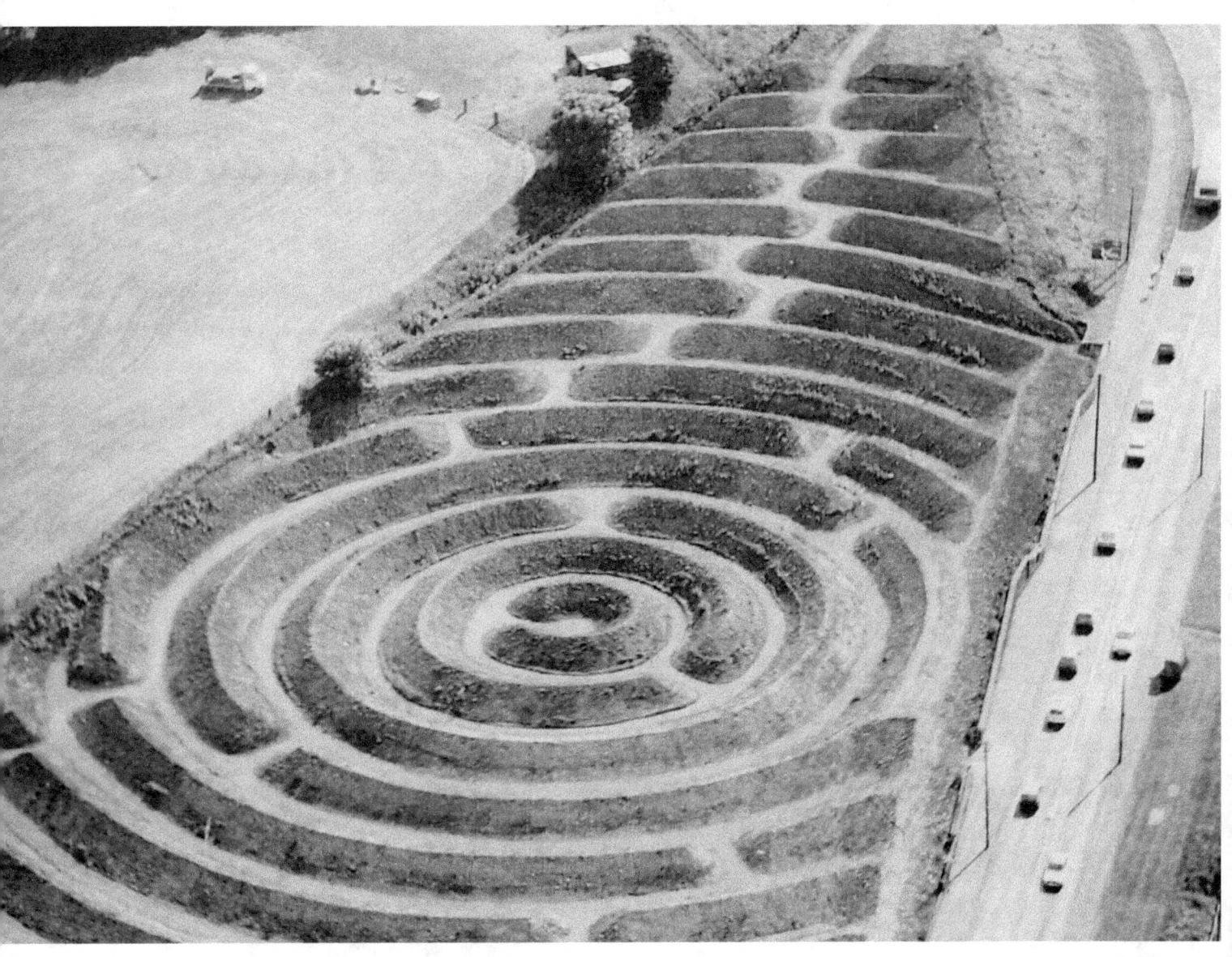

Poppy Petals Wrapped Around a Boulder (1989)

Andy Goldsworthy's sculptures are marked by a number of elements familiar in land art: transience, domination, penetration, circular forms (globes, circles, spirals, snakes, cones) and nature mysticism. The ephemerality of the pieces, for instance, is a key component. Snow and ice will melt away, leaves will disintegrate, stones will be blown over. Each Goldsworthy sculpture has a date printed with its title. Not just a year, as in the usual artwork, but a specific day. Thus, one of his best pieces, the delicious poppy covered boulder, has the title: *Poppy petals wrapped around a boulder held with water* (Sibobre, France, 6 June, 1989). The petal-covered rock, with its brilliant red colour, nestles in some mossy boulders, looking very much like one of Brancusi's 'cosmic eggs'. The red colour reveals the rock's shape, size and form, its position amongst and relation to other rocks. Not wishing to disturb or move the rock (it's not that small really), Goldsworthy's act of covering it in wet poppy petals draws attention to this particular egg-shaped rock, *this* one and not the others (although the surrounding boulders also become the subject of the sculpture: attention is drawn to them as well as to the red rock). In *Poppy petals wrapped around a boulder held with water*, then, the place becomes as crucial as the centrepiece, the red rock.

Goldsworthy is using a standard observation of natural science: red really does stand out. In the Japanese Zen garden, colours are carefully orchestrated, so that a single leaf can set off a vast acreage of predominantly green or ochre. In the Oriental garden, notions of *feng shui* and *yin* and *yang* control how a landscape is shaped by humans. In the system of *feng shui*, the elements of a garden or a building must be in harmony with natural forces of air, water and earth. Get it wrong and one messes up the creation. The Zen Buddhist or Taoist harmonizing approach is very much that of Goldsworthy's art. In the manner of the ecological follower, he speaks of wanting to be in harmony with nature. Goldsworthy, like other artists, can be seen as ecological artists, artists committed to ecological issues.

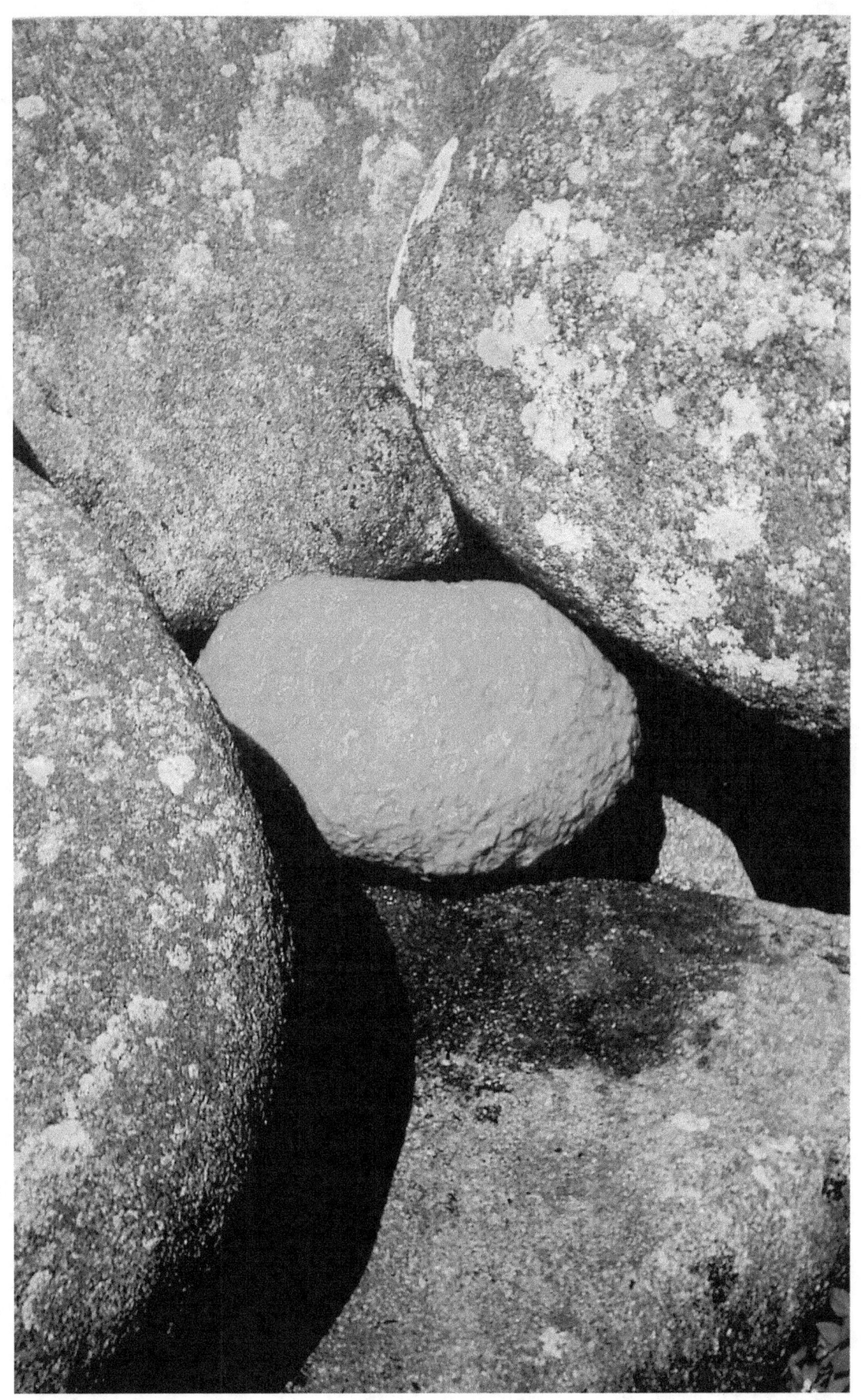

Snowballs

In some sculptures of Andy Goldsworthy's, the snowballs are small and look like seeds placed inside the trunks of broken trees (as in the 1993 piece in *Wood*, 24). Other snowball-in-tree works include *Oak tree snowball* and *Beech tree snowball* (both Dumfriesshire, both 1994). Goldsworthy photographed these sculptures from a distance, to include the whole tree and its snowy surroundings. These are atmospheric pieces, with the white of the sky and the snow predominating.

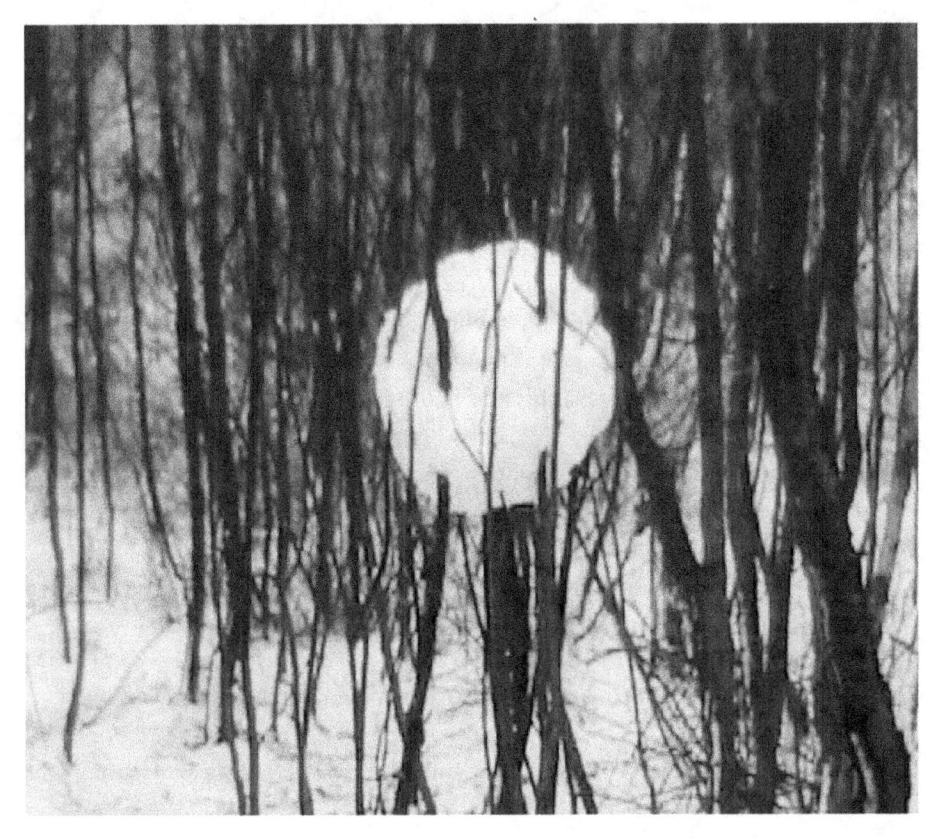

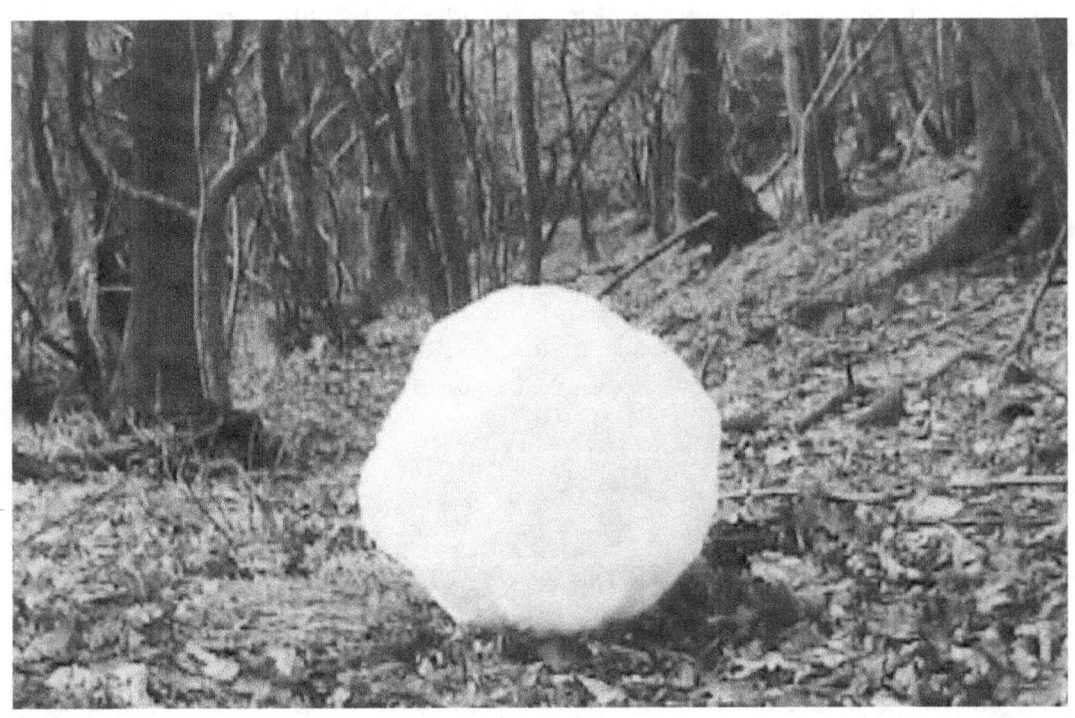

Snowballs In Summer (2000)

Snow melts, and Andy Goldsworthy's sculptures exploit the precariousness and impermanence of snow as a material. He speaks of being frustrated in making snow sculptures, of snow crumbling before he could complete the piece. Yet his snow works are some of his most exciting pieces: a snowball, for instance, caught in the branches of a tree. It looks impressive in the photographs, the ball of snow, so heavy and cold, floating, it seems, in the black, leafless branches of a tree. Goldsworthy has brought snow into the studio, most impressively in the series of large snowballs he brought from Craighall near Blairgowrie to Glasgow. Goldsworthy waited and waited for snow to fall during 1988-89. When it did, eventually, he made a series of snowballs which were exhibited in the Old Museum of Transport in Glasgow during the Summer of 1989.

In 2000, for the major London exhibition at the Barbican, Goldsworthy recreated the *Snowballs in Summer* event, this time located in various sites around the City of London. A video, *Midsummer Snowballs* (produced by University of Hertfordshire students) was shown at the Barbican.

The lines of snowballs, in rows in the museum space, recall directly the Minimal exhibitions of the 1960s. Each snowball was roughly the same size, but, like Minimal artists such as Donald Judd, Goldsworthy made each one slightly different. Within each snowball, Goldsworthy rolled in different elements, most of which are favourite Goldsworthy materials: willowherb stalks, pine needles, pebbles, reeds, oak sticks, and so on. Each snowball, then, was not just a sphere of ice melting slowly in Summer, it was a container of natural materials, each with their own properties, which affected the melting of the snow. The melting of the snowballs itself was a natural process which the environment of a museum made highly visible. Each snowball melted in a different way. The inner stalks and pebbles became gradually more and more apparent, appearing on the outside of the snowball as it decreased in size. A pool of water formed around the snowball. Slowly, webs of stalks appeared, or a covering of old orange pine needles, looking like a cake decoration.

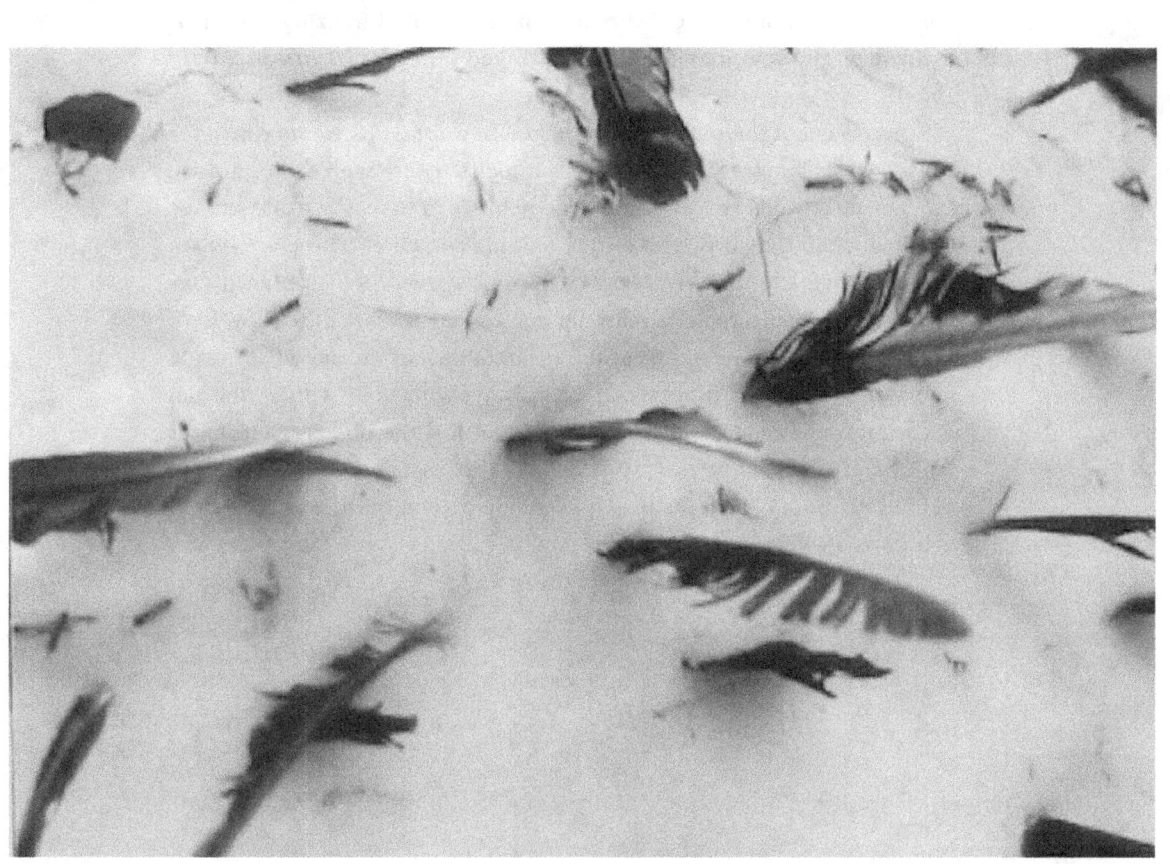

Each snowball became an alchemical vessel in which the arcane transmutations of nature were made visible. The secret processes of the natural world became apparent to all who visited the museum in Glasgow. Every stage of the melting transformation was captured on film – a record of alchemy. An associated snowwork, *Snow and mud layers* (1987) lasted two weeks: during the day the snow tower melted and slumped; during the night it refroze. Every day, in this cycle of freezing/ thawing, night/ day, the sculpted snow tower looked different (*Hand to Earth*, 152-3).

Vision was not the only sense activated by *Snowballs in Summer*, for snow, as one knows, makes noises as it melts. There were other noises, too, because Goldsworthy stuck large pebbles in the snowballs, so they clunked when they dropped off the melting snowball. These are noises that occur all the time in nature: dripping water, rocks falling, twigs cracking. To hear them in a museum context makes one newly aware of the natural world. The alchemical transmutations of the snowballs made one aware of nature's processes, for, as always with Goldsworthy, the aim is a greater understanding of nature. It's not just the object itself that is important, Goldsworthy says, but also the processes going on inside and behind them that are valuable. Not a single object, but the processes of 'nature as a whole'.[1]

1. In N. Sinden, 1988, 28.

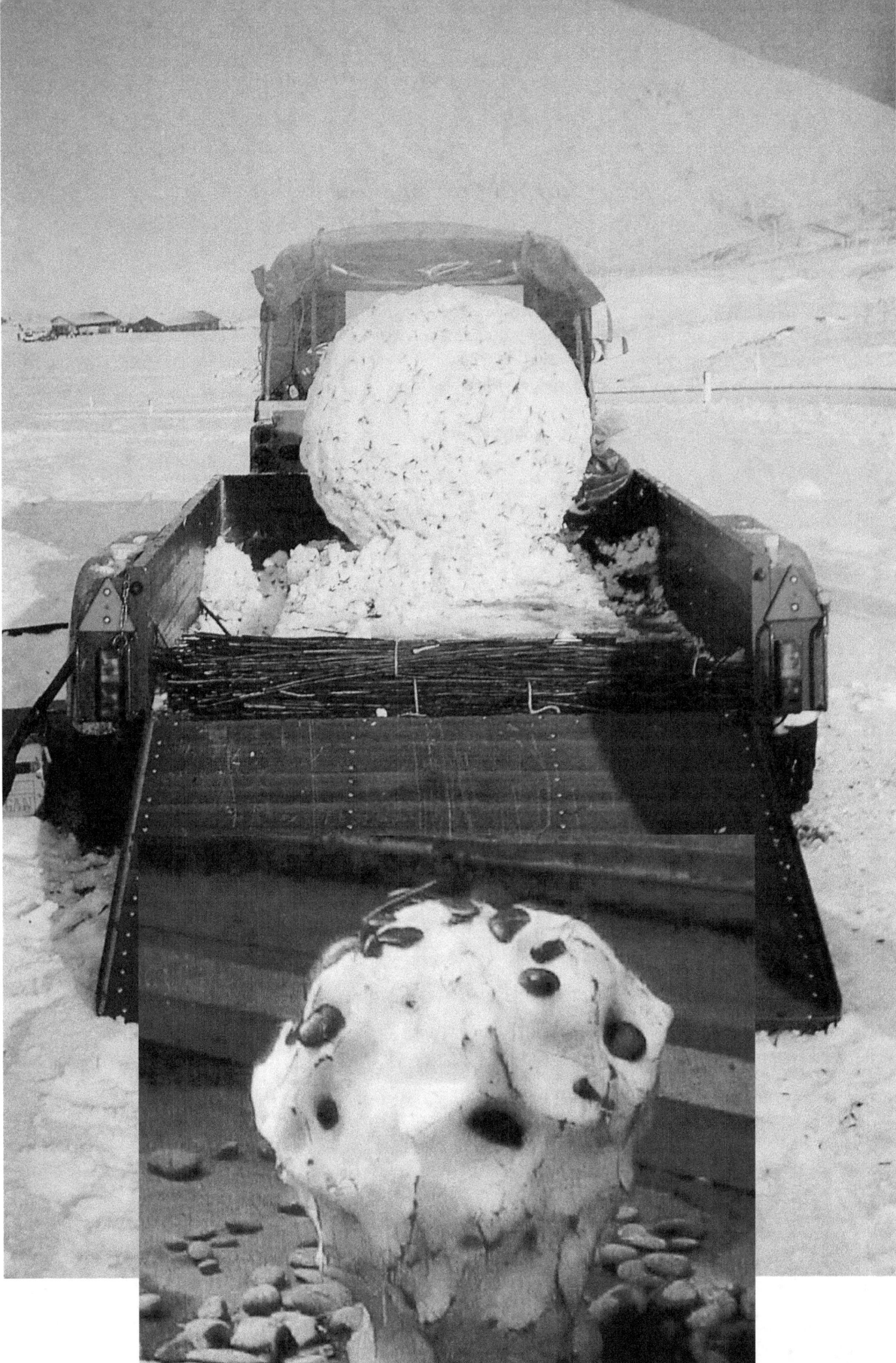

Slits Cut Into Frozen Snow (1988)

Some Goldsworthy sculptures are seen in a variety of lighting conditions –
stormlight, snowlight, misty skies (the snow wall is an obvious instance).
Goldsworthy reproduced (in *Andy Goldsworthy*) three double page
spreads of a snow wall made at a favourite spot, Blencathra in Cumbria.
The full title of the work explains some of it:

> *Slits cut into frozen snow*
> *stormy*
> *strong wind*
> *weather and light rapidly changing*

The title reads like a *haiku*, like many of Goldsworthy's titles. The title,
however, does not convey the Romantic power of these photographs
which directly recall the oil paintings of J.M.W. Turner. Behind the slitted
snow wall the viewer sees brooding cloudscapes, with the sun burning
through in the second shot. In the third picture, the wall, in the fore-
ground, is in shadow, while the sun shines onto a portion of a distant hill.
Above roam clouds with softened edges, as out of Mark Rothko's abstract
panels or Emil Nolde's watercolours of North Friesland.

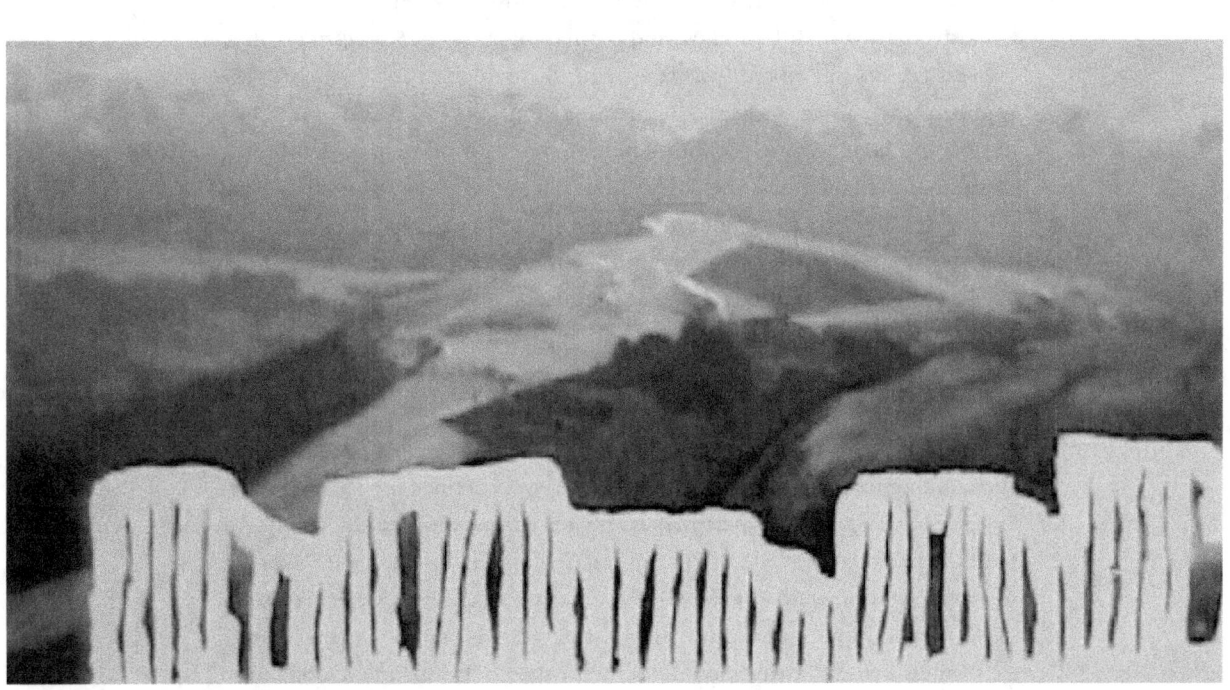

Sidewinder (1985)
and *Seven Spires* (1984)

Andy Goldsworthy's large-scale works, like Michael Heizer's or Walter de Maria's, are monumental works, which sprawl across the landscape. *Sidewinder* (1985) and *Seven Spires* (1984), at Grizedale (a Forestry Commission site between Windermere and Coniston Water), are trunks of trees stripped of their branches, and pinned together. In *Sidewinder*, the curved trunks are placed on the ground, to form a long snake-like sculpture: the form rests on the ground then curves into the air. The impression is of sliding, arching kinetic energy. In other words: a huge serpent slithering along the forest floor. In *Seven Spires* the trees are pinned together to form tall spires. The result is a series of enormous edifices made of wood in amongst other trees. Goldsworthy wanted to harness the sense of the 'almost desperate growth and energy driving upward' in the pine wood, and to evoke a cathedral-like atmosphere, with the spires stretching skyward with the brown gloom underneath.[1]

It is, at first, not clear which is a tree and which is sculpture. Both, of course, are made of wood: Goldsworthy has simply drawn together the surrounding trees, it seems, but in doing so, he redefines the surrounding forest. *Seven Spires* looks at first to be a gentle sculpture, blending in with the surrounding forest. 'In avoiding monumentality, however, Goldsworthy's sculptures do not forego grandeur' wrote Andrew Causey (1990, 128). Yet they do stand out, really, they are distinctly works of art, existing in a paradoxical relationship with the environment. A 'collaboration' is a polite way of saying what Goldsworthy's *Seven Spires* is about: a 'collaboration with nature', a phrase used about much of his art. Goldsworthy sometimes writes arrogantly about his art. For him, the human touch can improve on nature: combined with human culture and art, nature is made even more significant. It's not enough for nature to be existing on its own: it requires humans to make it complete. Or as Goldsworthy puts it:

> If anything, I am giving nature a more powerful presence in the mass of earth, stone or wood that I use. (N. Hedges, 71)

1. In R. Davies, 1984, 151.

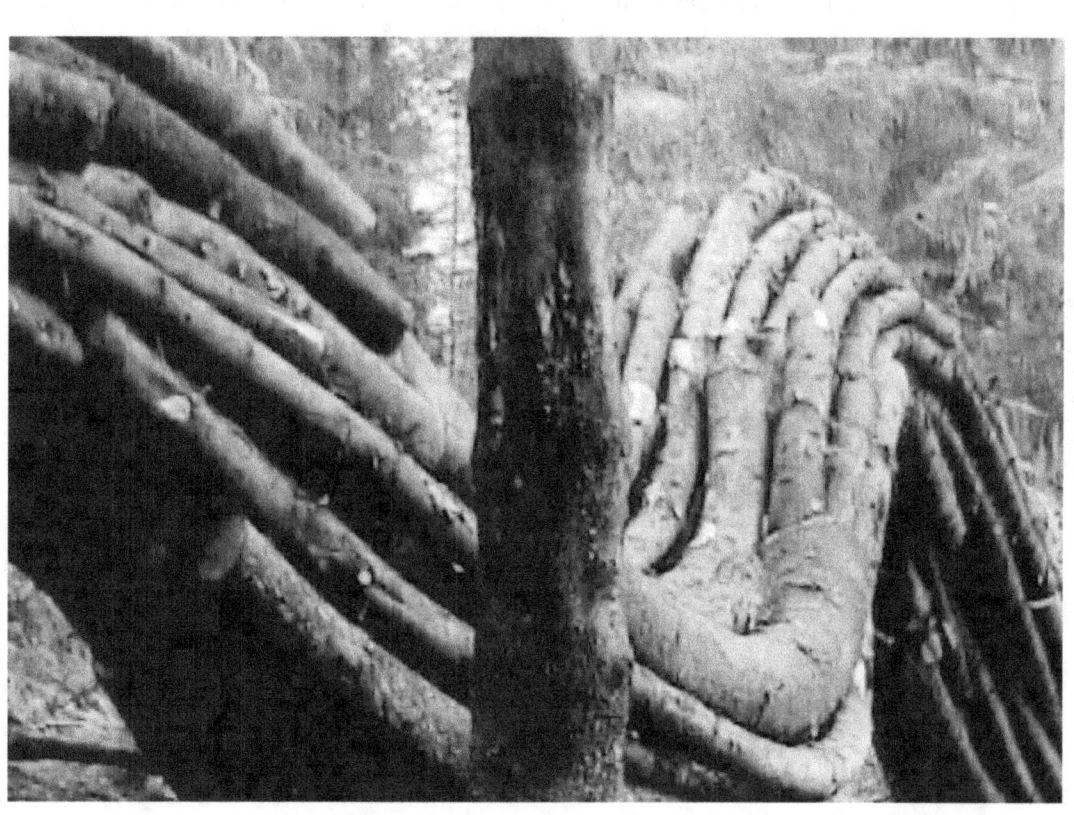

Ice Arch (1982)

The moment when the sculpture topples is a moment of crisis, which Andy Goldsworthy believes is a key point in a work. Not only it is an exciting moment, when all that effort is gone in a flash, but it actualizes the cycles in nature which are at the heart of Goldsworthy's æsthetics. Nature's cycles and times of change are very important for Goldsworthy. 'The earth as a whole is probably in these cycles, going through different speeds and changing. Understanding those cycles is understanding the processes of nature' he wrote in his Arctic diary.[1] When the sculpture collapses, one of the many transformations of nature is made manifest, is valorized. The collapse is an expression of cyclical change. Goldsworthy, ever the student of nature, knows that the collapse will soon be followed by another building, one stone on top of the other. Similarly, when something dies in nature, another thing is born. The moment of collapse in Goldsworthy's photographs thus makes vivid the birth-death-rebirth cyclical quality in nature and in his art.

Sometimes the sense of change is not shown, but is included in the work's title. For instance, one of his snow and ice sculptures, a wall made in Japan on Christmas Day, 1987, is described as 'a wall of frozen snow' which 'collapsed in the sunlight'. While it's obvious that any snow sculpture will (eventually) melt and collapse, Goldsworthy feels the event is significant enough to include in the title of the work. All the time with Goldsworthy's sculpture one is reminded that he is using (as with David Nash and Wolfgang Laib) materials that will not last: sand, snow, leaves, petals.

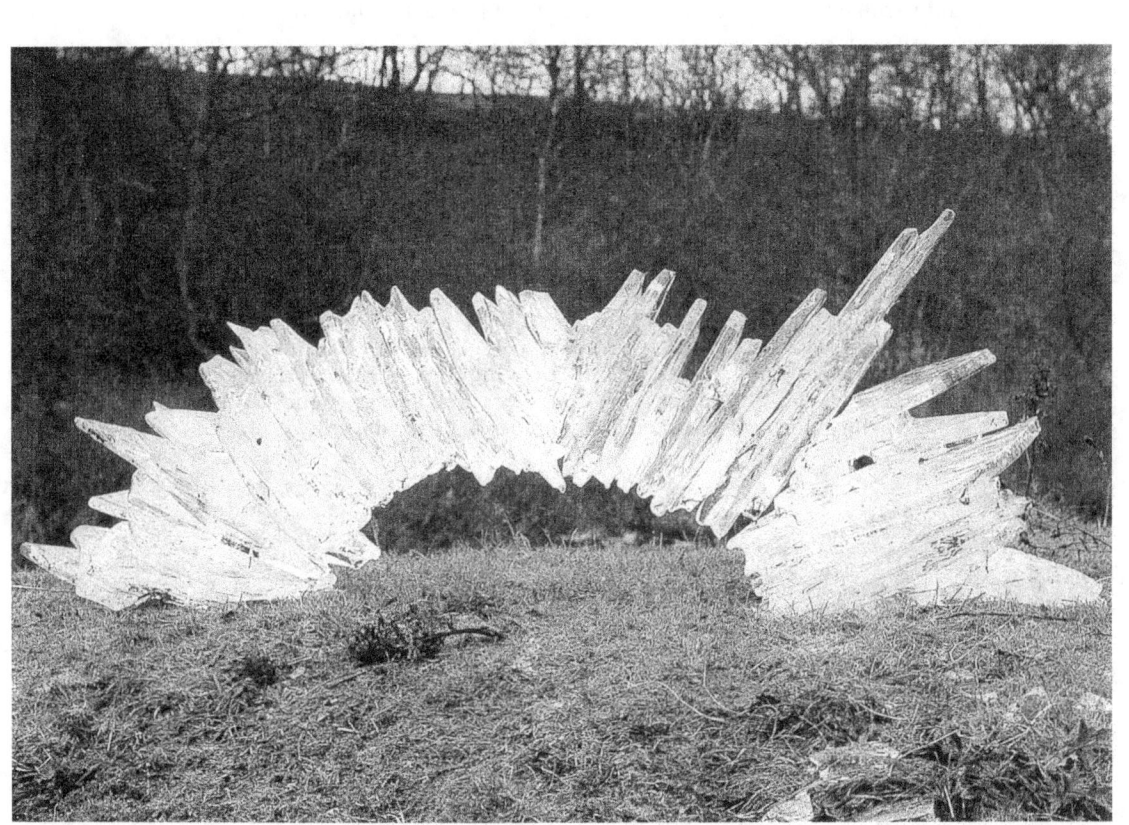

This notion of decay and entropy was an important element in Robert Smithson's earth art.[2] It's the same for Richard Long: 'my work is partly about change or disappearance, invisibility... all these strange states of matter' (1986, 1, 9). In his book *Stone,* as in the books *Andy Goldsworthy* and *Passage,* one finds photographs not only of sculptures that have toppled, but photographs of sculptures that are in the act of falling down. Goldsworthy loves to photograph works that have fallen to bits. 'I like to draw things out to a peak of intensity – hold them there – and let them go' he says.[3] So he has sculptures that are impossibly balanced. A line of rocks, for instance, placed on the slope of a quay that goes into the sea (Wales, 1993). The photographs in the book *Stone* depict not only the artwork as it is 'meant' to be – a line of stones on a quay – but also the various stages of its collapse. The stones fell as the tide came in and the waves pushed them over. Other Cibachrome photographs depict cairns or towers that fall over.

Ice workshop. Made arch over a pile of sticks – waited for it to freeze – temperature going up and down – thawing then freezing – managed to get out most of the sticks – lost concentration for a moment – all sticks loose but somehow knocked arch and caused its collapse.[4]

1. In *Hand to Earth*, 158.
2. R. Smithson: *Writings*, 56-57; C. Robins, 80.
3. In M. Church.
4. A. Goldsworthy, 1985, quoted in S. Clifford & A. King: "Hampstead Heath and Hooke Park Wood 1985-86", in *Hand To Earth*, 57.

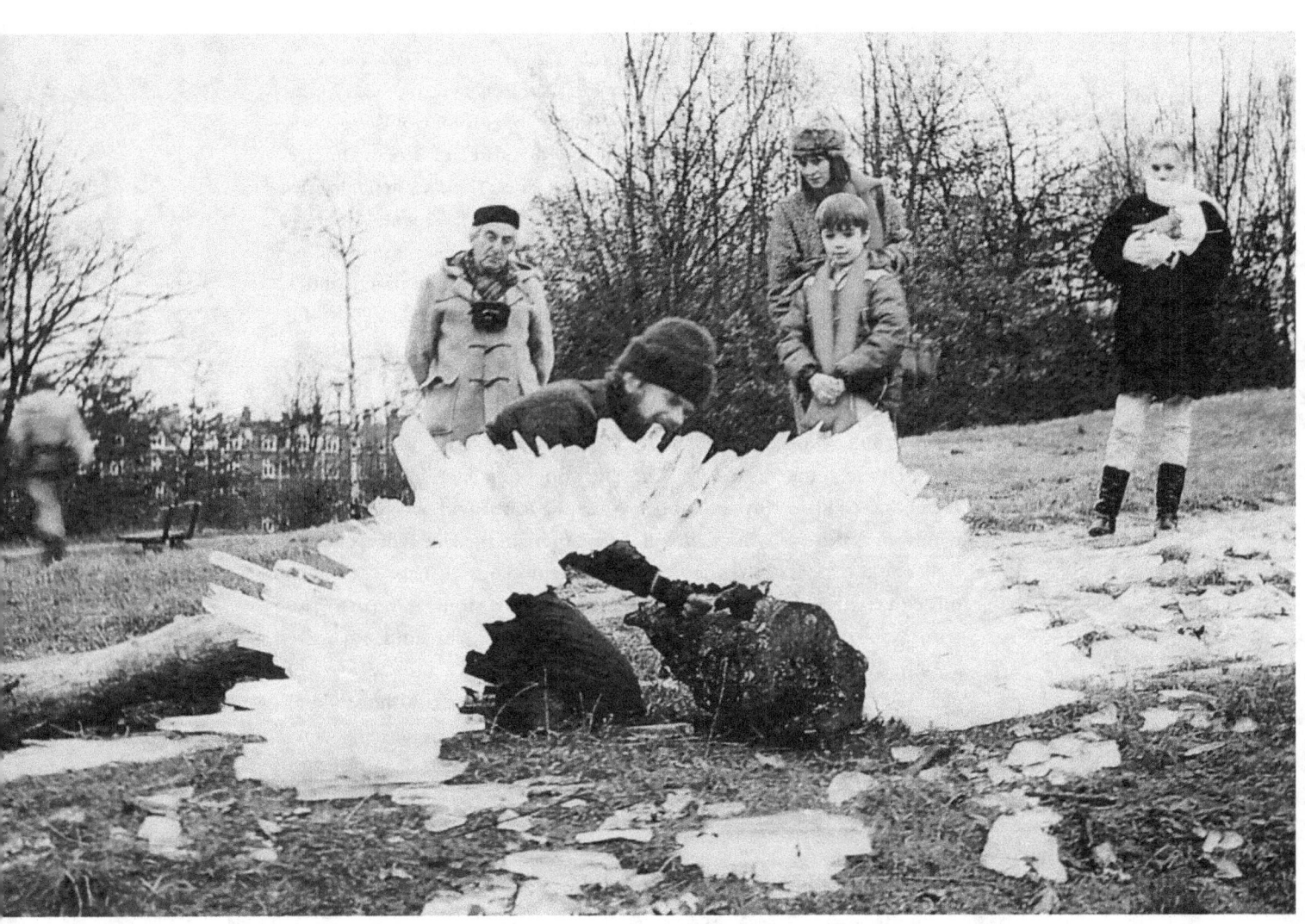

The Wall (1989)

This is a snake-like sculpture that Goldsworthy made between his land and a neighbouring farmer's at Stone Wood, Penpont. *The Wall* is a 'monument to walls',/ a neat way of creating, on Goldsworthy's side of the wall, a sculpture, and on the farmer's side, a sheepfold. Golds-worthy's walls have a dual purpose: practical, and æsthetic. The walls are boundaries or sheepfolds as well as artistic objects. Their æsthetic derives from their practical applications (*Stone*, 106). While later walls (such as *Room* or *The wall that went for a walk*) did not have a 'practical' or agricultural function, Goldsworthy still related them to the practicalities of stonewalling. Goldsworthy speaks proudly and sentimentally of the practice of stonewalling: he speaks of 'tradition', 'history', 'years of experience' (*Stone,* 106).

Another wall, related to the first, was made at Vassivière in France: *Two folds* (1992) was two curl-shapes, like two question marks, which mirrored each other, as in *The Wall*. The upper fold enclosed some trees, as in other Goldsworthy wallworks, while the lower fold became flooded with water. This is a work that will decay, though: the lake will erode the wall, and the roots of the trees may alter the upper fold. This wall unites three of Goldsworthy's favourite elements: water, stone and earth. The stone curves link together the earth and the water, and both the seemingly 'weaker', more transient elements – water and trees – will change and even destroy the apparently 'stronger' element, the stone of the wall. For Goldsworthy, stone is hard and unyielding, tradition's view, but 'flowing, changing, malleable', if, he adds, one is 'prepared to understand it in those ways' (*Sheepfolds,* 12).

1. A. Goldsworthy, unpublished notes, 1988, in *Hand to Earth*, 134-5.

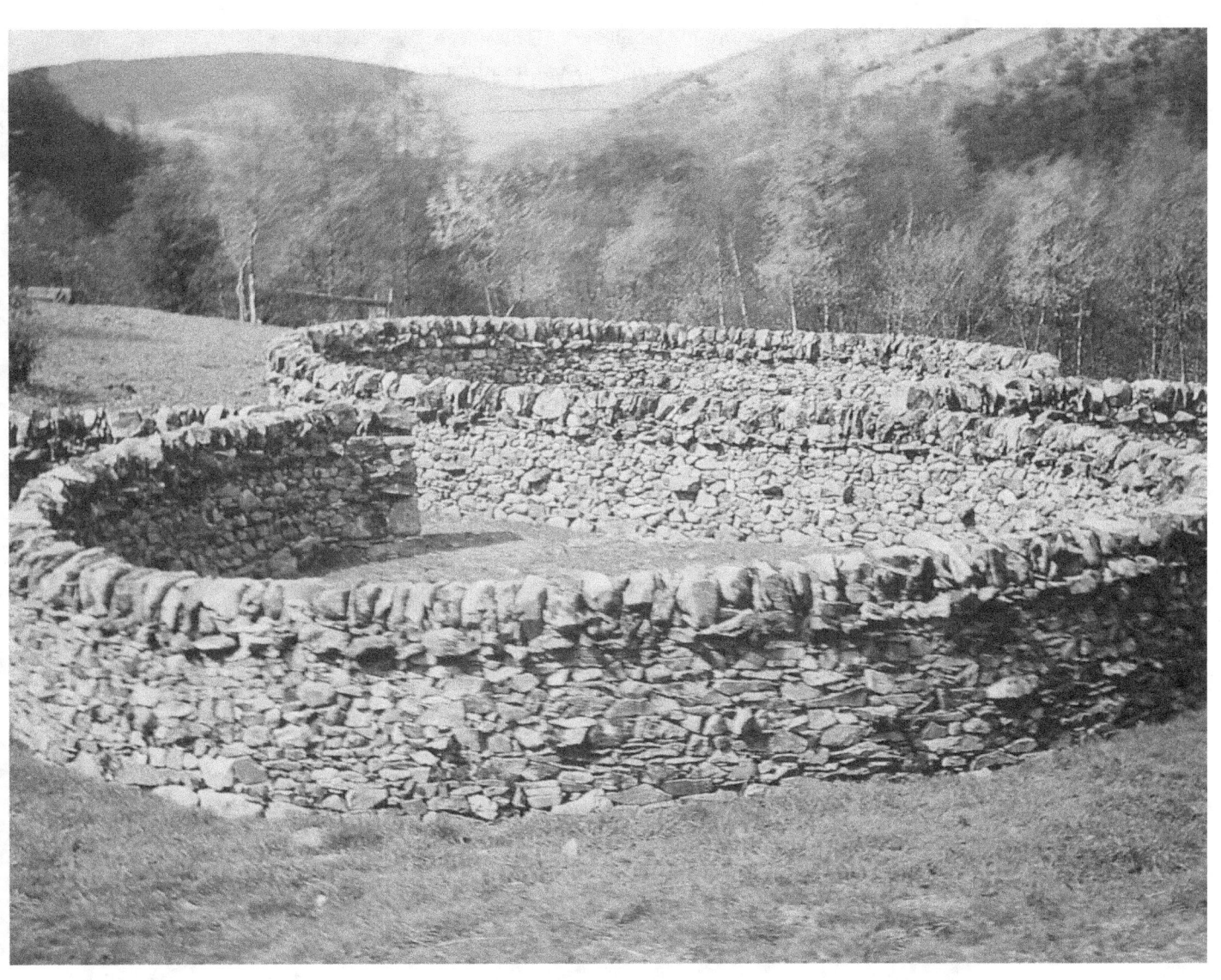

Leafshield (1986)

The 'shield' of sycamore leaves made on Hallowe'en 1986 in Glasgow glows bright gold. Goldsworthy was excited by the colours of this particular Autumn:

> I arrived during a week of the most intense autumn weather I have experienced and the most extraordinary range of colours in the leaves scattered everywhere – sycamore, elm, chestnut...[1]

The suspended leaf shield turned out to be 'one of the best pieces I have ever made', as Goldsworthy put it. The hanging leafworks enable light to become a key element in the sculpture: the translucence of the leaves was highlighted. The sun completed the sculpture, making the leafwork as 'extraordinary as going to the Arctic' (*Hand to Earth*, 167). Light is one of the key formal elements that Goldsworthy explores in his sculpture. Critics have spoken of Goldsworthy's 'stunning effects of light and atmosphere'.[2]

Because place is so important,[3] light (and colour) becomes a primary tool. Some works pivot very much on luminosity and opacity, not just the leaf shields, but some of the snow walls, the holes in sand, and so on, so that without the right sort of lighting, they do not work properly. Some sculptures are made in response to certain lighting conditions – the stick sculptures in the Lake District, made in the pale, liquid light of dawn, for example. 'When I work with the land I work with the sky. When I work with water I am working with the clouds', stated Goldsworthy (*Hand to Earth*, 167). The branches from a mulga tree in Australia (1991) were edged with red sand in order to catch the light of the setting sun: set end to end, the red-edged branches looked like a snake (appropriate for the Australian outback). Some of Goldsworthy's weakest works were made in Australian in 1991: *Mulga branches* had the branches laid on the red sand in two directions; they changed colour as the light changed.

1. Goldsworthy, sketchbook no. 13, and in N. Sinden.
2. Katharine Carter, "*Stone*", *New Welsh Review*, 27, Winter 1994-95, 100.
3. 'My strongest work is so rooted in place that it cannot be separated from where it is made' Goldsworthy wrote in *Stone* (6).

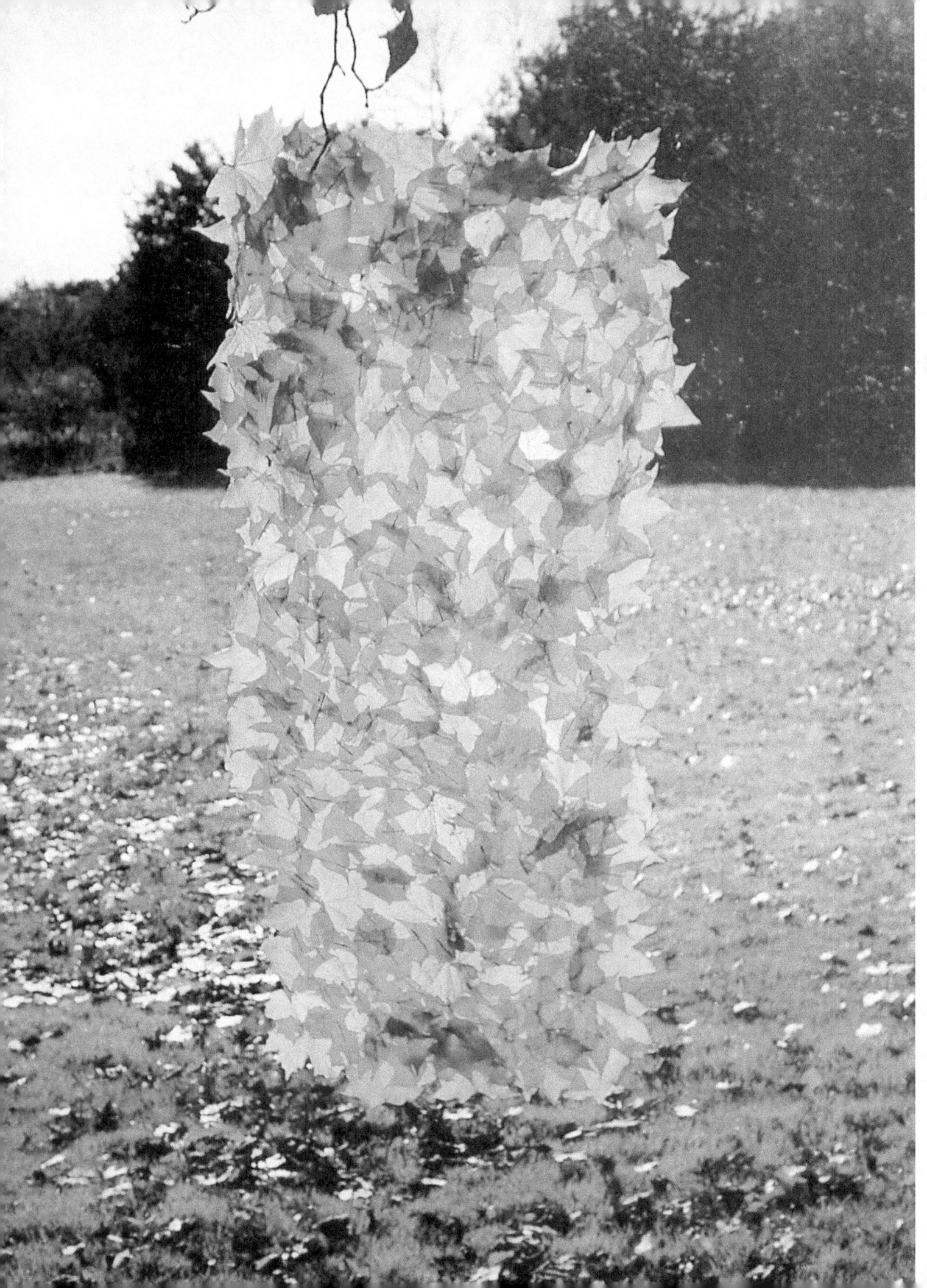

Hole (1976)

These are some of Andy Goldsworthy's sculptures earliest sculptures –
nothing more complex, apparently, than a hole dug in the Earth. The hole
would become one of the artist's recurring motifs – in leaves, in sand, in
clay spheres, or in the ground. On the following pages are examples of
the hole motif combined with the low, circular cairn or mound.

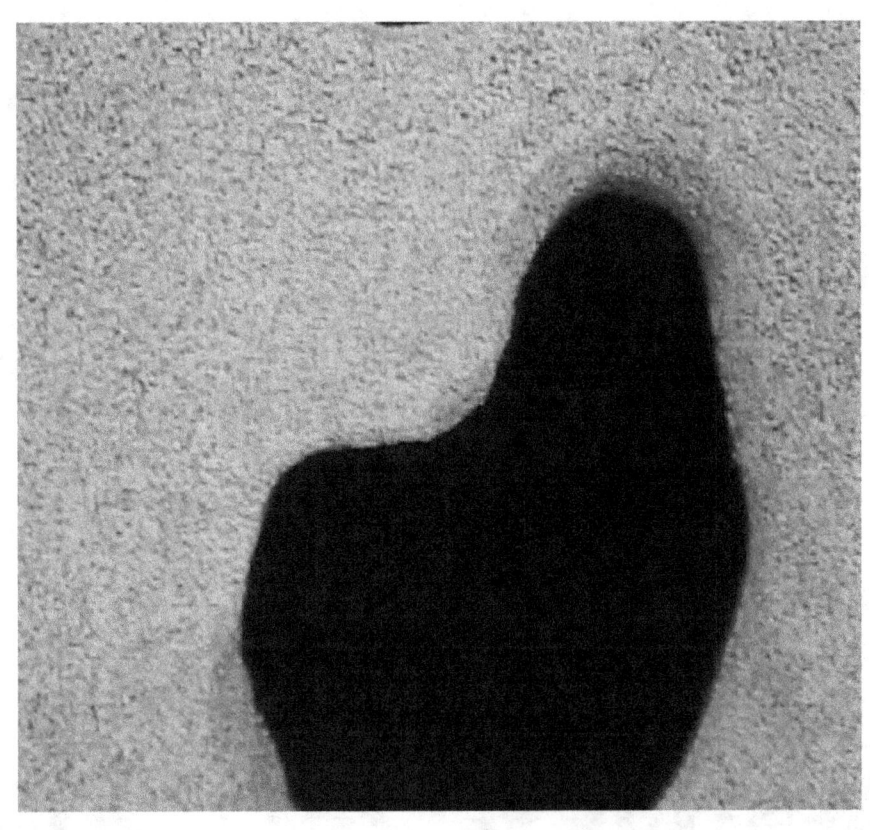

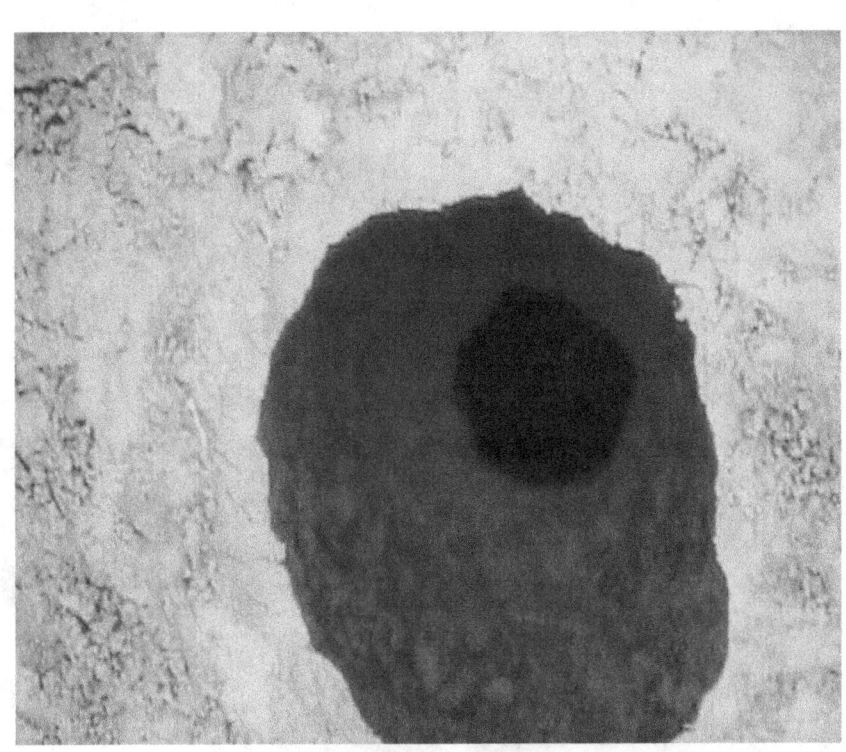

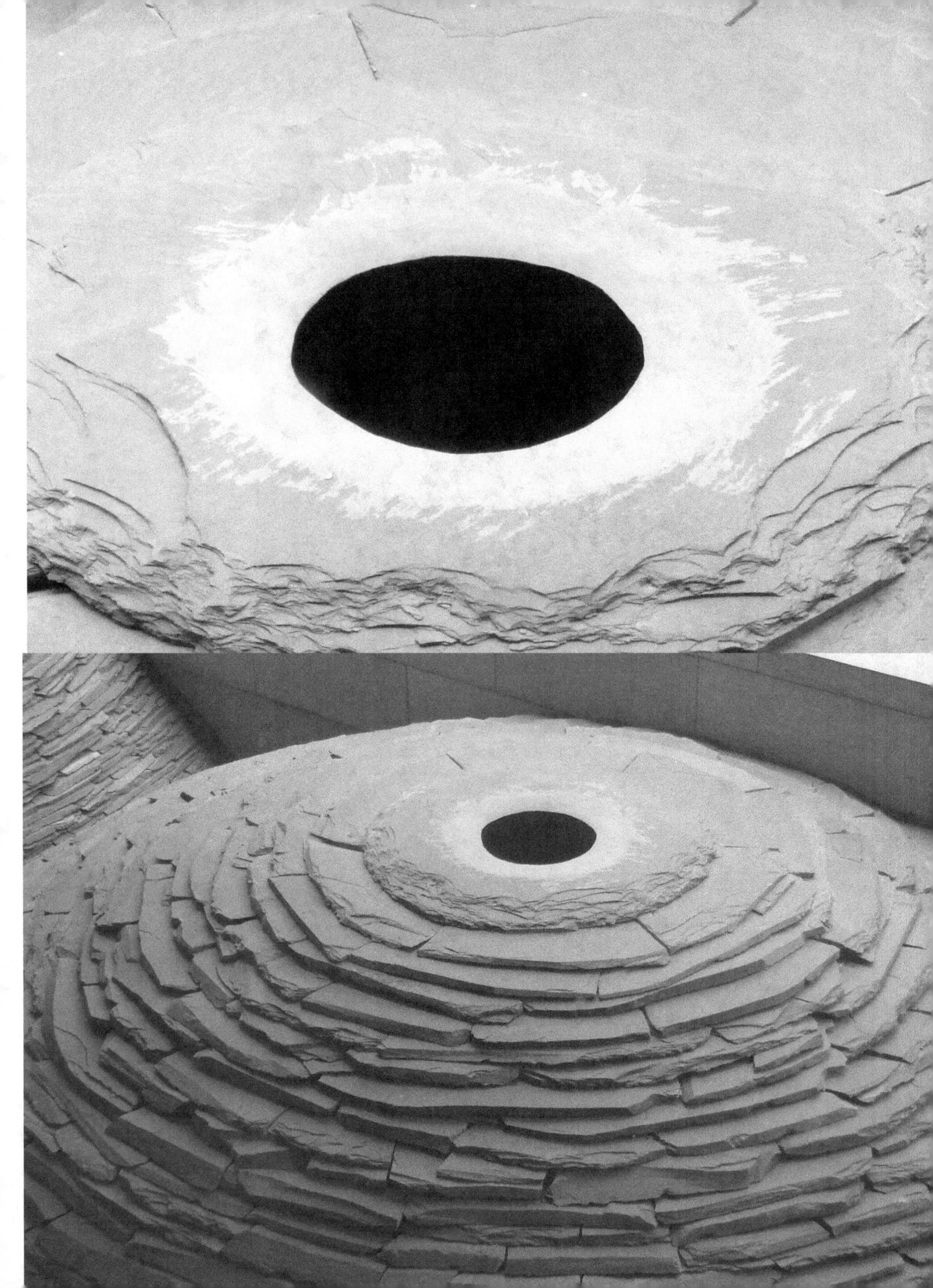

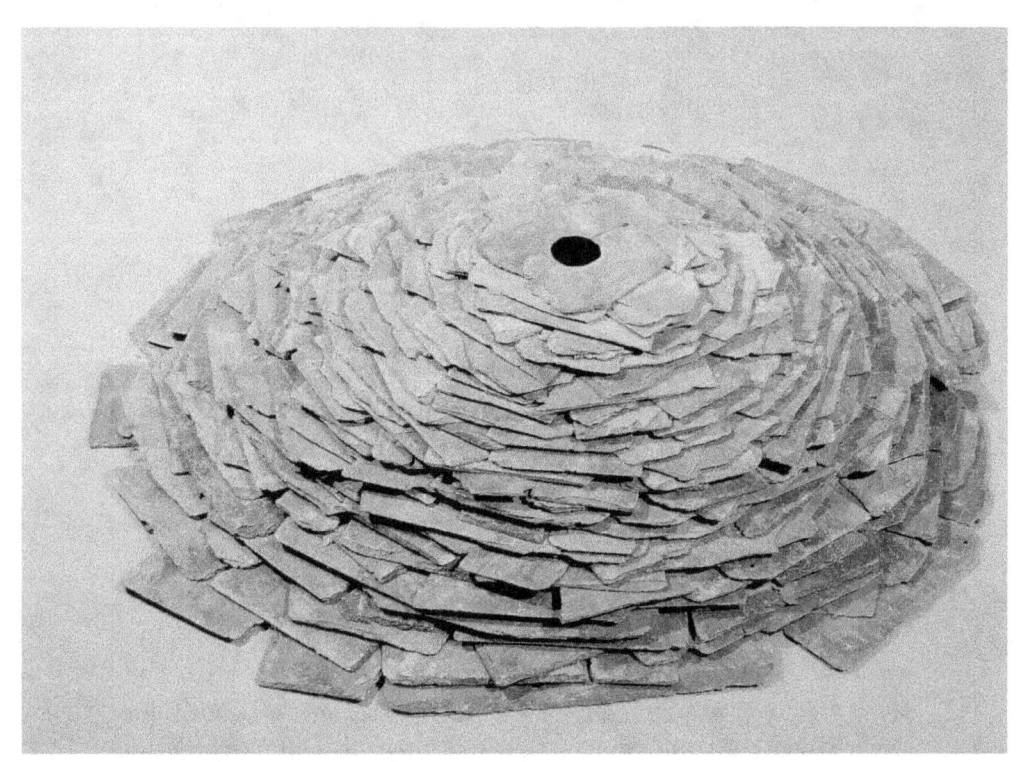

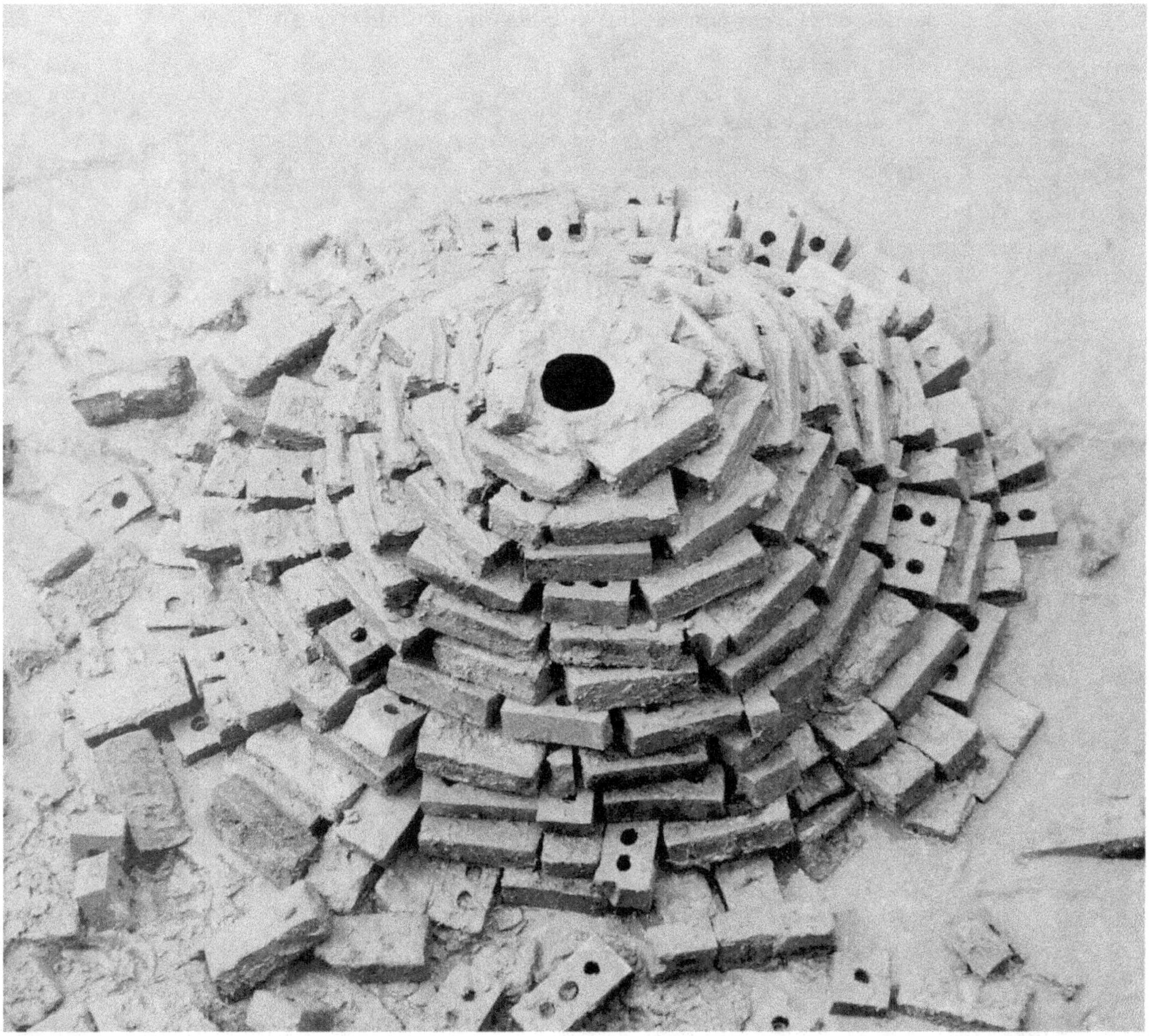

Hole (1984)

Andy Goldsworthy regarded his hole made at the Serpentine Gallery in the 1980s as 'perhaps the best work I ever made in a building', because he claimed he 'touched the nature of the building'.[1] The Goldsworthy hole is also a key element of many of his cairns: the holed cairns are usually low circular structures with a circular aperture on the small flat summit, as in *Black water hole,* or another water hole, in the Thames (1987), or *Slate hole* (1983) and *Stick hole* (1999). Sometimes the holed slate cairns recall hearths or alchemical vessels in which the energies of nature are being harnessed. One thinks of David Nash's 'hearths' and stoves (*Sea Hearth, Snow Stove, Wood Stove, Slate Stove*, etc), and Chris Drury's shelters. (Goldsworthy has fired stones in a kiln, in order to release the stone's essence, exactly as mediæval alchemists did. It is not the spectacular nature of fire and flames that intrigues him, though, but 'the slow intense powerful heat that is at the core of nature' [S, 65]).

1. A. Papdakis, 1991, 249.

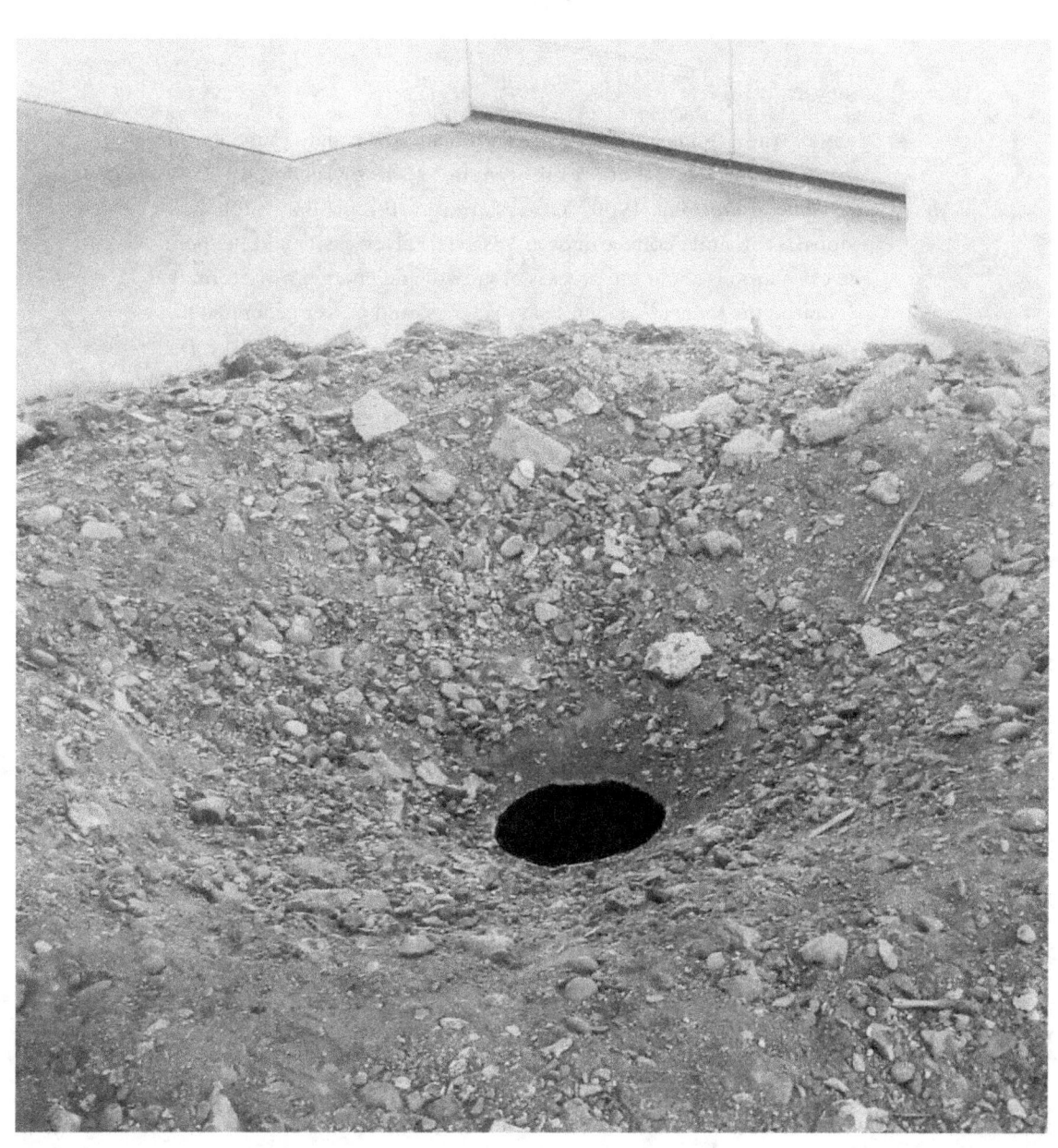

Slate Cones

Many of Andy Goldsworthy's cairns are made from slate (such as *Slate cone*, 1987, 1988); others from branches (*Oak branches*, 1990); or sandstone (*Sandstone*, 1990). Others are put into groups (such as the proposals for stone cone groups at Vassivière, Newcastle and Penpont). The cairn form is about the process of growth and energy. It is a form that celebrates 'the fullness, vigour, heavy ripeness and power generated from a centre, deep inside' Goldsworthy claimed (*Stone,* 37). Like D.H. Lawrence and Friedrich Nietzsche, Goldsworthy here makes the age-old links between 'ripeness' in nature and femininity and pregnancy. The Goldsworthy cone, then, can be seen as another expression of female fecundity, in the Lawrencean manner, an equivalent for a pregnant woman (like the prehistoric "Stone Venuses", the squat, callipygous figurines): in short, stone Mother-Goddesses.

'Cone' is perhaps not quite the right term for an image or expression of fullness and ripeness: Goldsworthy's 'cones' look more like fruit. The imagery of fruit would accord with Goldsworthy's ripeness discourse. 'Cairn' is also not quite the right word, though some of the 'cones' on rocky mountainsides (*Cone to mark day becoming night at Glenleith Fell*, and *Cone to mark night becoming day*, Scaur Glen, both 1991) have affinities with natural cairns and outcrops of rock. Some of the cairns were made at night, to be seen at night, as hymns to the night, or the dawn, or the sunset. Working on the Yorkshire *Ice hole,* Goldsworthy spoke of 'working with the moonlight' which was a 'very strange intense light' (1987, *Hand to Earth*, 147). Working at night, Goldsworthy spoke of approaching 'the most beautiful point, the point of greatest tension, as one moves towards daybreak'.[1]

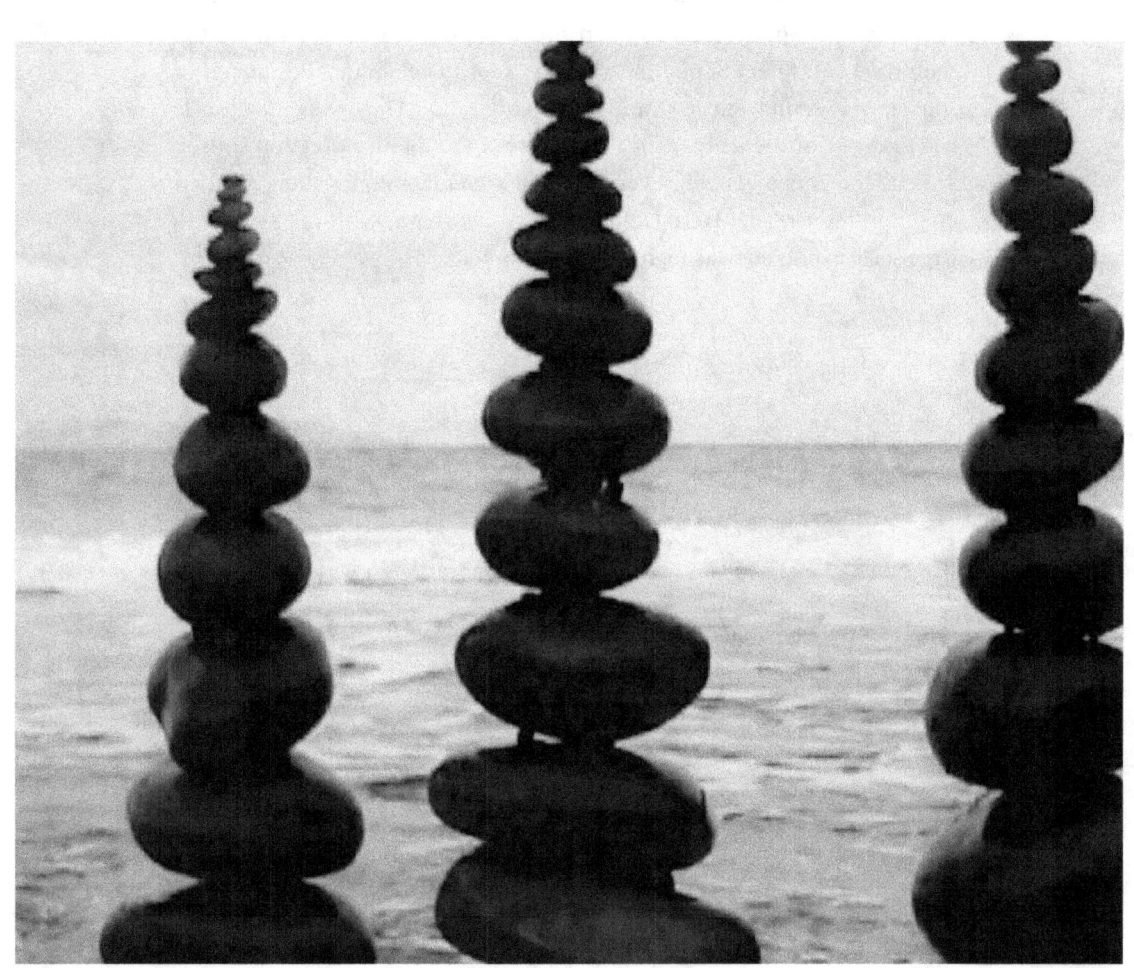

In Australia Goldsworthy constructed cairns 'for the moonlight', or 'for the day' (*Stone,* 43). Like the mulga tree branches edged with red sand to catch the setting sun, these stone cairns were made for particular lighting conditions: the orange-coloured stones made into a cairn were associated with (and completed by) the setting sun. The stone cairns were the sculptural equivalent of lighting a fire in order to celebrate Midsummer or sunset; or erecting a little shrine for a minor deity. They were small-scale celebrations of the daily festivals of dawn, moonlight, noon and sunset, sacred moments that occur every day, but which are no less holy for their common recurrence. Here Goldsworthy is working 'with the sky', with large-scale events such as nightfall and moonlight.

1. In Y. Baginsky, 1989.

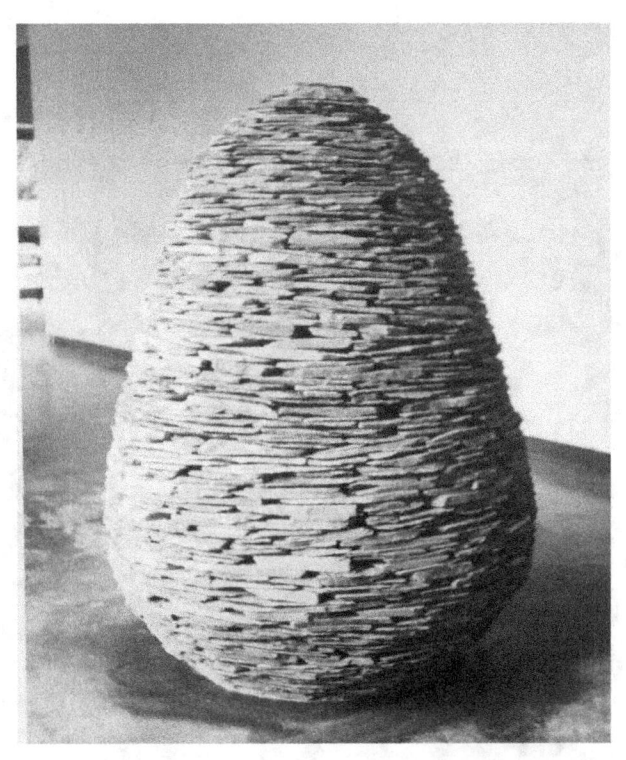

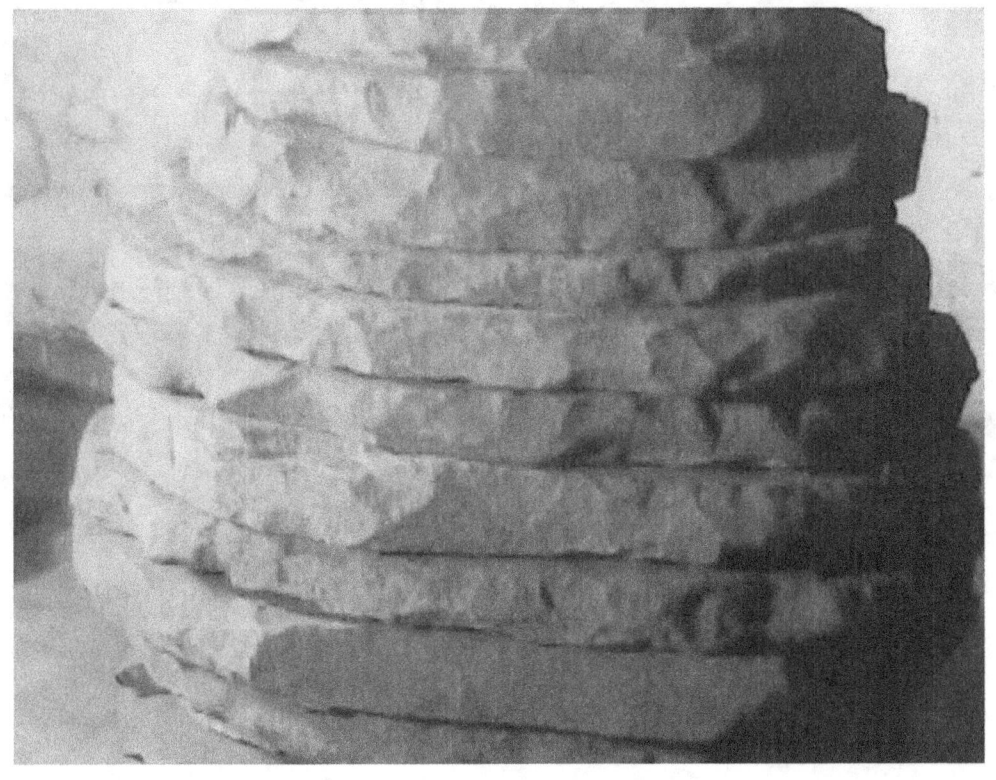

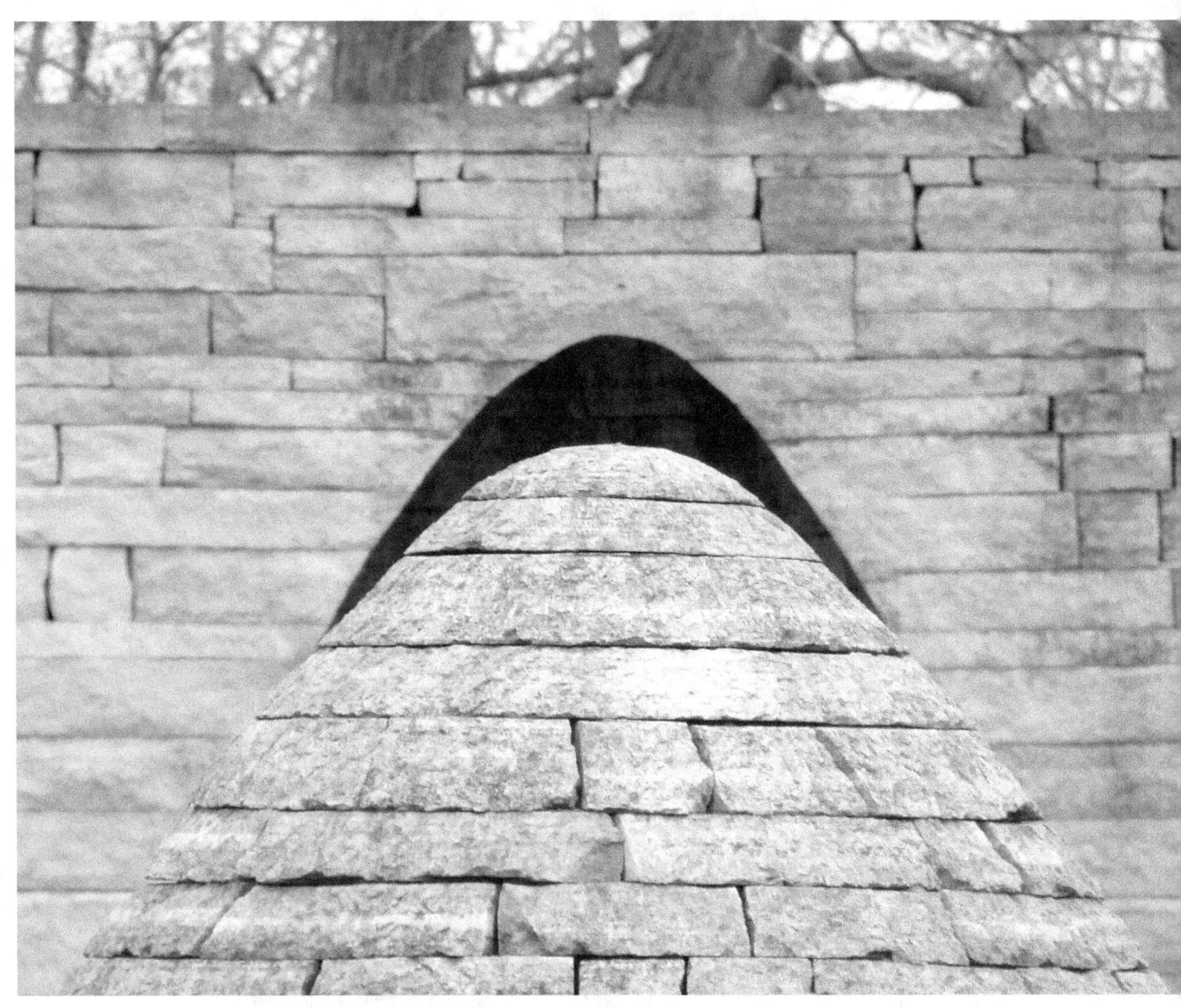

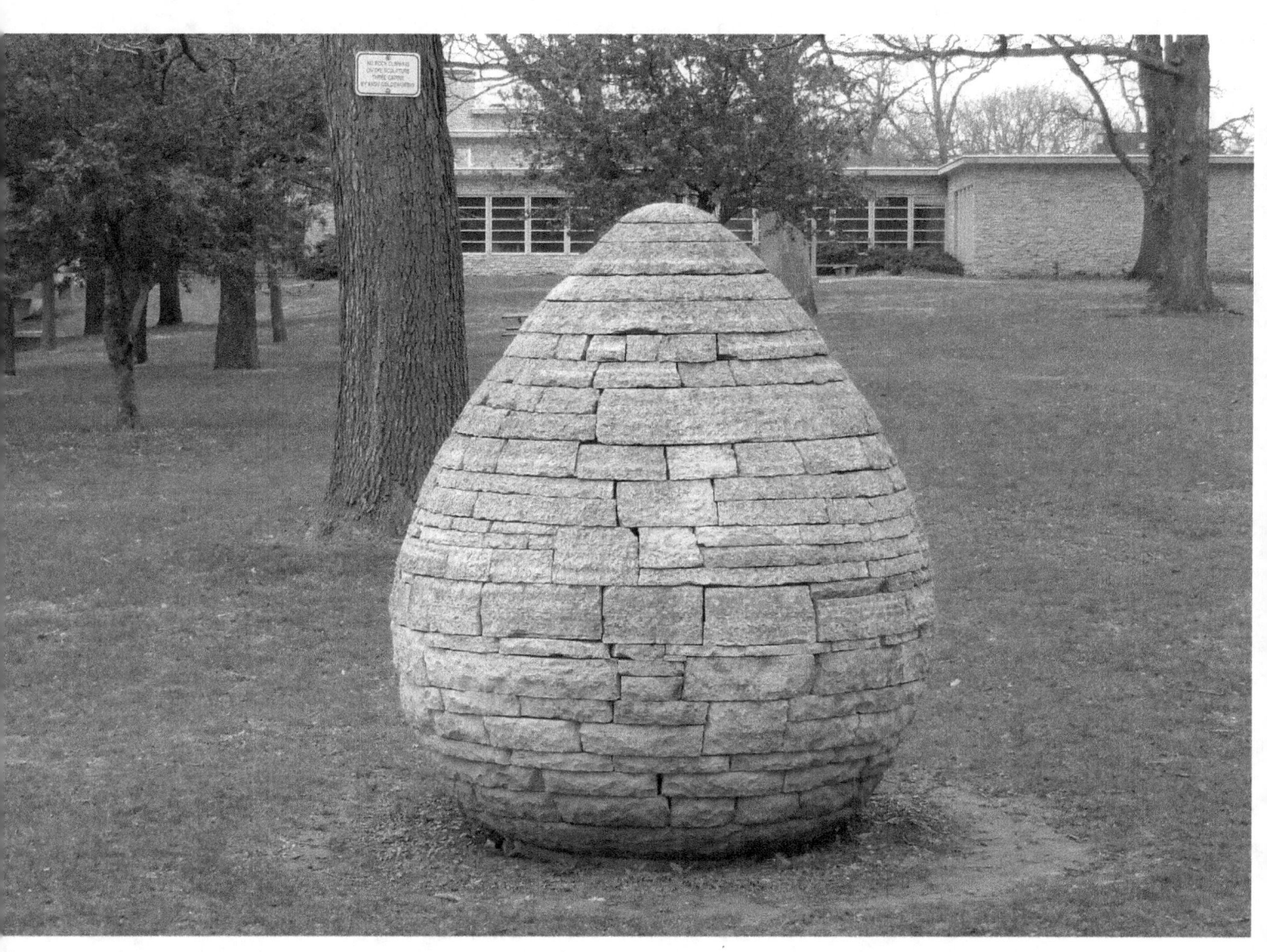

The Capenoch Tree (1996)

The largest section of the book *Wood* (1996) is devoted to the *Capenoch Tree* series of works, made between 1994 and 1996 in Dumfriesshire. The 'Capenoch tree' was an old oak tree standing slightly apart from other trees. Andy Goldsworthy concentrated not on the whole tree, its trunk or its branches, but on one particular branch that grew sideways out from the tree, horizontally, a few feet above the grass. The *Capenoch Tree* series was unified by its location: every work was centred on the tree and its long branch. The unity of the series was enhanced by Goldsworthy photographing each piece from the same angle, the same side of the tree. In nearly all of the photographic records of the *Capenoch Tree* series in *Wood* the same elements are present: the trunk on the right, the branch extending across the picture plane from right to left, the ground underneath and the background of trees. Goldsworthy returned to the Capenoch tree in all seasons, but favoured Autumn and Winter – the best works in the *Capenoch Tree* series are those made in Winter. Goldsworthy wrote portentously of the Capenoch tree and of trees in general in *Wood*:

> The stone grows within the – the seed. The column is a growth form, progressive. Tree is stone expressed in wood… The long branch that has grown horizontal to the ground has taught me that the tree is the land. The branch is like the landscape. It is the earth, it is stone… (*Wood*, 23, 85)

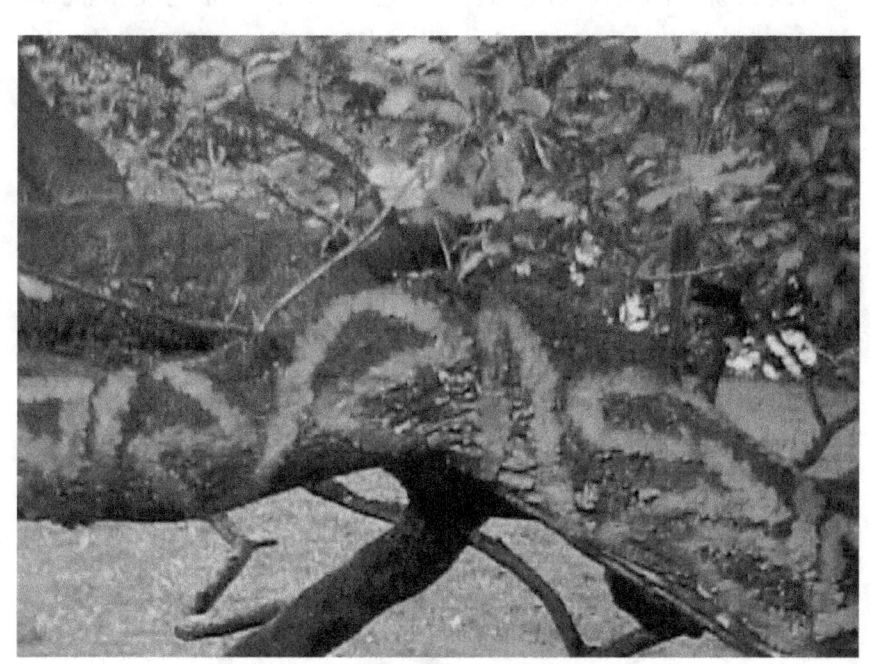

The Capenoch Tree (1996)

Apart from the hanging oak leaf lines, some of the less successful works in the *Capenoch Tree* series were the cairns and towers. The branches stacked against the tree trunk with a large circular opening (Jan 16, 1996), for example, looked out of place, as did the *Five Stone Arches* (March, 1994), a 'herd of arches', made from thick slabs of stone. The line of seven snowballs, meanwhile, balanced along the length of the horizontal branch in decreasing sizes, worked well: this is one of the most adaptable of Goldsworthy's forms.

The large hollowed snowball made in March, 1995 when the snow was thawing also suited the location and its place in the *Capenoch Tree* series. The two 'stone houses' made in August, 1995 consisted of a stack of branches leaning against the tree with a large oval opening. Inside the 'house' was placed a column of balanced stones in decreasing sizes. This Goldsworthyan form is complex and difficult to harmonize satisfactorily with its environment.

The simpler structures, such as the lines of leaves pinned to the branch, were finer realizations of Goldsworthy's explorations of the tree-in- the-landscape theme. Of the other stacks of sticks placed next to the Capenoch tree, the simpler forms worked best: not the cone with a hole through which the branch was glimpsed, but the globe of sticks next to the trunk, and the tower of sticks through which the branch passed (Nov, 1994). The *Two holes* (1995), one made with leaves, attached to the branch, and one dug in the ground, was a weak work. The *Oak tree snow cairn* (1996) was a simple but effective form: a shallow cone located underneath the upward curve of the long branch. Goldsworthy capped the snow cairn with mud, then covered it with mud. Goldsworthy admitted to a 'deep sense of spirituality', but said 'it doesn't manifest itself in any sort of religion'.[1]

1. A. Papadakis, 1991, 250.

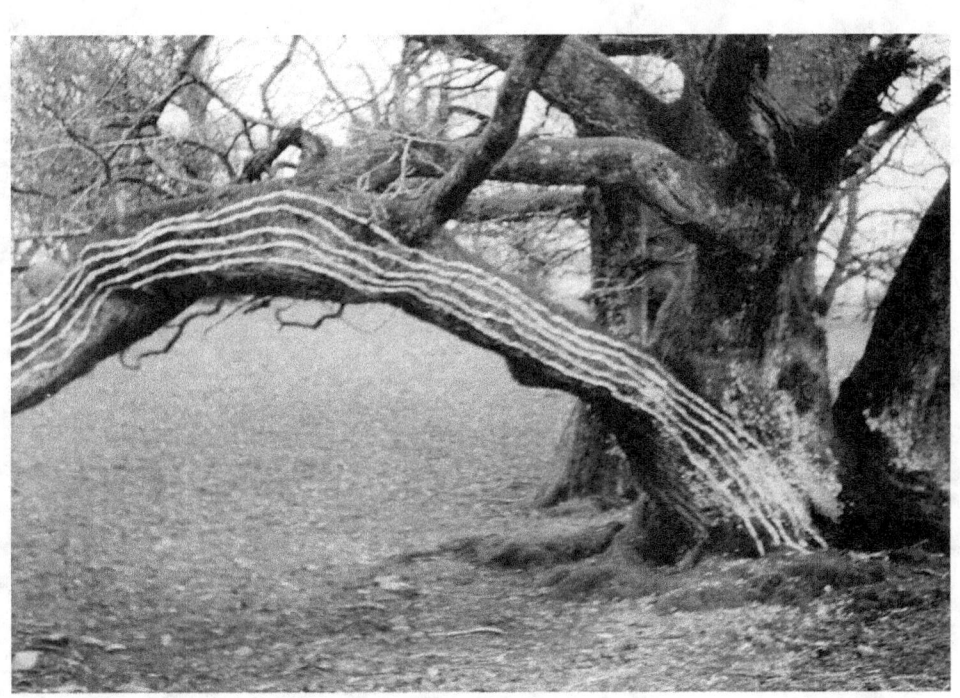

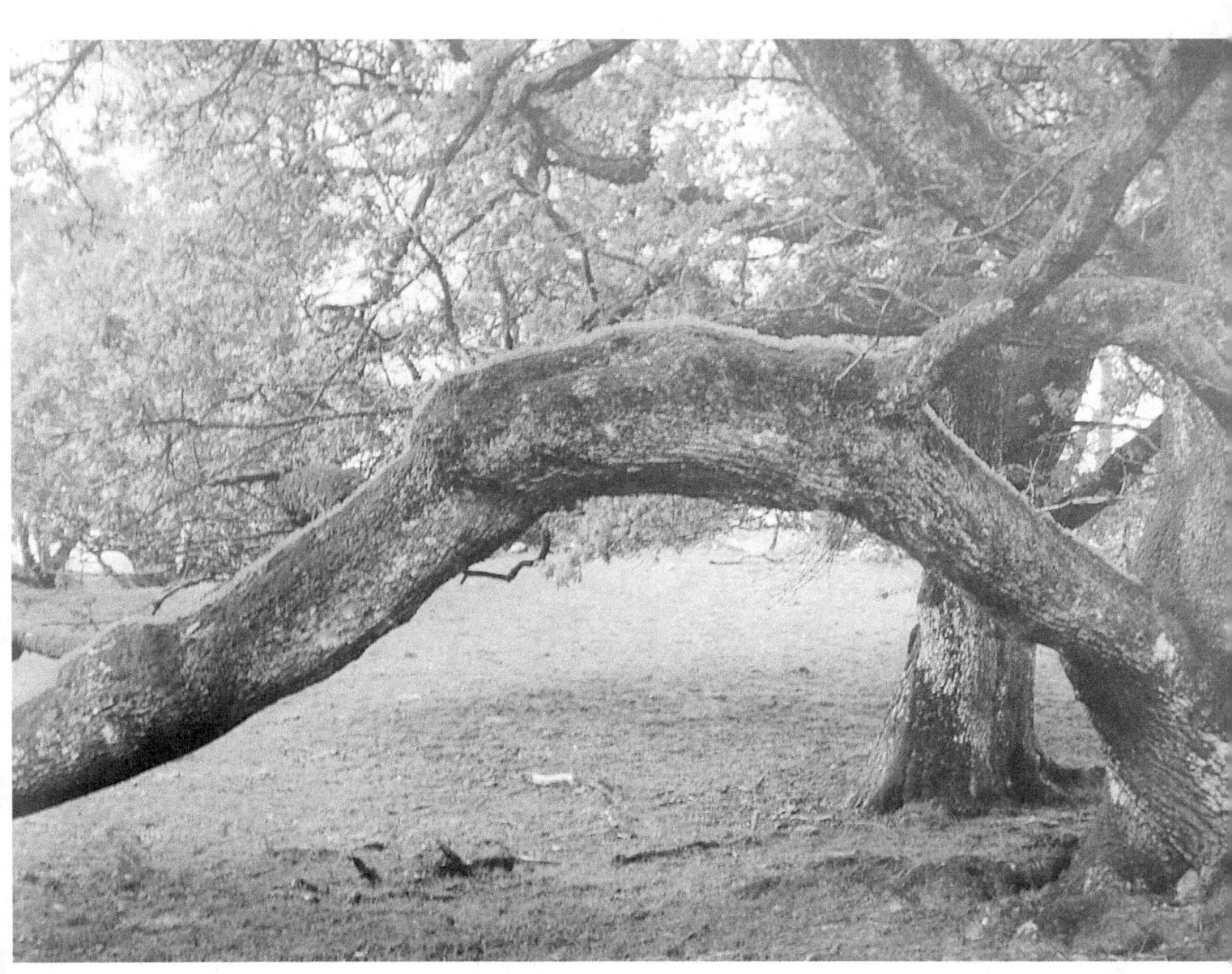

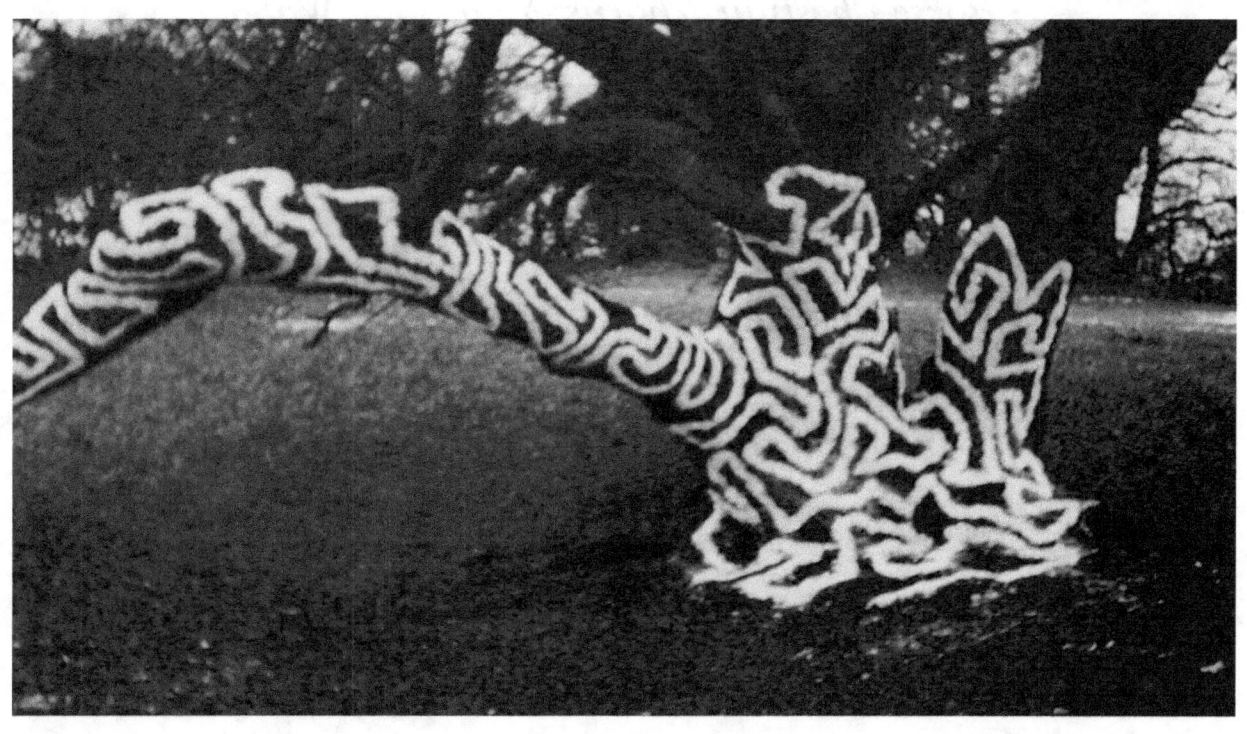

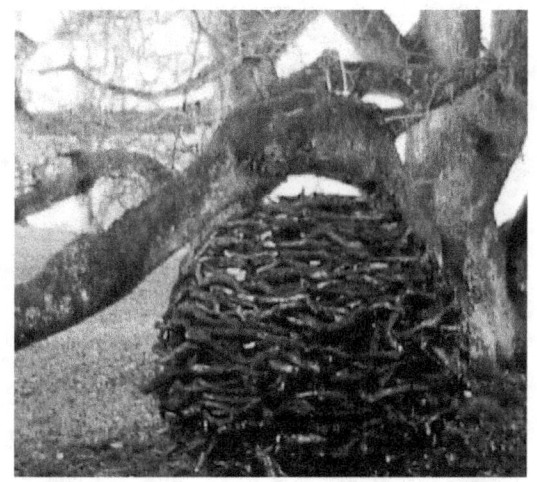

Horse Chestnut, Thorns, Mud, Soot, Water (1989)

Andy Goldsworthy has made more 'traditional' forms of art in galleries: his bracken, fern and horse chestnut stalk works, for instance, were produced by pinning the materials onto white gallery walls. These works – *Bracken fronds* (Ecology Centre, London, 1985), *Reeds, bracken and horse chestnut stalks* (Centre d'Art Contemporain, Castres, and Galerie Aline Vidal, Paris, 1989) and *Reed line drawing* (Paris, 1990) – were essentially free, open wall drawings, often employing basic motifs such as the circle and open curve. Screens of plants that Goldsworthy created in galleries include the *Susuki grass* and *Horse chestnut leaf stalks* (both made in Japan in 1993), and *Rushes thorns* (1992, San Francisco).

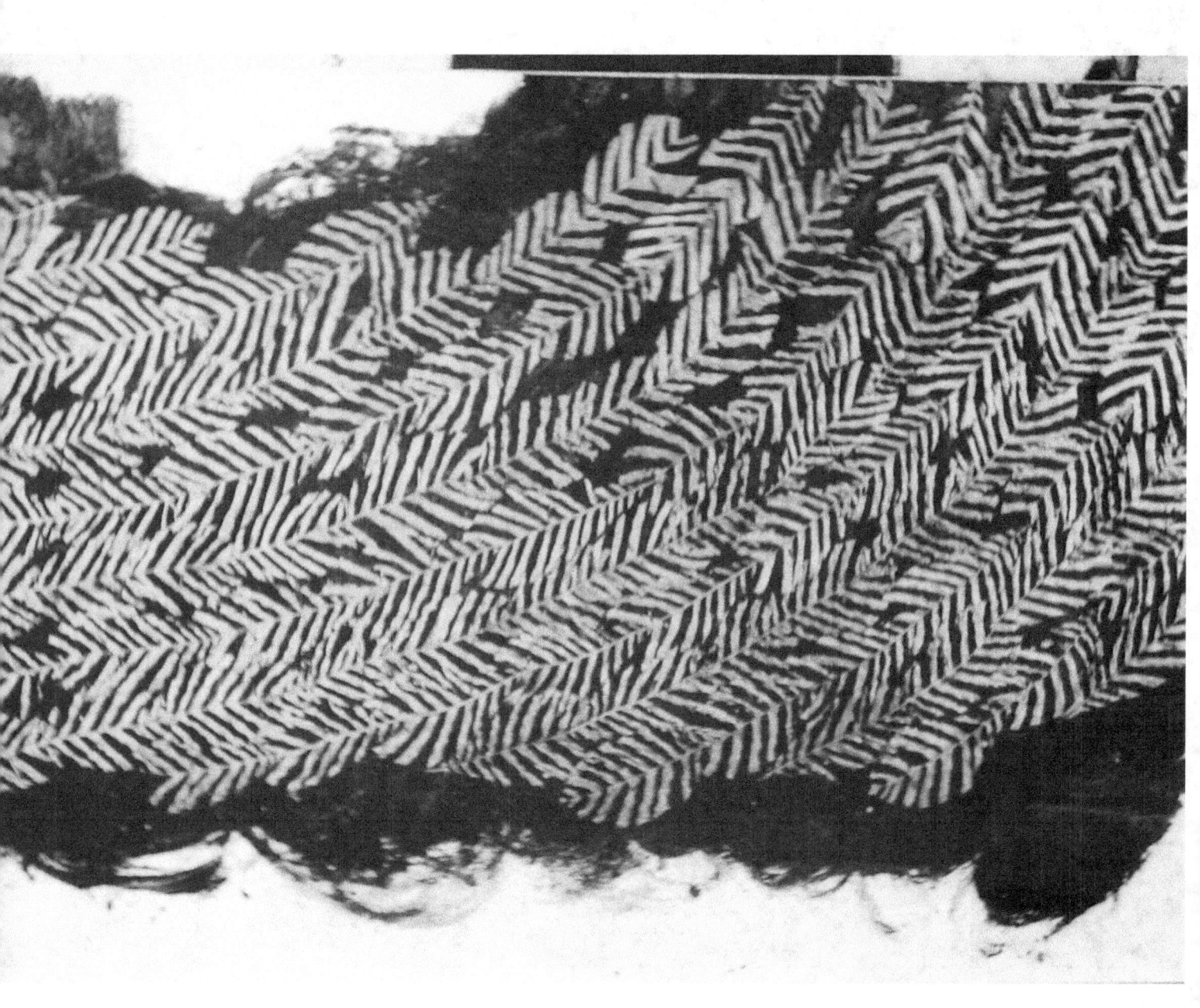

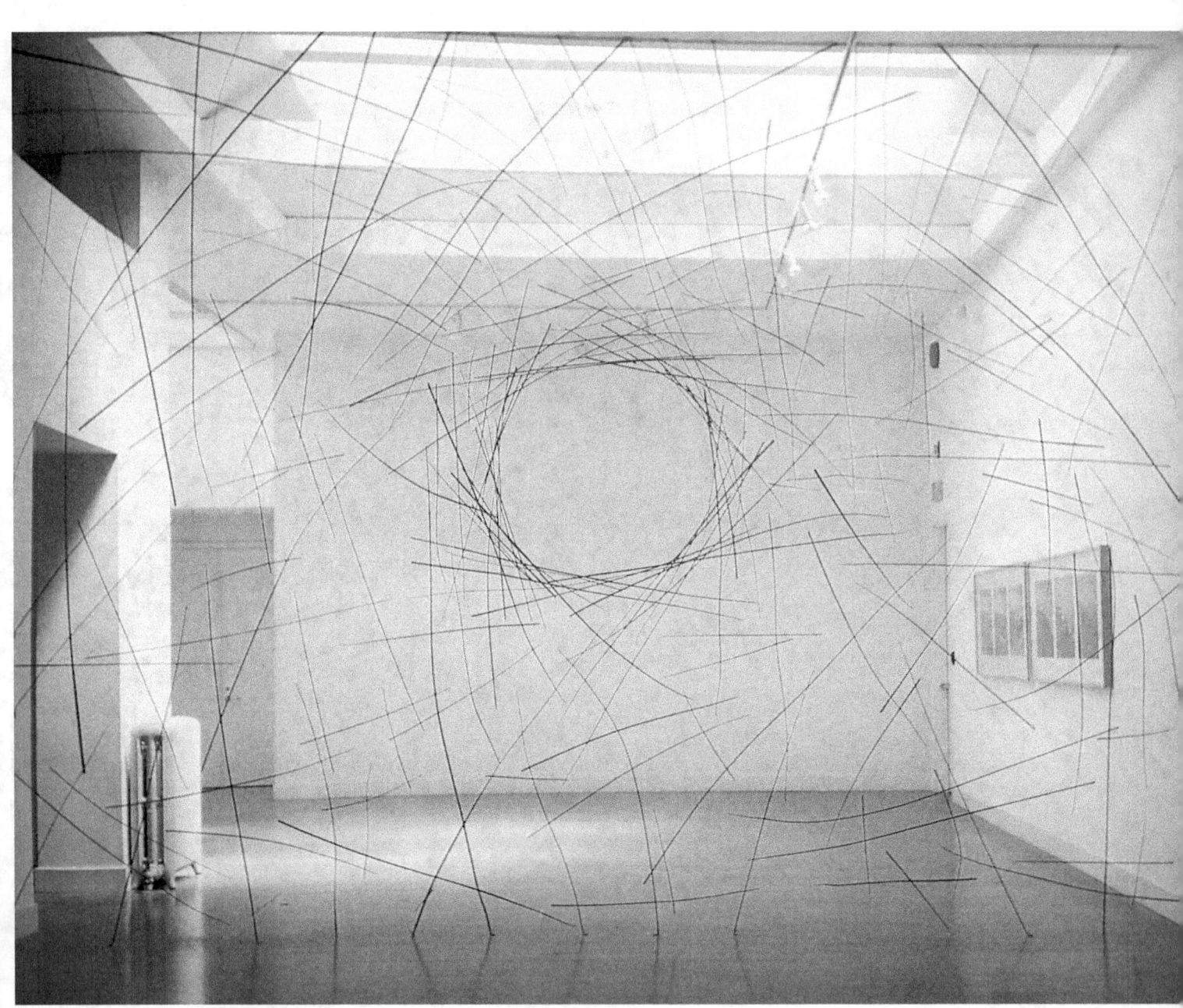

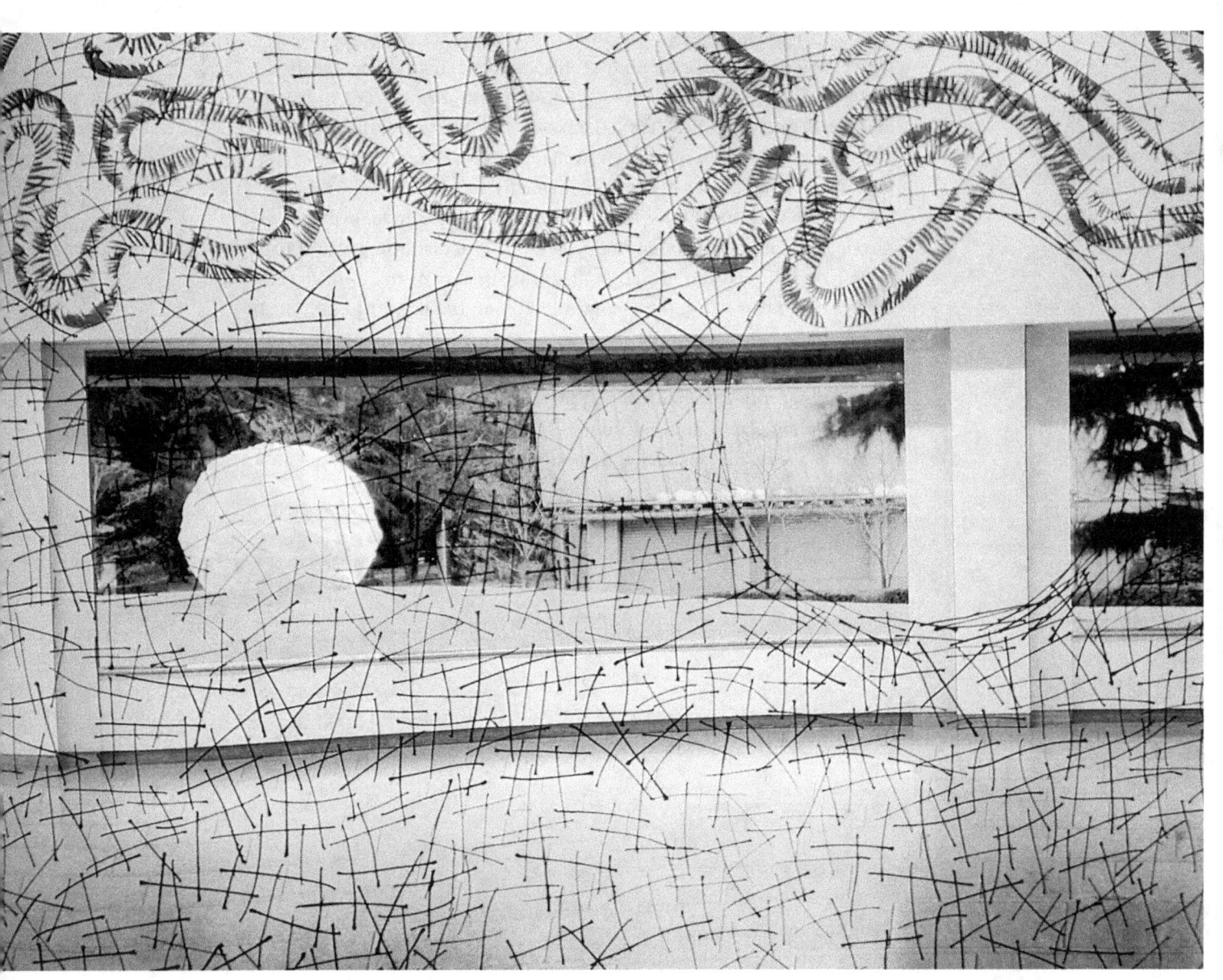

Clay Wall (1998)

Other large-scale works by Andy Goldsworthy include the installations *Slate Wall* and *Clay Wall* (1998, Edinburgh), *Clay Wall* (1996, San Francisco) and *Clay Wall* (2000, London). For his dance collaboration, Goldsworthy had one of his clay walls filmed over ten days to form a backdrop to the performance. Goldsworthy found he was not wholly happy with the filmed *Clay Wall*: 'I found the flicker and movement of the image as it goes through the projector more disturbing than I had anticipated'. It was the unstable, flickering quality of the footage that unsettled Goldsworthy, the changes in colour and light: 'the physical nature of the film and its projection makes the medium more present that I would like it to be' (T, 84). That's an interesting remark that suggests that Goldsworthy prefers recording media to be transparent. He doesn't want his photographs drawing attention to themselves as photographs; he wants the viewer to look through them to the sculptures and places he's photographing.

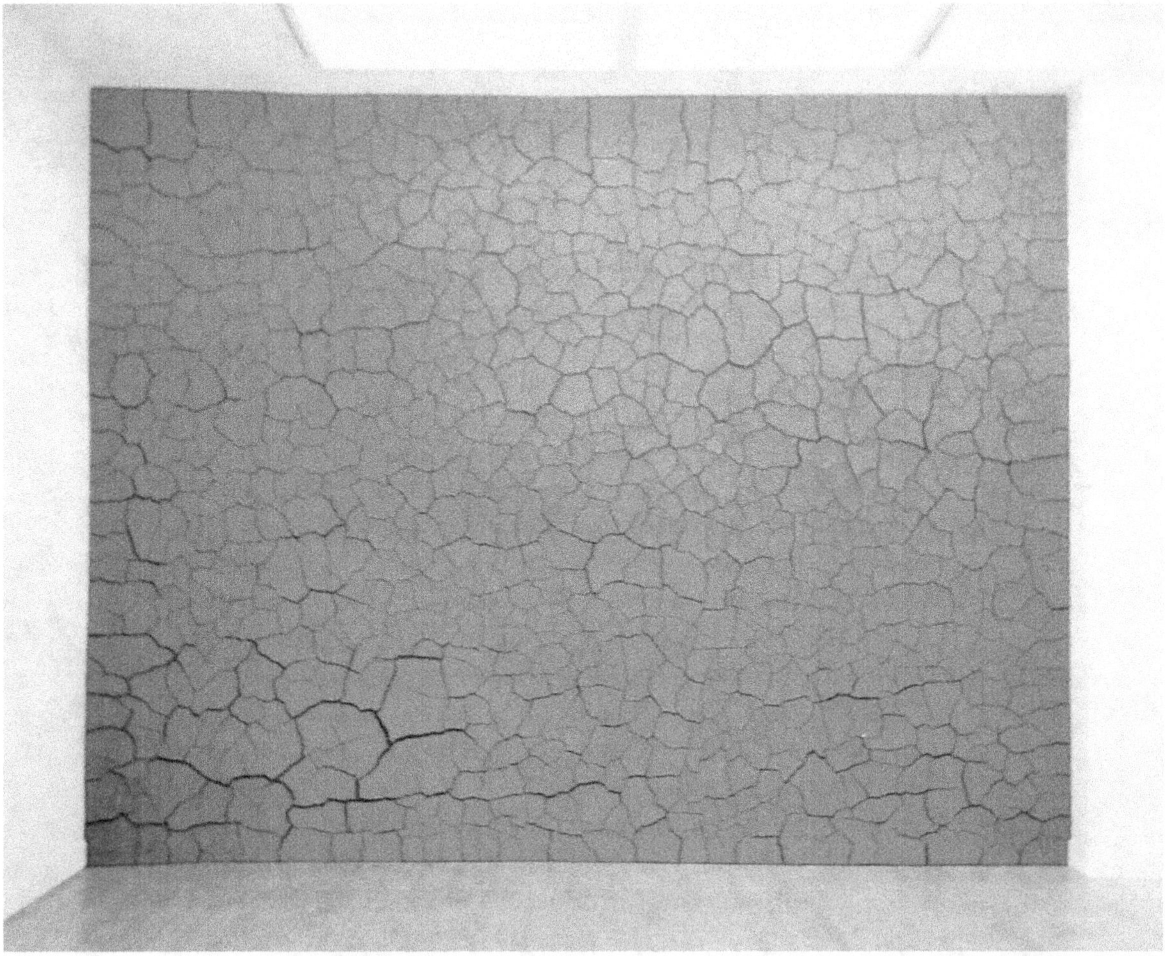

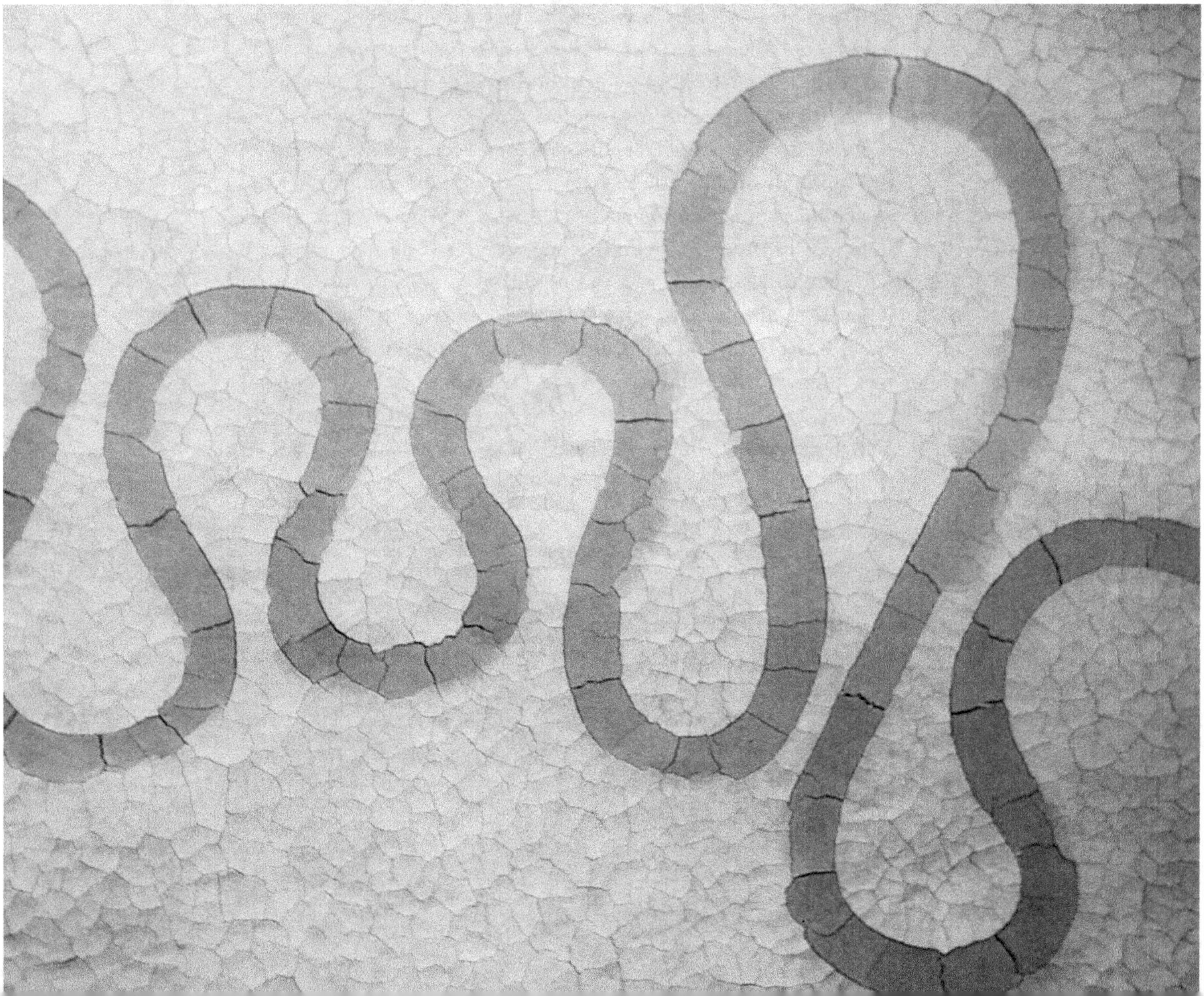

Broken Pebbles (1987)

The spiral and snake employed by so many land artists down the ages (in ancient Peru, or on the doors of Neolithic tombs, or in the Mid-West of America) is associated with the Goddess and with the energies of life. The circles and spirals of Goldsworthy, Nash, Oppenheim and Smithson are also those of the Goddess, the ancient Earth Mother. In the eco-neo-pseudo-pagan view, the land artists, then, make marks upon Mother Earth, upon the surface or skin of the Goddess. Goldsworthy speaks inadvertently of phallic penetration when he says: 'I want to get under the surface... At its most successful, my 'touch' looks into the heart of nature' (*Winter Harvest*). The Earth, which is seen by some as female, is penetrated – by Michael Heizer gouging vast chunks out of the American desert, by Walter de Maria thrusting a kilometre-long brass rod into the earth, and Goldsworthy, seemingly so gentle, has cut trenches into the earth, or smashed slabs of slate or pebbles or leaves, to make lines of broken, shattered material on the earth. He has torn leaves apart to form a line, and has broken pebbles, making a line, like a fault line in continental structures (*Leaves Torn in Two*, 1986, and *Broken Pebbles*, 1987, in *Andy Goldsworthy*). These are violent gestures, destroying the organic make-up of the natural forms he so adores.

Sometimes the violence of a split-apart rock is emphasized by Goldsworthy highlighting the rough edges of the crack with red – as in *Granite boulder found split open* (1990, *Stone*, 76). The red leaves stuck on the edges of the split make the jagged edge look like a wound. Another rock Goldsworthy marked out with red, the *Soft red stone* at Heysham Head in Lancashire (1991, *Stone*, 82), was chosen perhaps because it was a rock that had recently fallen from the cliff above. It was not smoothed by water and weather: its sheared-off edges and planes were exaggerated by the red colour. All land artists, all artists, must break up and reform materials, but these cracks and holes can look like scars.

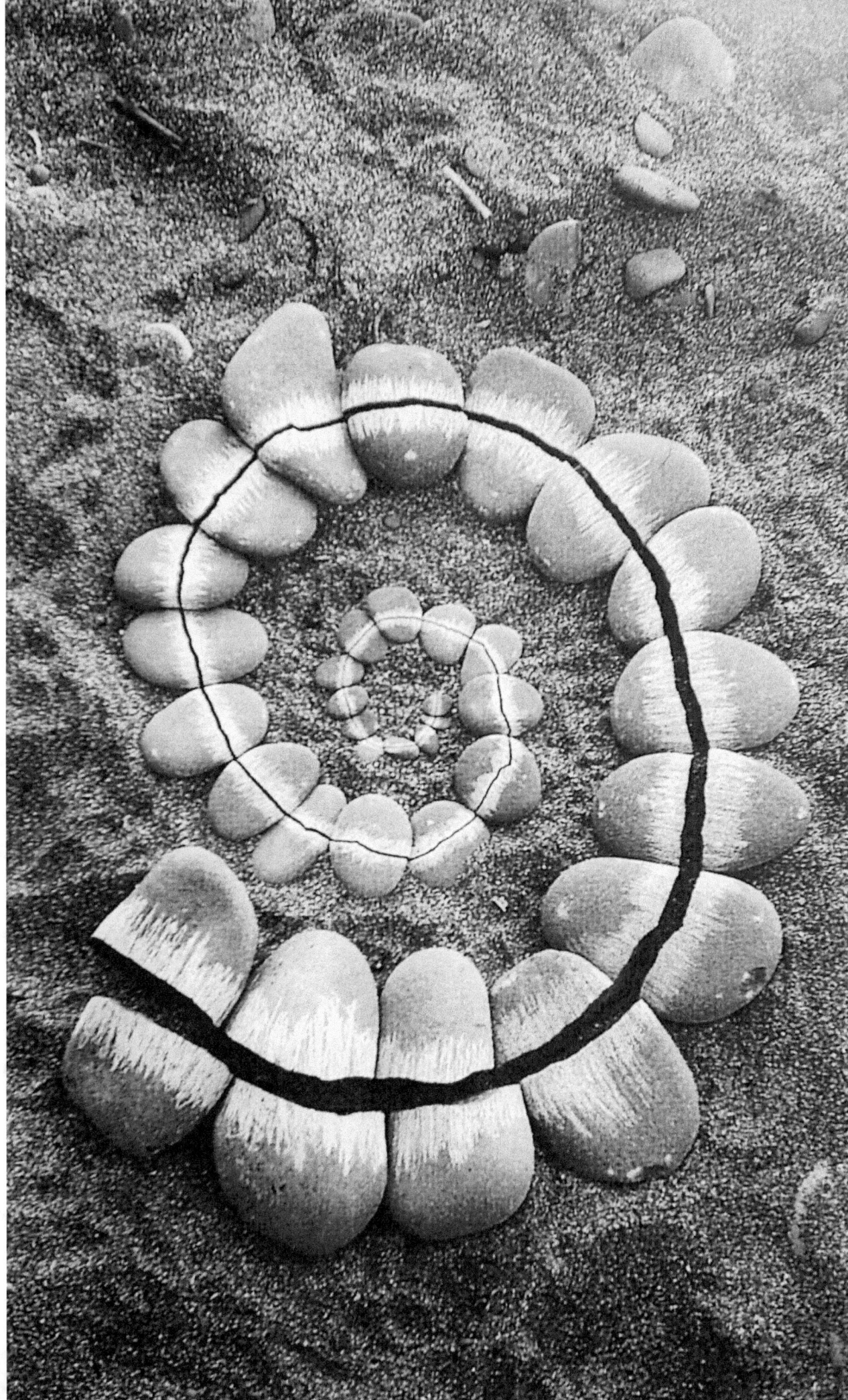

Cairns (1988)

Andy Goldsworthy has fashioned circular mounds out of leaves, slate, bracken and sticks which echo prehistoric monuments such as Silbury Hill in Britain, which have been interpreted as 'feminine' or womb images. Goldsworthy has made hollow snowballs – large snowballs, a few feet across, which are hollowed out like fruit: their hollowness is one of their central attributes. Goldsworthy cuts a circular hole in them (at Blencathra, Cumbria, 1988, *Andy Goldsworthy*). Like stone age people who covered the white bones of the dead with red powder (red as the colour of life, of blood, passion, rage), Goldsworthy often uses red as a colour in his art. He has red leaves, stones rubbed with red stones, a boulder covered with red poppy leaves, sand dusted with red powder, petals wrapping a branch, and red rowan berries dropped into pinned-together iris blades.

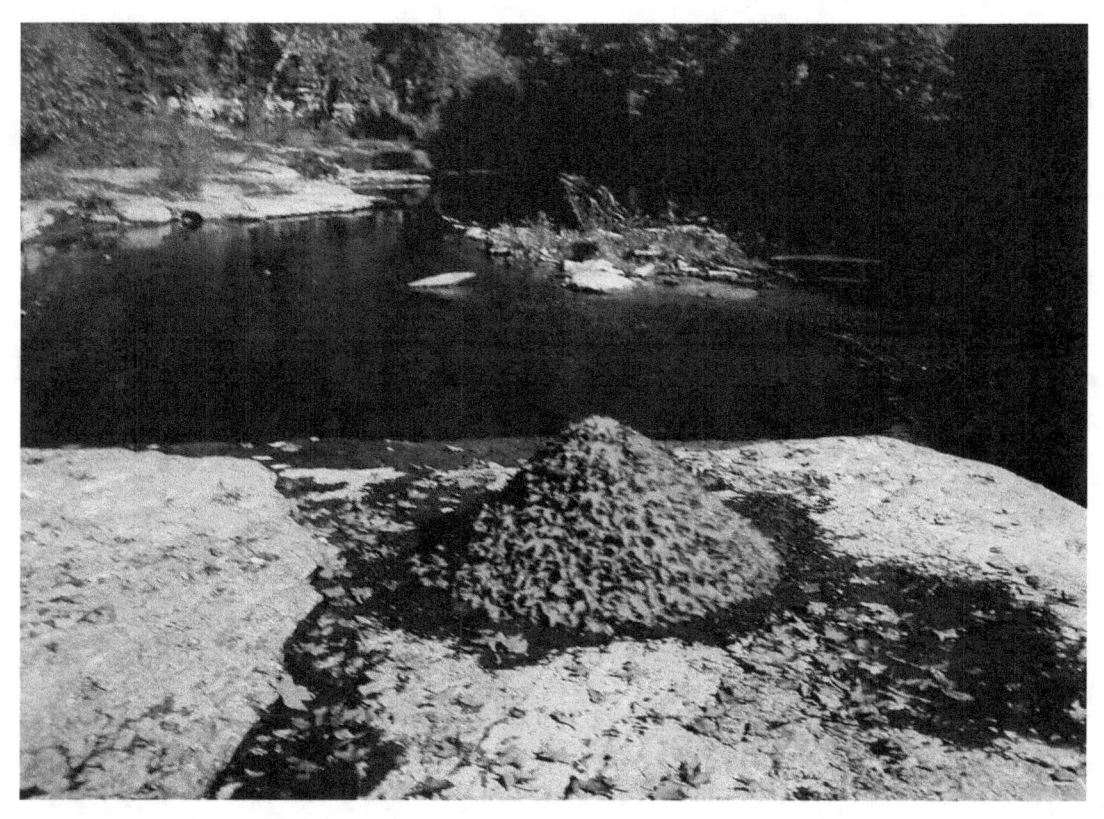

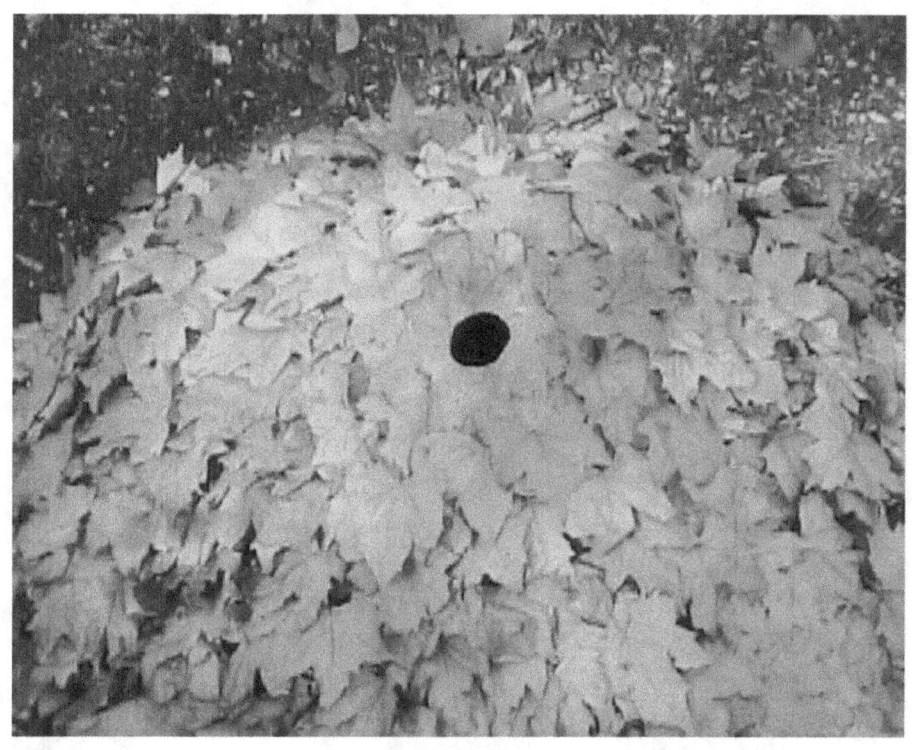

Entrance (1986)

In 1986 Andy Goldsworthy was commissioned by Common Ground (the New Milestones Project) to work at Hooke Park Wood near Beaminster, in West Dorset in the UK. He made *Woven beech*, a large arch that recalls his 'drawing in air' stick sculptures: a demi-circular arch provides an entrance point: but instead of shaping the branches above the arch, Goldsworthy allowed them to splay out in every direction. The inside of the arch is a rough half-circle, but the upper half of the arch is a tangle of branches and slender tree trunks.

For *Entrance* (also 1986), Goldsworthy used the technique of strapping tree trunks and branches together that he employed in *Sidewinder* and *Seven Spires* at Grizedale. Aided by John Makepeace (of Parnham Trust in Dorset) and some students, Goldsworthy created a barrier or gateway to Hooke Park Wood from two circles of overlapping tree trunks. Drop-bar barriers were fixed on each standing circle, so they would cross in the middle, echoing Goldsworthy's icicle sculptures. Goldsworthy's concerns were that the sculptures would blend in with the environment, as well as being functional.

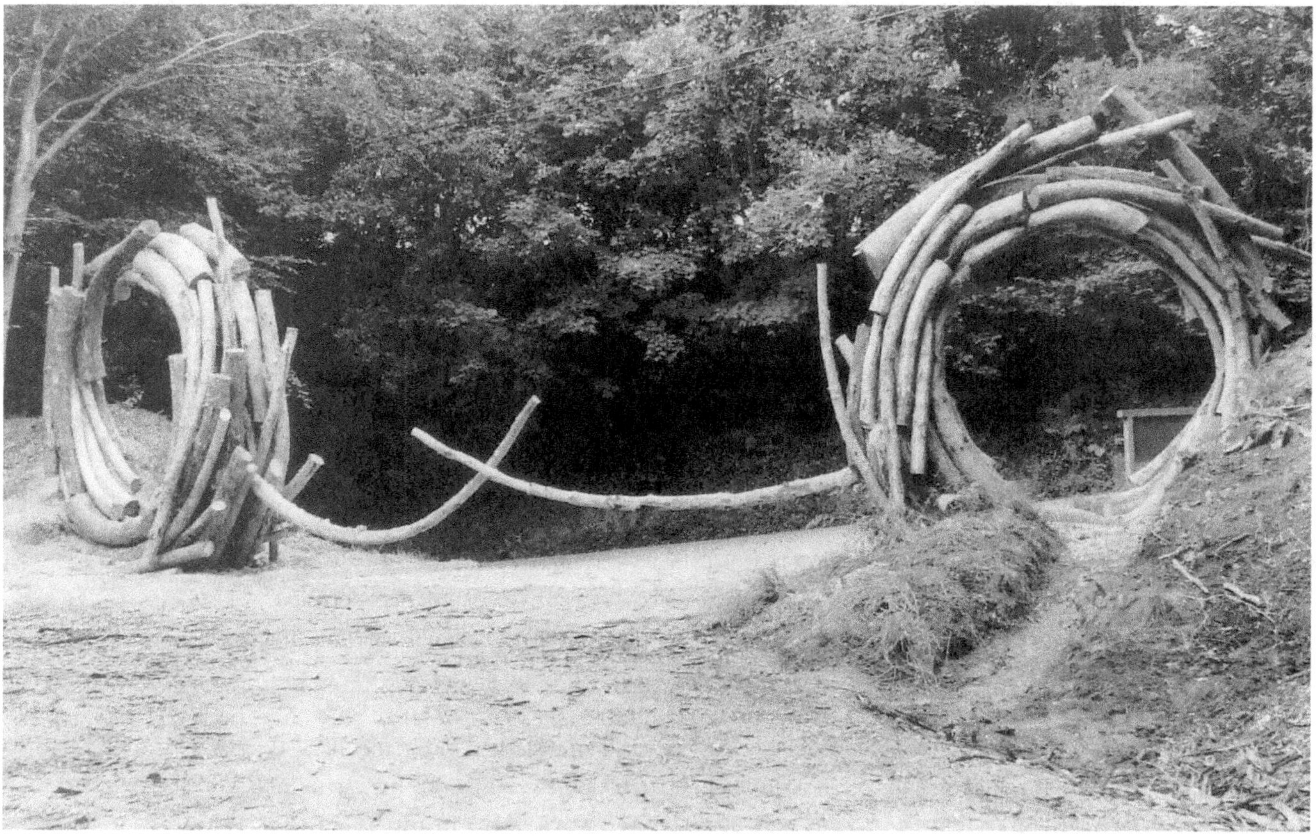

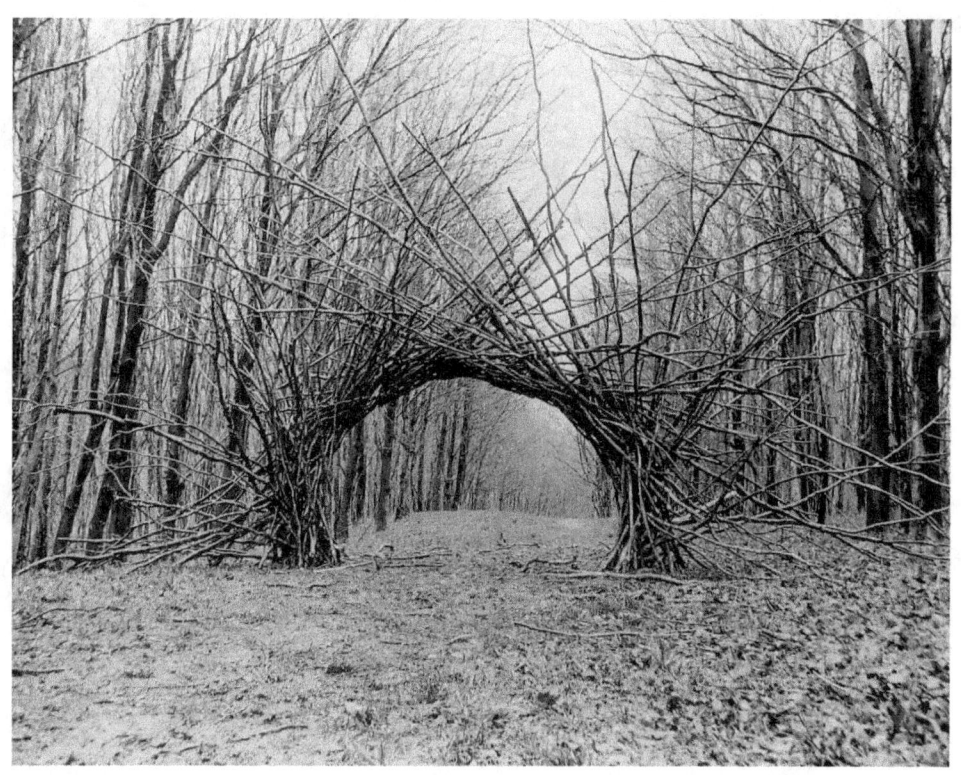

Oak Leaf Globe (1985)

Andy Goldsworthy's main visual motif is the circle, whether as a globe made of leaves, slate or snow, or a cone or cairn (often made of slate or snow), or circles made of leaves half-frosted or stone rubbed with red powder, or circles cut into snow or leaves. The circle is 'such a fundamental form, one can never get away from it altogether' says Goldsworthy (*Hand to Earth*, 19), though his circles are usually deliberately slightly irregular – he avoids the connotations of traditional symbolism.[1] There are many 'negative' circles, made by the surrounding material.

The 'feminine' quality of this primary circular symbol has already been mentioned. It sounds too obvious to say that Goldsworthy's circles, globes, cones and rings should have 'feminine', maternal connotations, but it is precisely in this sort of simple world of equivalents and responses that Goldsworthy operates. The simplicity of the structures, such as a circle, cannot be improved upon, but no matter how 'natural' the circle is as a shape, it always looks humanmade in Goldsworthy's art. His circles of white leaves in amongst dark leaves always stand out from the surroundings. The viewer is always aware that a human has made those marks, or arranged the leaves in that way. The globe made from oak leaves, for instance, is typical of Goldsworthy's melding of the 'natural' and the human. Yes, the viewer has perhaps seen oak leaves many times, or any sort of leaves. Yes, the viewer has probably admired the multi-coloured leaves of Autumn. But Goldsworthy's sphere of leaves in the forest is not an object the viewer might expect to come across on a walk. The oak leaf globe asserts itself instantly as *art*, as a humanmade artifact. Yet how right these globes of ice, snow, slate and leaves can appear. The simplicity of the structure (the circle) makes these sculptures seem curiously 'obvious' and 'natural'. Like a really good pop song or film, one wonders: why haven't they been made before? Goldsworthy's globes, whether made out of stacked rocks (Blaenau Ffestiniog, 1980), or snow (Lancashire, 1980), or from redwood sticks (California, 1995) seem so 'obvious' to the viewer. They look simultaneously 'out of place' and quite at home in their settings.

1. Goldsworthy dislikes geometry being 'imposed upon nature' (*Hand to Earth*, 162), though all his sculpture (like all art) can be seen as something 'imposed upon nature'. Even the most ephemeral and minuscule of Goldsworthy sculptures, such as the tiny flower or leafworks, are impositions and additions to the natural world. They are events which do not happen 'naturally'.

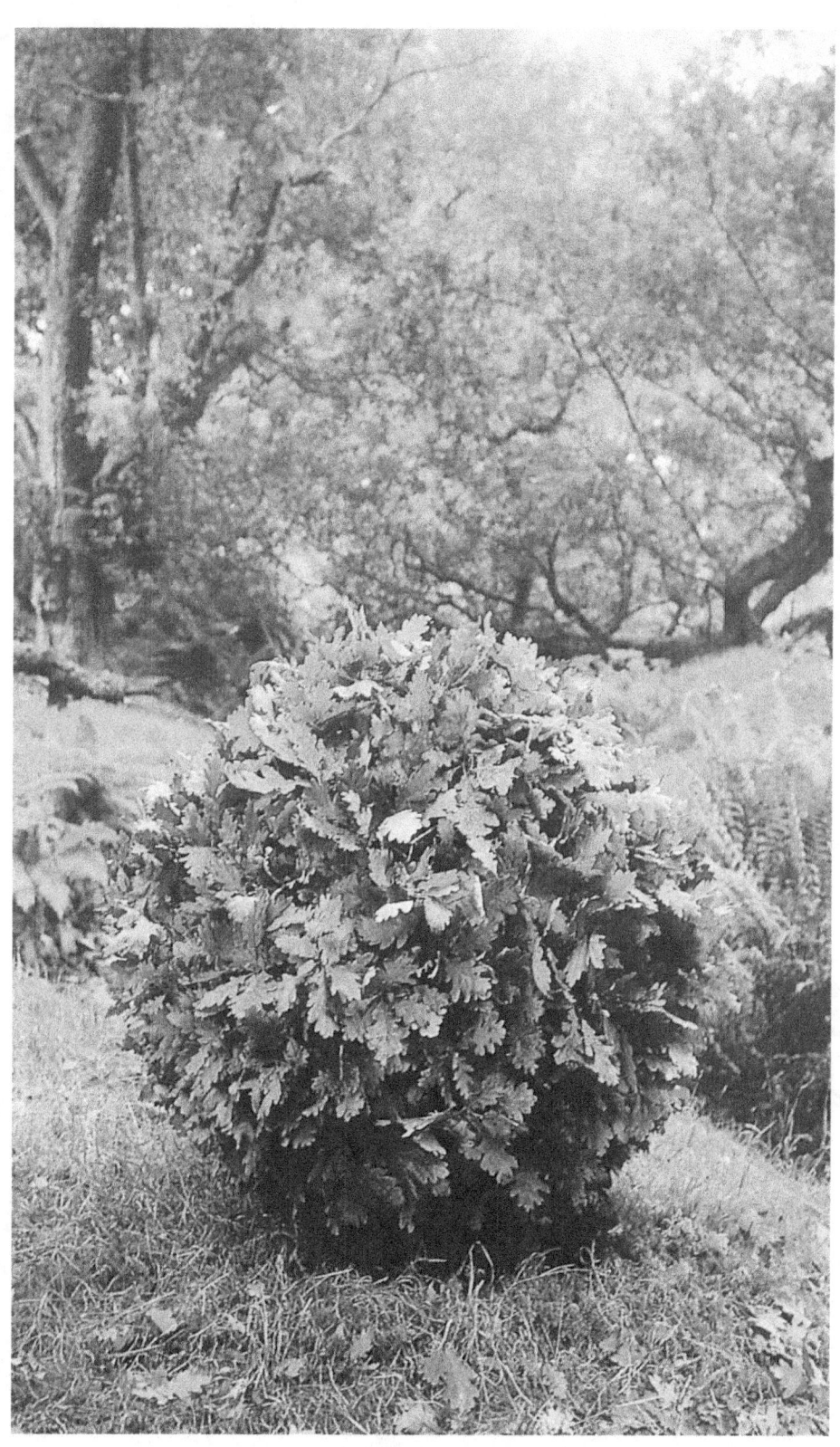

Snowball Prints

Upstairs at Andy Goldsworthy's London (27, Old Bond Street) show in 1994 were photographs and snowball prints. The latter were smears of ochre-coloured stone dust and water on large sheets of paper. Like other land artists, Goldsworthy works in the landscape, so there are numerous problems when he shows work in a city. The city is definitely not the obvious Goldsworthy place. The photographs and prints, then, point always towards the outdoors, towards the ideal Goldsworthy space, which is some wilderness – the North Pole, Cumbria, Scotland, and so on. The snowball prints are disappointing, really. A snowball melting on a sheet of paper is too random and easy, perhaps. The combination of a natural act of melting and the framed piece of paper in a gallery, with the latter's art historical background, is problematic. The viewer might prefer to see Goldsworthy making these prints. Then they would make more sense. Perhaps a photograph of the artist making the print would suffice. As it is, the snowball prints are full of suggestions of things they cannot deliver. They are, like Goldsworthy's photographs, a record of something that occurred elsewhere. And what occurred elsewhere is of course what *really* interests Goldsworthy.

No land artist can be satisfied with written accounts of art made in the landscape (unless they are purely Conceptual works), just as no painter would be satisfied with photographs or written accounts of their paintings. No, they must have the paintings themselves, the actual flesh and blood of the painting, so to speak, the very feel of the oil on canvas, the shape and size and texture and reflectivity and proportion and tactile qualities of the actual painting. Photographs of paintings only disappoint the artist. Ditto with the land artist. Goldsworthy's photographs and prints are not what they're really interested in: the work is elsewhere, in the landscape (note that Goldsworthy has participated – in Cardiff and Bristol – in group shows which focus on photography as sculpture).

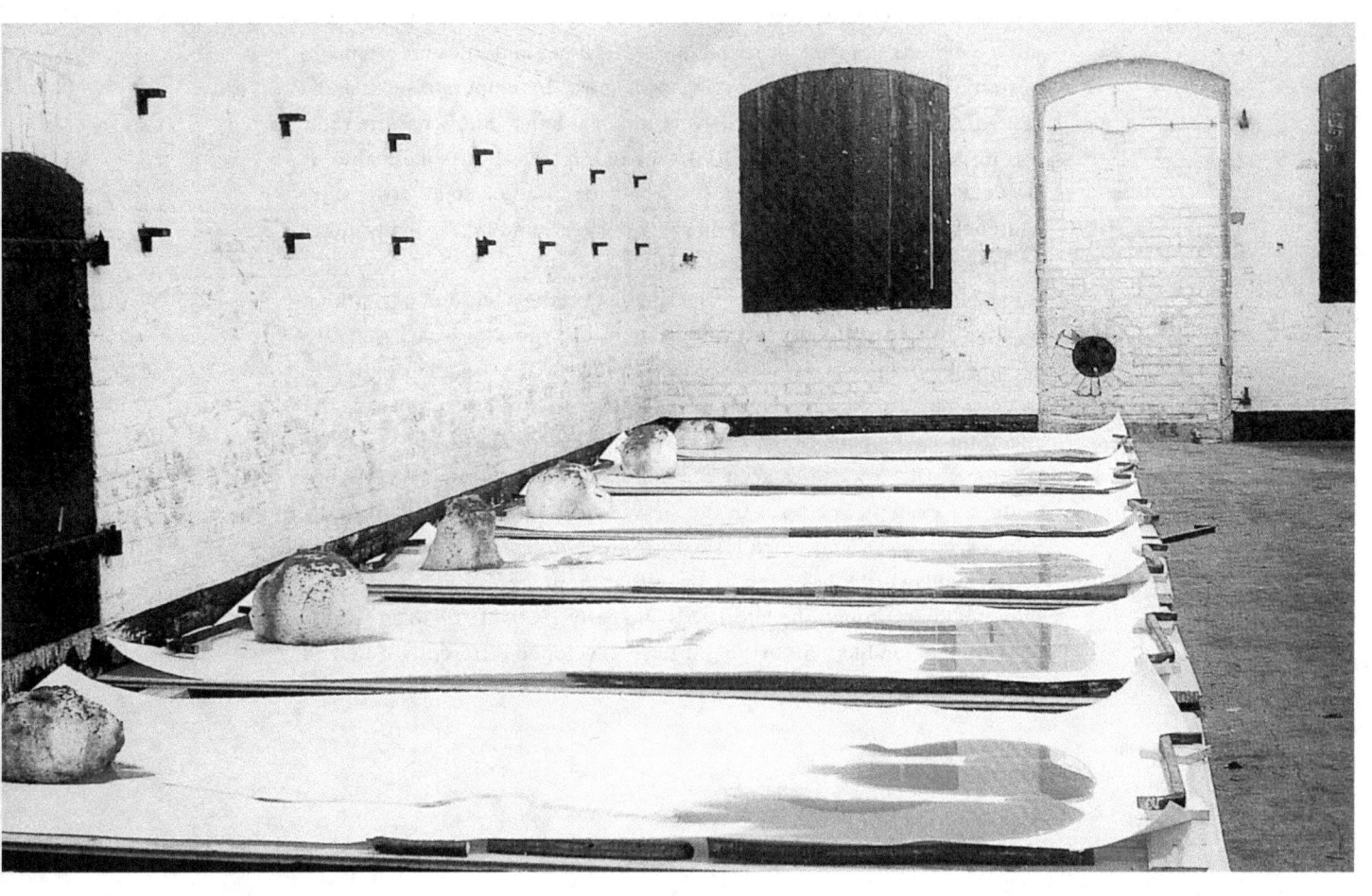

Snowball Trail (1982)

One wonders whether Andy Goldsworthy would like to work in snow and ice more than in any other medium. His notes and titles record many frustrations stemming from working with snow. In temperate snowlands, though, one feels Goldsworthy is very much at home. Snow has the right sort of qualities Goldsworthy looks for in a material: it is malleable, it melts and changes, it's cheap, it's good for large or small works, its whiteness makes for striking, contrasty imagery, and it seasonally alters the landscape, and later dissolves into it.

In Goldsworthy's snowworks one senses also the sheer fun of working with snow. For people in most of Britain, snow is not a definite occurrence each year, as it is in Northern Russia or Alaska. For children, snow can be an exciting event. Goldsworthy speaks like a child of 'the effect, the excitement' of the first snowfall (*Hand to Earth*, 165).

Some of this joy comes across in Goldsworthy's snowworks. He has made, for example, patterns in the snow by rolling a snowball around a field, exactly as kids do when it snows (*Snowball trail*, Brough, Cumbria, 1982). Goldsworthy has been lucky in that there were some good, cold, snowy Winters around the late 1970s and early 1980s. 1977-78 and 1981-82 were memorable – his art might have developed differently if he had made work during milder, snowless Winters.

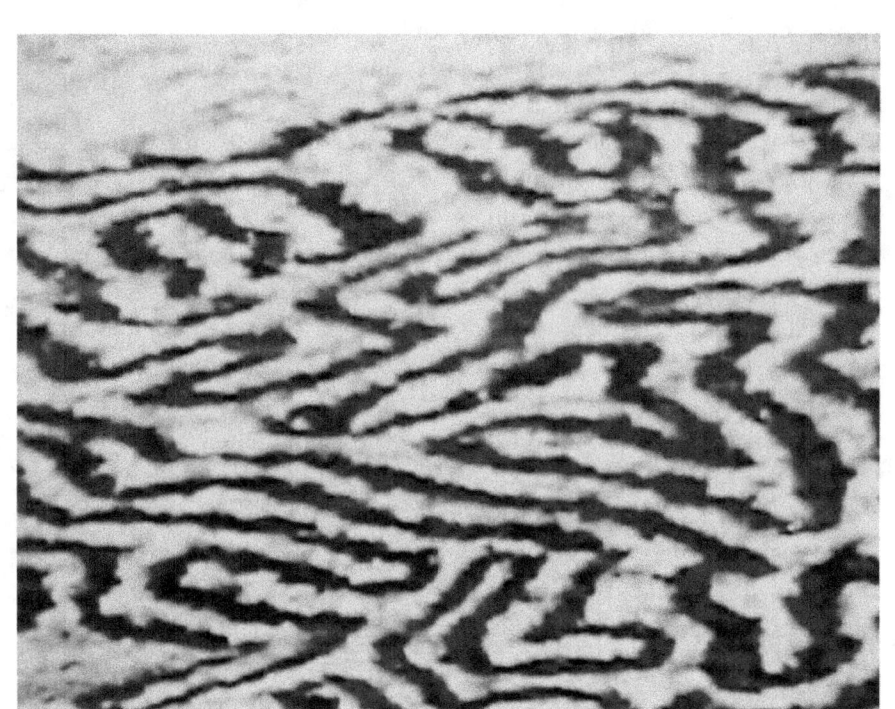

Splashes and *Throws*

Andy Goldsworthy says that he is really working with time. 'If I had to describe in one word what I do, I'd say I work with *time*'.[1] Although it seems, at first glance, to be all about space, about particular spaces and how materials react with certain locations, time is an important element in Goldsworthy's art. He speaks of adding another layer to preceding layers of 'human understanding and character' when he makes work in the landscape.[2] He is conscious of the past and its layers of time on/in the landscape. 'The land is an expression of its past' he says (*Hand to Earth*, 189). He investigates moments, the instant of a splash; then there are works that last a few minutes or hours: the soil drying after Goldsworthy's laid on it after rain; or days – the rocks covered in clay; then works that study seasons (Autumnal leaves, snow and ice works); and works that explore the slow, cosmic time of enduring media – stones, the sun, the sea. What counts, Goldsworthy says, is not the duration of the work, but 'the experience of making.'[3] 'I've always been interested in the moment a work is made' (*Sheepfolds,* 15).

Many of the photographs in his exhibitions document very brief occurrences: the red earth in the river, or mud being thrown in the shallows on a beach, or on a misty hillside: *Rainbow splashes* were made with a stick in Yorkshire (1980), *Slate throws* (Cumbria, 1988) consisted of throwing slate into the air, like *Hazel stick throws* (1980) and *Leaf throws* (Tayside, 1989). *Maple leaf throw* was made in Japan in 1990. In 1995, Goldsworthy had the Ballet Atlantique dance troupe throw sticks and soil into the air at once. In California (1994), Goldsworthy threw dust into the air against the sun, which he called *Breath of Earth* works. It is the shapes the mud and earth and sticks make in the air that fascinates Goldsworthy. He is seen in various photos, throwing the mud and earth, his legs and arms raised high, caught in a moment of release. These photos are about time, about letting something go, and capturing the trajectory. Mud and earth is not 'alive', as a bird is, but Goldsworthy seems to throw the mud and earth as if he's releasing a bird. He wants the earth to fly. It doesn't: it arcs back to the ground, but these arcs are elegant, and become the subject of many photographs. The 'throws' are also very dependent on particular lighting conditions. In the Lake Michigan photographs (1991), Goldsworthy is shot against the light in a

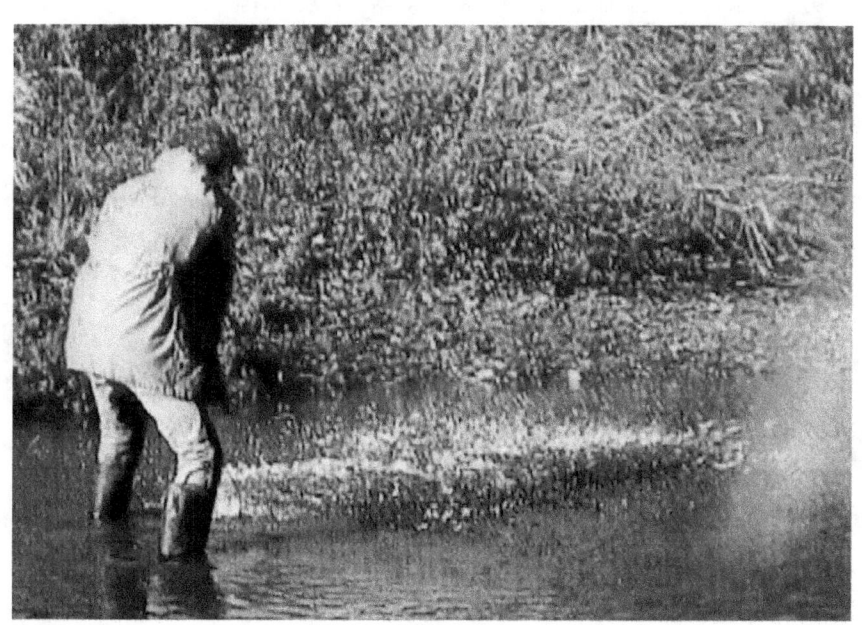

dusky sky, so that the trajectories of the wet sand in the air can be clearly seen. The red mud throws at Scaur Water occur against bright green foliage, which contrasts with the red. Colour contrasts are also central to the Mount Victor Station throws, which were made with red sand ejected into the clear blue Australian sky (1991).

1. In M. Church; and *Stone*, 120.
2. A. Goldsworthy, sketchbook no. 19, Feb, 1988. *Hand to Earth*, 150.
3. A. Goldsworthy, *Rain sun snow hail mist calm*, 4.

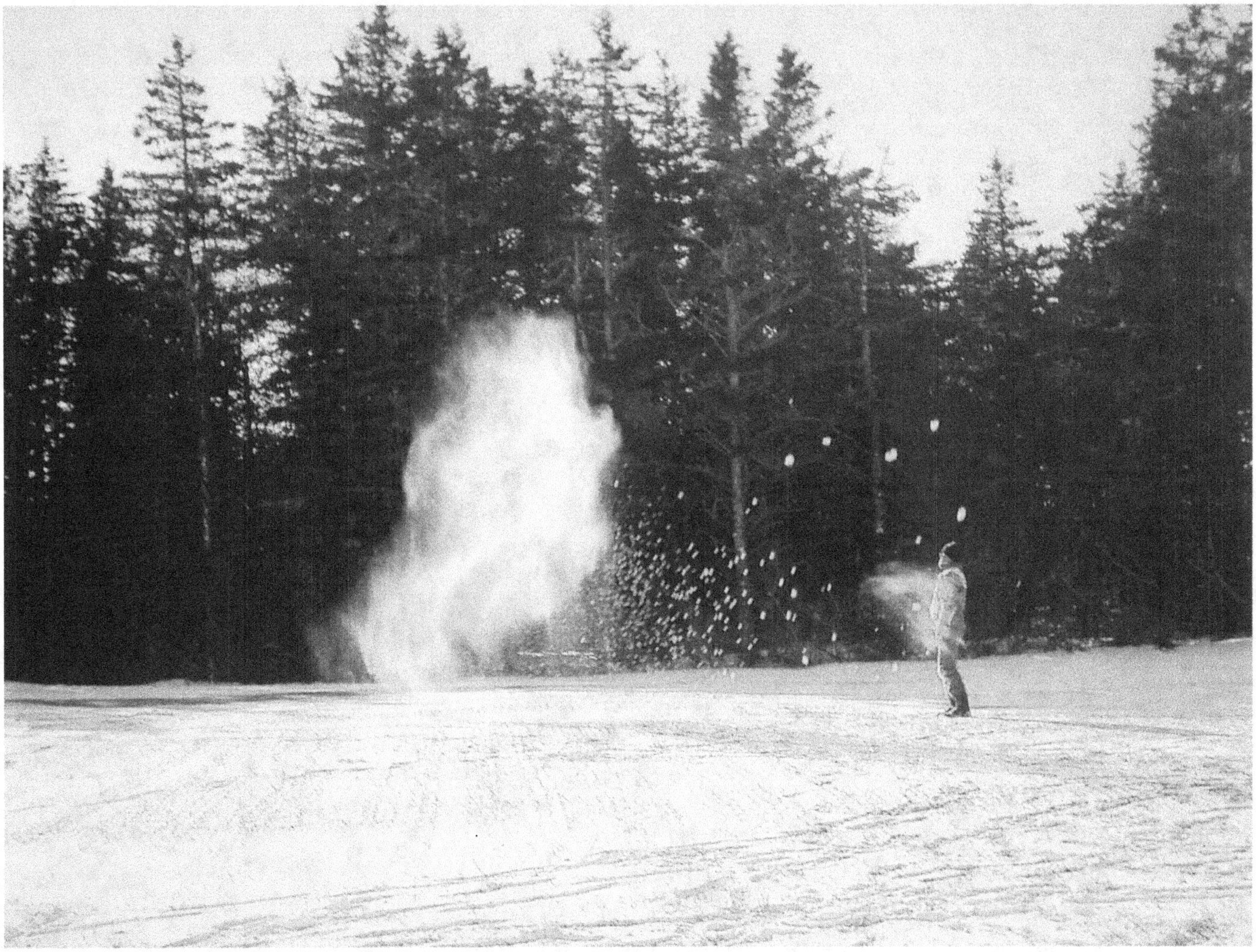

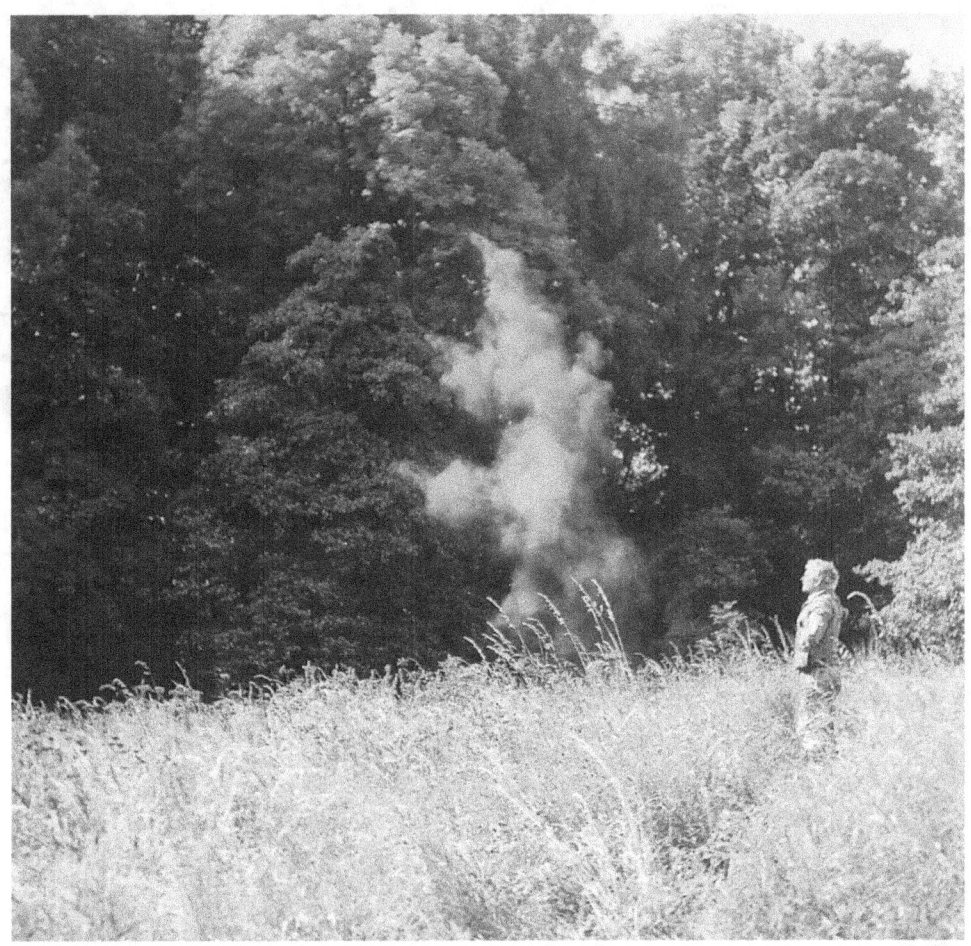

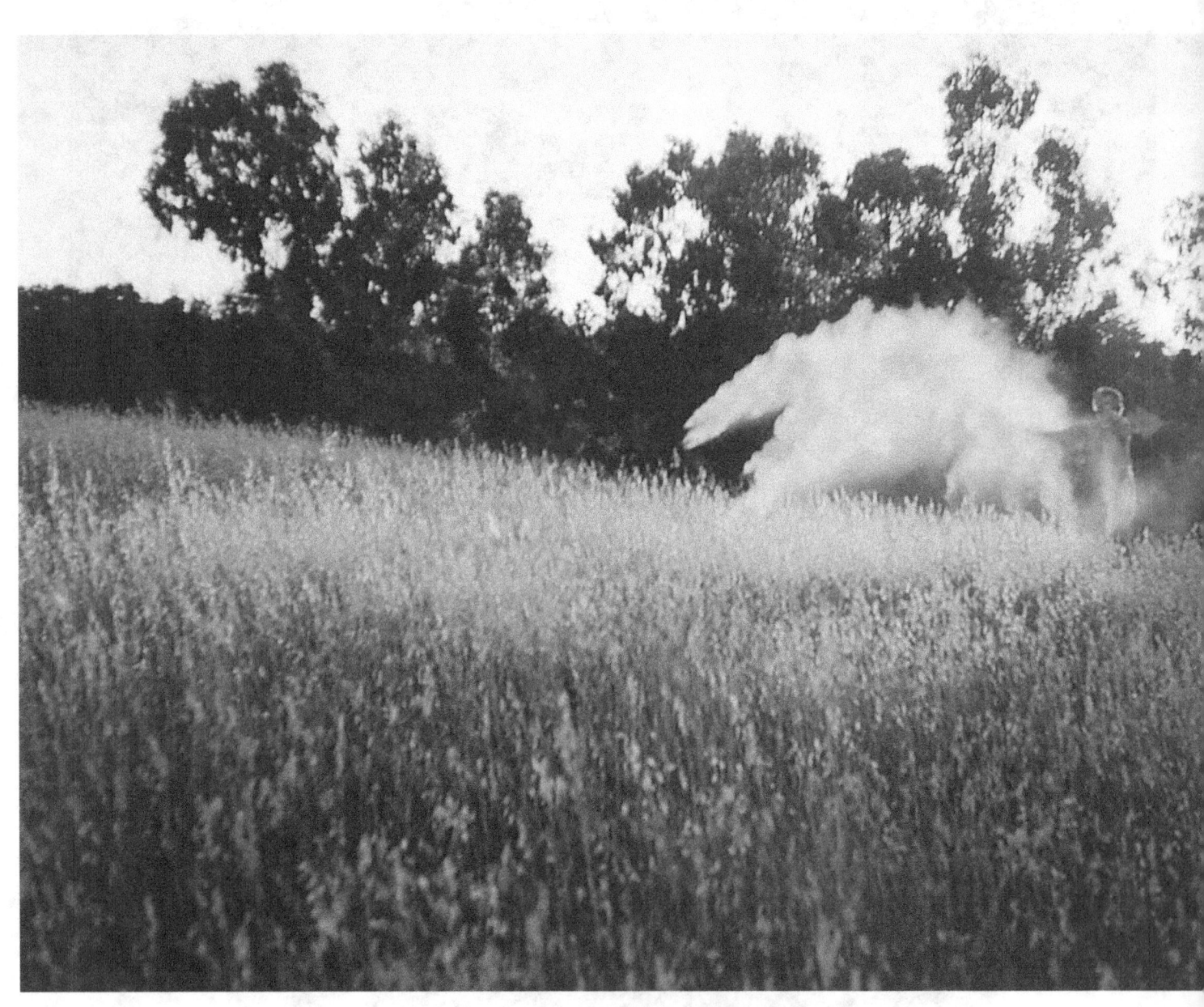

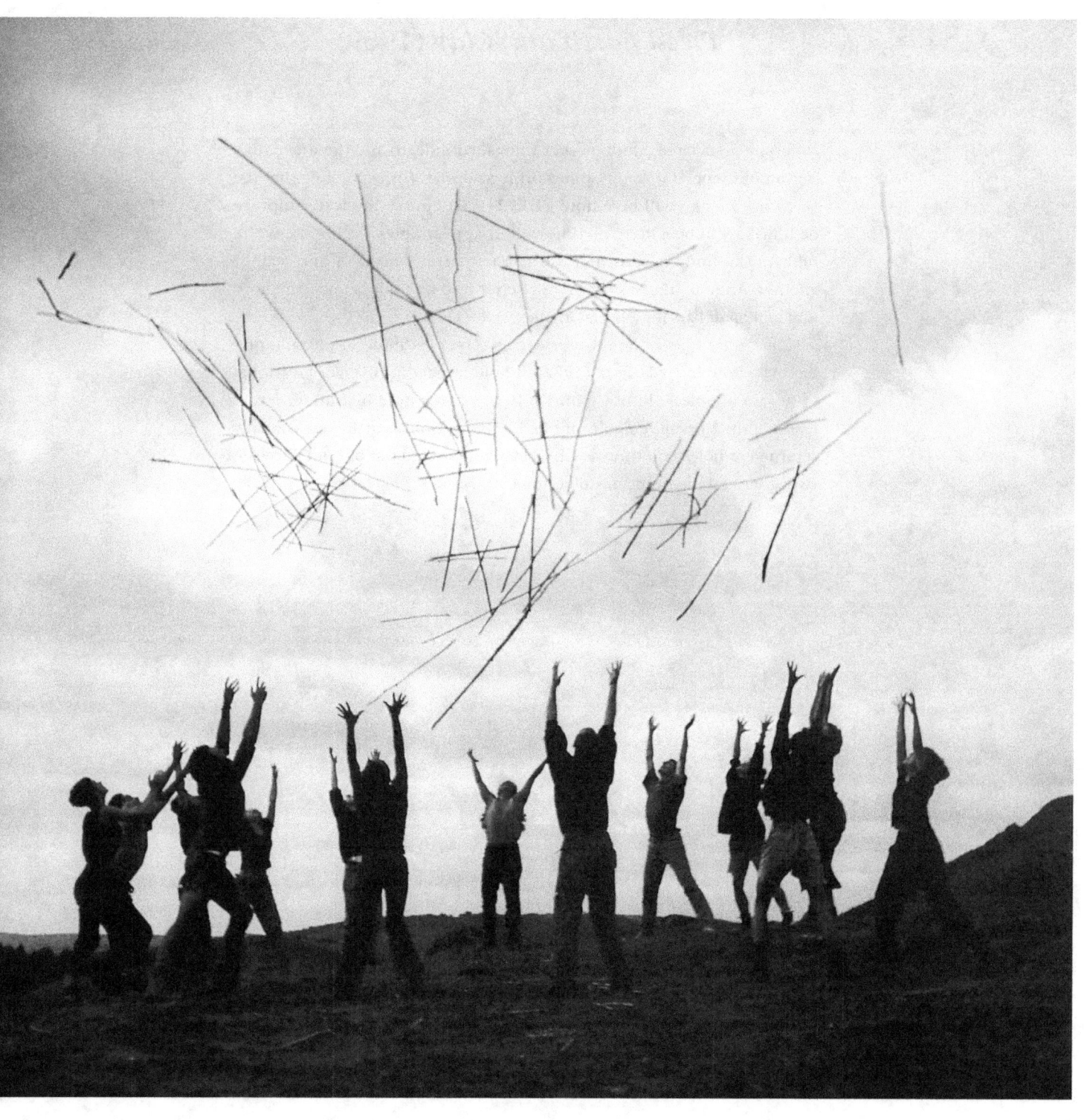

Fired Earth and Clay (1989)

Holes are associated, among other things, with death and the grave. In a portentous moment, Andy Goldsworthy said that '[i]t is possible that the last work I make will be a hole' (HE, 24). Of course the last sculpture he'll make will be a hole: then he will disappear down it, like the white rabbit. The body is returned to the Earth after death, in one way or another. After all, there's nowhere else for it to go (unless one can afford fifty million dollars for a burial in outer space).

Like a gravedigger, then, Goldsworthy scrabbles about in the soil, producing a hole in Hyde Park (1982), a hole in peat in Blaenau Ffestiniog (1980), a double hole in Cumbria (1980), and a hole just under a tree trunk in the Yorkshire Sculpture Park (1983). Goldsworthy occasionally returned to hole sculptures, such as in a hole carved out of sand between two stones on the beach at Collieston (2000).

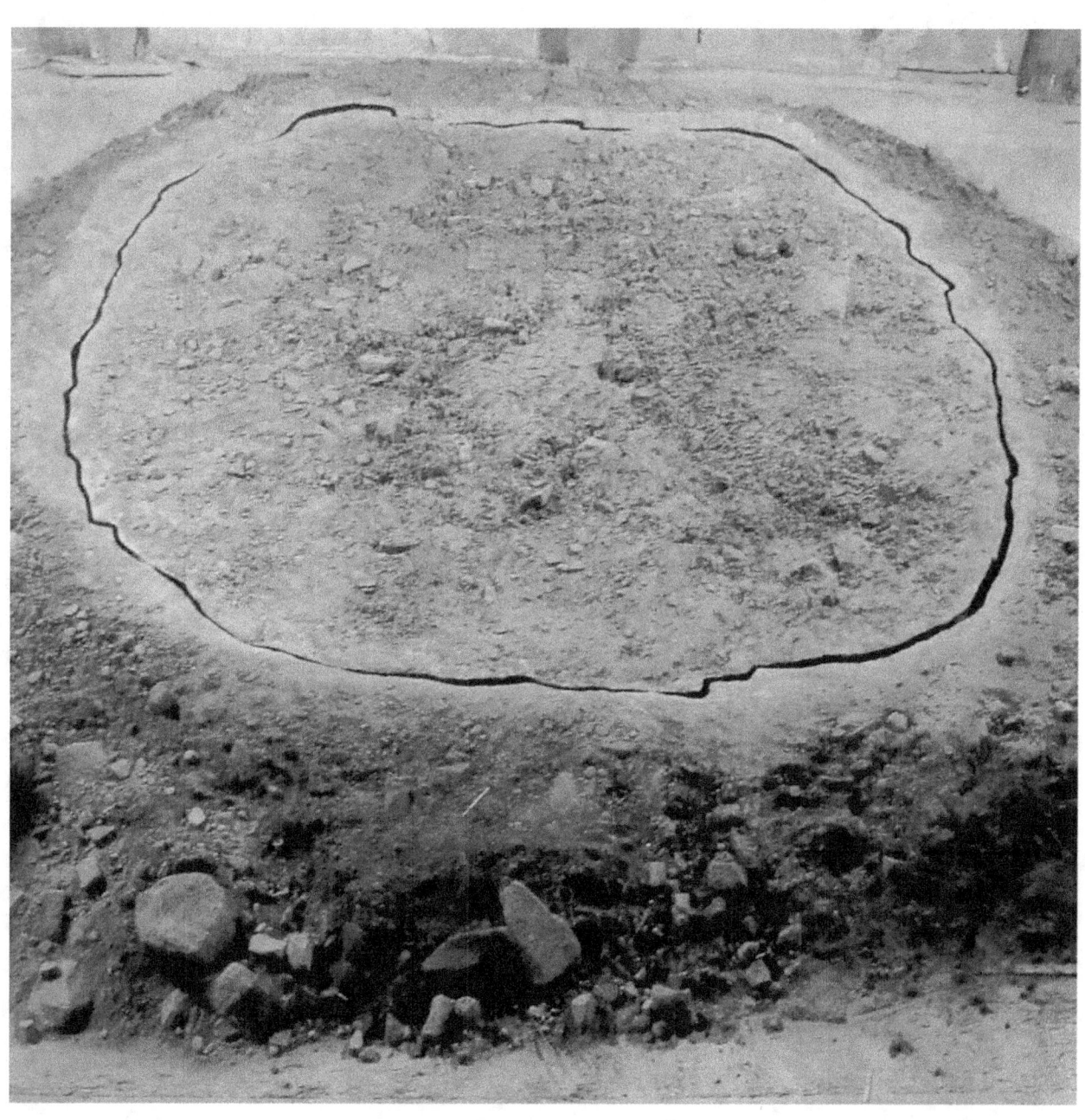

Slate stack (1988)

Slate stack at Stone Wood in Scotland was a simple idea, on a grand scale: built next to (in 'partnership' with) a hollow tree, it consisted of a rectangular structure of flat pieces of slate (HE, 147). The slate was set horizontally, but in the middle of the thick wall was a circle shape (actually a cylinder) made by placing the slate vertically. It looked a lot simpler than it sounded in a verbal description. Like many of Goldsworthy's sculptures, the viewer gets the idea instantly. It is simple, but constructed on a 'monumental' scale.

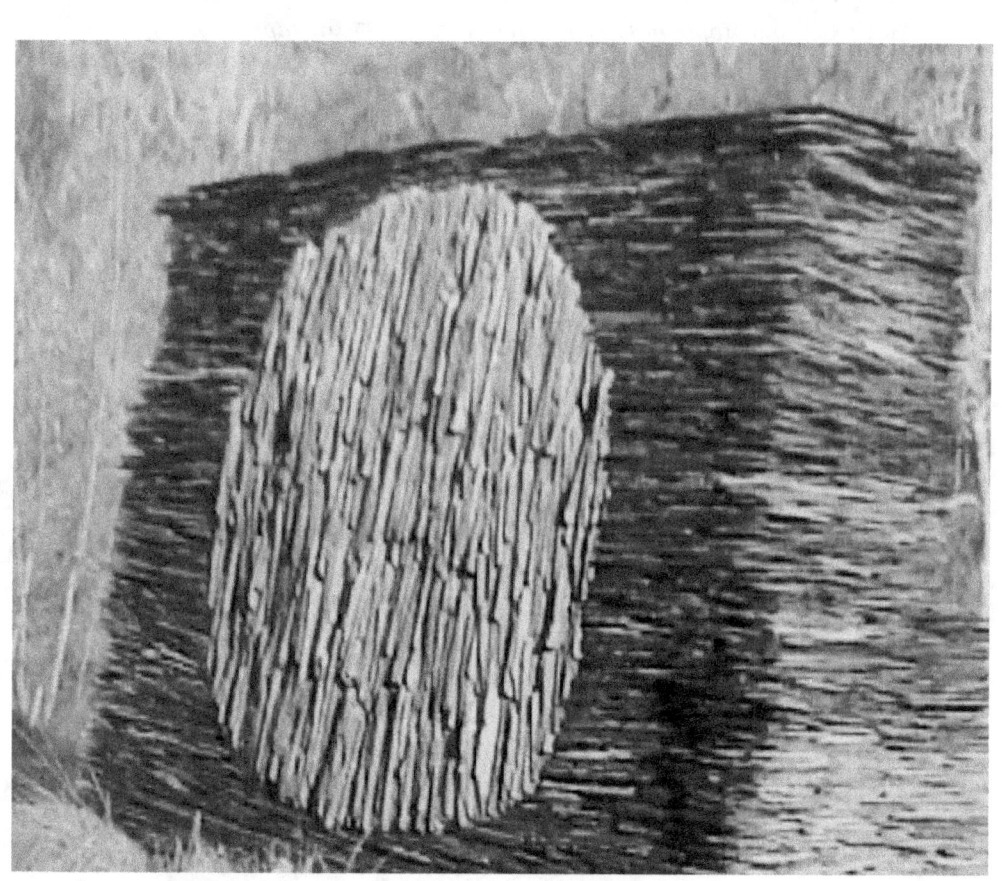

Japanese Maple (1987)

Some of the brightest of Andy Goldsworthy's leafworks were made in Japan, where the maple leaves are dazzling in October and November (in, for example, *Maple patch*, November 22, 1987, or *Japanese maple*, November 21-22, 1987). These have become some of Goldsworthy's signature pieces among his early works.

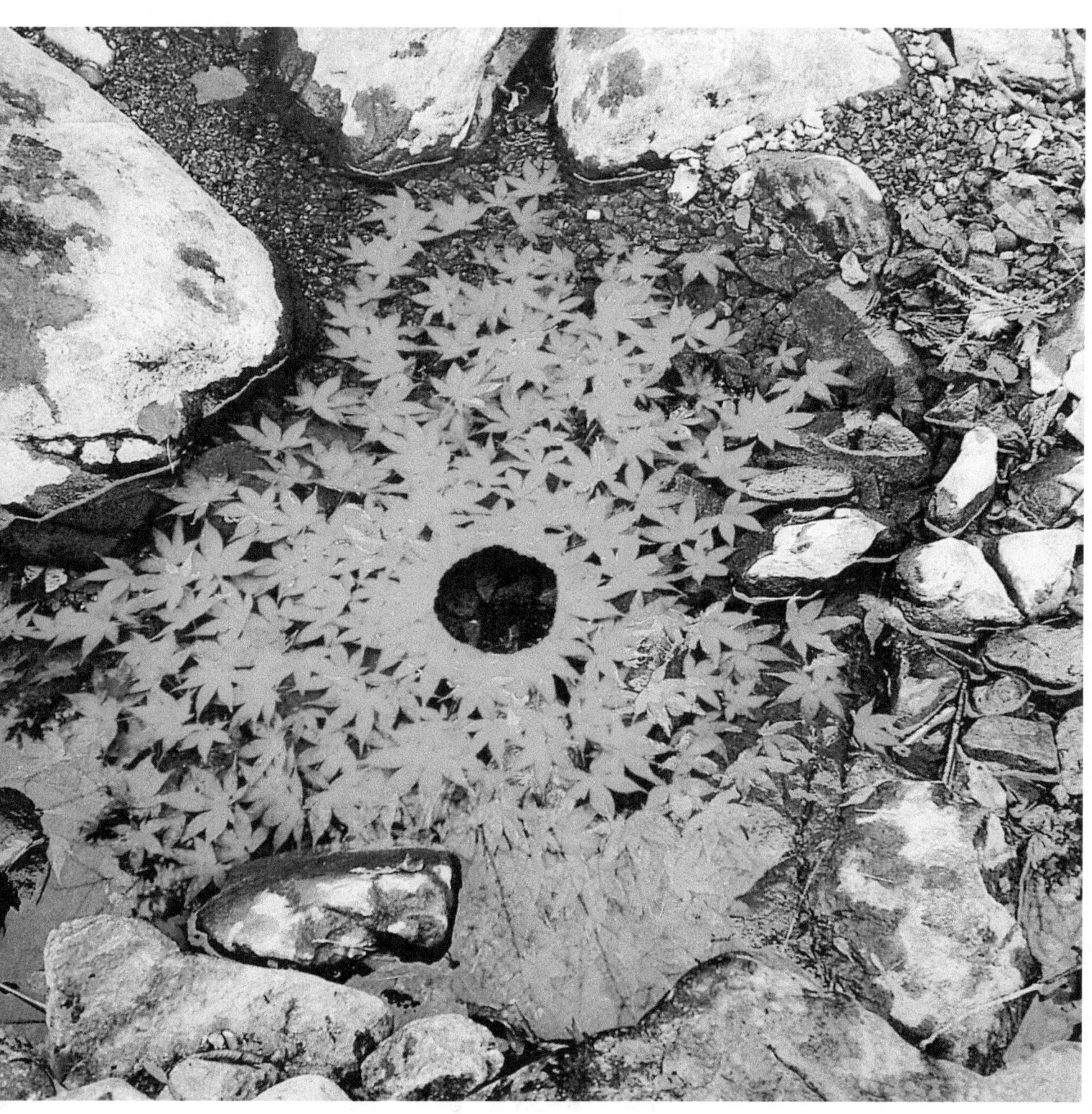

Red Pools (1993)

Andy Goldsworthy put a red object in amongst the soft, muted colours of green moss and grey, wet rocks of Scotland. The colour red stands out even more on wintry, overcast days, when there is hardly any deep colour in the surroundings. In 1993 Goldsworthy made a number of sculptures in small pools of water he found on the rocks at his beloved Scaur Water in Dumfriesshire. He stained the pools with some red stones. The manufacture of these sculptures consisted of nothing more elaborate than rubbing some stones together to stain some water. The results, though (photographed in *Stone*, and later exhibited in *Black Stones, Red Pools*), are dramatic: as Goldsworthy said, often a good sculpture needs only a delicate or small-scale touch in the right place to make it work (*Stone*, 95). In amongst the weather- and water-worn boulders of the Scottish stream the mid-red stands out vividly. It reveals the contours of the surrounding rock; the relation between the pool of water in its isolation from the rest of the stream (which formed it); and the elegant ovals and circular shapes of each pool. These are the landscapes of Goldsworthy's art, these bleak, grey, wintry scenes, beside a lake, or the sea, or a river, or halfway up a mountain. The Celtic fringe, in short. Beside a mound of grey slate, the colour red stands out, like 'a wound', as Goldsworthy remarked, emphasizing the flesh-and-blood nature of his art.

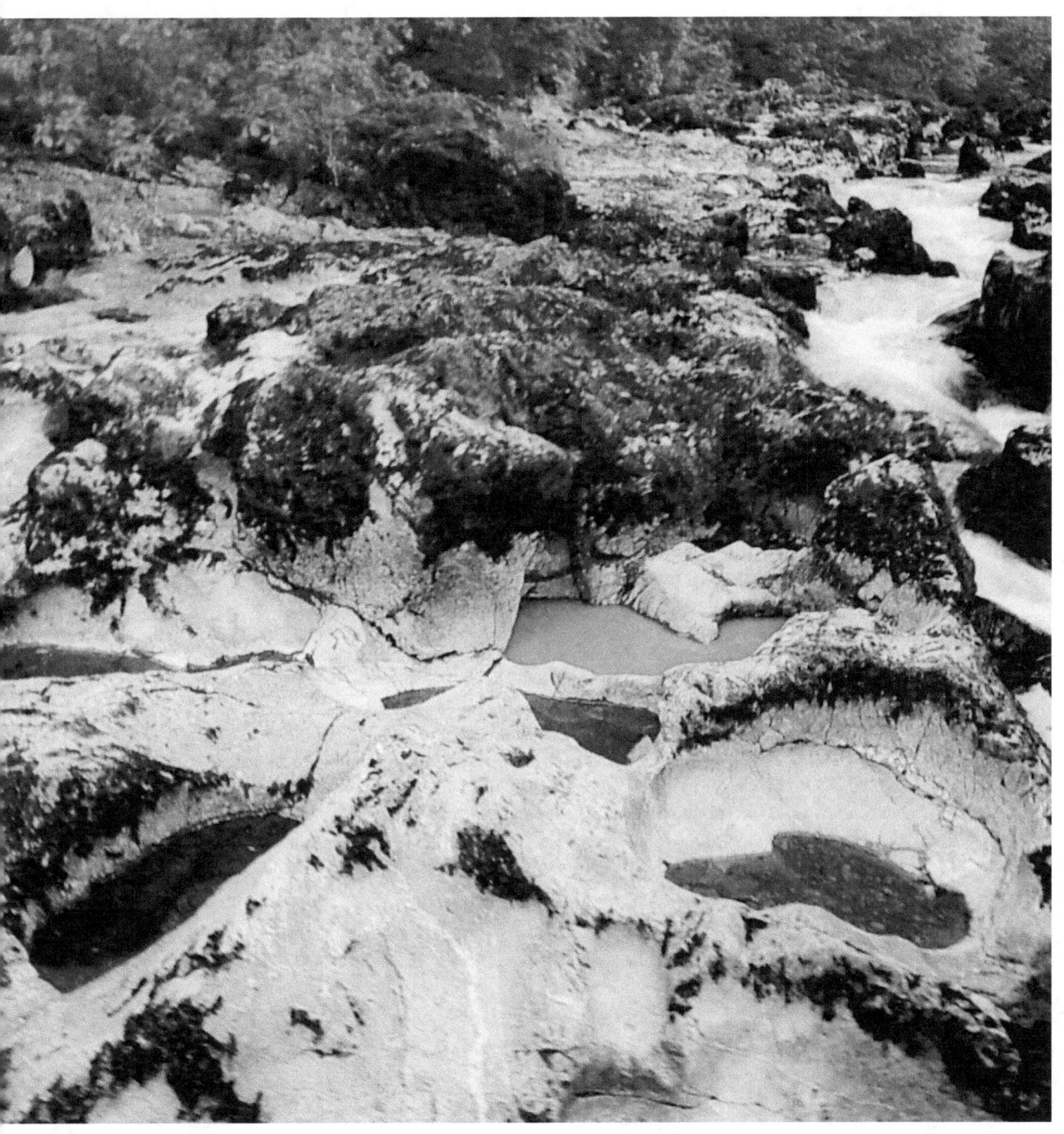

Alaska (1995)

In Anchorage, Alaska, in 1995, Andy Goldsworthy built a series of lines from branches frozen together. The forms – curving and zigzagging columns – were familiar Goldsworthyan motifs. Later, Goldsworthy took down the stick towers and used them to form a long line of 114 sticks which stretched out over the Alaskan snow. Goldsworthy related the line of sticks to the tree line, the line of distant mountains, and the line of the estuary:

> I want the line to be made up of wood, ice, wood, ice, wood, ice. Winter, summer, winter, summer, winter, summer. I like the idea of many pieces being joined together in a continuous line, just as the seasons are' (*Wood,* 49)

This series of works culminated in a stick house in which Goldsworthy hung a 3 foot icicle made by dripping water. In his journal Goldsworthy said that the icicle was meant to be like a knife with the surrounding wood as a sheath. He also related the vertical icicle to the spine of the dancers in *Végétal*, and to the stone columns (*Wood,* 10). The ice house was about the relationship between trees, water and the cold. 'The tree needs water, yet water makes it vulnerable to the cold. Water at its core, its spine: delicate, fragile and vulnerable' (*Wood,* 49).

Goldsworthy spoke of the relation between stone and wood, stone and trees. 'It is no accident that I called the piece of land near to where I live 'Stone Wood'. I've always been aware of the relationship between these two materials' (*Sheepfolds,* 22). Note that two of Goldsworthy's major art books are entitled *Stone* and *Wood*.

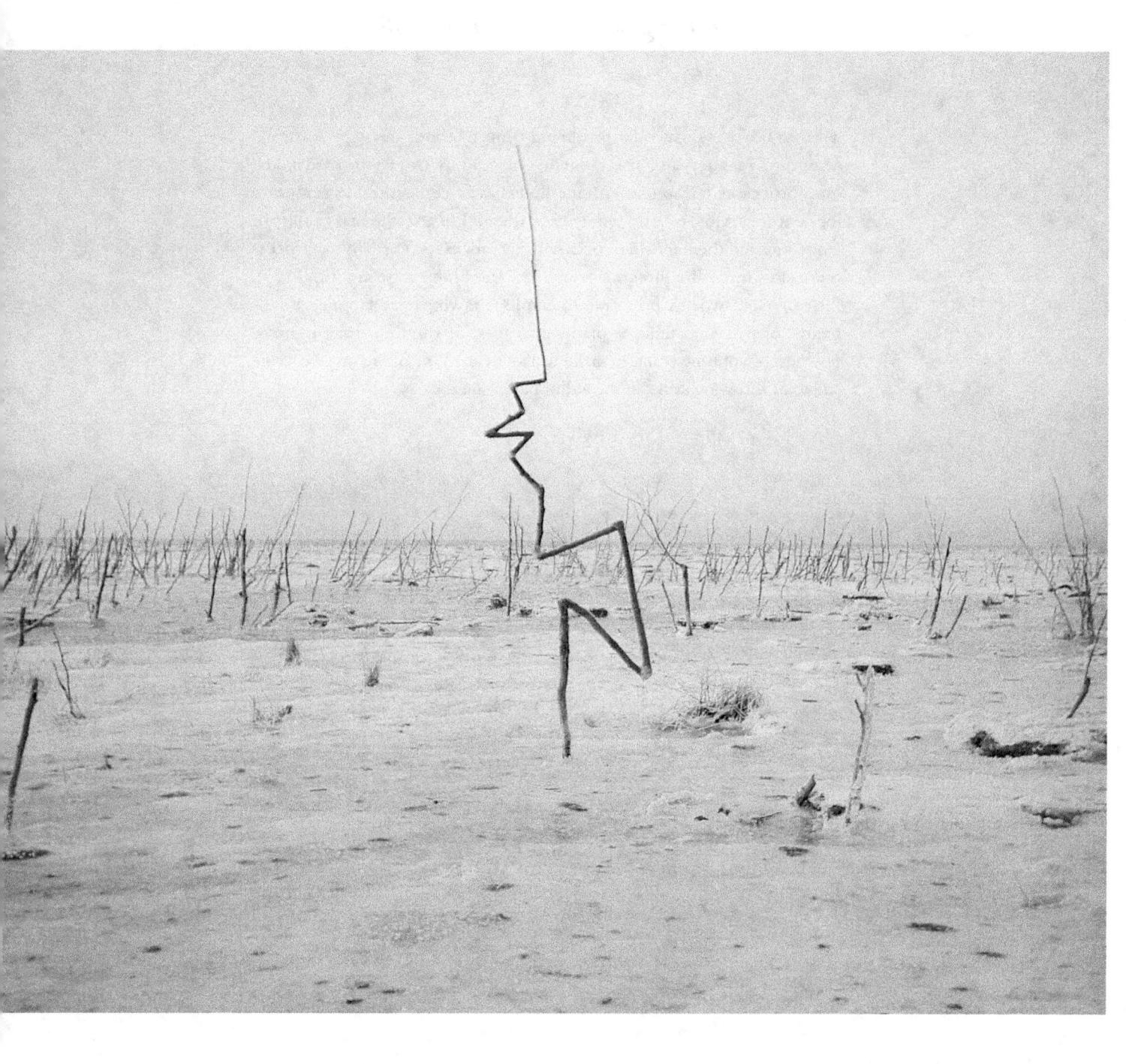

Carving Frozen Snow (1987)

Although he has carved stone from time to time, in the traditional sculptural manner, and also modelled clay, Andy Goldsworthy disliked both processes. Although both methods have been central to sculpture for centuries, Goldsworthy rarely used them. 'I dislike the malleability of modelling and the imposition of carving as processes. Carving is a process that relies upon the integral strength of the block of stone' (RA, 105). Instead, Goldsworthy preferred to employ drawings or shaping with his hands, or weaving stalks or plants or leaves, or rubbing stone to make powder, or splitting stone to make walls or cairns, or piling up or carving snow, or throwing stalks in the air, or balancing rocks.

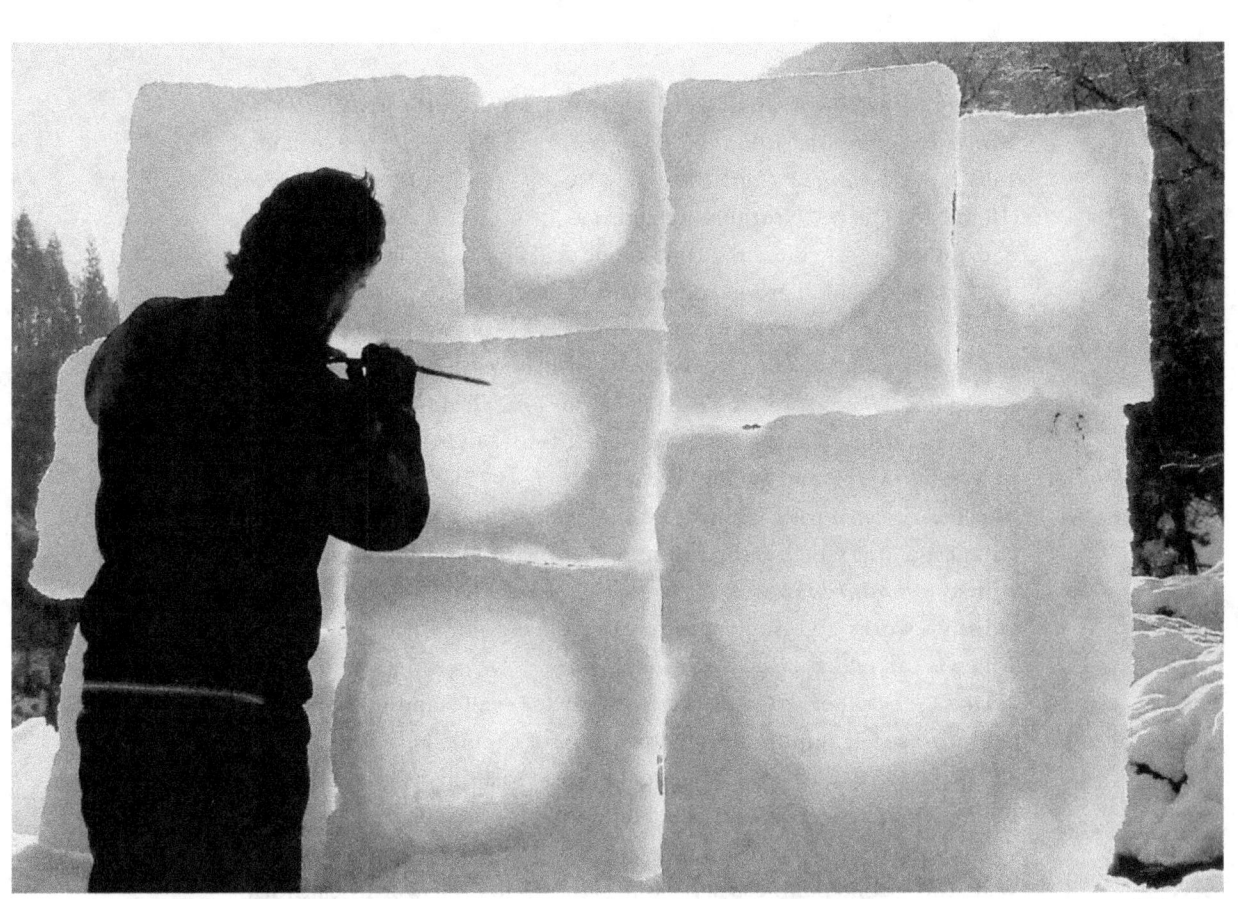

Balanced Rocks (1988), Balanced Rocks (1988), Cairn (1989)

Balancing works of Andy Goldsworthy's include the two *Balanced Winstones, Balanced stone* and *Balanced rock*. *Balanced rock* (Cumbria 1977), like *Balanced stone* (Heysham Head, 1978) and *Balanced rocks* (High Nick Quarry, Northumberland, 1993), is basically a 'logan stone', one of those rocks (there is a famous one at Treryn Dinas in West Penwith in Cornwall) which are balanced so delicately they can be rocked by hand. The 1987 *Balanced rocks* (Japan) was a group of three columns of four stones each, recalling Henry Moore or Barbara Hepworth sculptures.

Another *Balanced rocks* piece (Cumbria, 1982) had four slabs teetering above and below a small spherical stone (*Andy Goldsworthy*). *Balanced rocks* at Bow Fell and Scafel Pike (Cumbria, 1977) explored problems usually associated with architecture and engineering – the idea of counter-balancing and weight, for example (*Hand to Earth*, 22-23). Goldsworthy's *Balanced rock* is shot against the sky, like so many of Goldsworthy's works, to bring out the fundamental point of the work: a rock which is carefully balanced.

Like Richard Serra, Goldsworthy has made wall-standing sculptures, sculptures that require a wall to complete them, such as in the first *Balanced Winstone* (1988). This sculpture is, basically, two largish rocks, both with pointed ends, connected only at their points. One stands on top of the other, with the rest of the upper stone leaning against a studio wall. The second *Balanced Winstone* is the basic Goldsworthy cairn with a sharp-ended stone at the summit. On top of this balances another stone, the equivalent in large scale would be a huge boulder the size of a multi-storey car park on top of the Great Pyramid of Cheops.

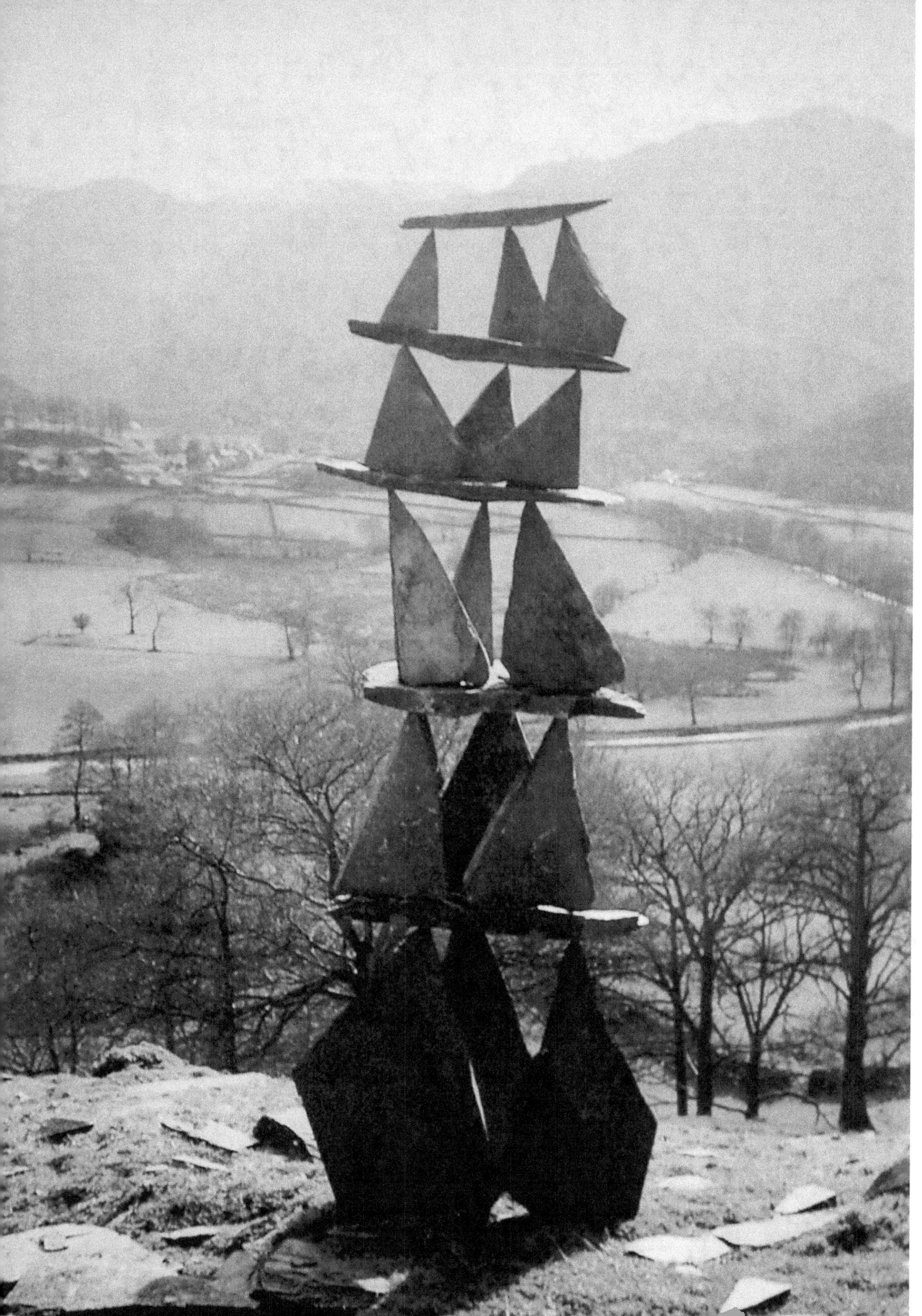

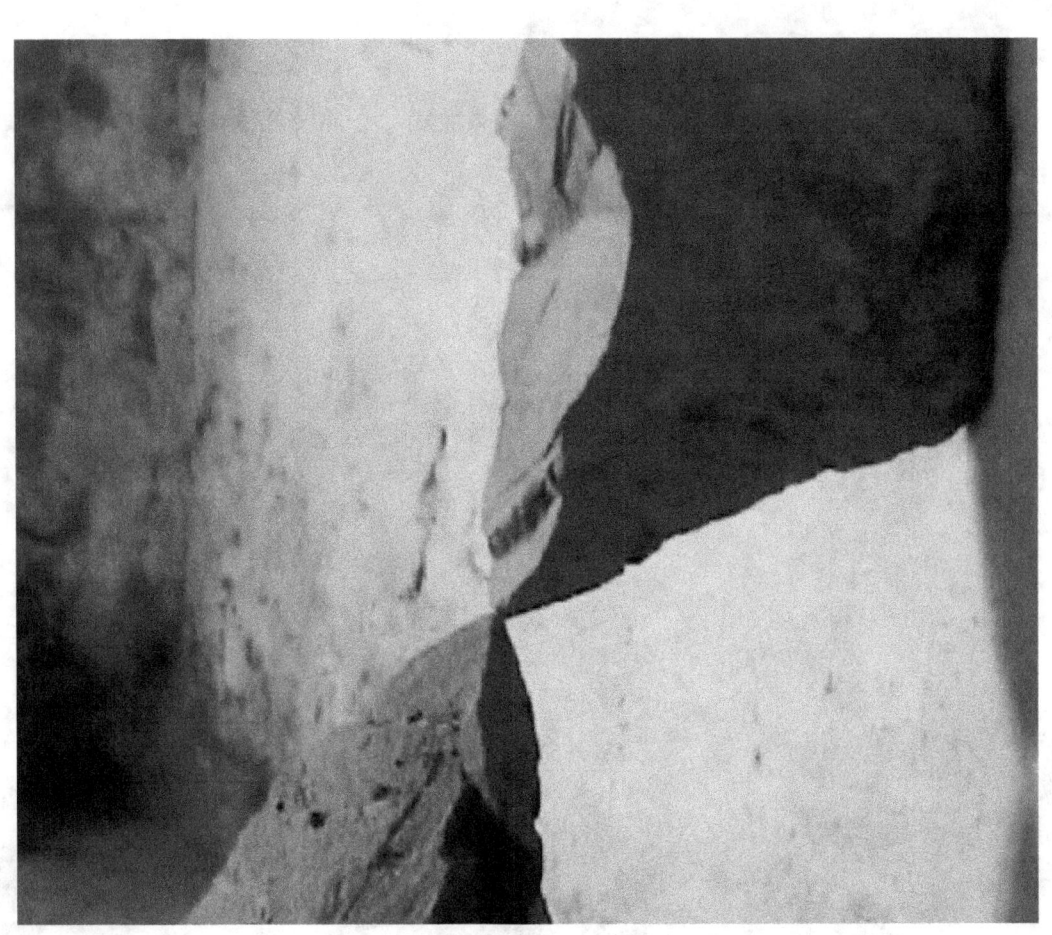

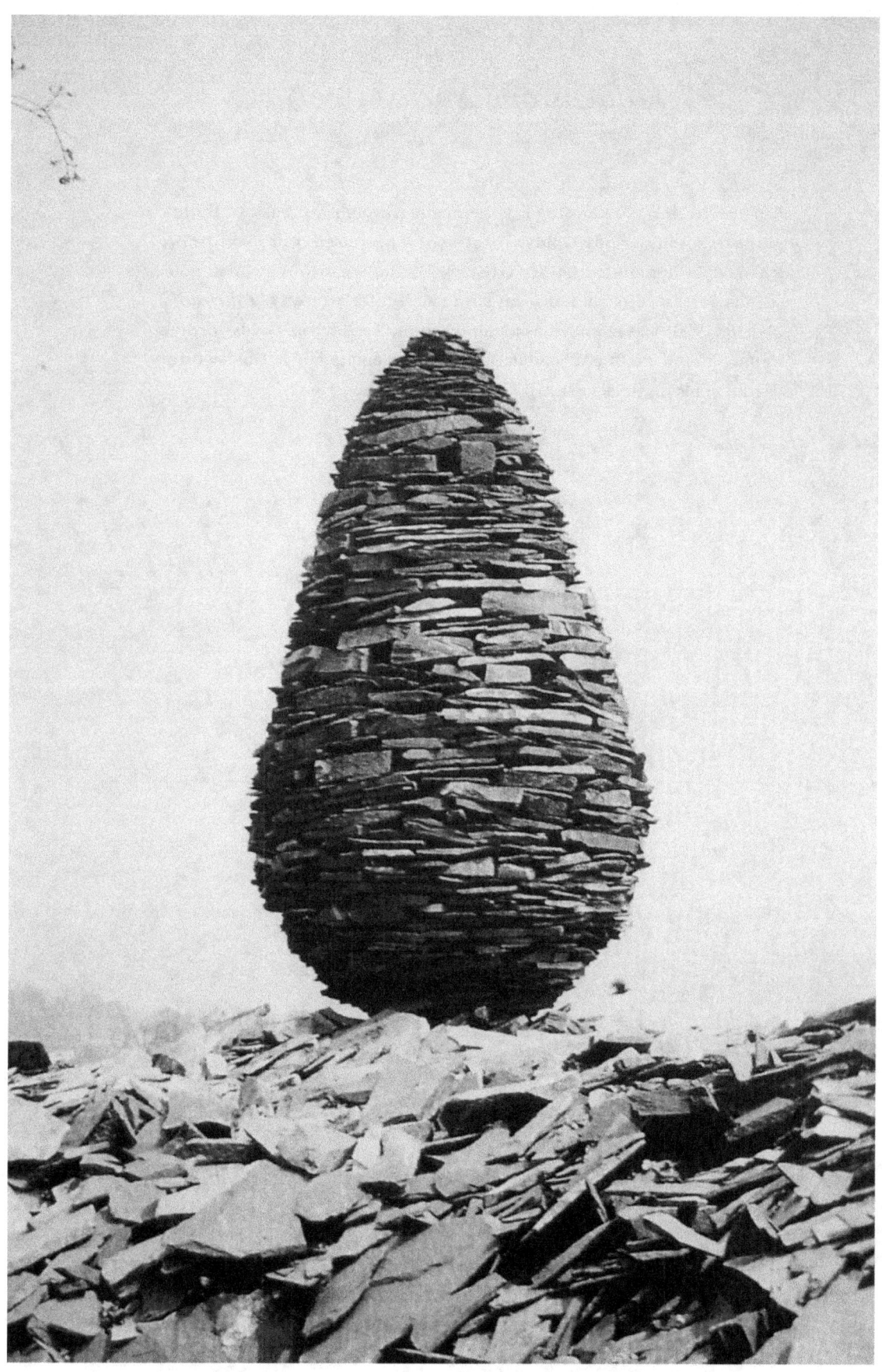

Touchstone North (1990)

The arch form, so simple yet so elegant (though not easy to build), appears often in Andy Goldsworthy's art – he's used it probably more than any other contemporary artist. Before he went to the North Pole, Goldsworthy constructed from stone a circular archway. *Touchstone North* (1990) was intended as a pointer to the Arctic from Goldsworthy's home in Scotland. It is a 'landmark that will orientate north' Goldsworthy wrote in his Arctic diary.[1]

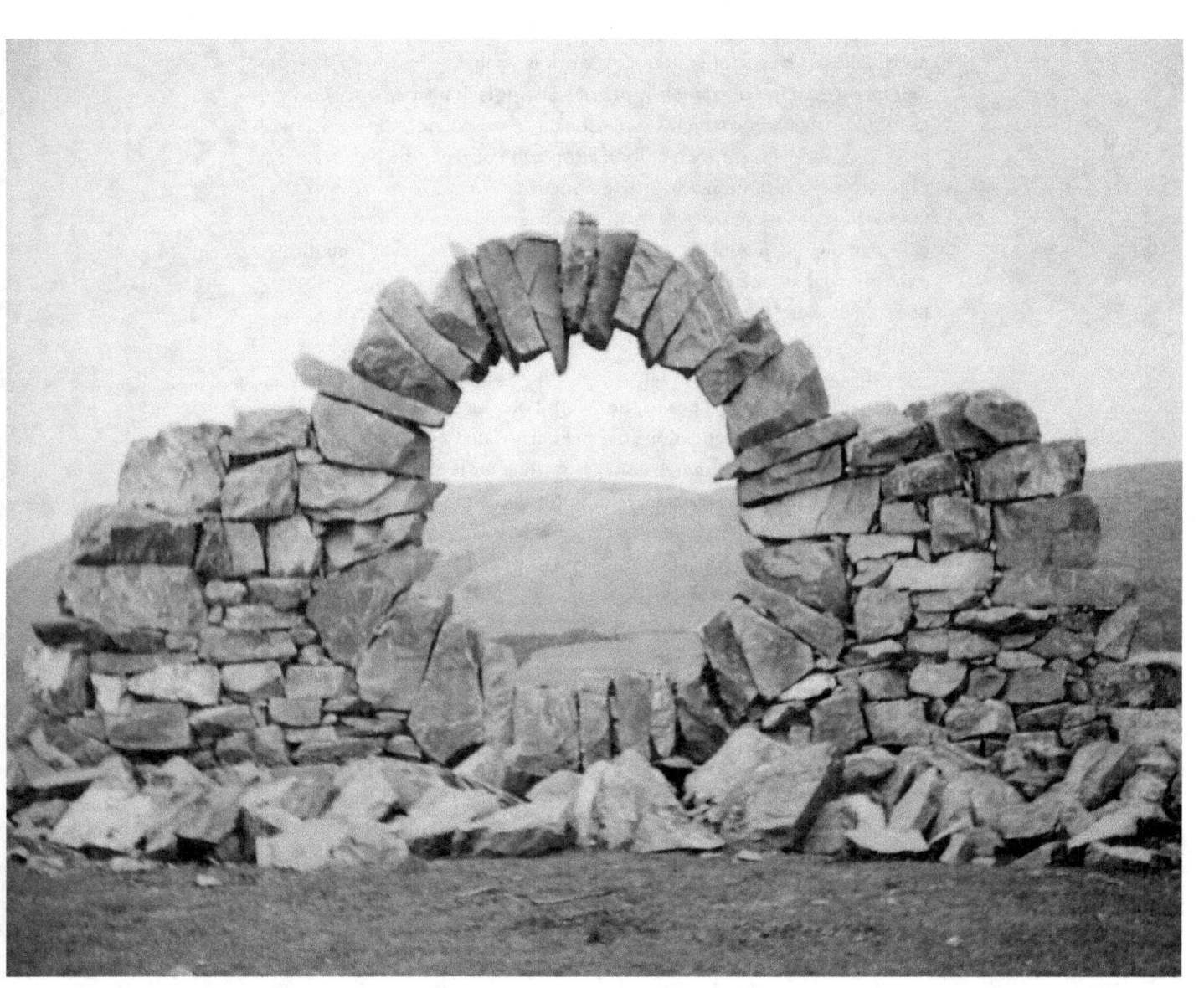

Touching North (1989)

Andy Goldsworthy's most dramatic work is probably *Touching North*, four circular arches or tunnels made of snow. It is dramatic partly due to its location, that space which's so thoroughly a masculine 'wild zone', the place of macho adventures, colonization and courage, the North Pole. Goldsworthy's intention with the grandeur of *Touching North* was 'to follow North to its source'. He had already encountered 'North' in 'the cold shadow of a mountain', he said, meaning he had already found the extreme cold associated with the North Pole in Scotland or Northern Britain. But there was a practical reason for going all the way North to the North Pole, and that was so that Goldsworthy could enjoy 'the luxury of constant freezing'. For, in Britain, snow comes and goes: it does not stay for months on end as it does in the North Pole. As Goldsworthy writes: 'so much that I have made in ice has been frustrated by a rise in temperature. I have held ice seemingly for ages waiting for it to freeze only to let go and see it drop off.'[1] Apart from the four arches of *Touching North*, Goldsworthy made a series of ice and snow works at the North Pole: ice walls with slits and zigzags cut in them; large stacks made from slabs of snow; long rows of snow slabs.

1. A. Goldsworthy, *Touching North*, 1989, and in *Hand to Earth*, 75.

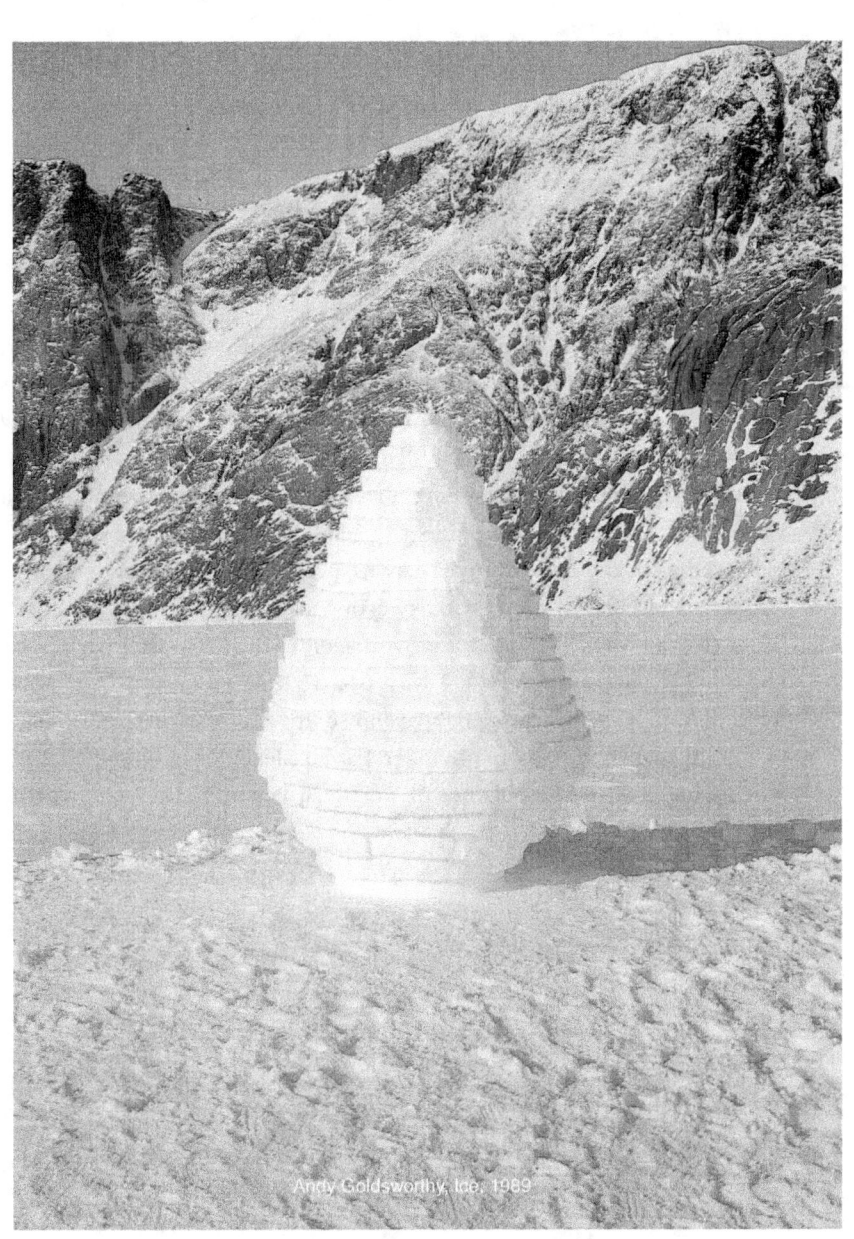

Andy Goldsworthy, Ice, 1989

Dark Dry Sand Drawing (1987)

For Andy Goldsworthy, as for any number of sculptors, the personal touch, of hands on materials, is crucial:

> The work itself determines the nature of its making. I enjoy the freedom of just using my hands and 'found' tools – a sharp stone, the quill of a feather, thorns. I am not playing the primitive. I use my hands because this is the best way to do most of my work.

Indeed, when it comes to drawing on the sand on a beach, Goldsworthy will not use a stick, as many folks would. Instead, he uses his hands, kneeling or crouching on the sand. His *Dark dry sand drawing* is worked by hand, dribbled onto the sand on the Isle of Wight (1987). The result, all swirls and curves, comes directly from Jackson Pollock (the beach drawing has the sense of harmony, of each part balanced with the rest, not part having precedence over any other, of Oriental landscape painting). Goldsworthy has also drawn lines on frozen water (Nova Scotia, 1999). A lot of work Goldsworthy has done in deserts has been with carved sand (in New Mexico, Arizona, California and Australia). In a way, these drawings and sculptures of sand (in the shape of spirals, snakes, zigzags and boulders) are basically developments of the work with sand on the beaches of Northern England that Goldsworthy undertook in the late 1970s.

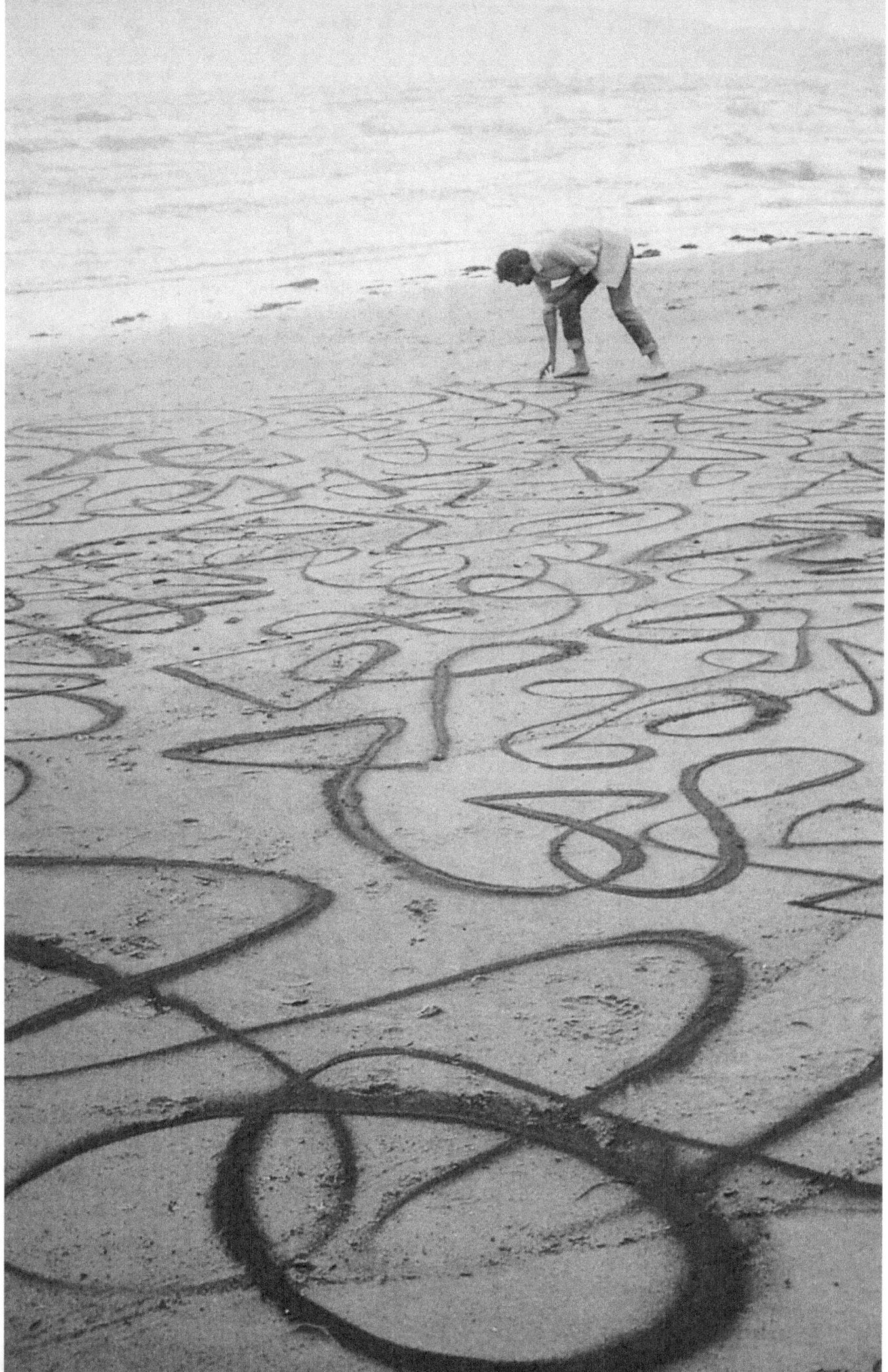

Arches

The notion of balance, of objects being held aloft, defying gravity, fascinates Andy Goldsworthy so much it becomes one of the central motifs of his work. He makes arches from thin pieces of slate (such as the *Slate Arch* of 1985, Cumbria, and *Slate Arch*, Wales, 1982) or has arches stretching up four steps (*Slate Arch*, 1990, Tarbes). *Over the stone* is a large arch made from loose stones found on the hillside at Scaur Glen: it is built over a large boulder, the internal form of the arch echoes the shape of the boulder. *Over the wall* is an arch that leaps over a stone; *Tree arch – river stones* is an arch of three components, leaning up against a tree; *Between two trees* is a shallow arch wedged between some trees; *Out of the stones* is an arch leaning against the boulder used in *Over the stone*: it is two-thirds of an arch (these arches were made in the winter of 1992-93 in Dumfriesshire [*Stone*, 98-99]).

In the late 1990s Goldsworthy took his arch out on the road, constructing it in a variety of locations along ancient drove roads in Scotland and Cumbria. The journey (a.k.a. *Drove Arch*) was linked to the *Sheepfolds* project, and was recorded in the 1999 book *Arch*.

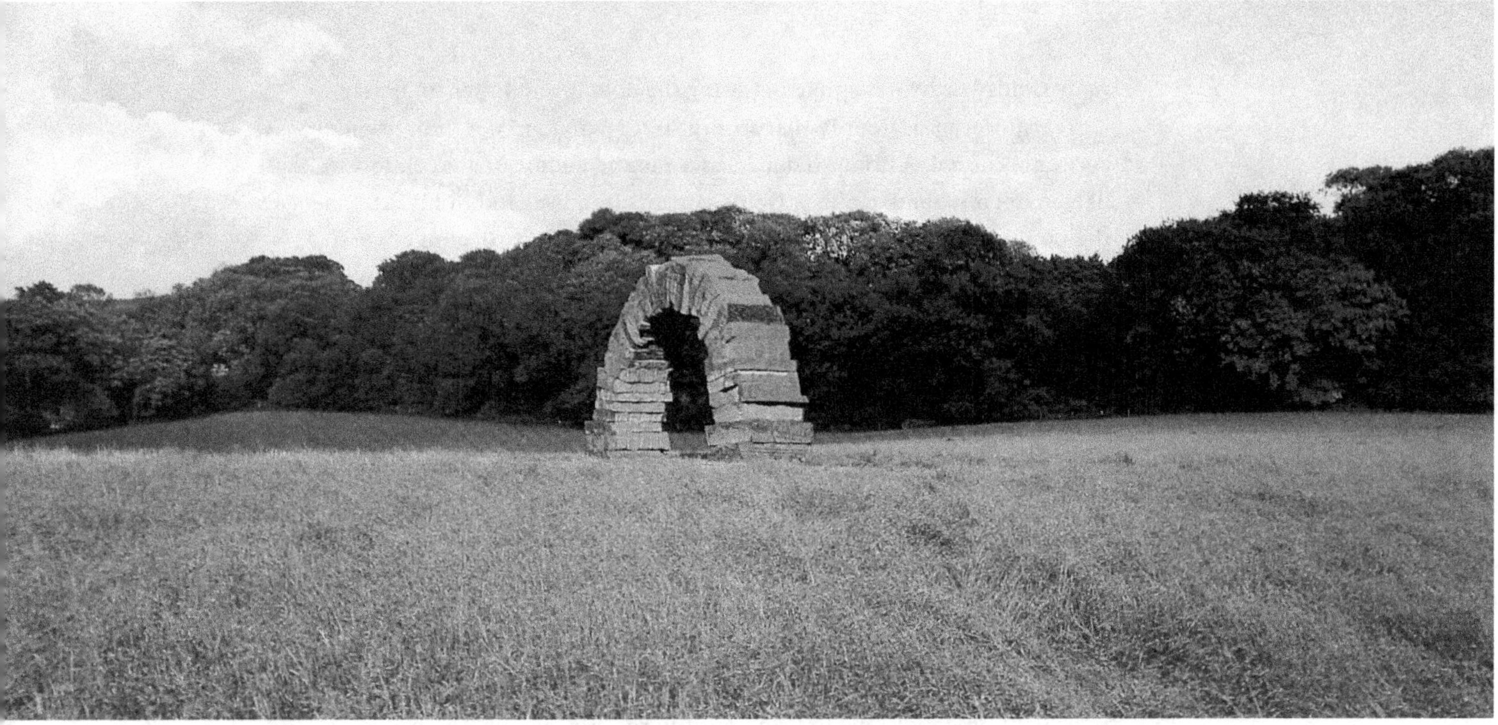

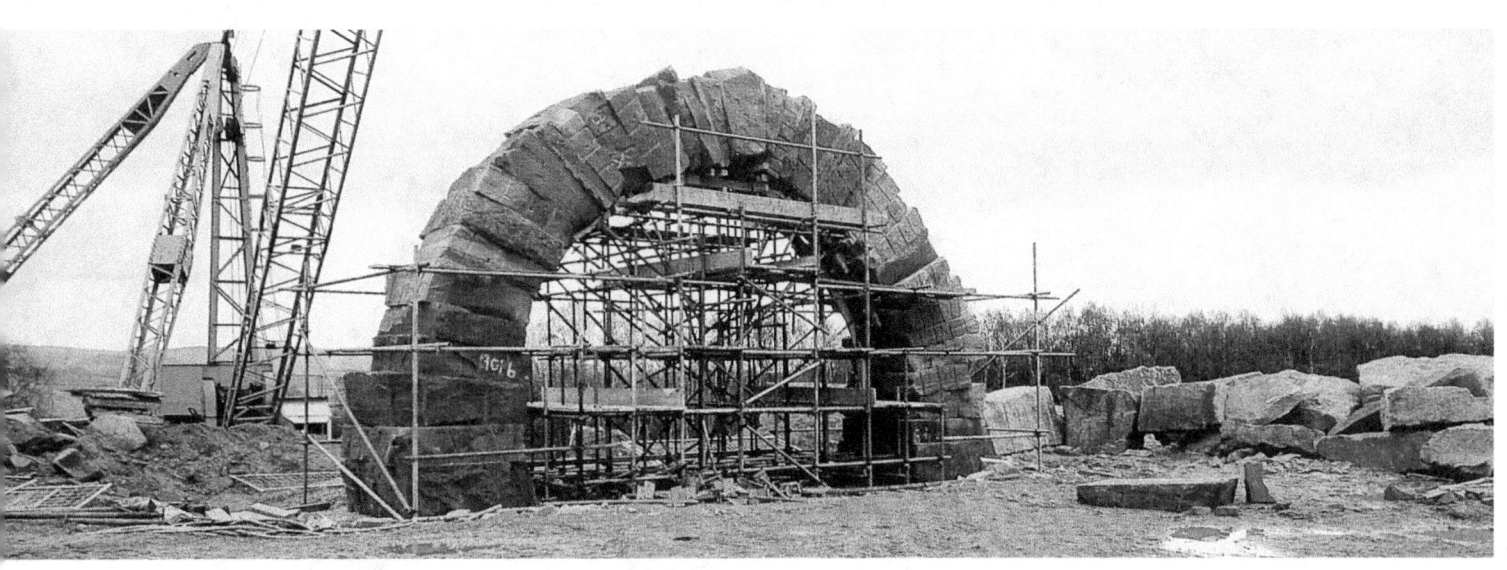

Leafworks

Andy Goldsworthy has spoken of using the colour red: in Japan, he says, he learnt about a 'deeply disturbing' red (*Wood,* 15), a 'heightened awareness of red. A bright red maple tree in the middle of a green forest, like an open wound' (in ib.). Goldsworthy often uses red in his art – in the boulders covered in red maple leaves or the poppy-leafed covered stones, or the ridged holes made on the beach at the Isle of Wight with red edges (1987, *Andy Goldsworthy*). Red maple leaves climb up rocks or are layered on top of little rockpools. Goldsworthy relates red to the iron in human blood. The Harrlemmerhout work, *Poppy petals,* was a seven-foot long line of poppy petals held together with spit which was hung from an elderberry. It was, a critic said, 'one of the most impressive and poetic works' Goldsworthy made during his time at Haarlem.[1] At Hampstead Heath an associated work, a line of beech leaves, was floated over a pool (1985, *Hand to Earth,* 59). In Australia the colour red did not come in Goldsworthy's work, as one might expect, from flower petals or red stones, but from red sand: Goldsworthy rubbed the sand into the bark of a mulga tree. Gathering rain clouds and a brilliant, low sun created the right lighting conditions to bring out the red tree against the brooding grey sky (*Stone,* 54-55). Goldsworthy said that the red of the Australian outback was 'deeply moving spiritually'. 'I have tried to touch that colour not just with my hands, but also with light' (*Wood,* 15).

1. H. Voegls: "Haarlemmerhout", in HE, 54.

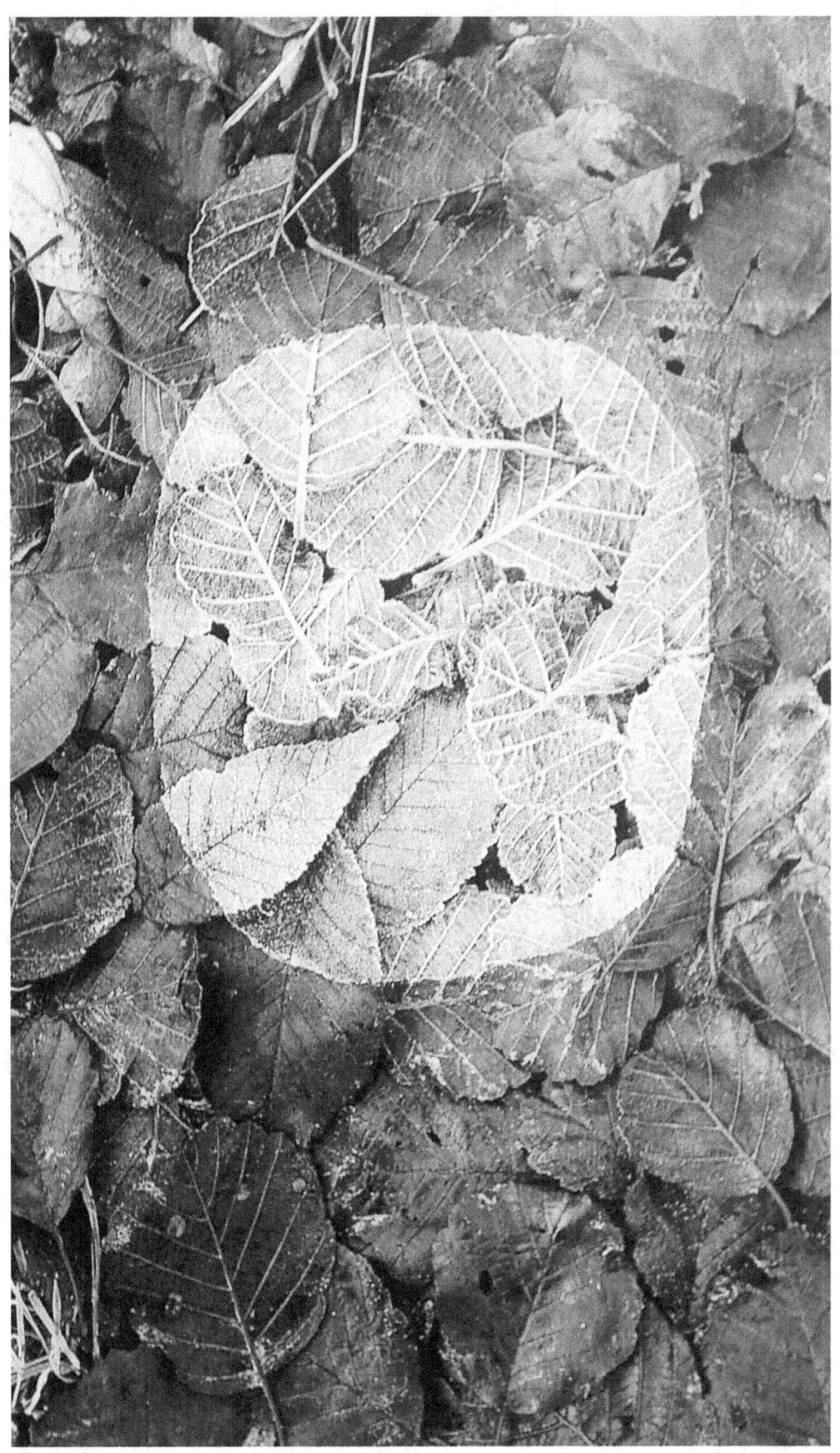

Holes

Andy Goldsworthy's anxious, ambivalent attitude towards holes in the ground recall the views of (usually male) philosophers on the negativity of holes and voids, which are associated with the sexual identity of women. These fears and ambiguities are found in much of Western culture: in Sigmund Freud's castration myth; in the belligerent misogynist theology of St Augustine, Tertullian, St Paul and Origen. Another religious view sees women as Mother Goddesses, identified with nature, the seasons, vegetation and the powers of the earth. One deity which some feminists and British poets (such as Robert Graves and Peter Redgrove) have worshipped (though they would not use that term) is the 'Black Goddess', a divinity of darkness, night, the unknown and the supernatural.

The psychologist Jacques Lacan's notion of the 'lack', which subsequent feminists have criticised, is another obvious reference. What women lack is the phallus, the 'transcendent signifier' as cultural theorists call it. The art object is thus (in Julia Kristeva's interpretation) a fetish, a stand-in for the imaginary maternal phallus. Friedrich Nietzsche had similar views of the 'feminine': it was not menstruation or lactation that scandalized Nietzsche so much as the lack or absence of a visible (sexual) organ. 'What Mother Nature needs so urgently to hide from view is not so much what she has as what she lacks. Nietzsche suspects a void at the center of the body of nature.'[1] In French feminist Luce Irigaray's reading of Lacan what women lack is the ability to speak from/ with the phallus: the genital lack suggests an ideological or æsthetic lack, the absence which becomes cultural silence.

This masculinist fear of the black hole or void at the heart of nature is very apparent in Goldsworthy's statements: 'looking into a deep hole unnerves me' he writes; the black holes of his sculptures are openings into the 'deep insecurity in nature – a fragile, unpredictable and violent energy' (Stone, 64). He is fascinated by holes: 'I enjoy the seductiveness of a hole' he says, 'which always makes me want to explore the spaces inside or beyond' (Hand to Earth, 61). Goldsworthy admits to being frightened as well as fascinated by the powers of nature. He speaks of the blackness under the Earth rising up and buckling the rim of the holes he makes in the ground and in the floors of art galleries. He makes a hole in a gallery floor to remind the spectator that just below the

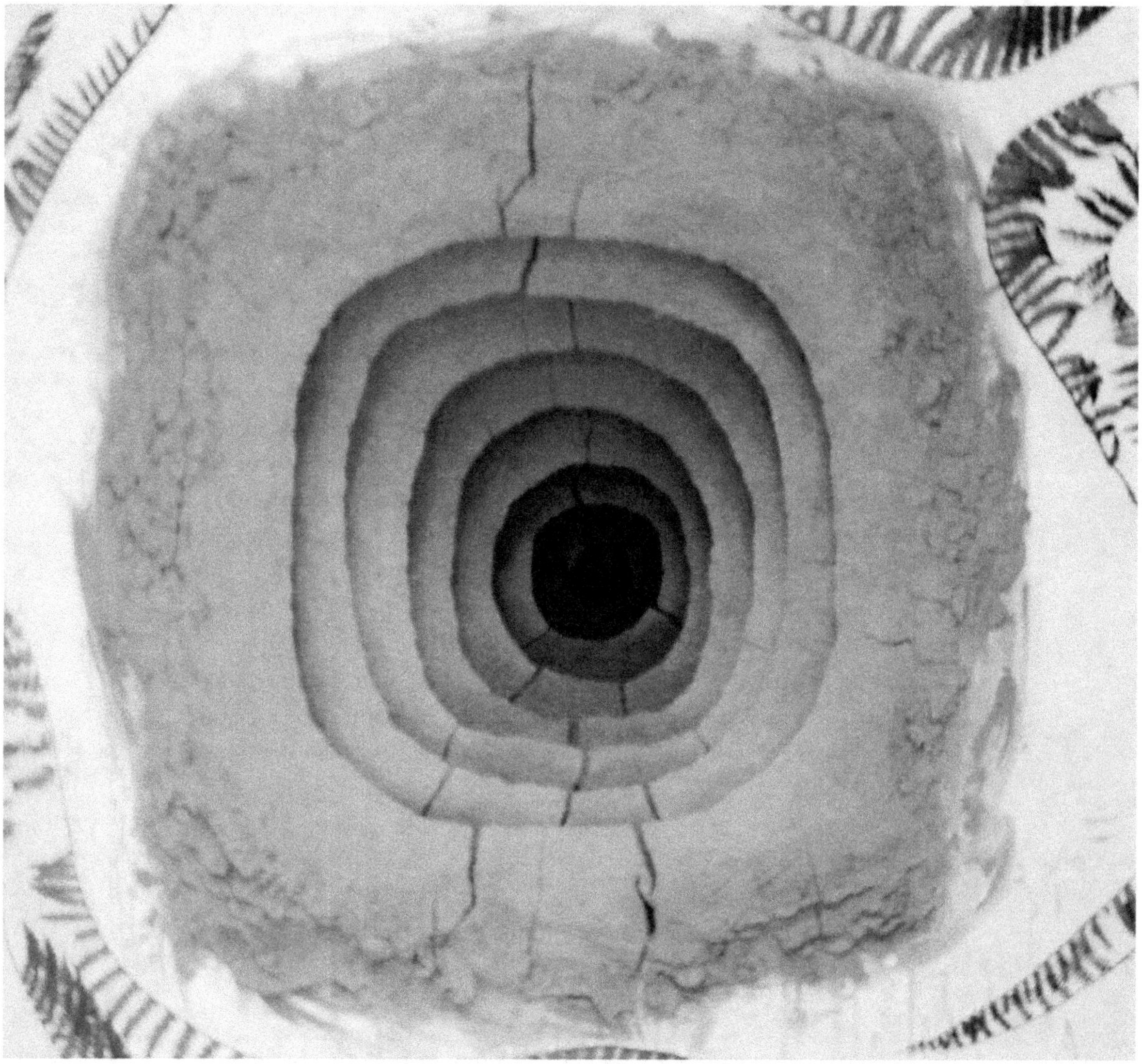

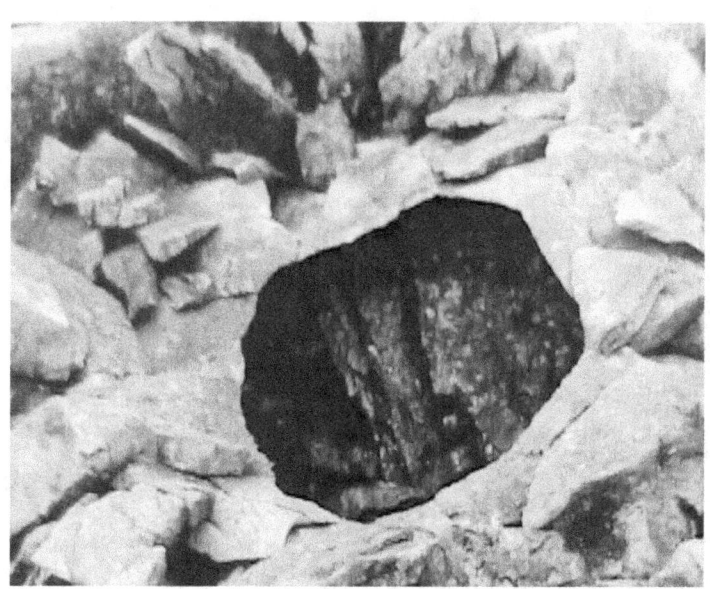

building is the unpredictable and immense energy of nature and the Earth. Goldsworthy built holes at the Serpentine Gallery (London) in 1981, and at the Frank Hals Museum (in 1984).

Sculptures such as the Greenpeace office commission, *Seven Holes* (1991), are obviously about the Earth's energies. The sculpture *Black Water Stone* (1993) makes explicit the identification between the Earth and 'feminine' discourses: the low cairn with the small hole at the summit is placed under water: the presence of the 'feminine' element, water, adds another layer to the already symbolically rich sculpture (the cairn or mound; the circle; blackness; the hole; the submerged or partially out of sight setting). Another 'feminine' cairn is the *Welsh sea cairn* (1993), built on a pile of barnacled rocks right next to the ocean: when the tide came in, it surrounded the cairn. The sculpture was another 'before and after' work, and could hardly fail: like the cover of *Stone* (*Balanced rocks*), *Sea cairn* was seen against and beside the ocean. The presence of the surging waves gives the stone sculptures a grandeur they certainly would not possess if they were sited in a slate quarry. Other holed cairns include ones made from rowan leaves (Yorkshire, 1987) and pebbles (Japan, 1987).

1. C. Koelb, "Castration Envy", in P.J. Burgard, ed. *Nietzsche and the Feminine*, University Press of Virginia, Charlottesville, VI, 1994, 79.

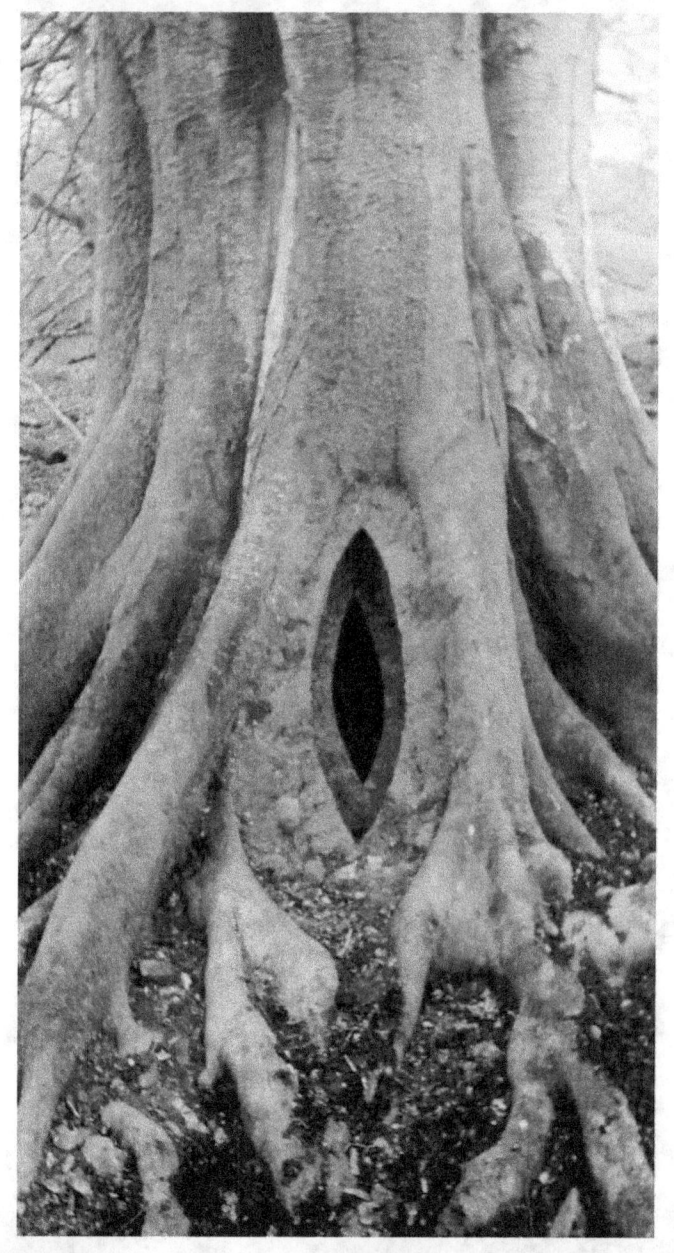

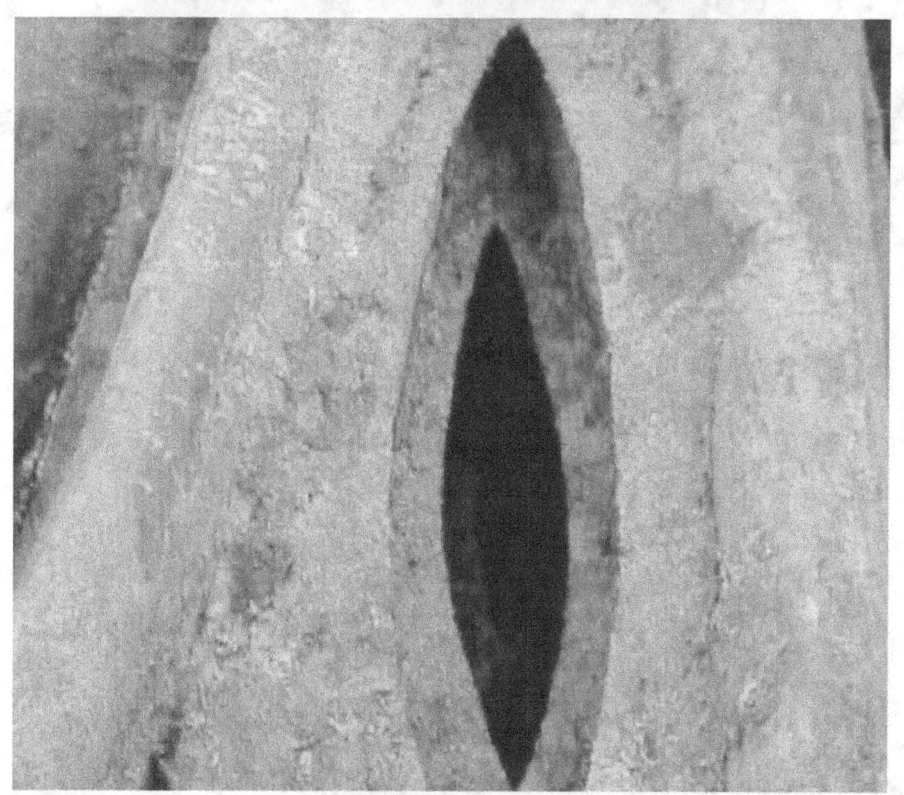

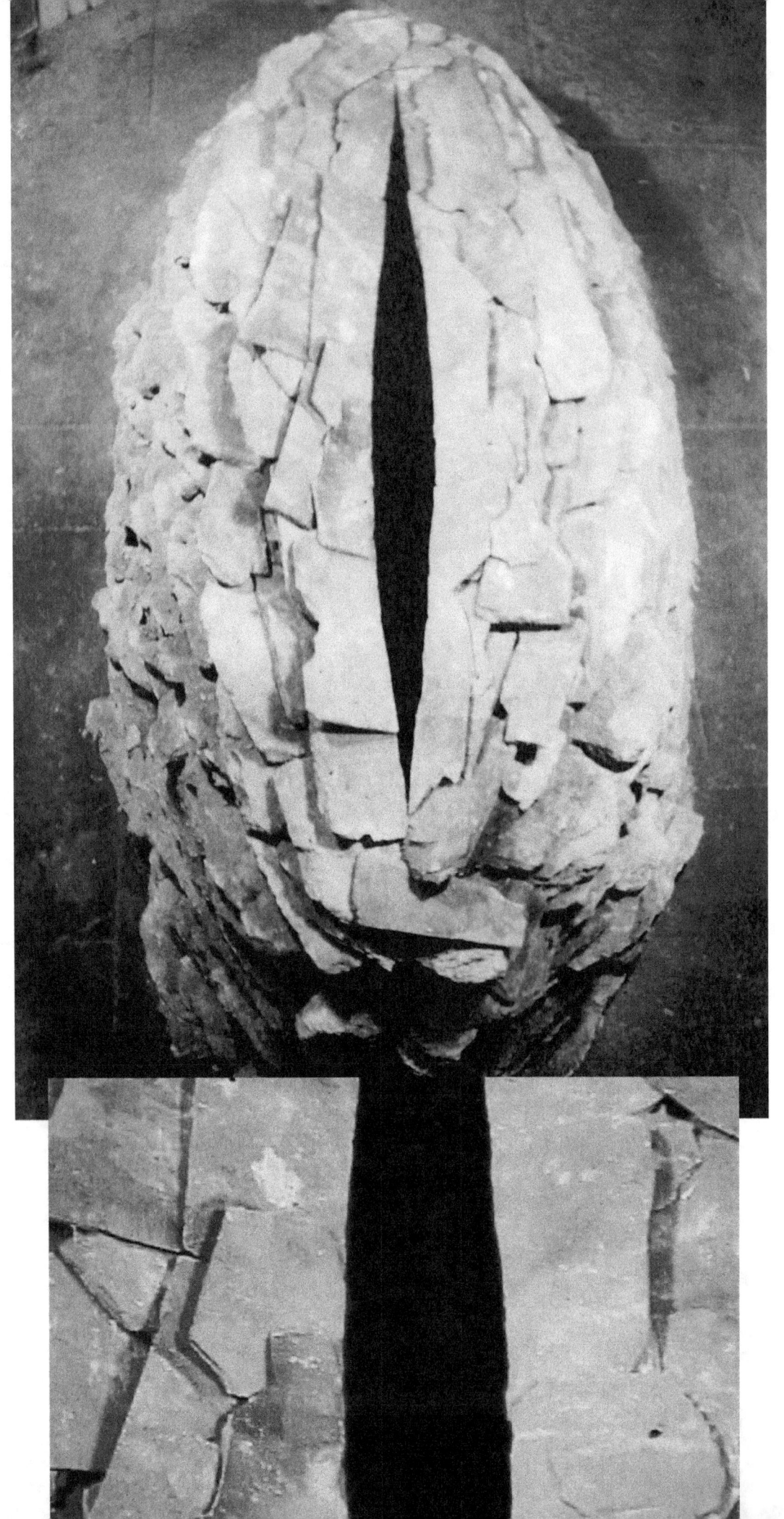

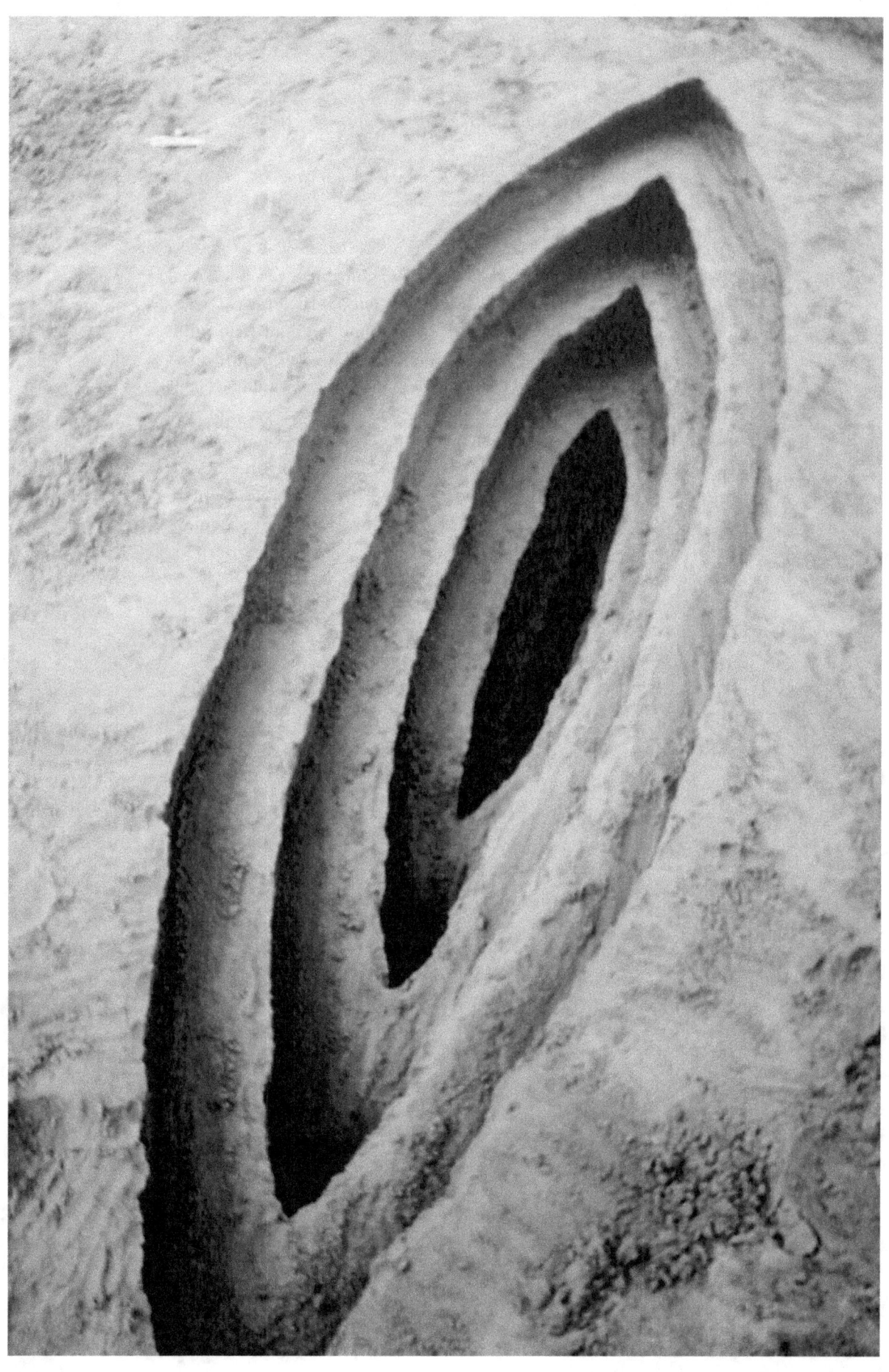

Thin Ice (2004)

'Some places I return to over and over again, going deeper – a relationship, made in layers over a long time' commented Goldsworthy (AG). For an artist like Andy Goldsworthy, the land around Penpont, Thornhill, Burnhead, Keir Mill, Cleuchhead, Carronbridge, Closeburn and Tynron would be very, very familiar. Weeks or perhaps months would be spent each year fashioning sculpture in this part of the South-West Scotland. One can bet that Goldsworthy will be out there making art in the area, if he's not working on a commission in Digne or California or wherever, or dealing with admin, or on vacation. Goldsworthy's sculptures will be situated all over this part of the world. Some will be extremely ephemeral, and some might last a little longer than a day or so.

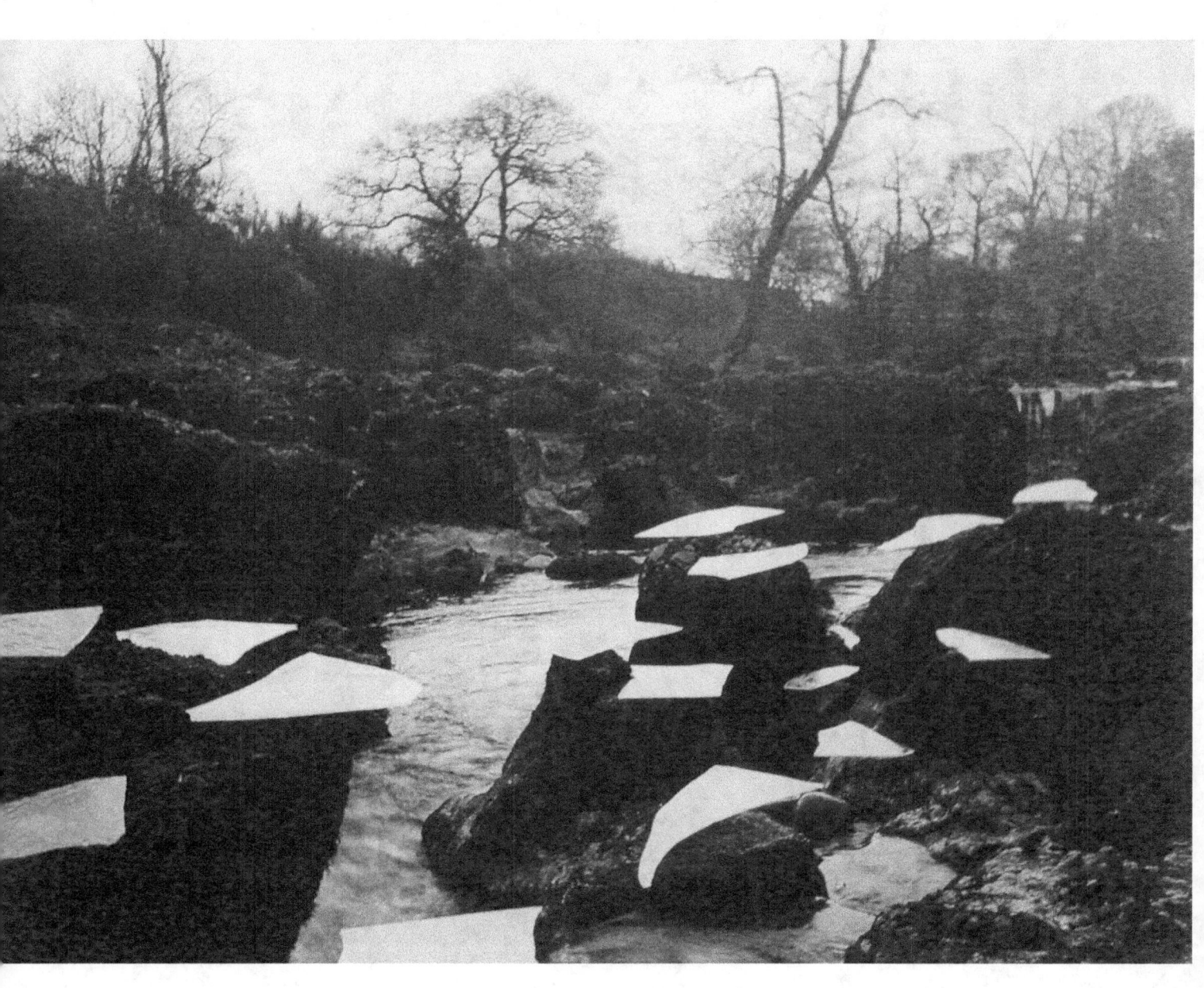

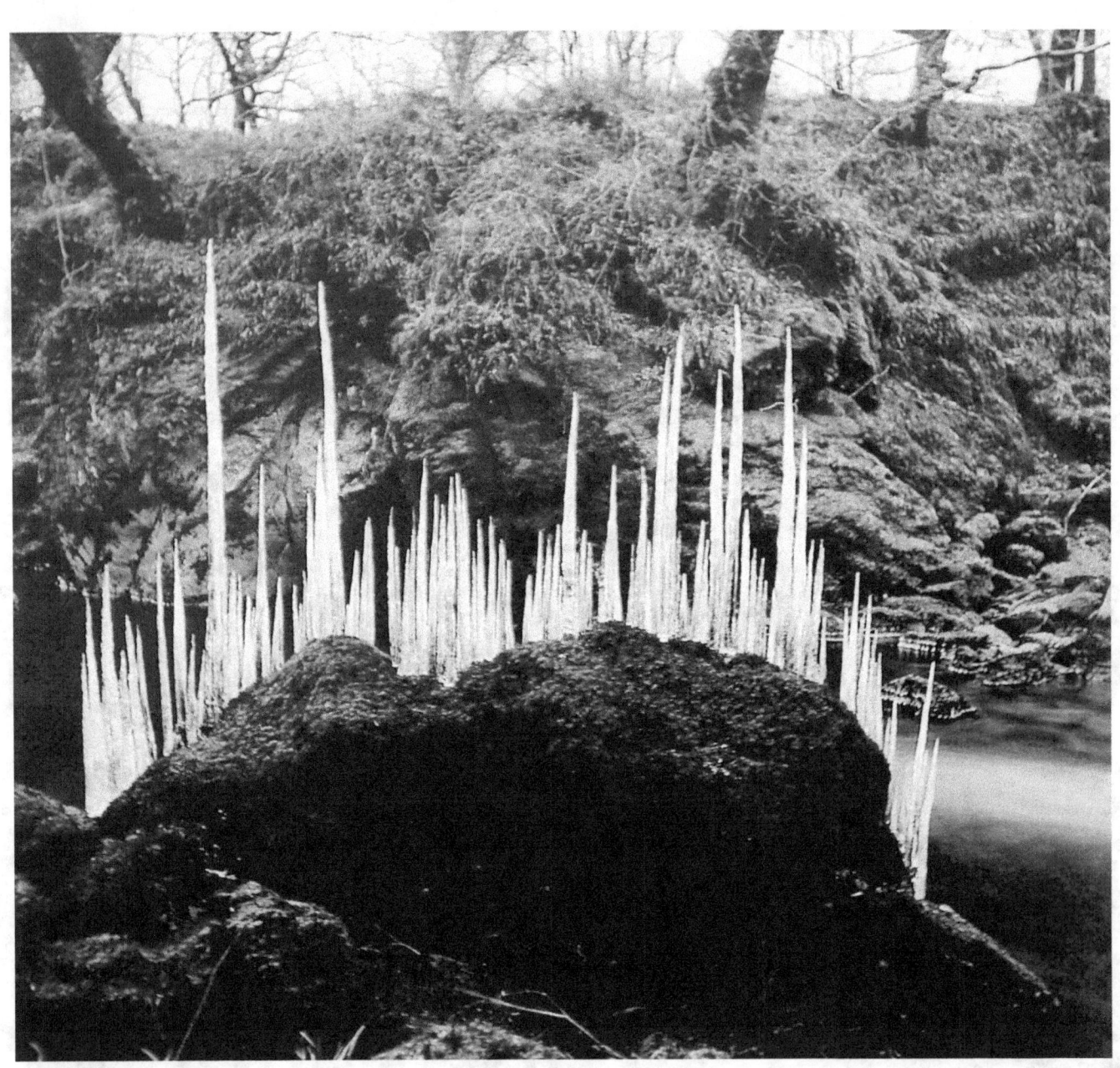

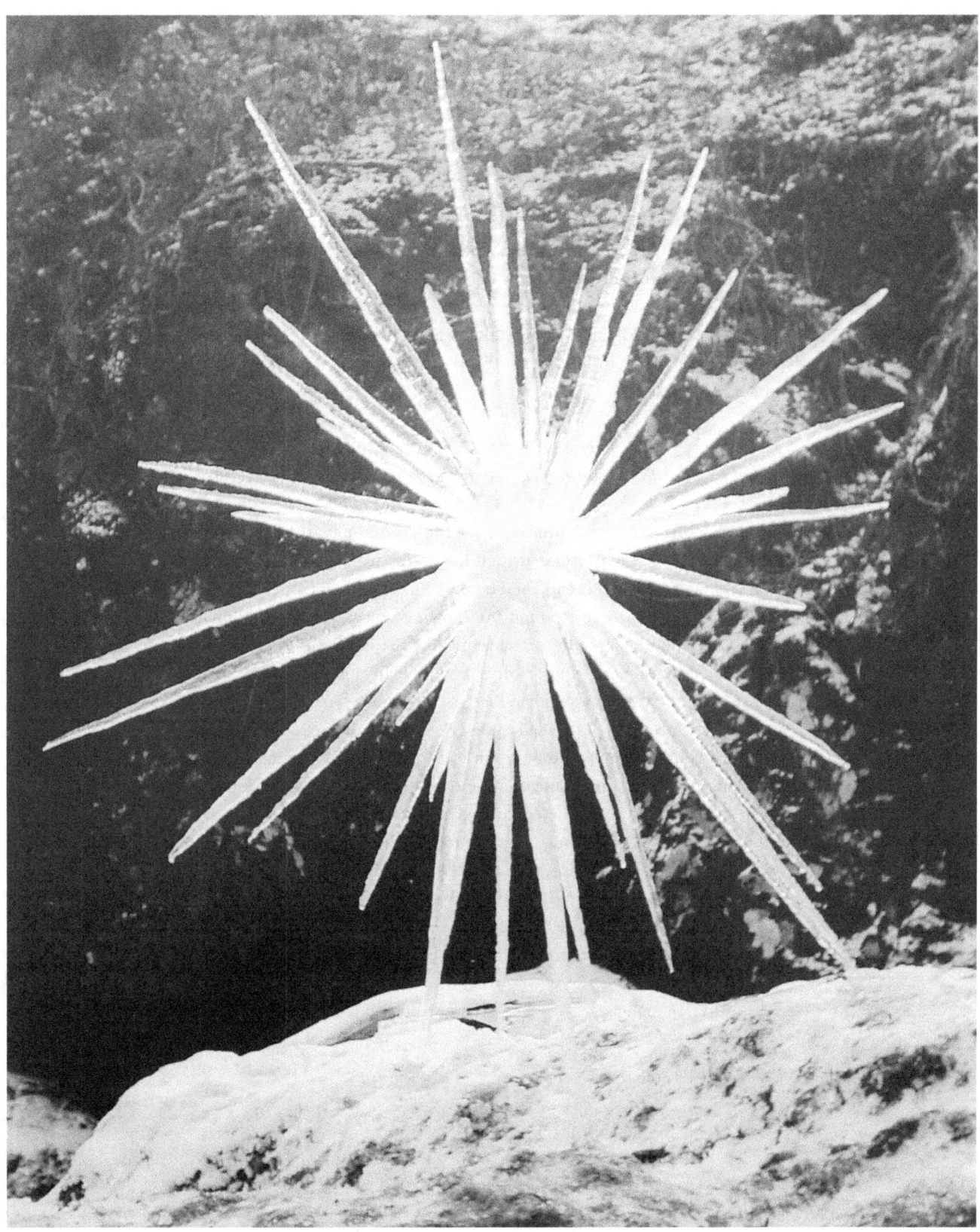

Rain Shadows

Andy Goldsworthy produced a series of works, beginning in the 1980s, which directly recall Yves Klein's *Anthropometries*. Goldsworthy laid down on the ground when it was raining or snowing: the result was the outlines of his body left upon the ground. Sometimes he produced frost shadows in the early morning, creating a man-shape on the frosty ground. A typical the title for these works (reproduced in *Andy Goldsworthy* and other books) is:

> *Lay down as it started raining or snowing*
> *waited until the ground became wet or covered before getting up.*

Goldsworthy 'printed' himself onto the ground negatively, his body covered the dry earth, while around his body the earth (usually stones, but also grass and soil) is darkened by the rain. This wasn't a performance, though: Goldsworthy published the finished work, the rain shadow or body print, not the artist in the act of making the work. Goldsworthy also performed these pieces fully clothed, while many another performance artist would be tempted to create these works nude.

The body prints and rain shadows were spontaneous works; they could not be planned; one has to be open to the weather, knowing it is just starting to rain or snow. One could never – in Britain or any country, – plan such a work inside, then go outside and execute it. One would have to be already out and about. These works are always dependent on the weather, which is always unpredictable. For this reason, though they appear to be the most 'passive' of Goldsworthy's works – the easiest to produce (the artist just lies on the ground) – Goldsworthy finds them challenging, because the conditions have to be just right. On many occasions, the rain is the wrong sort, or (as in a work planned in New York City), though forecast, it doesn't come at all.

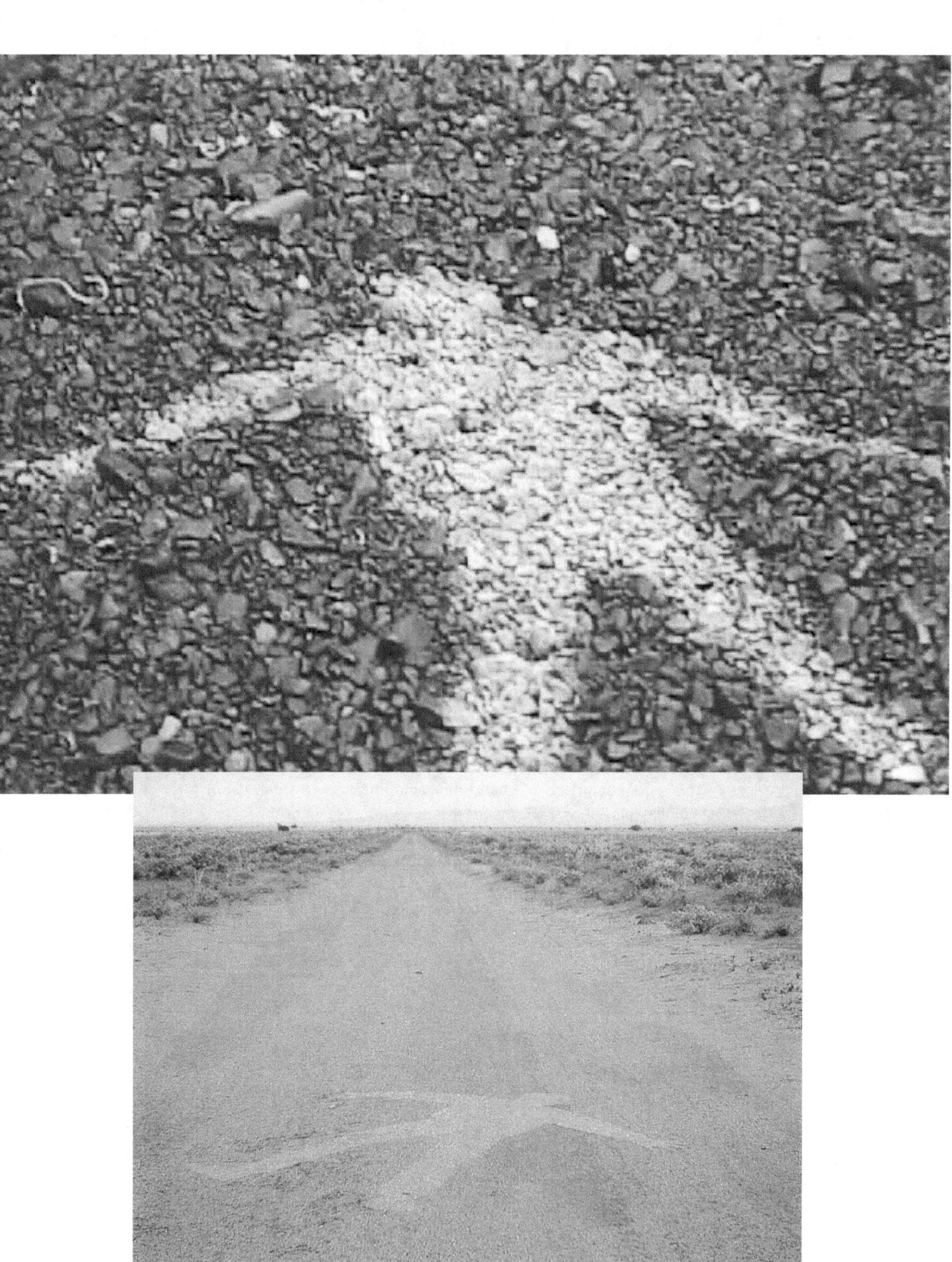

Night Path (2002)

Night Path (a.k.a. *Moonlit Path*, 2002) was constructed at Petworth Park in Sussex in Southern England (at the Leconfield Estate). It was a long path built from white chalk culled from the Sussex Downs that snaked through a wood. *Night Path* was meant to be experienced at night, though not necessarily a moonlit night (Goldsworthy also said that the path could be visited at other times of the day, and perhaps a clear moonless night, or a full moon obscured by clouds would be better [P, 153]). The idea of walking along a path by moonlight might have appeared as too romantic, Goldsworthy said (P, 156). In the event, it wasn't: '[t]he sculpture has become a far darker piece, in all senses of the word' (ibid.). Much more significant than the path itself was the experience of being out in the trees at night. As Goldsworthy put it in *Passage*:

> A place is so different at night – it is like being somewhere else. Perception, feeling and senses are changed by darkness. A different range of emotions and senses is released. (P, 153)

Plenty of land artworks have been made specifically for the night, of course: James Turrell's sky-viewing spaces, for instance, or the walks that Hamish Fulton has undertaken throughout a whole night. Golds-worthy's *Night Path* also recalls the spaces in Oriental gardens which were fashioned for contemplation in moonlight.

A work associated closely with *Night Path* was *Chalk Stones Trail*. This work comprised 14 chalk stone sculptures, each spherical or rounded, placed on a trial about five miles long (some of the stones weighed 14 tons). *Chalk Stones Trail* was situated at West Dean in West Sussex (North of Chichester). Goldsworthy intended to produce a book featuring this work and others in Sussex.

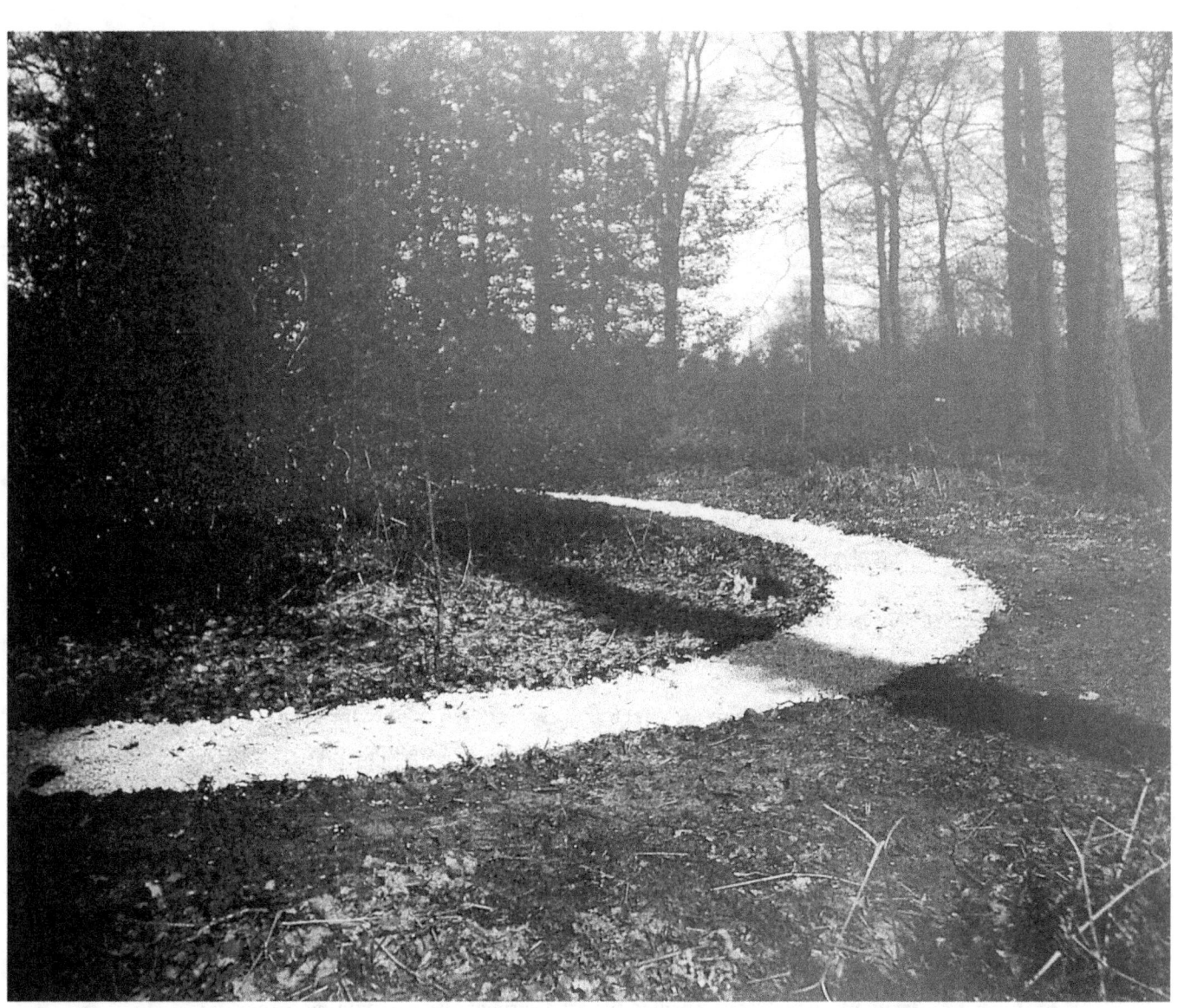

Serpents or Snakes

Andy Goldsworthy, like Michael Heizer, Walter de Maria and Robert Smithson, has made some huge pieces, such as the long 'snake' and the 'pool' or maze, in Country Durham, large works which take up a lot of space, and certainly dominate the surrounding landscape. Goldsworthy's large-scale outdoor works often use the serpent coil as a fundamental form. Goldsworthy maintains, however, that his 'snake-like' or serpent-shaped sculptures do not refer directly to snakes.[1] Whatever the artistic intention, however, it is impossible to limit readings of sculptures such as *Sidewinder, Lambton Earthwork* or the serpentine shapes in the British Museum's Egyptian Hall to responses to the environment. The serpent connotes time, change, seasons, birth-and-death-and-rebirth, eternity, sexuality, evil, the cosmos, and so on. Goldsworthy might wish to determine how viewers read his serpent-shaped forms, and emphasize the response he makes to the natural environment, but consumers of art will make any interpretation they like, and some they might wish to suppress (snakes also connote dirt – they slide on the dust; and excrement; the alimentary canal; eating and defecating; poison; reptile life, and so on).

The theme of the winding serpent was especially pertinent to Goldsworthy's installations in the Ancient Egyptian galleries of the British Museum and the Museo Egizo in Turin. Goldsworthy's large sculpture was made with local sand on the floors of the museums, snaking in between the exhibits of Egyptian artefacts. It was there for one day then dismantled (after being photographed, of course – the photographic record incorporated the themes of time and death just as piquantly as the sculpture itself). Even if not explicitly like 'snakes', these sculptures evoked the Ancient Egyptian preoccupation with time, death, eternity and immortality. Goldsworthy spoke of the sand snake flowing 'through the room – touching the sculptures and incorporating them into its form to give a feeling of the underlying geological and cultural energies that flow through the sculptures' (*Time Machine*). The sweet chestnut leafworks which accompanied the sand serpent also evoked time – they were spiral shapes, set in an Egyptian sarcophagus and a libation bowl.[2]

1. 'Some works have qualities of snaking but are not snakes. The form is shaped through a similar response to environment.' (*Andy Goldsworthy*)
2. Goldsworthy wrote that a 'work made with leaves is a celebration of growth, yet cannot work without expressing some anticipation of death, in a way that understands that death is a part of growth. The sarcophagi are not just containers of death, they are containers of life, in that out of death comes life' (TM).

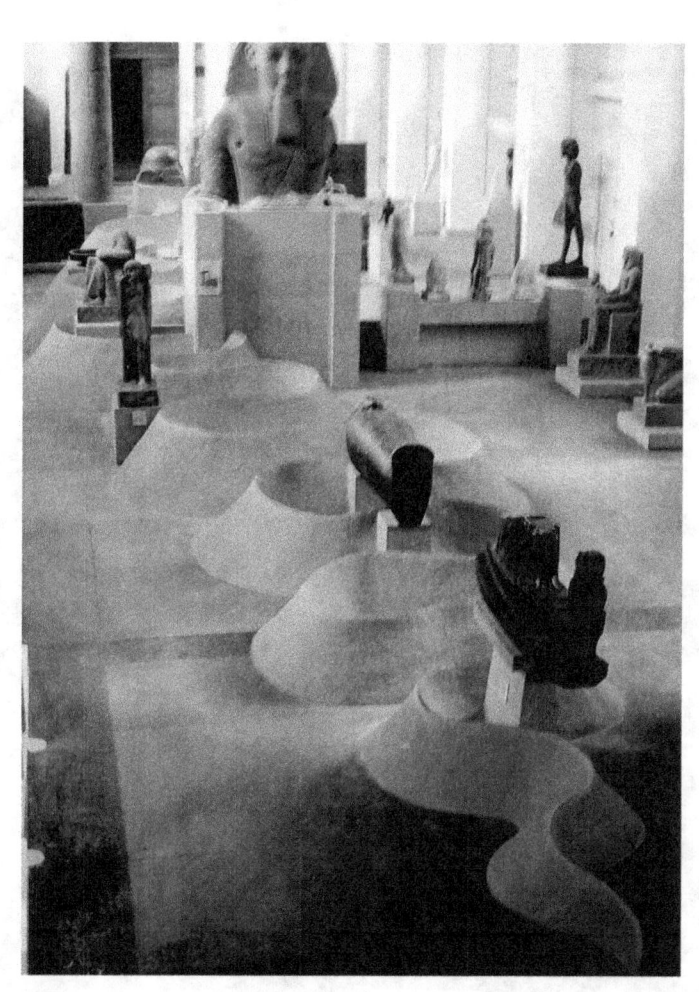

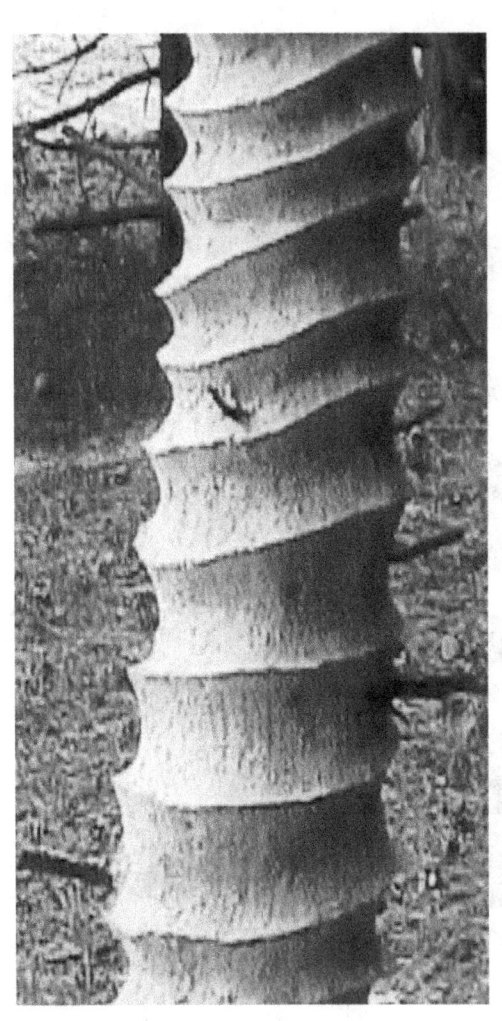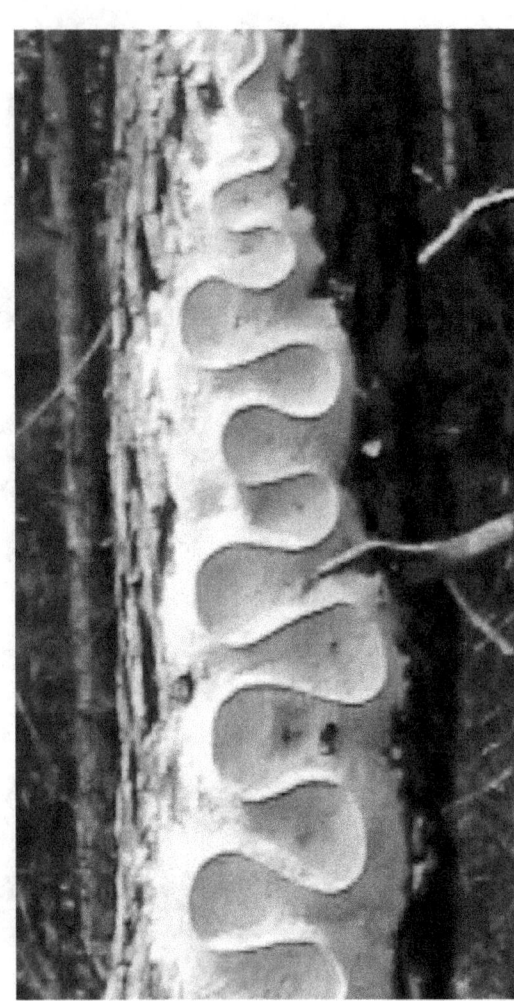

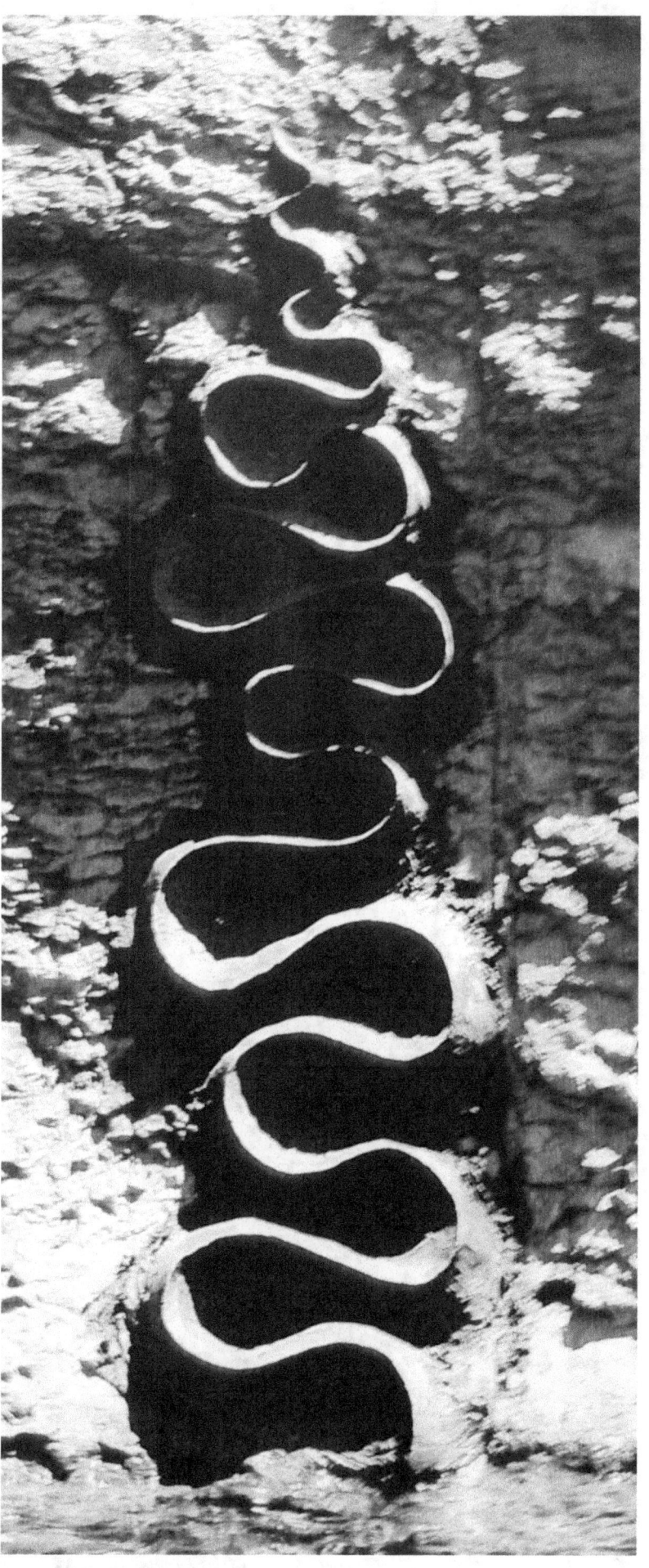

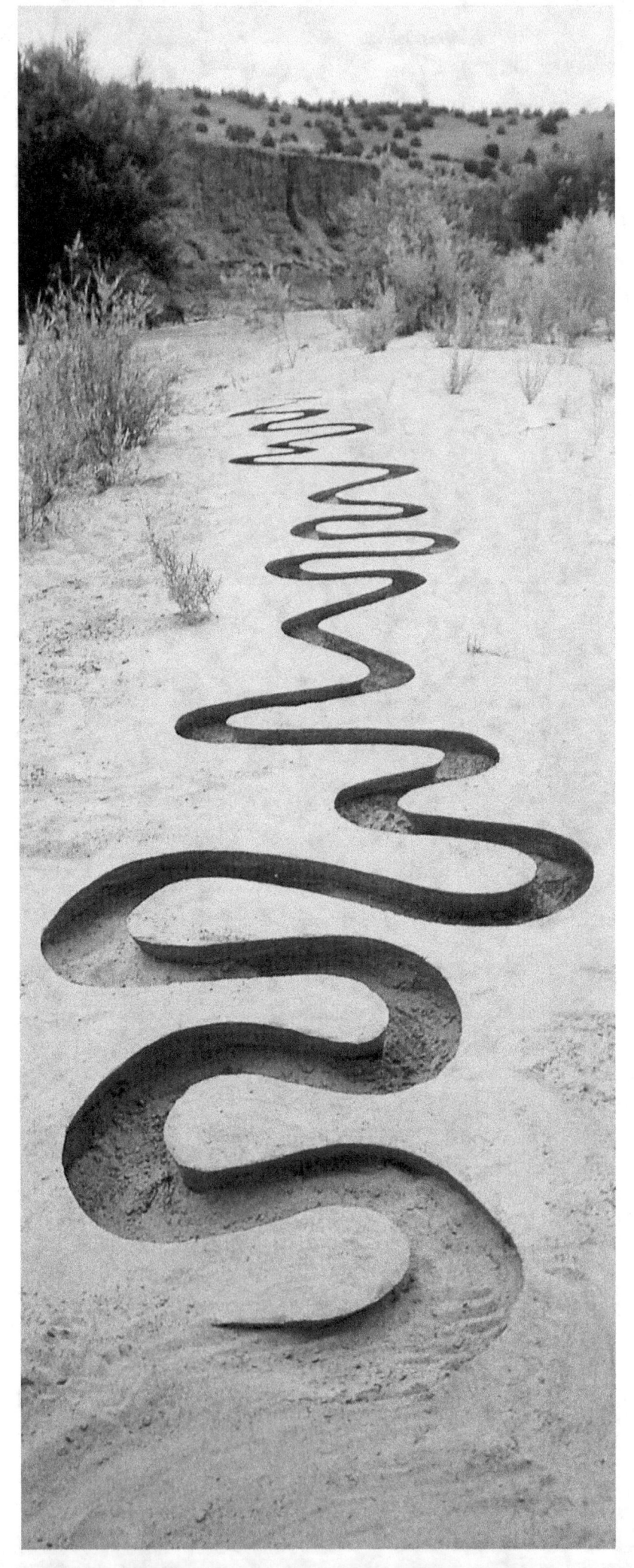

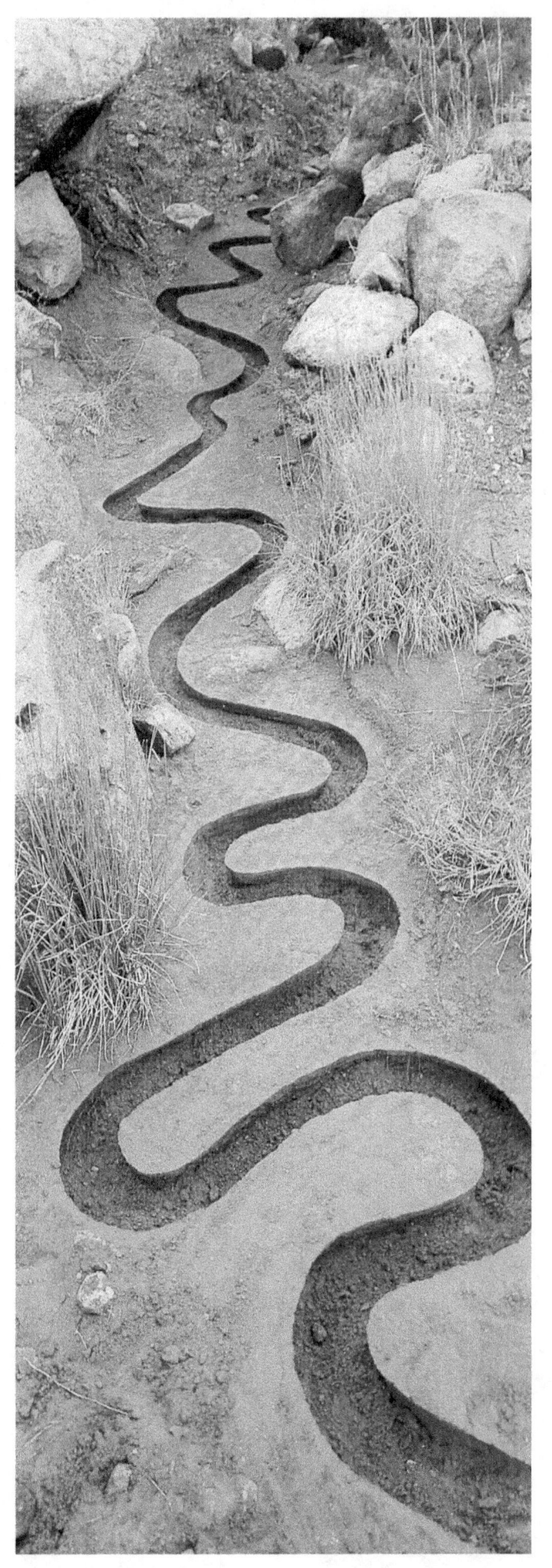

Fine Dry Sand (1989)

Andy Goldsworthy's *Fine dry sand (edges and ridges softened by the breeze)* is worked by hand, shaped in the sand in the Arizona desert in 1989. The result, a series of wavy congruent ridges, again recalls the serpent motif. Many sculptors have spoken of the importance of the making of the sculpture, its actual construction, with real (and sometimes organic, living) materials. In some artists, the material employed also has a symbolic or added meaning, as in Joseph Beuys' *Fettecke* or 'fat corner', a sculpture with powerful autobiographical and semiotic associations.

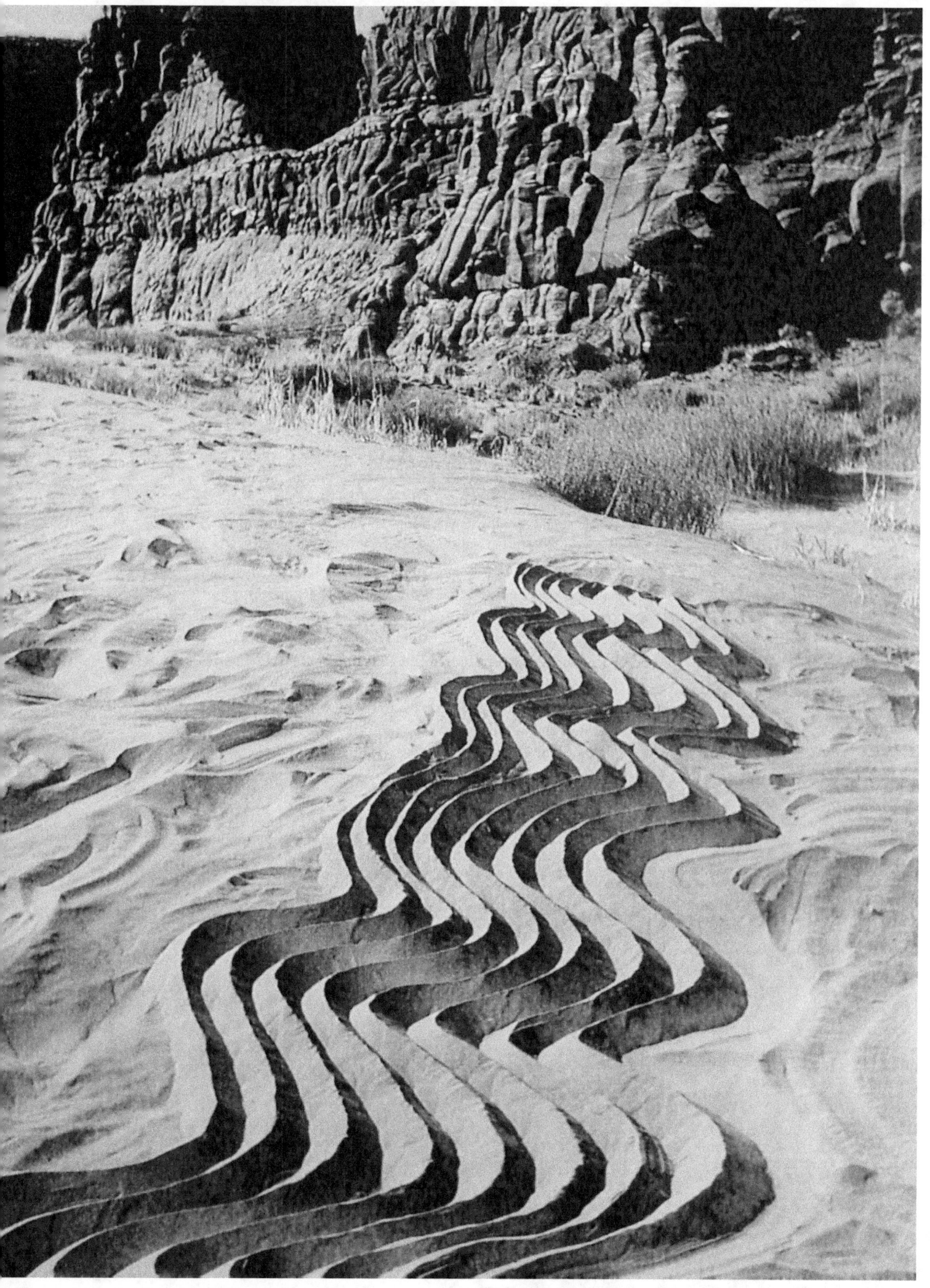

Leafworks

Andy Goldsworthy's leaf sculptures are often at their most effective in Autumn, not surprisingly, as the dates for many of the leaf pieces demonstrate (November 1, 1986, November 22, 1987, November, 1977, October 22, 1992, November, 2003, and so on). Works such as *Line to follow colours in maple leaves* (1992) use the changing colour of leaves in Autumn as their basic structure: the leaves pinned to the fallen tree change from green through yellow to orange, red and damson. One of Goldsworthy's best leafworks was made in Illinois in 1992. It comprised of a shield of red maple leaves set in the 'V' of two tree trunks. The importance of light was emphasized in *Maple leaves* in the book *Wood* by the decision to include a photograph of the sculpture from both sides, showing the sun shining on the leaves from one side, and shining through the leaves from the other.

Sometimes the wind is a problem, blowing away works which Goldsworthy has painstakingly constructed (Goldsworthy often chooses valleys or woods or more sheltered spots for his leafworks – there are few leaf pieces on an open mountainside in the Goldsworthy *œuvre*, for instance.) Making the leafworks enables Goldsworthy to learn about leaves – leaves blown from trees, or cold, brittle leaves, or 'wet frost-fallen' leaves, or freshly grown leaves. He is careful to take only a 'few leaves from each tree.'[1] He follows the seasonal development of leaves closely, most especially in and around his studio in Scotland. Leaves, like stones or snow, teach the artist much.

> The sycamore has taught me most [Goldsworthy said]. The biggest lesson being that so much can be found in something common and ordinary. Its leaf can turn all colours; its stalks can go bright red and within its leaf structure I realised my first leaf construction.[2]

1. Quoted in *Leaves*, Natural History Museum, London, 1989, 18.
2. *Leaves*, op.cit., 18.

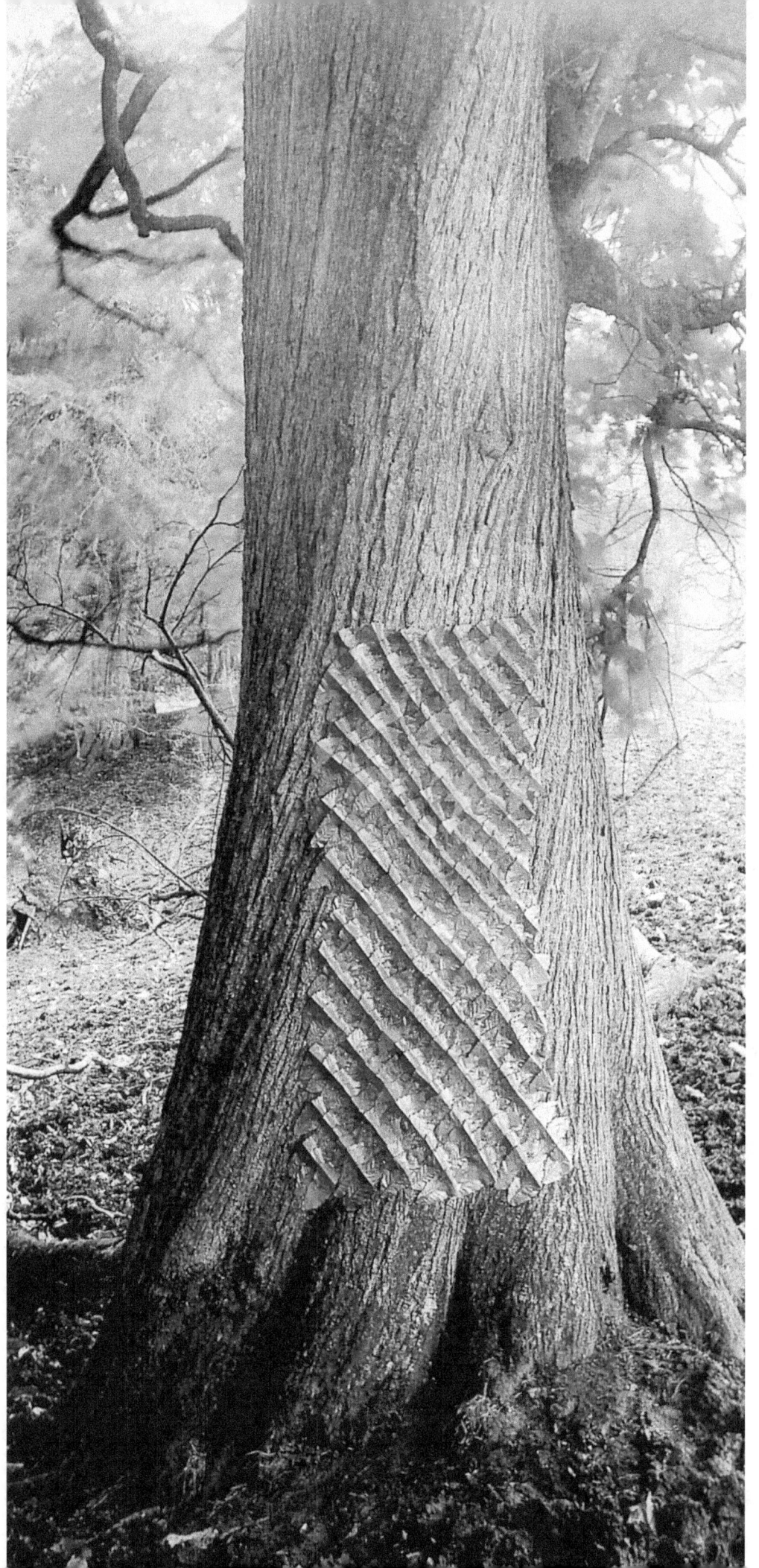

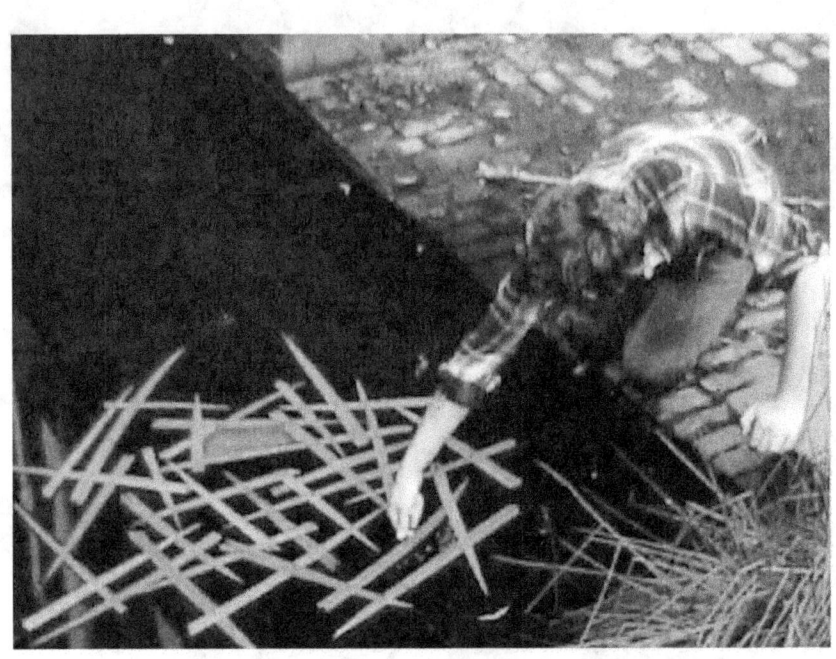

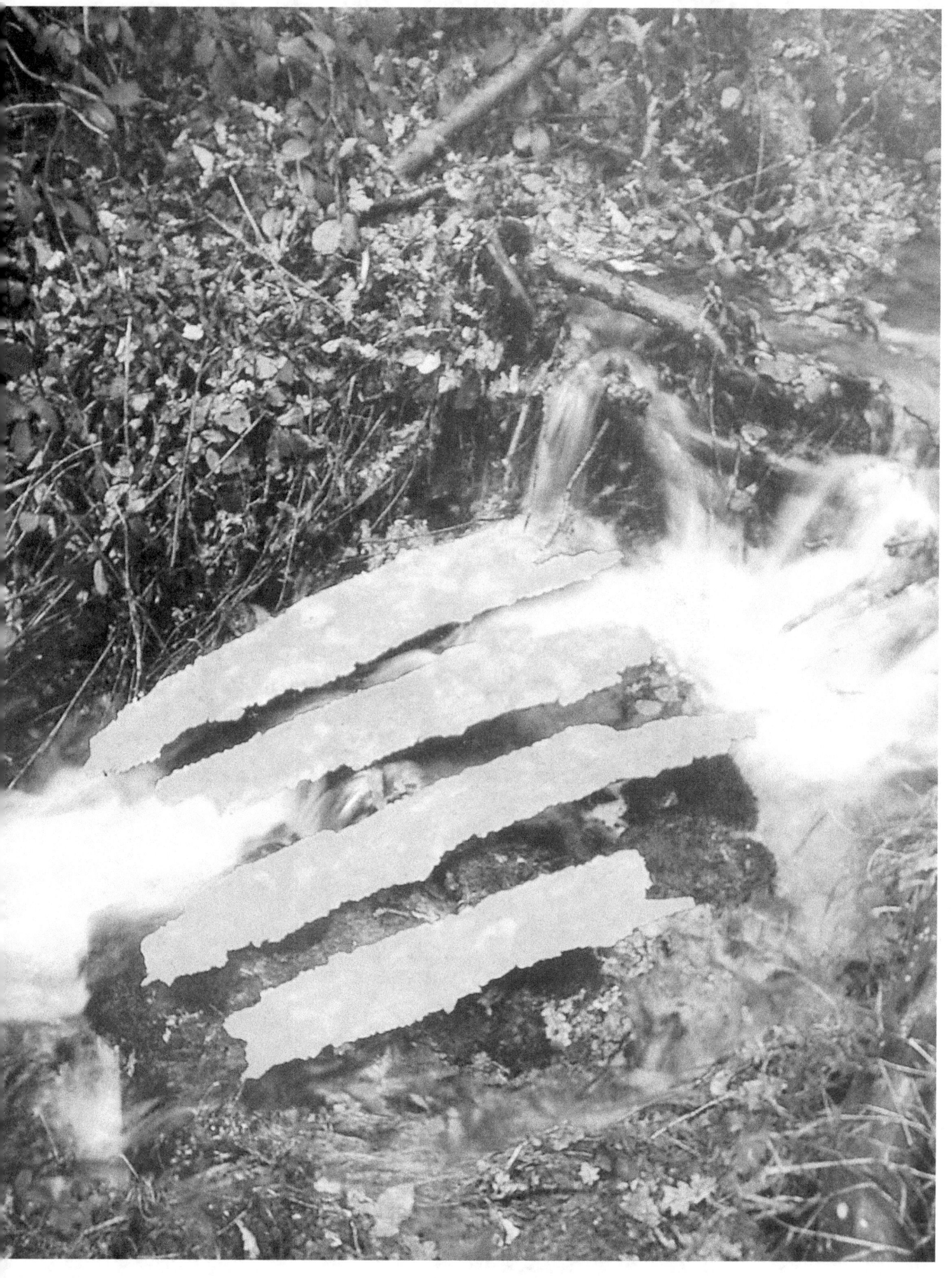

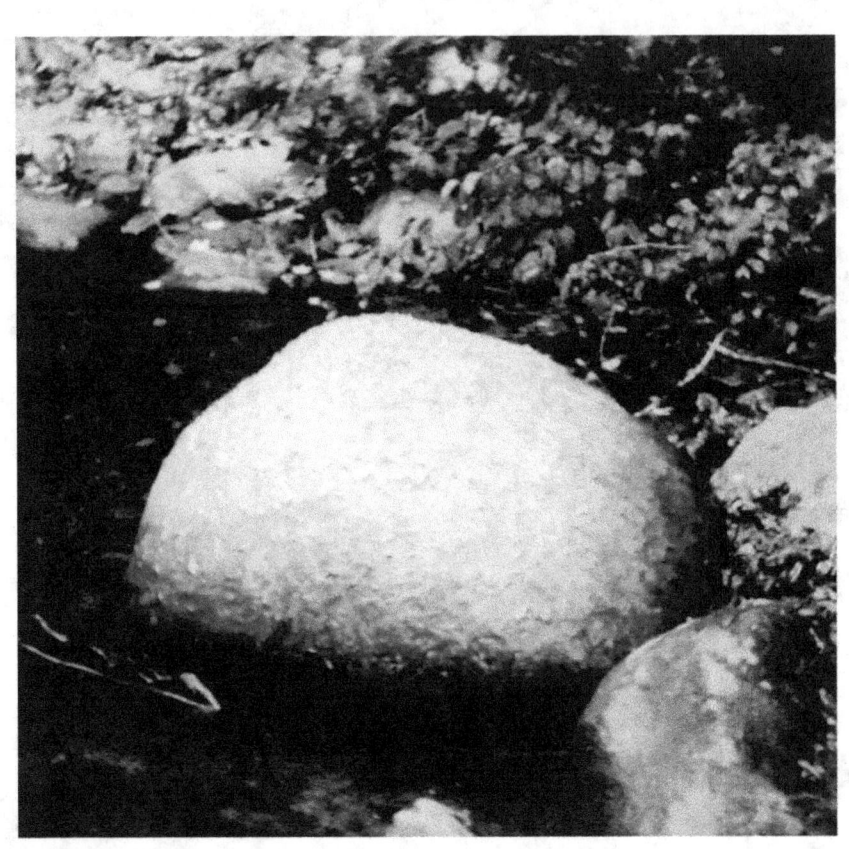

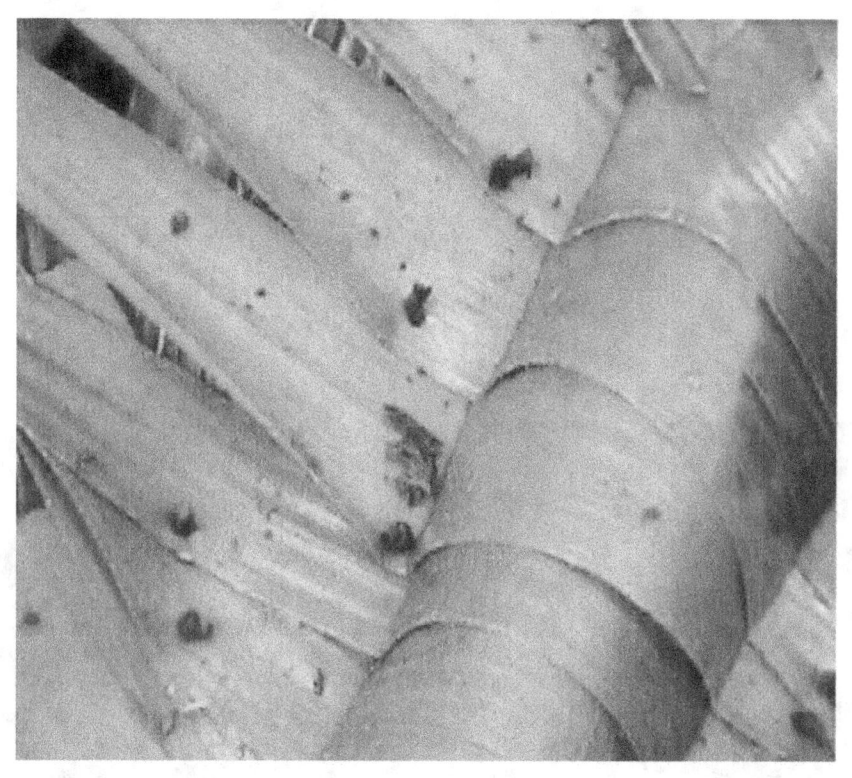

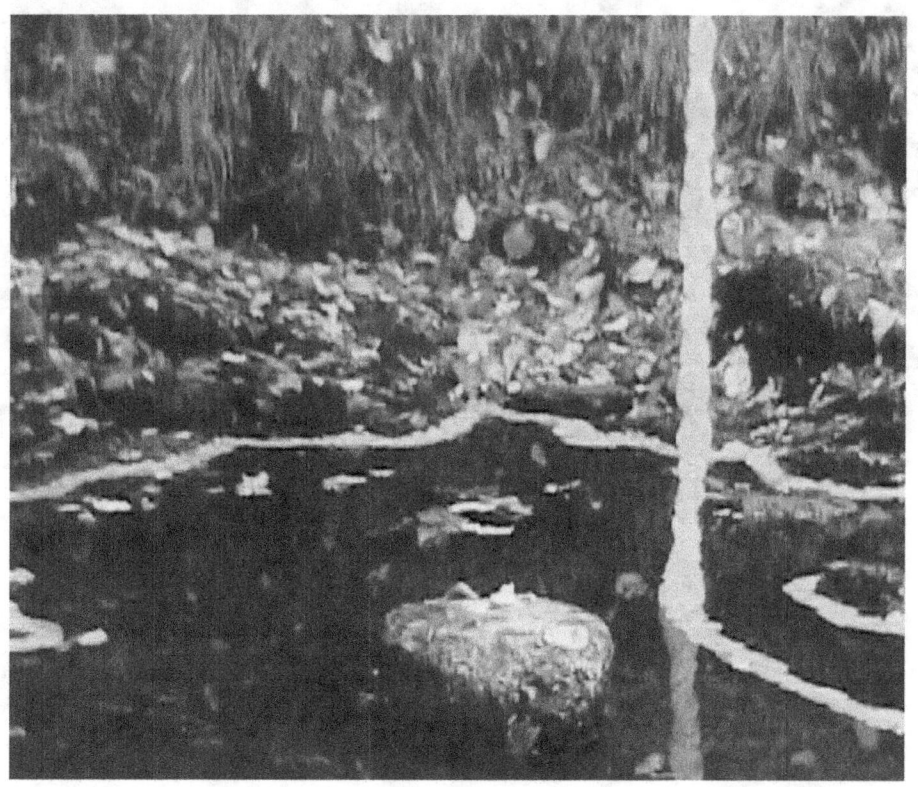

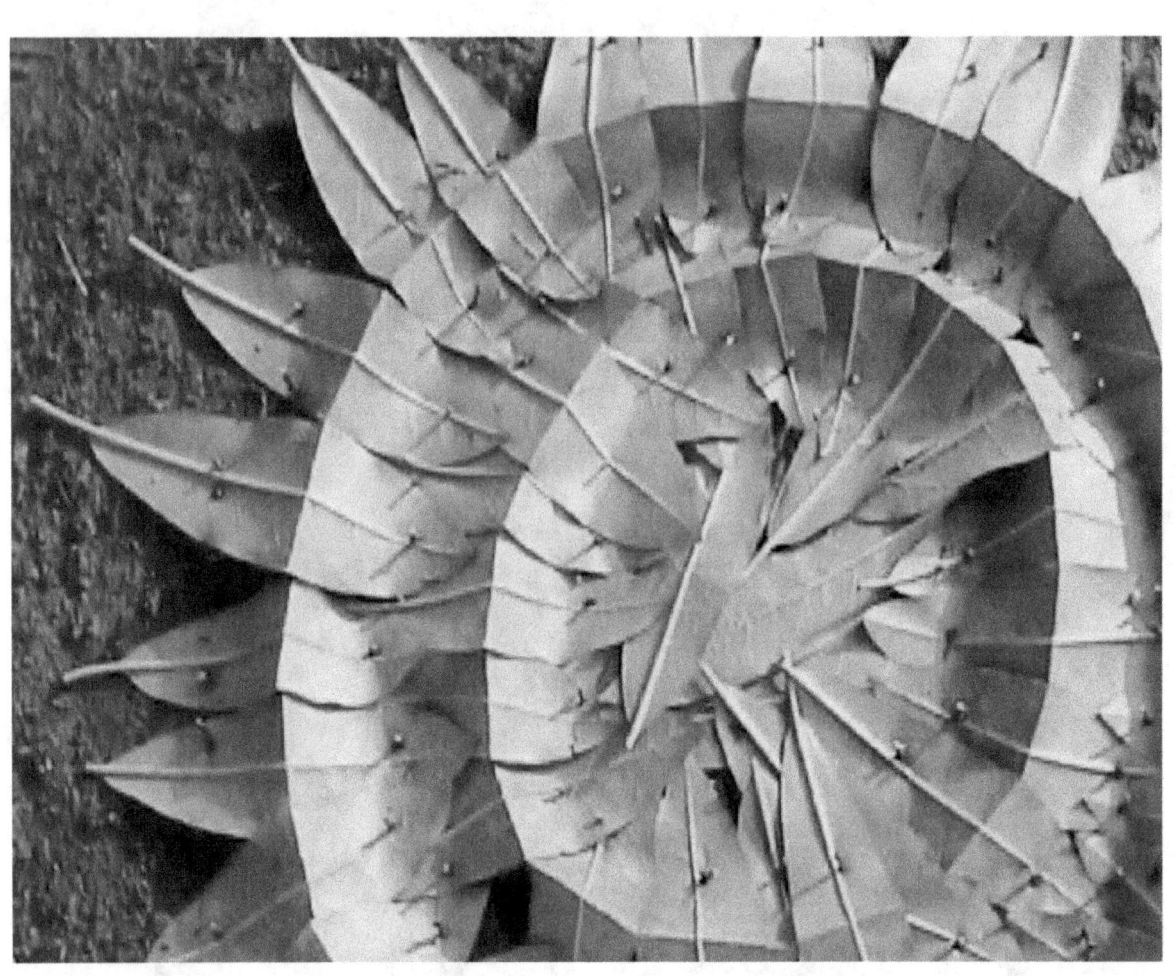

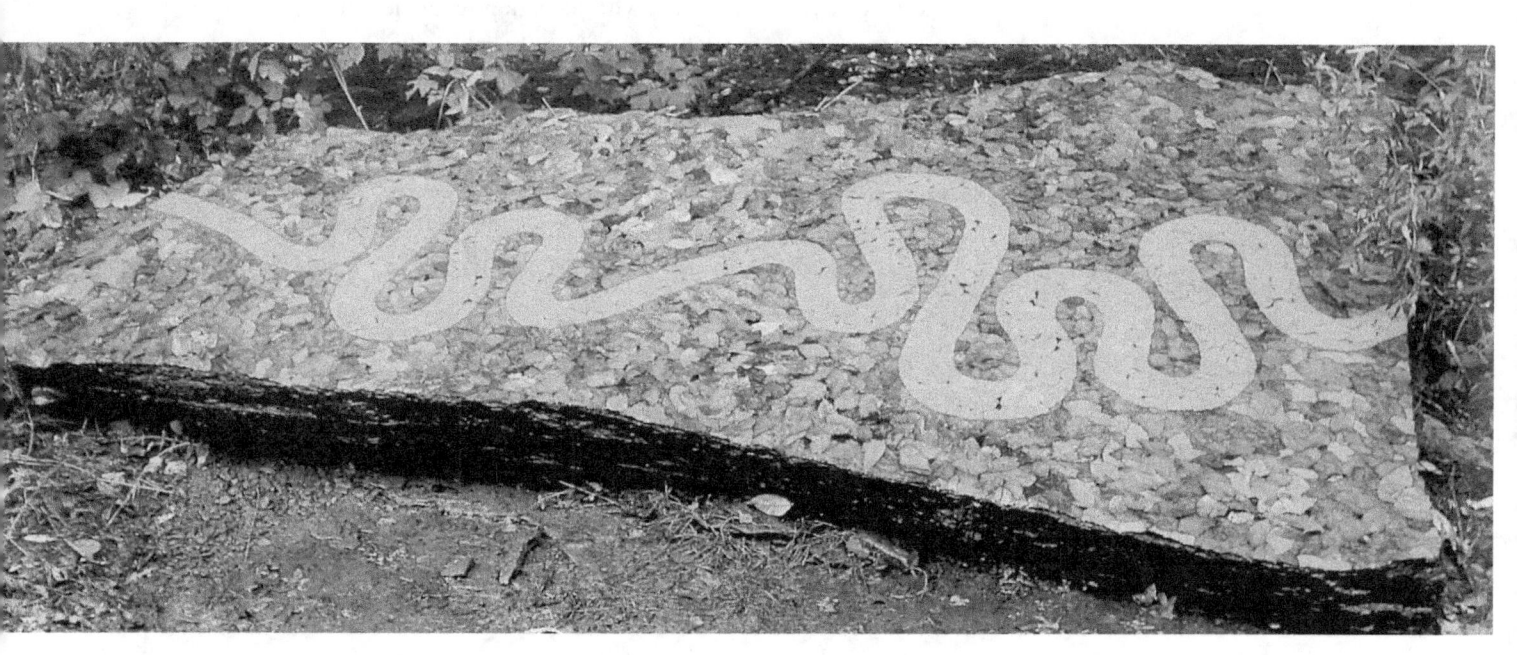

Branch

Many of Andy Goldsworthy's sculptures are about a 'before' and an 'after', and the interval between, the difference, the changes. For instance, there are two photographs which depict a stick in a 'before' and 'after' setting (an early work, made in January, 1981 [in AG]). In the first photo, the sycamore branch is shown on top of snow; it's one of those images of contrast (black stick against white snow) which Goldsworthy likes so much. The second picture shows the stick with its bark now peeled off, so it looks white. Meanwhile the snow has melted, so the white shows up against the dark earth. Twenty years later Goldsworthy was fabricating the same sculptural idea: a fallen branch in a stream covered with powdery snow (2001), and branches wrapped with leaves in a Massachusetts brook (2001) or a Scottish stream (2003).

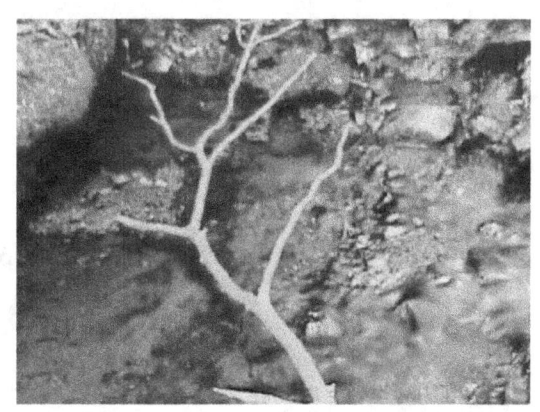

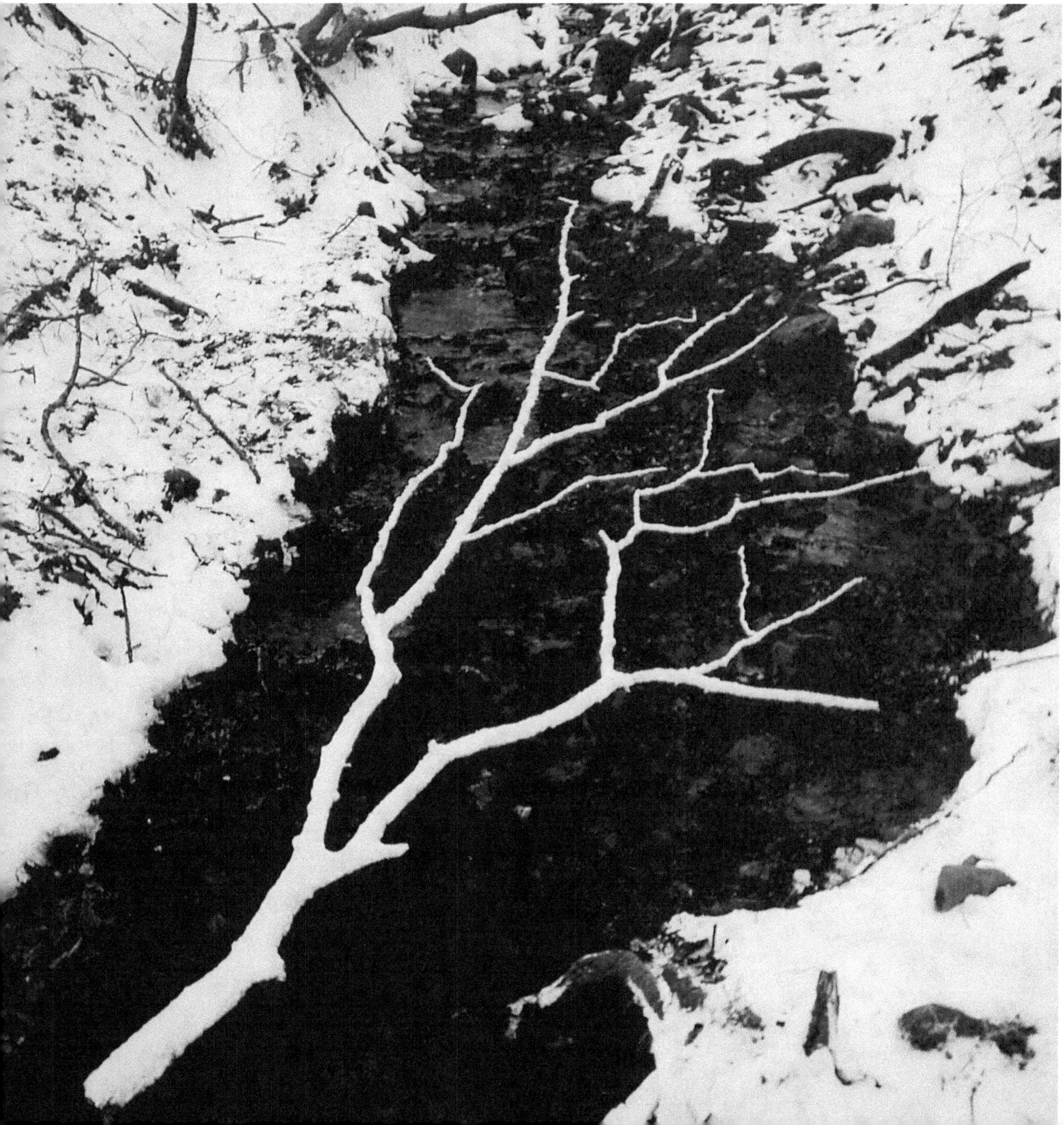

Wet feathers wrapped around a stone
(1999)

Andy Goldsworthy rarely uses animals in his art; stones and vegetation are his usual materials. Some sculptures refer to animals (such as sheep and cows). One or two pieces were made from feathers (*Goose feathers* [1983], *Wood pigeon wing feathers* [1977], *Feathers plucked from a dead heron* [1982], and *Wet feathers wrapped around a stone* [1999]). And some from wool (*Wool line*, 1995).

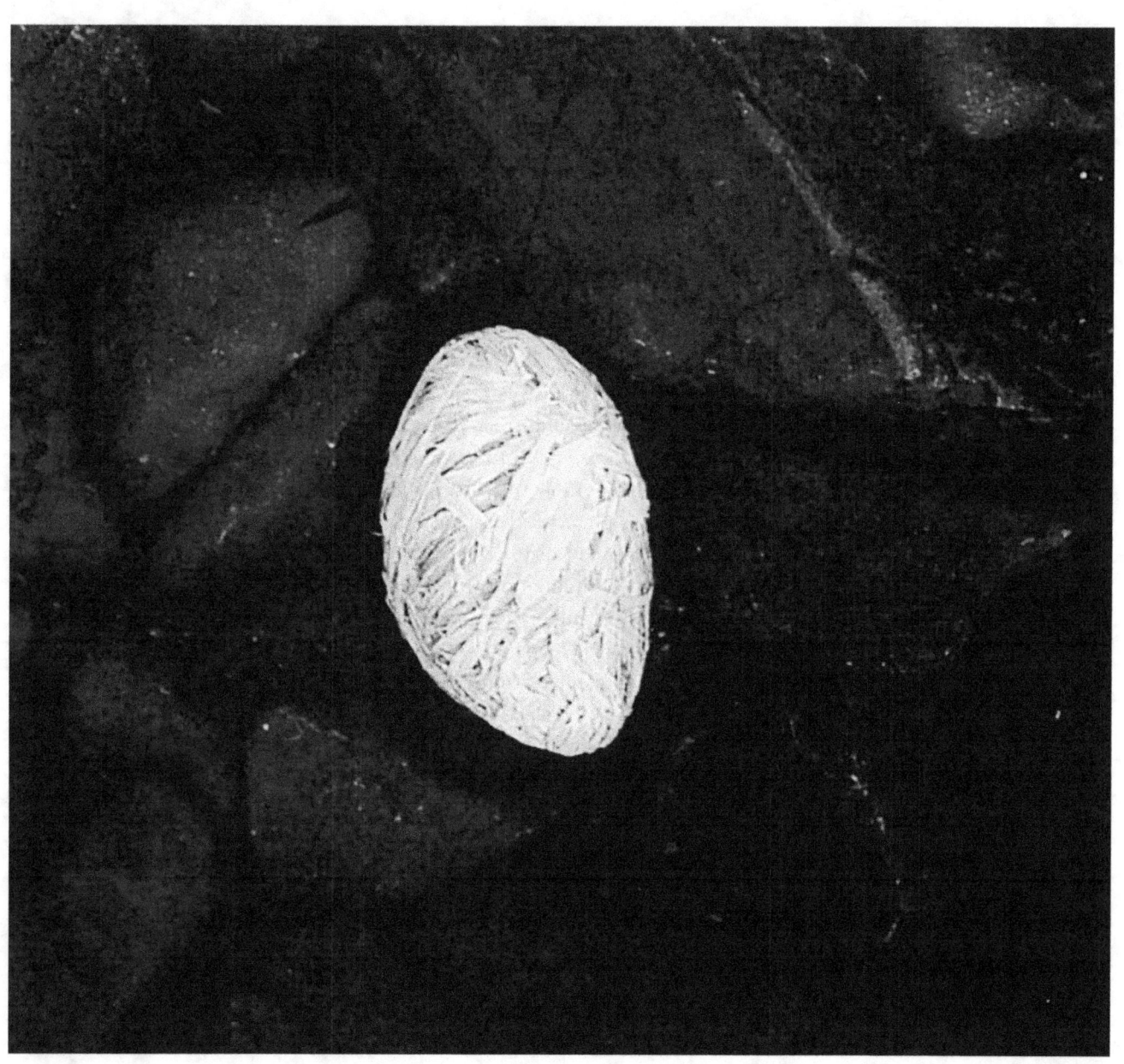

Beech Leaves (1999)

It's noteworthy that Andy Goldsworthy has only used a very small selection of flowers in his sculptures: poppy, foxglove, dandelion. He's far more inclined to use leaves or grass or stalks (such as hogweed or willowherb). Also, when Goldsworthy does use flowers, he avoids the hugely symbolic flowers of the Western tradition, such as the rose, lily or iris. And the flowers of Britain are also sidestepped: the daffodil, the primrose, the snowdrop, the carnation, the gladioli, the tulip, the forget-me-not, and so on. In addition, Goldsworthy has not made many flowerpieces in his later work.

Notice also that Goldsworthy tends to produce work outdoors with a very small number of plants: he has his favourite materials, such as willowherb stalks, or yellow beech or elm leaves, or green sycamore leaves. He has not fashioned many sculptures from nettles or brambles (for obvious reasons, perhaps). Or thistles. Or ferns and bracken. Cowslips, gorse bushes, ivy, pine cones and mistletoe are other plants Goldsworthy doesn't use much (although he has put some of these elements in his snowballs). And among trees, Goldsworthy hasn't employed the following trees much: yew, laurel, willow, hawthorn, holly, vine. Goldsworthy may avoid certain plants and flowers for all sorts of reasons, some practical, some æsthetic, some social, and some symbolic. Some of the plants noted above are loaded with thousands of years of symbolism: rose, lily, willow, laurel, hawthorn, mistletoe. Goldsworthy really likes the colour red, for instance, and it would be so easy for him to employ rose petals: instead, he opts for the poppy.

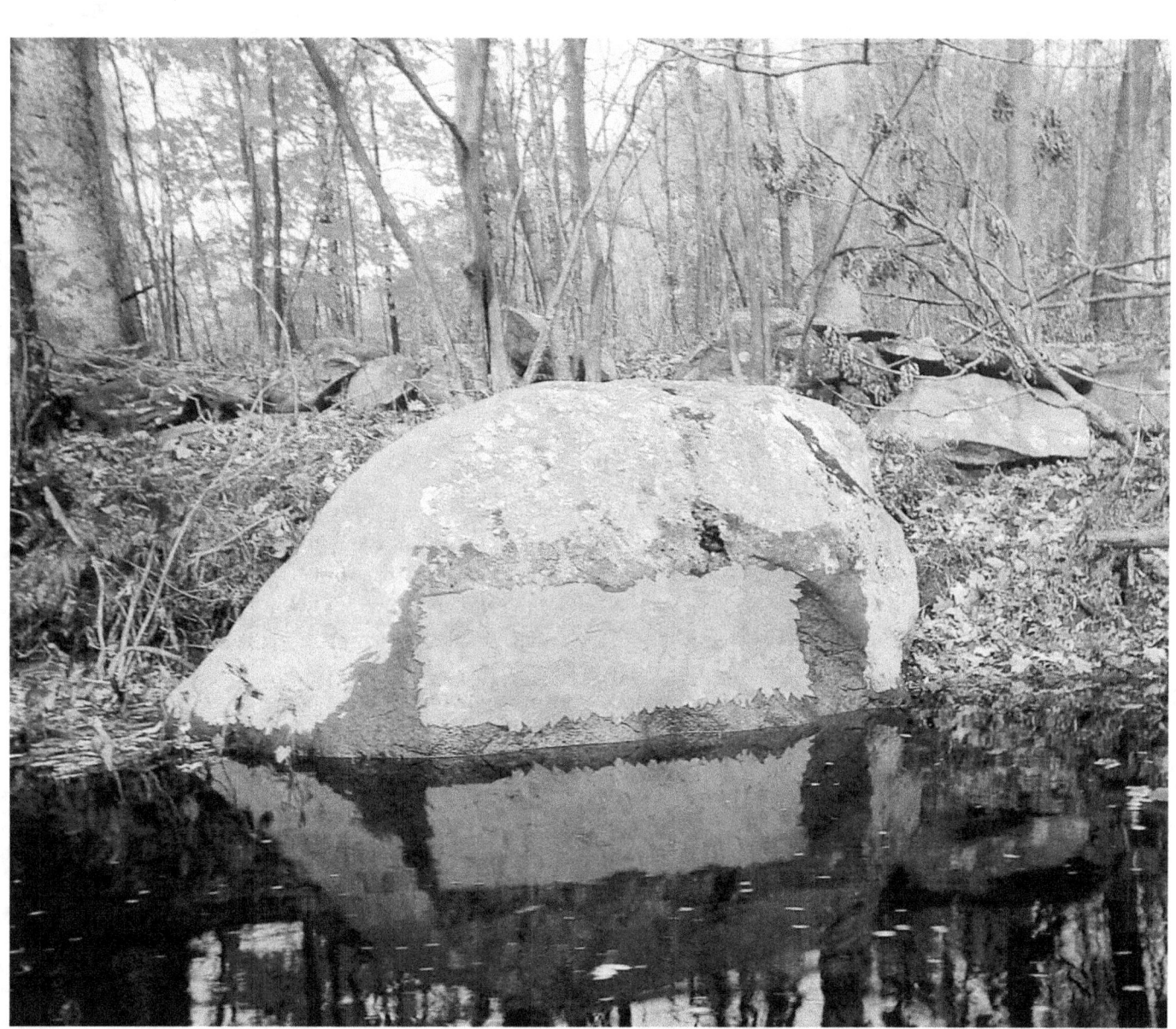

Penpont Cairn (2000)

The cairn that Andy Goldsworthy built in 1999-2000 was commissioned by the village he had lived in since 1986: Penpont in Dumfriesshire. Goldsworthy acknowledged that he was nervous and self-conscious about making a work that was so close to his home, that he would have to live with, that he'd often see, that would be seen by locals and neighbours (P, 6). It was one sculpture he'd have to get right; if it went wrong, he'd be always reminded of his mistakes. Goldsworthy said he had 'given enormous thought to its making' (P, 6).

Penpont Cairn was sited on the summit of a low hill in a farmer's field. Its situation on the hill's brow meant that it would be visible from many spots in the neighbourhood. It was a location that was very open on all sides: 'I have never made a cairn in a place so open, not just to the view, but to the rising and setting sun' Goldsworthy wrote in *Passage* (P, 8). Goldsworthy wondered if the siting of *Penpont Cairn* was perhaps a little *too* prominent; 'it might be too imposing and appear as if it were shouting for attention in a 'look at me' kind of way' Goldsworthy remarked (12). Silhouetting was particularly strong with the *Penpont Cairn*: because it was raised up from the ground on a large stone, the sky was always visible behind the sculpture. 'Although the making of a sculpture is obviously out of the ordinary, this particular work has a wonderful sense of the normal and everyday about it' Goldsworthy said during the construction of *Penpont Cairn* (P, 8).

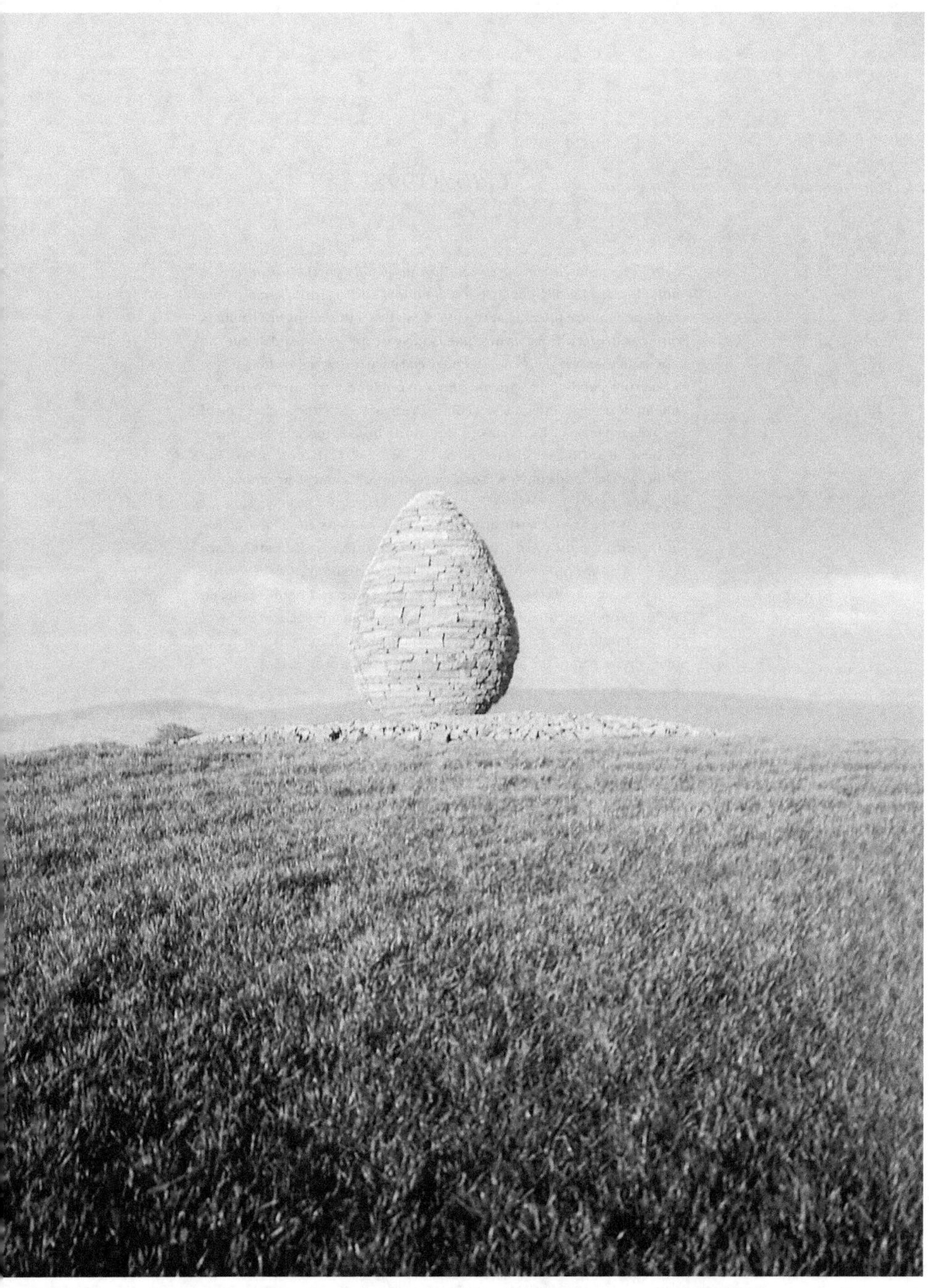

Cairn (1995)

In 1994-95 a new form appeared in Andy Goldsworthy's *œuvre*, the 'stone house', usually consisting of a hollow stick cairn or cone with a round or elliptical opening at the top. Sometimes the cairns or chambers were constructed from stones, like Goldsworthy's stone walls, but the basic structure was the same: an enclosed space, often with a hole to see in (and out), and often with an object (a boulder, a tree, or a balanced column of stones) sitting inside. (Chris Drury has made the shelter one of his primary forms). Examples of the 'stone house' include sculptures constructed at Digne les Bains and Mt. Kisco, New York (both 1995); the 'stone houses' built in New York were among the most prominent in Goldsworthy's *œuvre*. Like Chris Drury, Goldsworthy has occasionally enclosed his cairns with other materials, such as the slabs of ice surrounding a stone cairn (1996), and the stone spire inside a stick cairn (1995). A *Stone House* made in Melbourne (Australia) in 1997 took the form of a rectangular wall with a circular opening and boulder placed inside. 'Every stone that I place on a sculpture contains some of my own energy: the lifting, the cutting, the placing. Part of me stays with the stone, just as part of the stone stays with me' Goldsworthy said (P, 8).

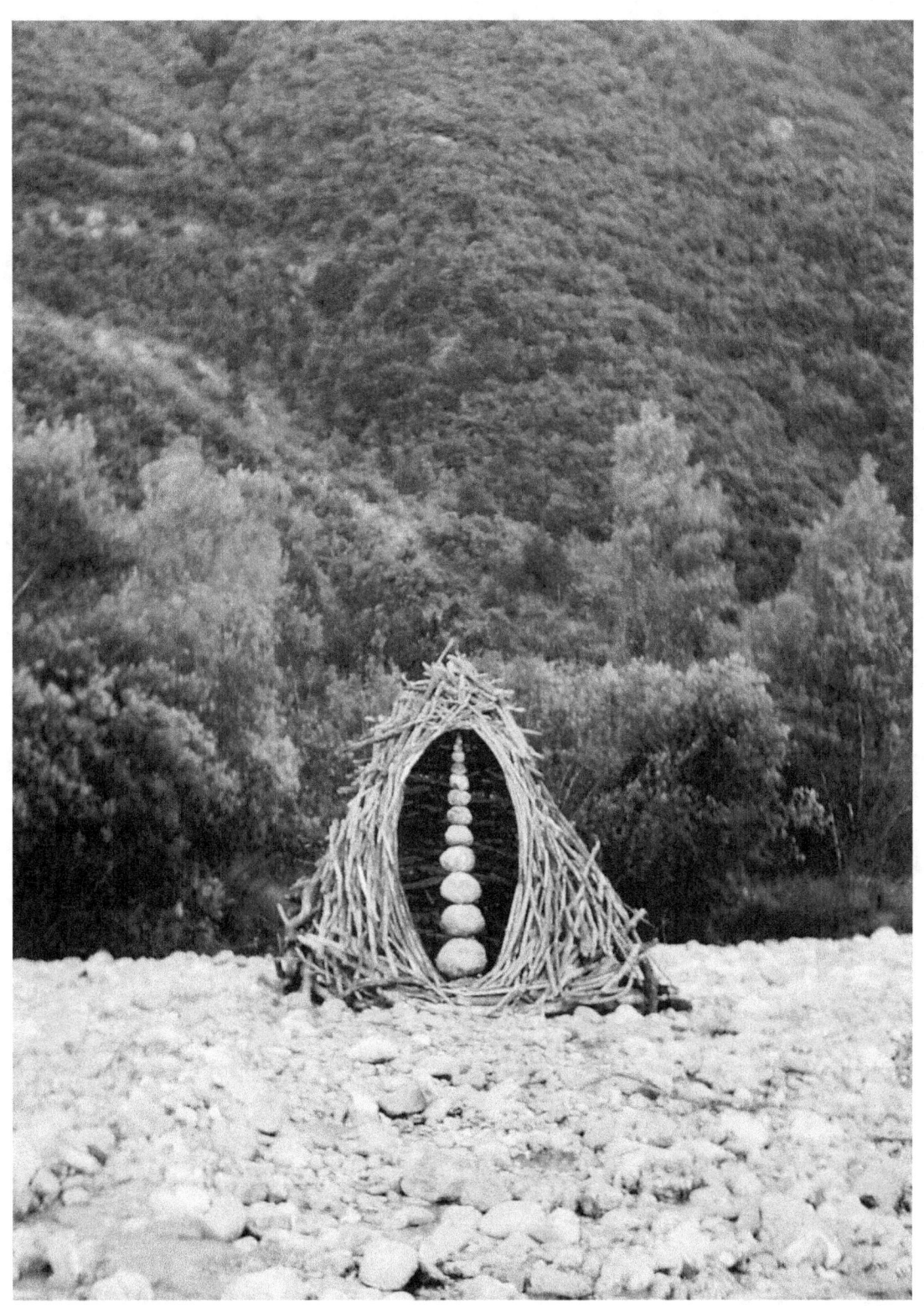

Sand Stone (2000)

In Collieston (Aberdeenshire) in 2000, Goldsworthy produced a group of ephemeral beachworks: a rock covered with smooth sand, or ridges of sand, or a negative circle of sand. Each sand work was washed away by the tide. Goldsworthy's very early works were consciously irregular and 'organic' in shape and form, rather than the more geometric forms he later adopted (such as circles, spirals and lines).

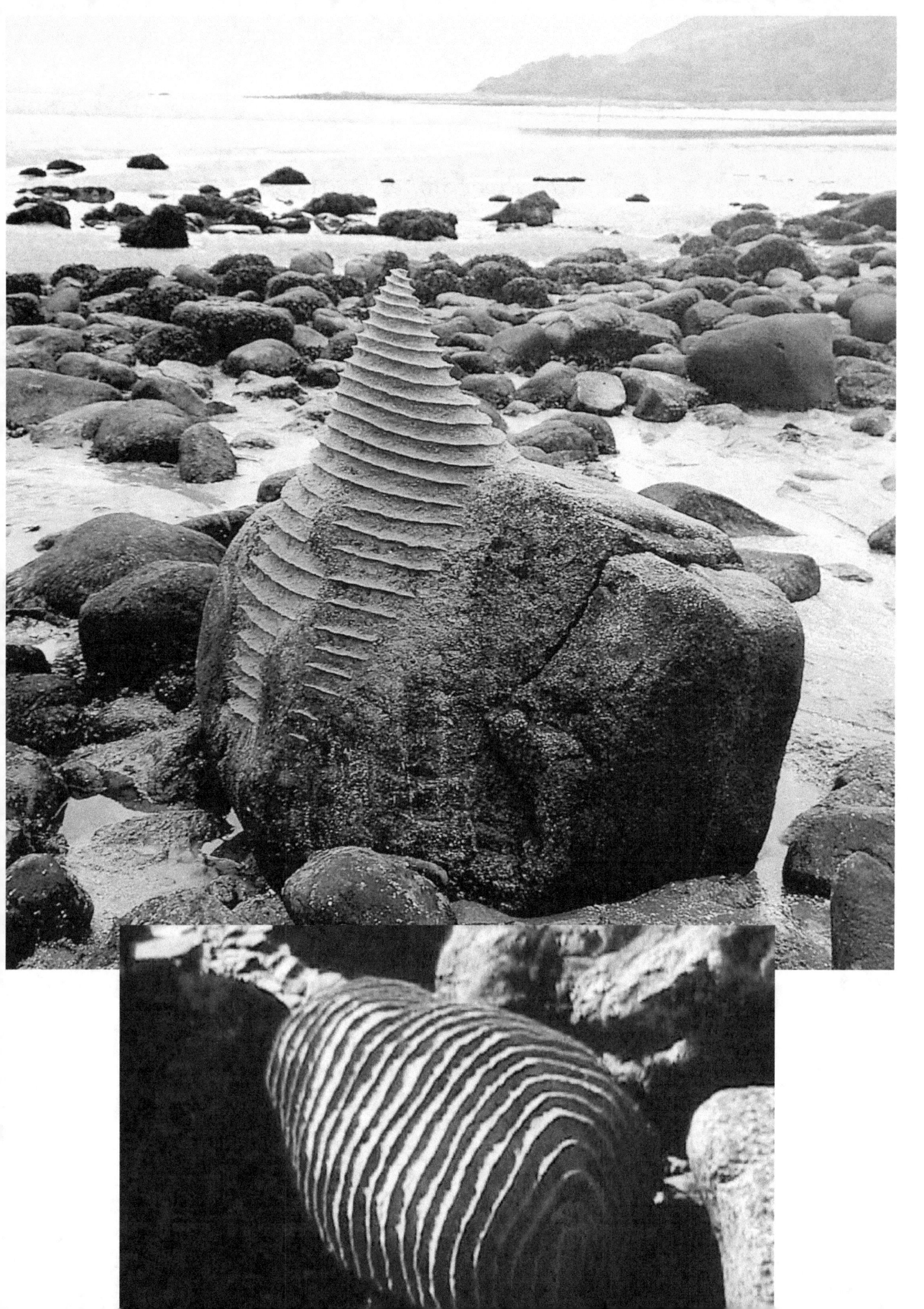

Two River Stones (2001)

In *Two River Stones* (2001), Andy Goldsworthy enclosed some rocks on the edge of a river with bands of curved sticks. The continuous lines could be associated with the notions of 'aura' or the astral plane of occultism, the envelope of supernatural energy that surrounds objects and animals. The 'aura' or astral plane is another manifestation of primæval animism, associated with the concepts of *mana* and charisma.

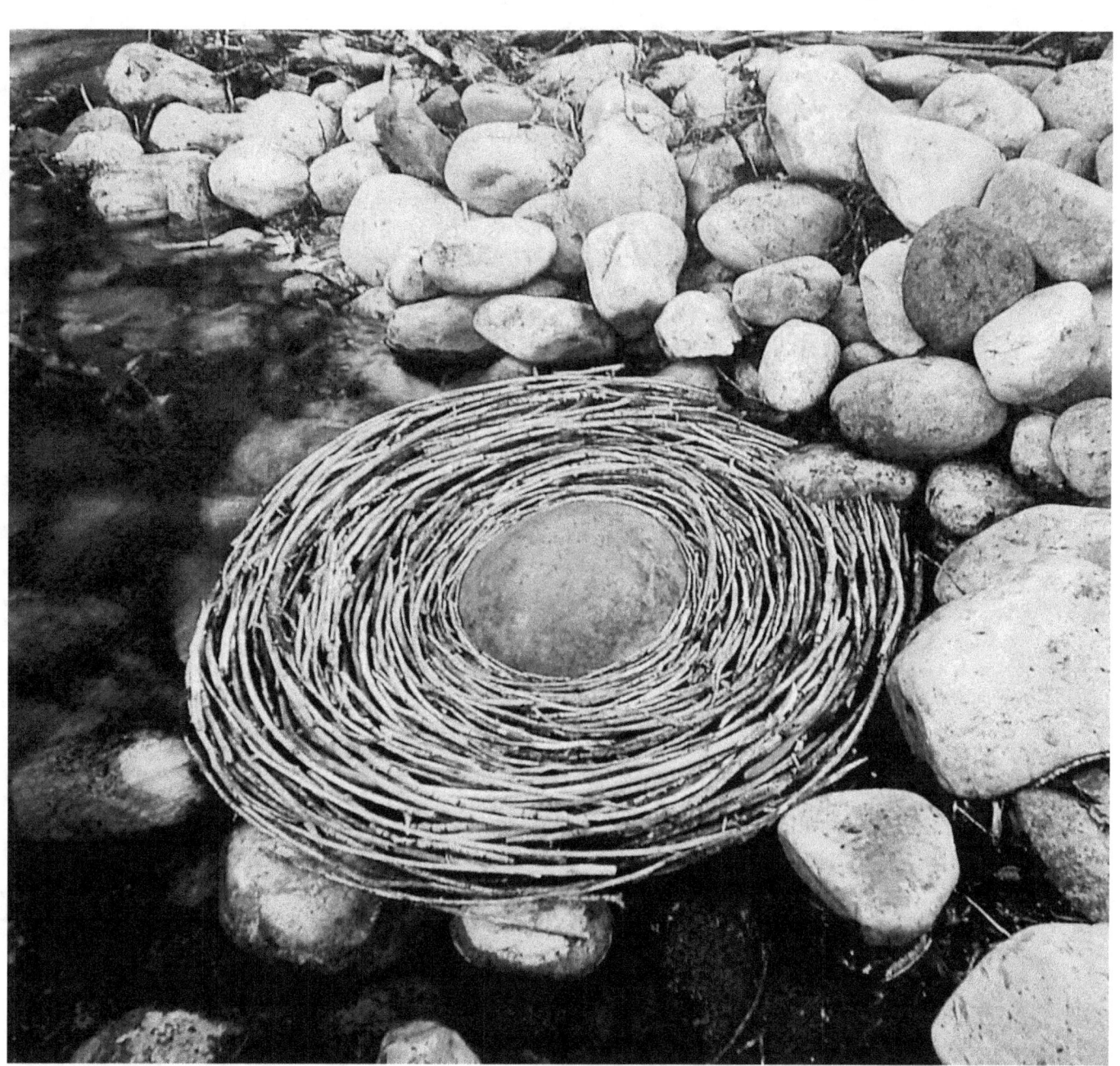

Trees

Andy Goldsworthy has worked intimately with trees since the beginning of his career as a sculptor and land artist. He has his favourite trees (oak, beech, elm), with sycamore trees favoured for their leaves (for building objects such as the leaf boxes). Elm trees, for example, are Goldsworthy's chief source of yellow in Autumn (P, 127). Some of Goldsworthy's most important works have used trees as their focal point, such as the *Capenoch Tree* series, and *Sidewinder* and *Seven Spires* at Grizedale forest. Goldsworthy has employed trees in countless works, using leaves and branches as materials in hundreds of sculptures, or trunks as easels or scaffolding. He's hung many works from trees: snowballs, shields, and lines of leaves. He's decorated trees with dandelions and snow. He's pressed leaves and sand into boles. He's extended trees with sand and clay. He's wrapped branches with petals and leaves. He's created footpaths winding between trees. He's used trees as backgrounds for carved sand drawings. He's built branches into stone walls. He's let trees define the path of his major works, such as the stone walls. He's worked in many, many forests and woods. Indeed, if you took trees out of Andy Goldsworthy's art, there would be a huge gap. In Goldsworthy's art, trees embody time, change, beauty, mystery, and place. Trees are, in short, the 'architecture of the planet'.[1]

1. Film director John Boorman's phrase.

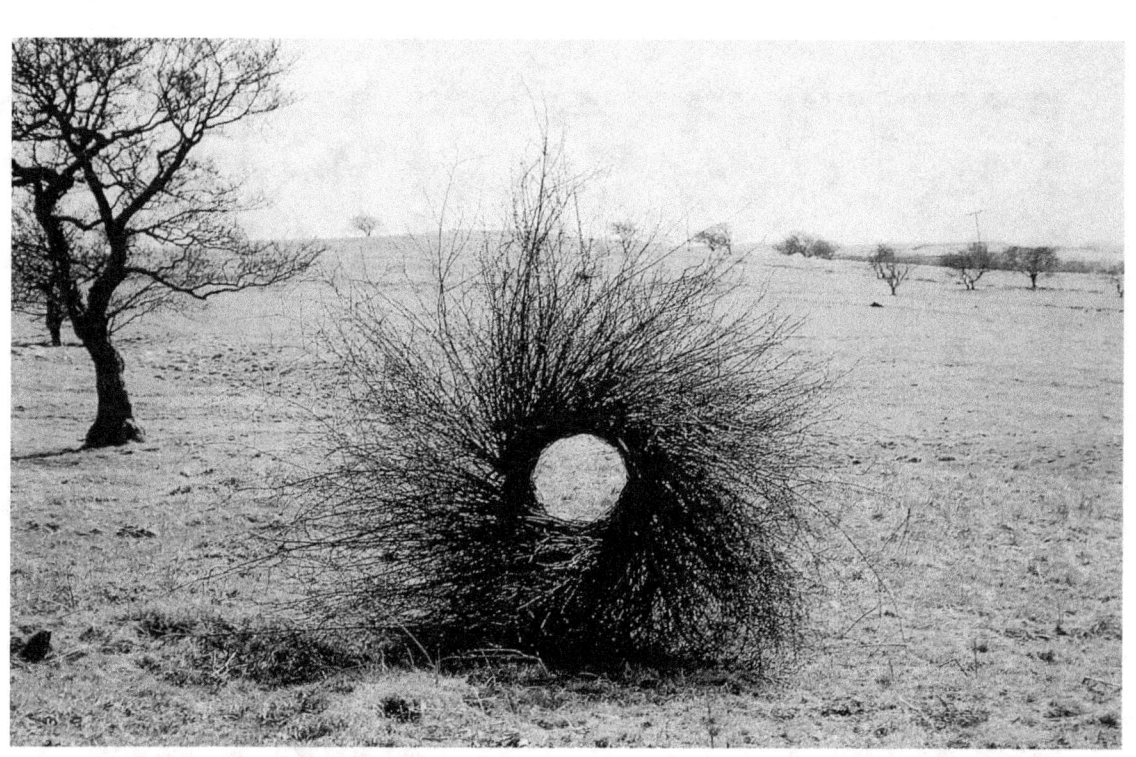

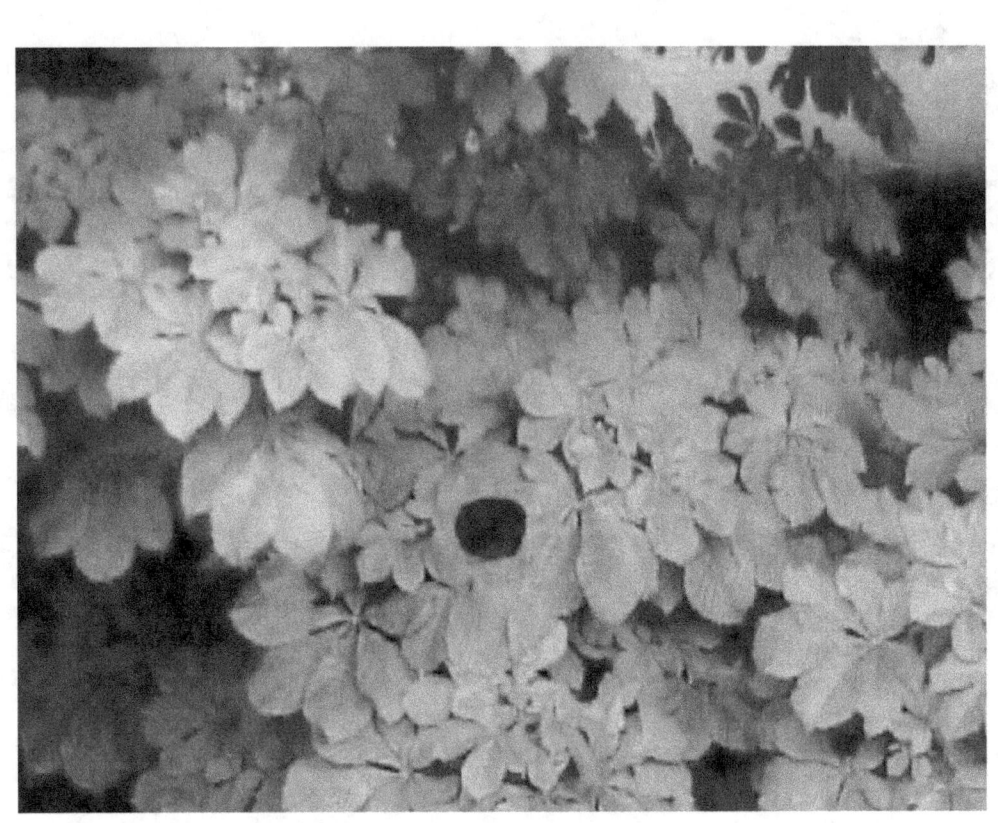

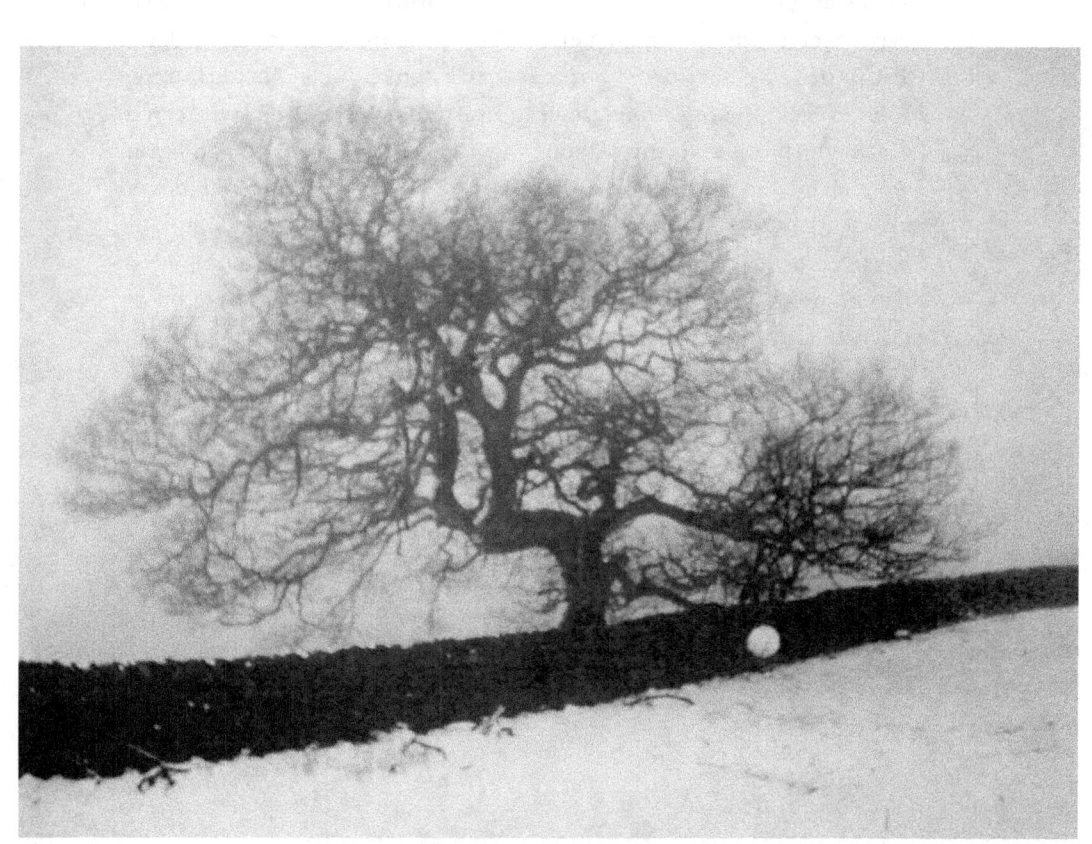

Clay Installation

An installation using clay (at San Jose, California) consisted of hollowed clay spheres, with the characteristic Goldsworthy sharp interior edges. The series of globes dried out and shed chunks of clay. Later hollow spheres include *Sand stones*, built in Holland in 1999. The clay-covered rocks which Goldsworthy exhibited in 1993 in San Francisco and Japan were aligned to the melting snowballs. The stones were covered in wet clay which was rubbed smooth: they looked like huge brown dinosaur eggs. As the clay dried, it cracked and fell off. The exhibits highlighted natural processes – such as the apparent randomness of nature (a bit of clay falling off the stone here, but not on that rock over there).

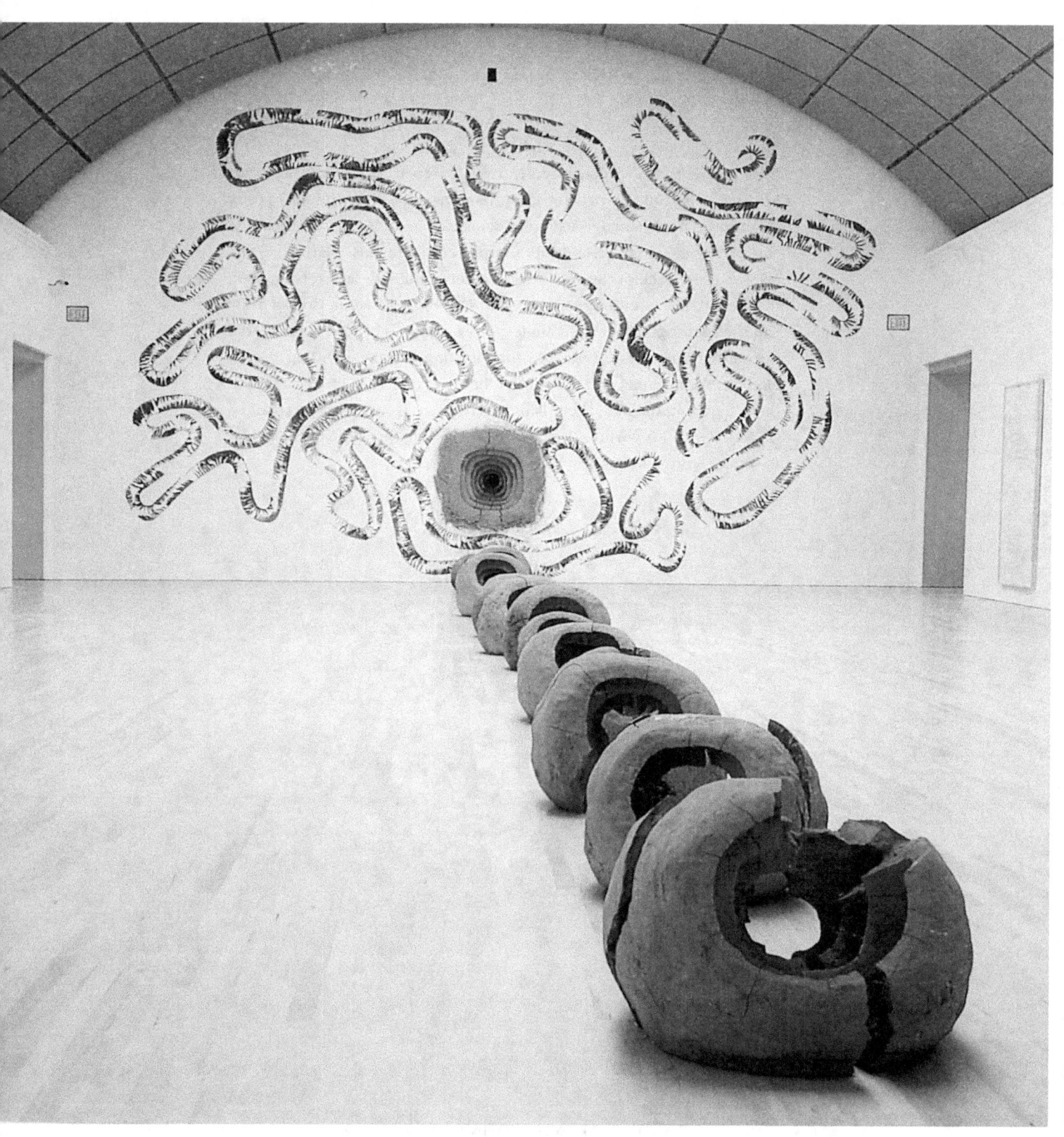

Pool of Light (2001)

Pool of Light was constructed in the Charente region of France (at Bioussac) in 2001, a private commission from Philippe and Libby d'Hémery. They wanted to use trees damaged and felled in a storm at the end of 1999. Goldsworthy built a large rectilinear installation on the terrace at the back of the *château,* using chestnut logs laid in parallel on the ground. In a circular area in the centre of the installation Goldsworthy had the split logs laid at right angles to the others. The logs would catch the sunlight in different ways in the morning and the evening: 'a dark circle in the morning and the reverse in the evening. At midday, and on those days without sun, there is no circle at all' Goldsworthy explained (P, 88). For Goldsworthy, *Pool of Light* was 'an expression of the ability to survive storms and upheavals' (ib.).

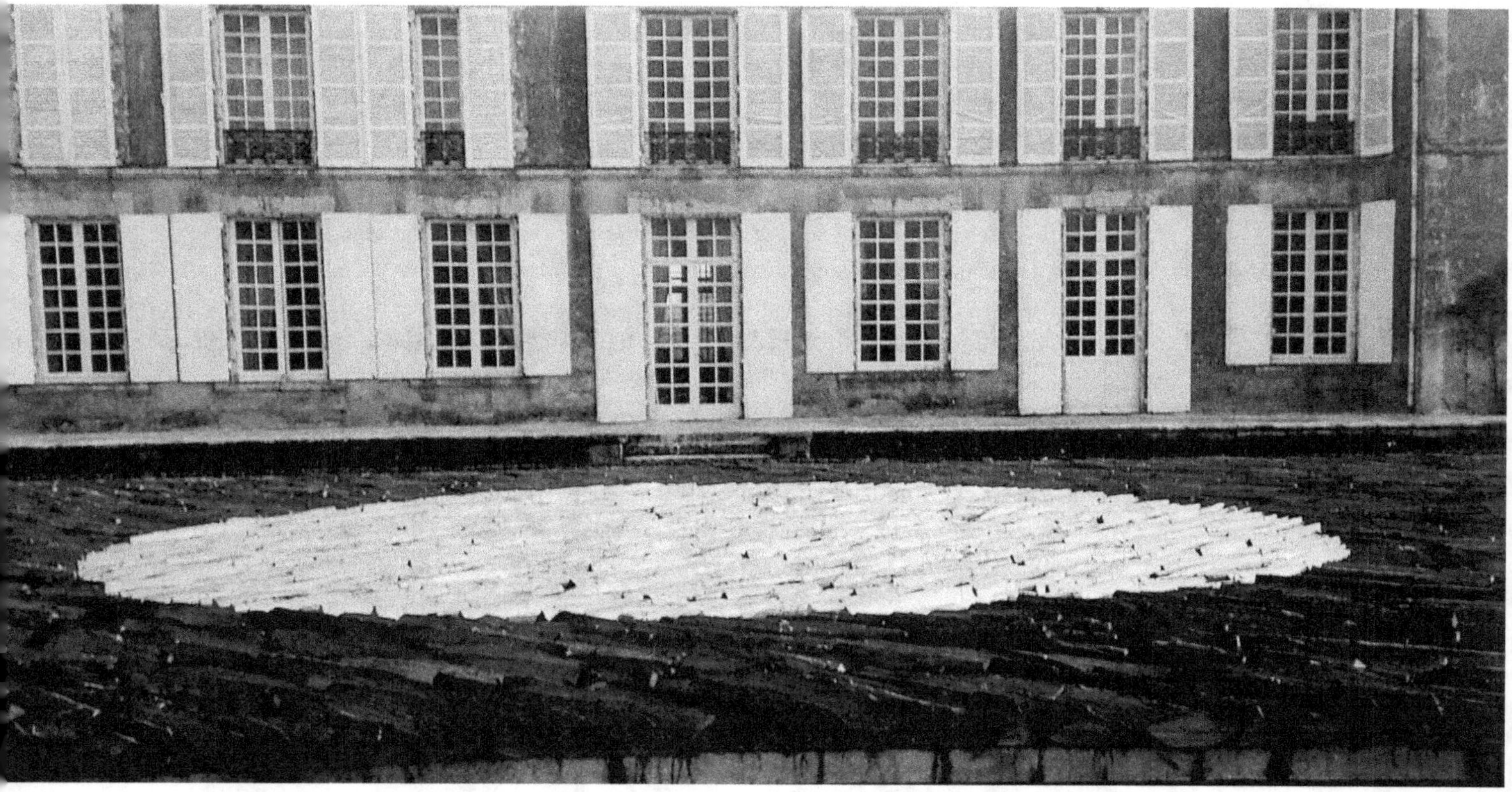

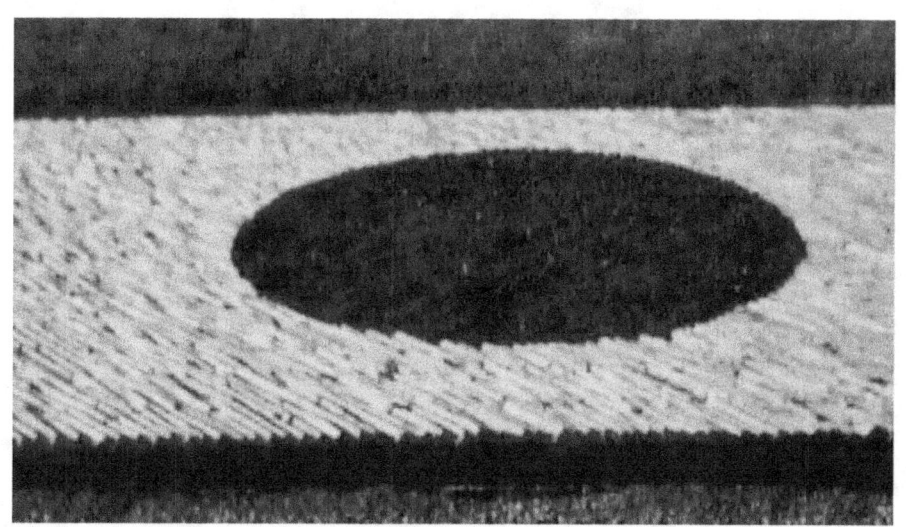

Icicles (1987)

Some iceworks of Goldsworthy's include icicles stuck onto a wall (made on New Year's Eve, 1992) and *Icicles frozen to a rock* (1991). In these pieces, the icicles are clustered together, like a mini forest of trees. The icicle works, like the mound of stones which were dipped in water then frozen onto a rockface (*Stone,* 44-45), are testaments of endurance: the artist had to keep returning to the same place to pull the work off. *Ice 'fish'* was a flat curve made from little sheets of ice; *Ice column* was also constructed from sheets of ice refrozen together: the result looked like a Naum Gabo tower (both 1991, Dumfriesshire). There was also an *Ice star,* two icicles aimed at each other ('pointing their frozen energies towards each other'),[1] an *Ice hole* made in Yorkshire Sculpture Park and a hollow *Ice ball* (1987).

1. Goldsworthy, sketchbook, January 22, 1983, *Hand to Earth,* 146.

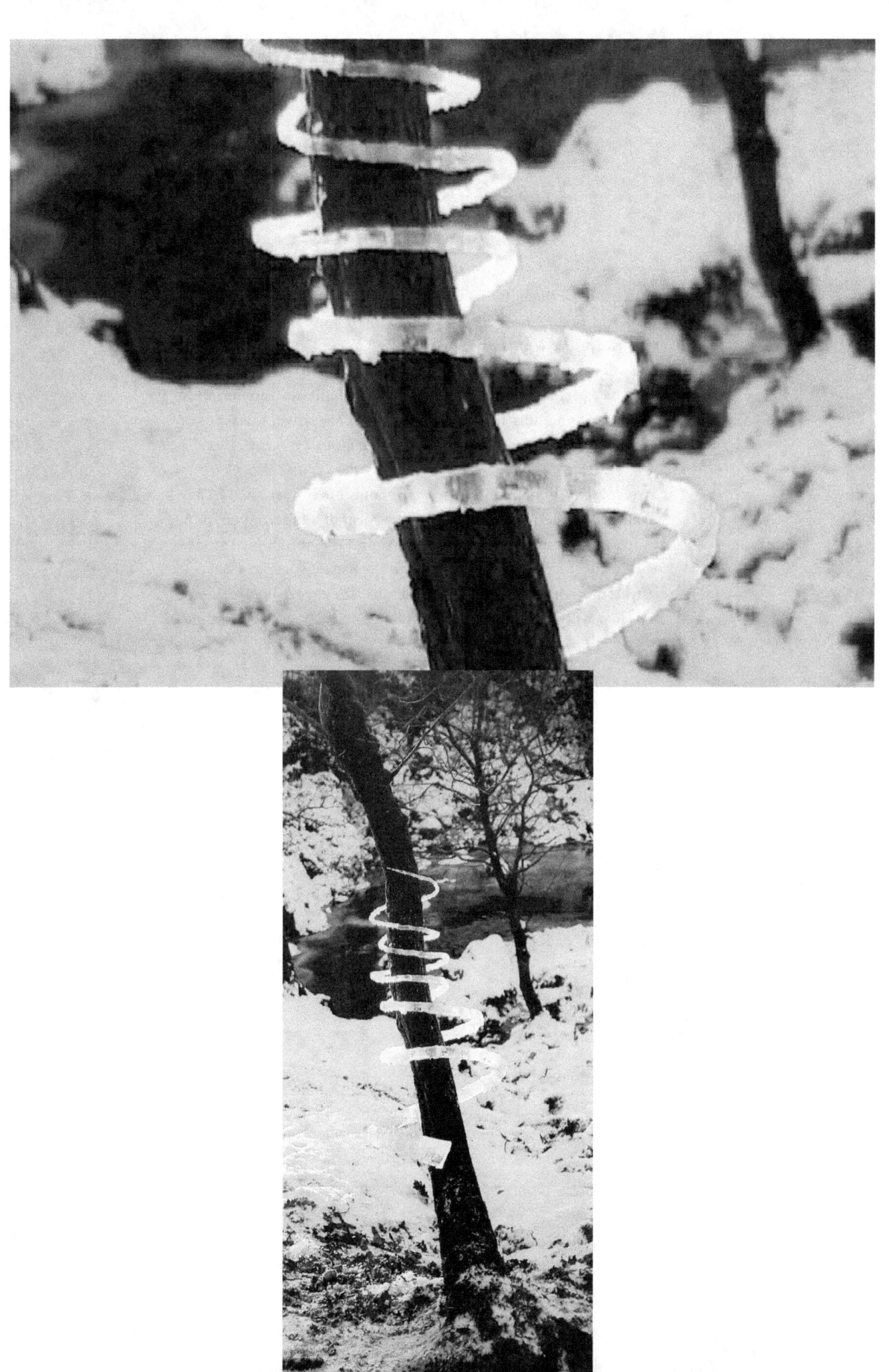

Stone Houses (2004)

Stone Houses was a prestigious commission from the Metropolitan Museum of Art in Gotham, for its roof garden. The rocks were taken from Glenluce Bay in Scotland and transported to the US, but the wood (white cedar) for the *Stone Houses* was from New England. The roof garden overlooked Central Park and the formidable skyline of Manhattan, so the sculptures had plenty to contend with visually. This setting certainly wasn't the undulating hills around Penpont or the windswept beaches of Scotland or California, but one of the most famous cityscapes in the world.

The two columns of granite stones were about thirteen feet high. They were fashioned in the familiar Goldsworthy form of a tapering column, so that the topmost stone was a pebble. Around the columns of stones Goldsworthy constructed an octagonal 'house' – basically a domed-shaped shelter structure which enclosed the columns (they were eighteen feet tall). The cedar wood had been split into rails, with each end overlapping.

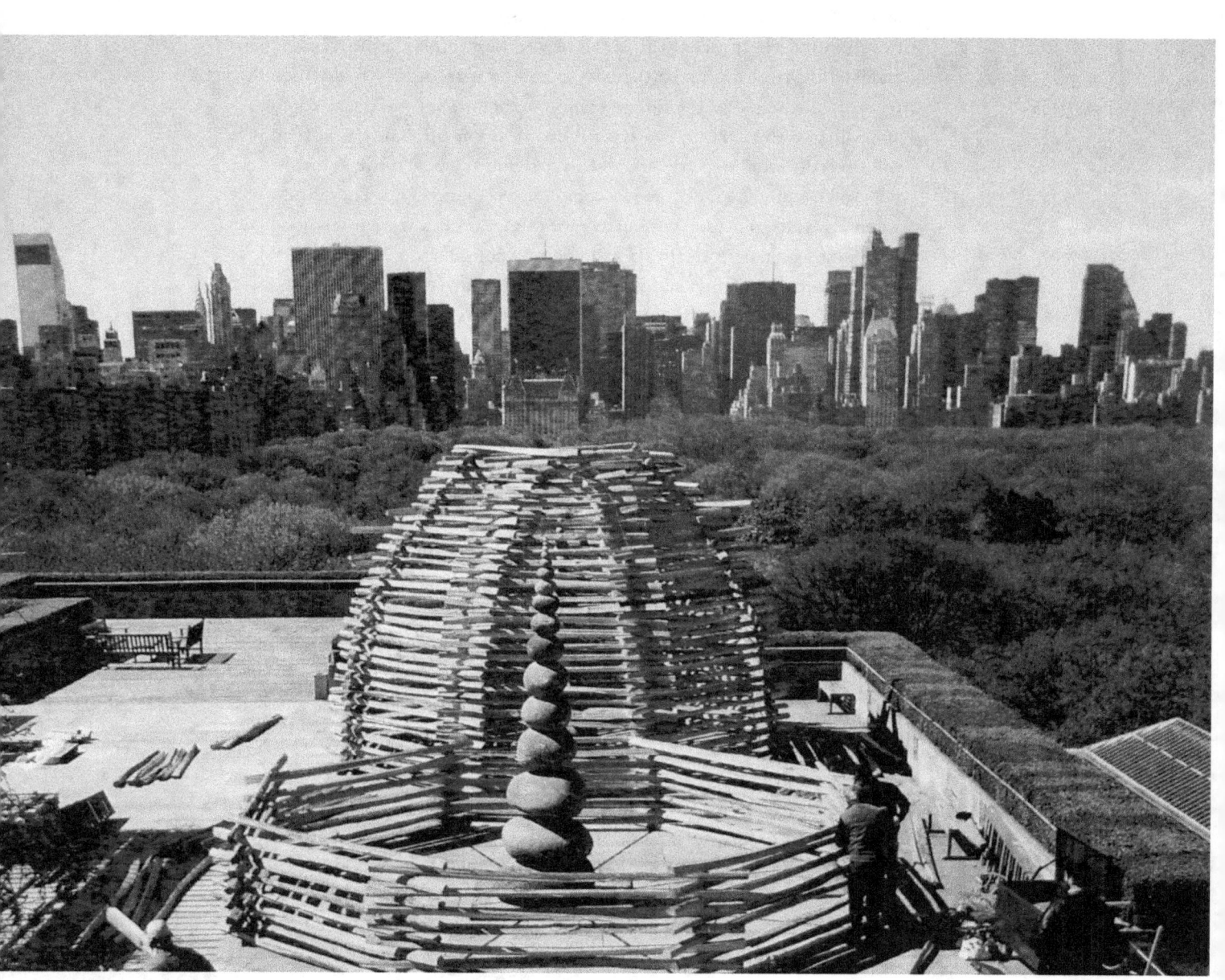

Tides

Some of Andy Goldsworthy's earliest works (of the 1970s) were tidal, beachbound sculptures which relied very much on the power and majesty of the sea to make them work. Some were sculptures which required the action of the tide to complete them. They were fabricated specifically so that the sea would cover them up. They involved Goldsworthy working very fast, usually arriving at a beach site at lowest tide, to give him the most time to complete a sculpture (it was thus best when low tide coincided with early morning). Beaches were often good places for materials, too (always an important consideration for an artist): sand and stones aplenty, and wood, and flotsam and jetsam. Building the sculpture was only half of the work, though: Goldsworthy always stayed around for the moment when the tide came in, photographing the sculpture throughout its immersion. The moment of collapse was particularly important for Goldsworthy, and he was disappointed if he didn't witness it.

Although the tidal works are dealing with big themes, of time, change, decay, the sea, nature, lunar power, and so on, there is also something undeniably childlike about such sculptures. They're reminiscent of children (and adults) who build castles, boats and walls from sand below the high tideline, so they can watch them (or stand in them) when the waves approach. Thus, Goldsworthy's tidal works are some of his most fun art: they can be regarded as serious explorations of nature and time, or larking about on a beach, building stuff then watching it disintegrate.

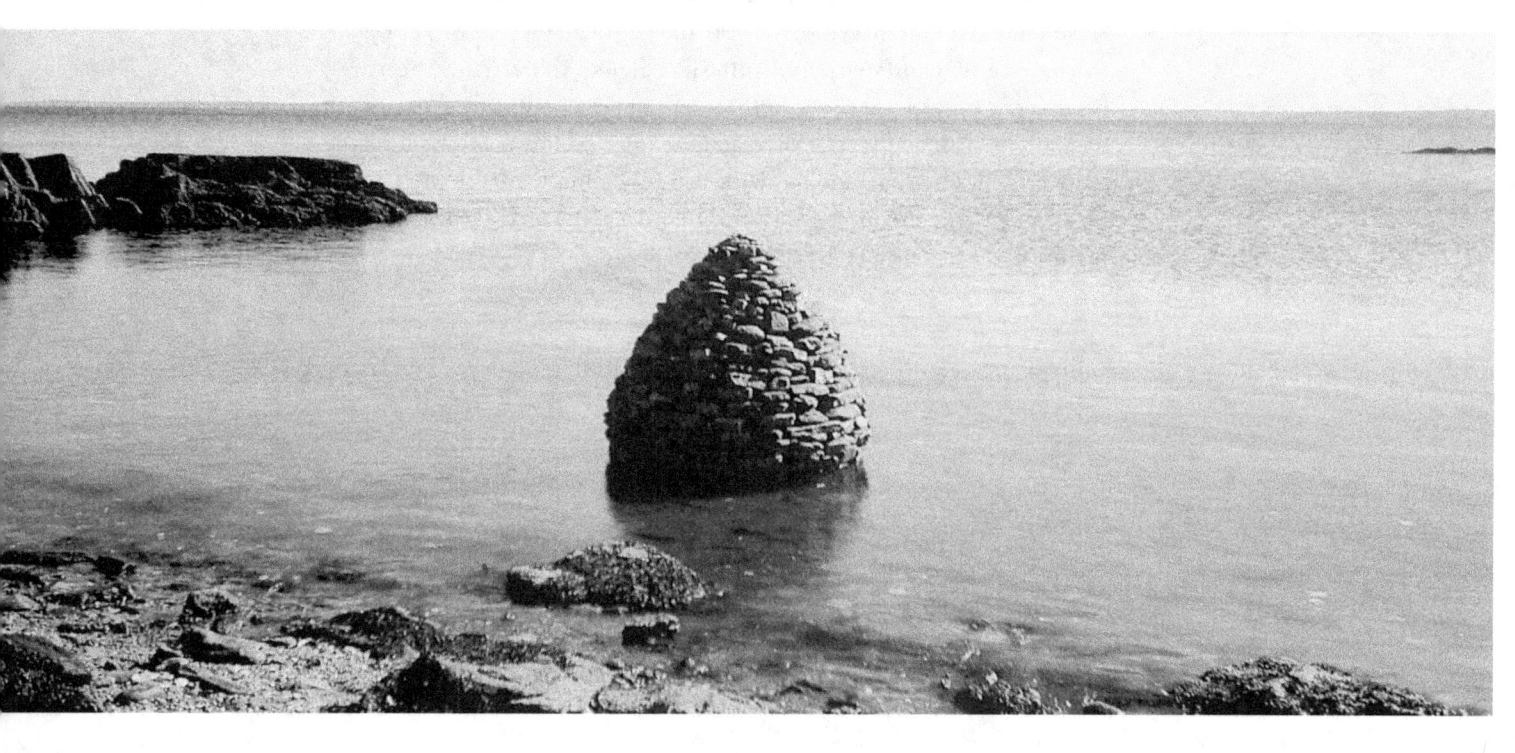

Three Cairns (2000-02)

Three Cairns (2000-02) was an important large-scale commission to construct three cairns in the United States of America: one on the West Coast (in California), one on the East Coast (in New York state), and one in the Mid-West (at Des Moines, Iowa). *Three Cairns* was a collaboration with three cultural institutions: Des Moines Art Center, Neuberger Museum of Art, Purchase, New York, and La Jolla Museum in San Diego. In the event, Goldsworthy built six cairns: apart from the three permanent pieces, there were three ephemeral sculptures: two were tidal, on the East and West coasts, and the third, in Iowa, was built on the prairie, which was set alight (with fire replacing water as the natural force which engulfed the sculpture. However, the stone cairn survived the fire).

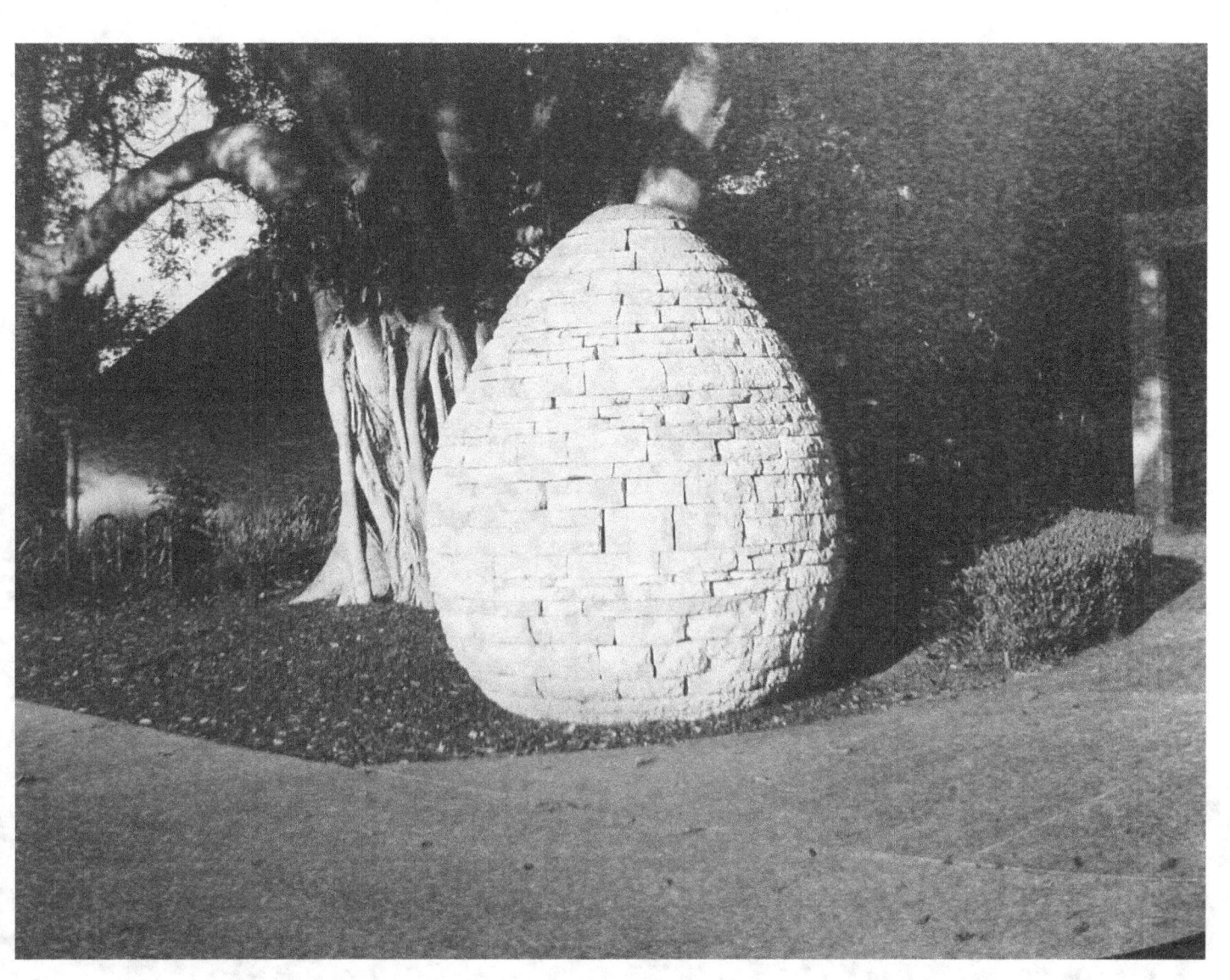

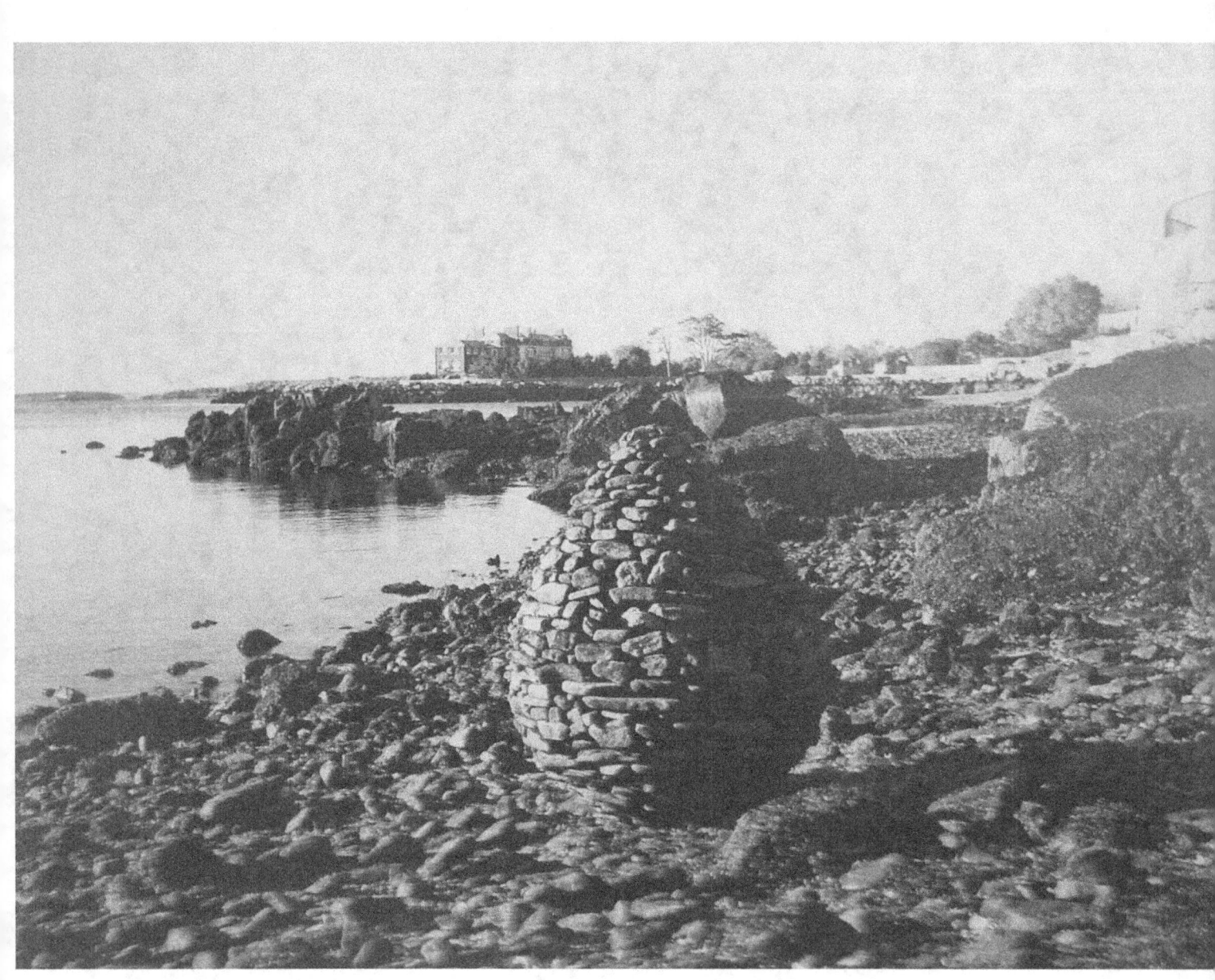

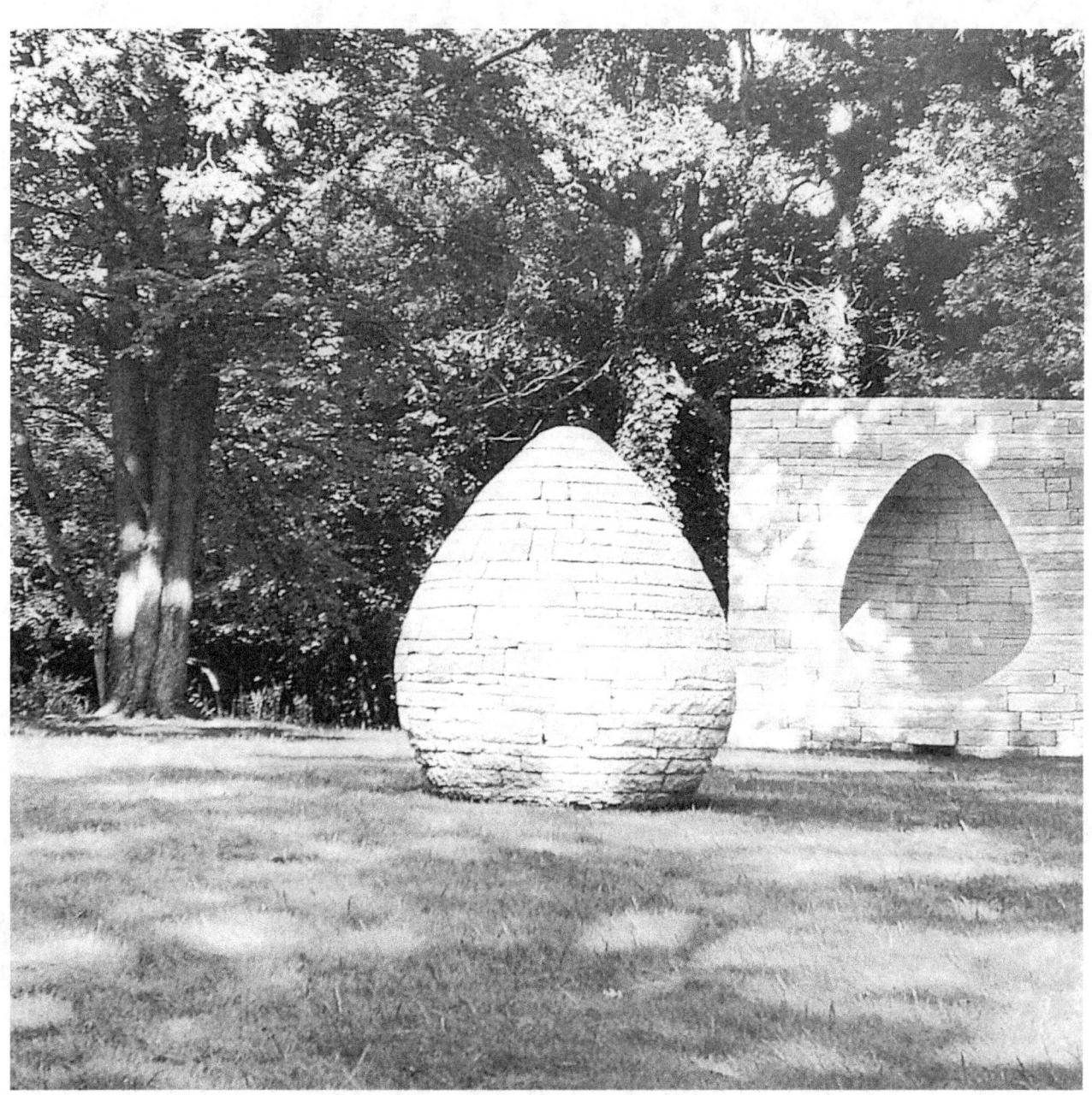

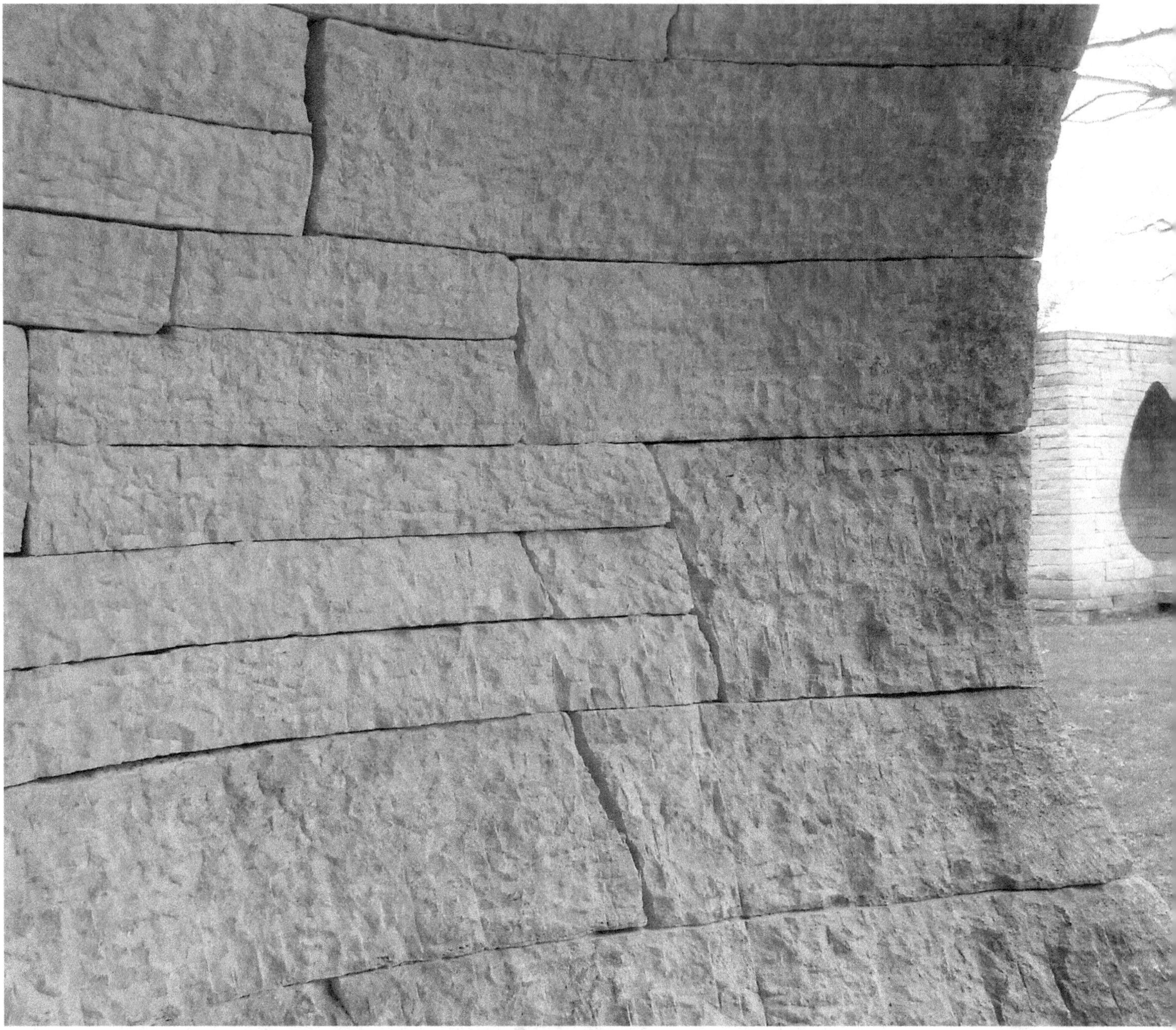

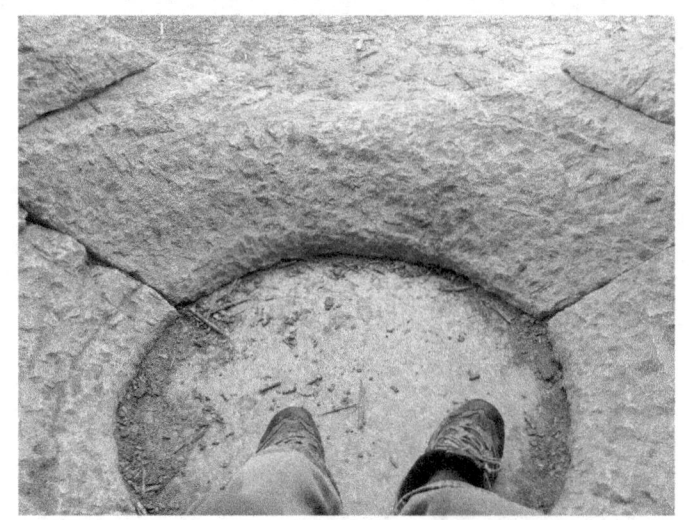

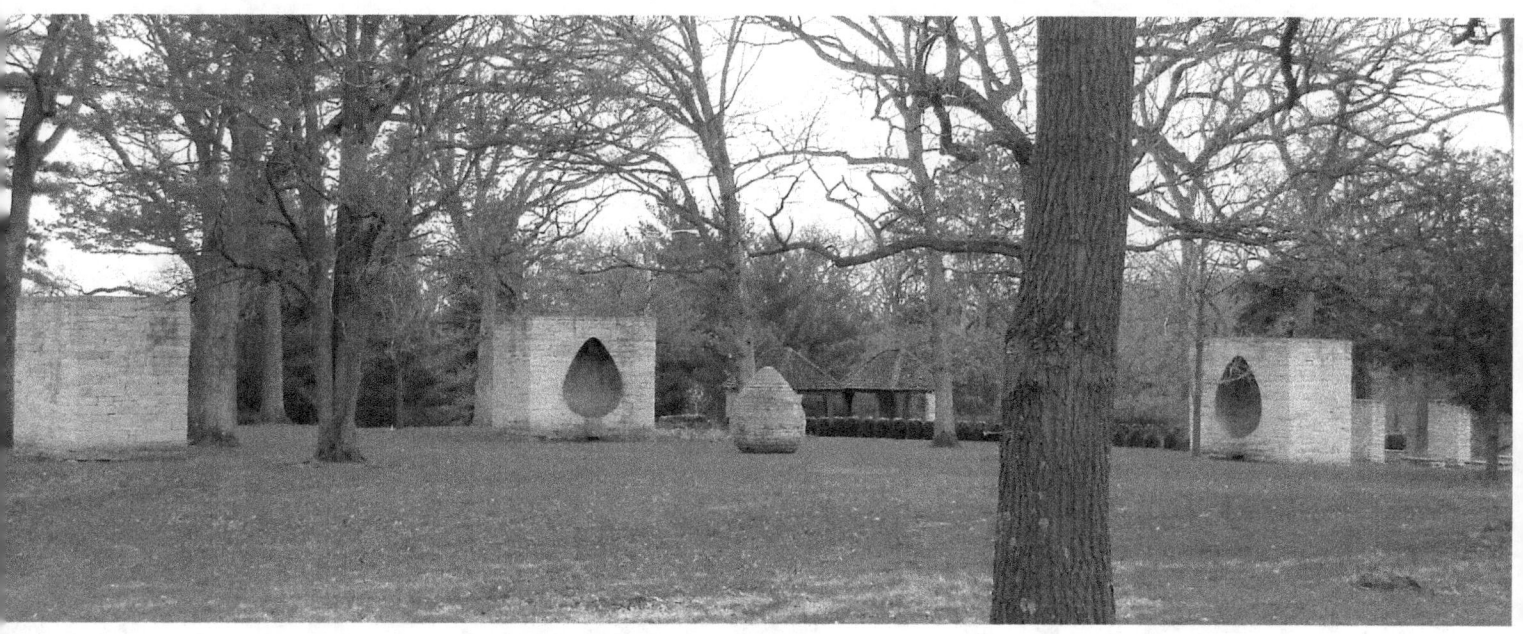

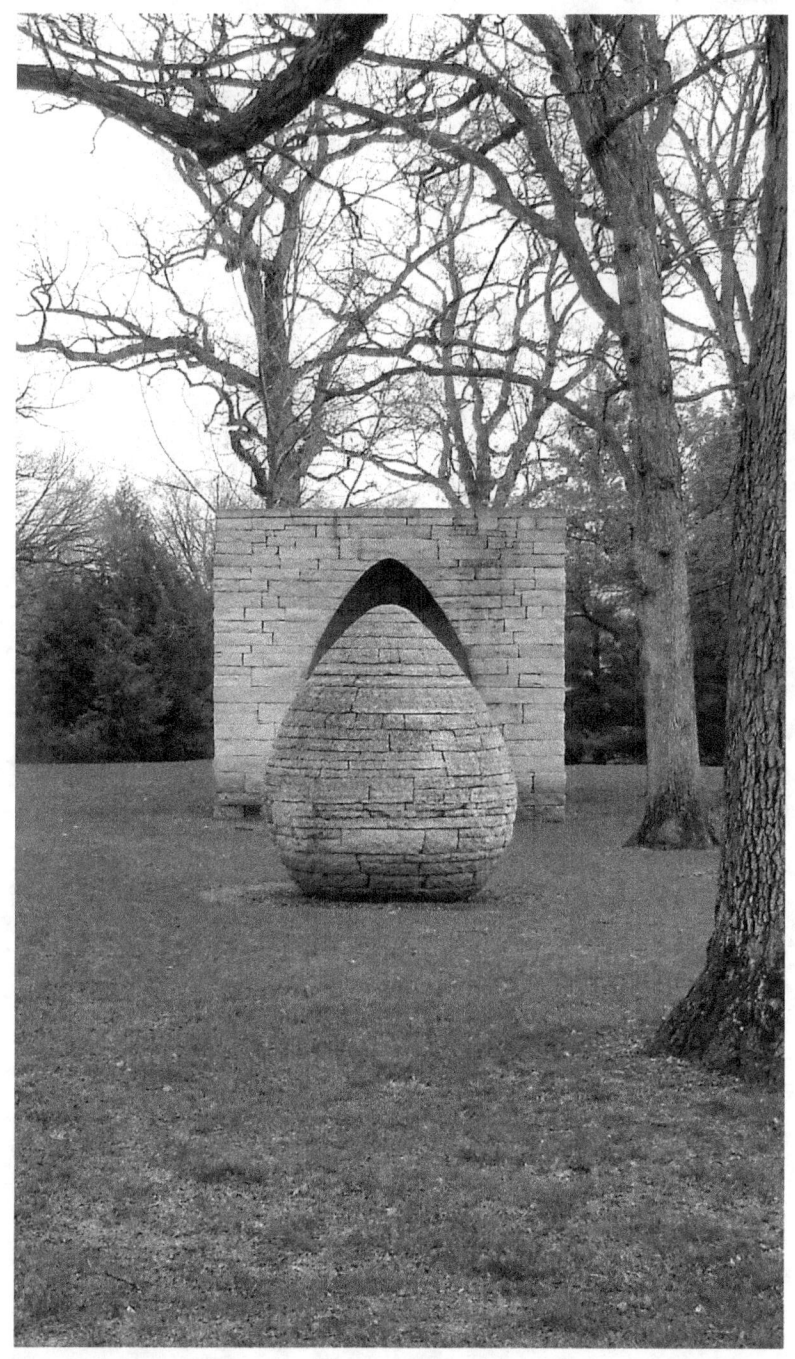

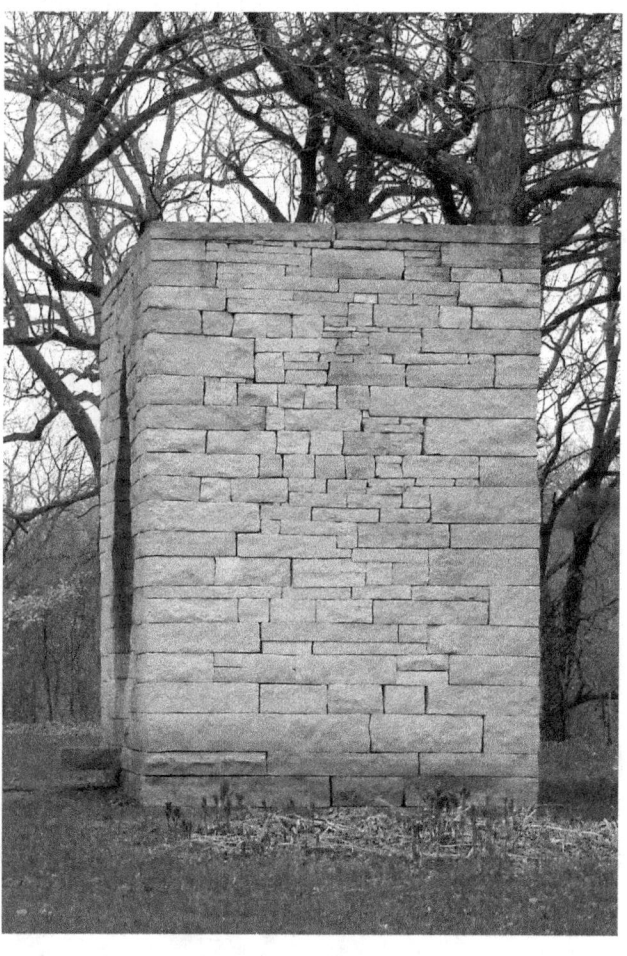

Arch (1997)

The *Arch* project of Summer, 1997 (a.k.a. *Walking Arch* and *Drove Arch*) expressed many of Andy Goldsworthy's æsthetic concerns. It consisted of Goldsworthy and his team building a red sandstone arch at twenty-two key sites along the old tracks and roads where sheep and cattle were driven, between South-West Scotland and the North-West of England. The route was from Locharbriggs Quarry, North of Dumfries, via Longtown, Carlisle, Penrith and Shap, across Cumbria, to Kirkby Lonsdale.

Arch was about ancient traditions, the history of the landscape, old economies, sheepfolds, and the contemporary landscapes of South-West Scotland and North-West England. Goldsworthy saw his art as just another layer of history on top on many layers of human history. 'I work in a landscape made rich by the people who have worked and farmed it. I can feel the presence of those who have gone before me' (T, 8). It wasn't simply nostalgia in reconstructing old agricultural buildings and structures either, Goldsworthy maintained, it was about finding new uses for them (RA, 107).

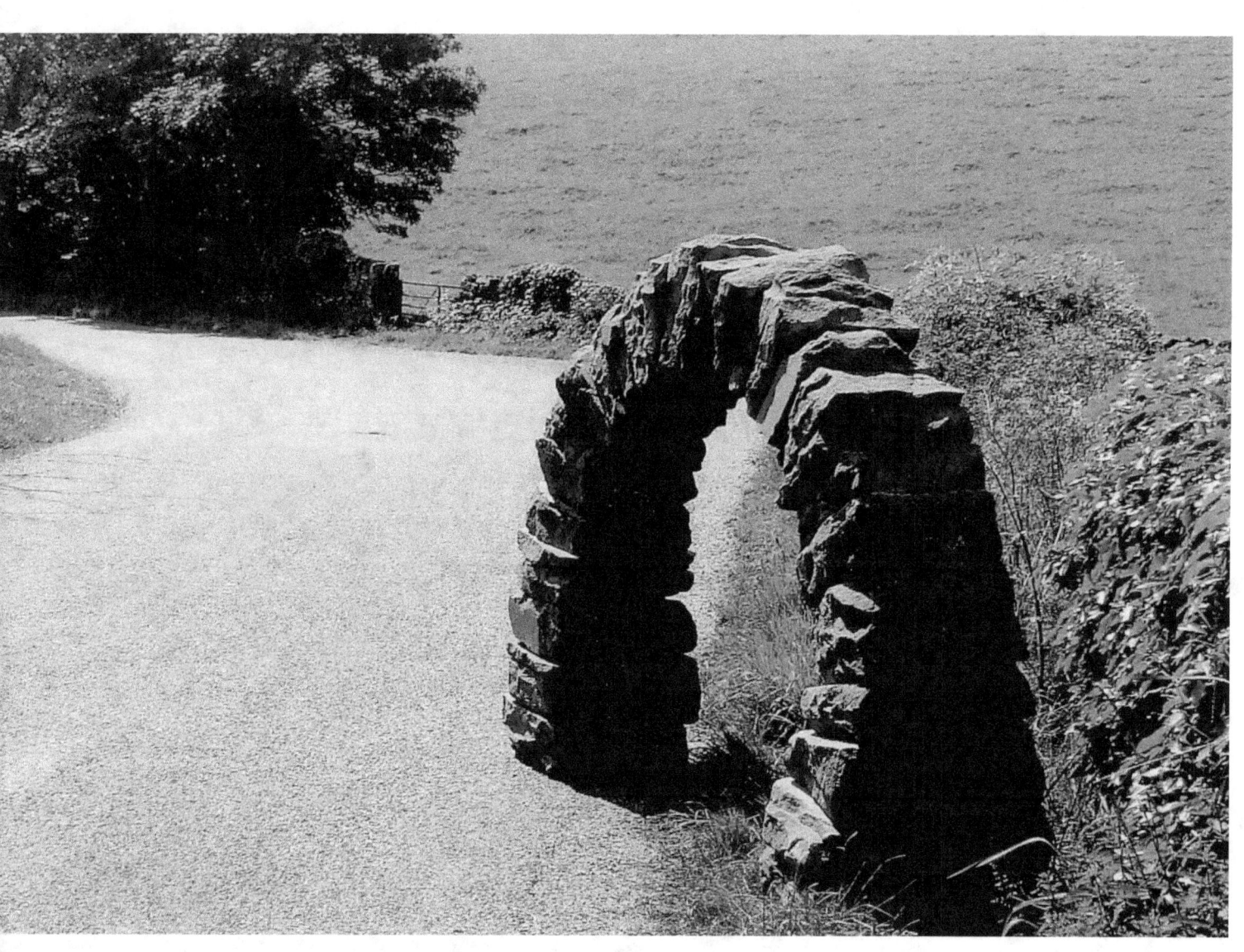

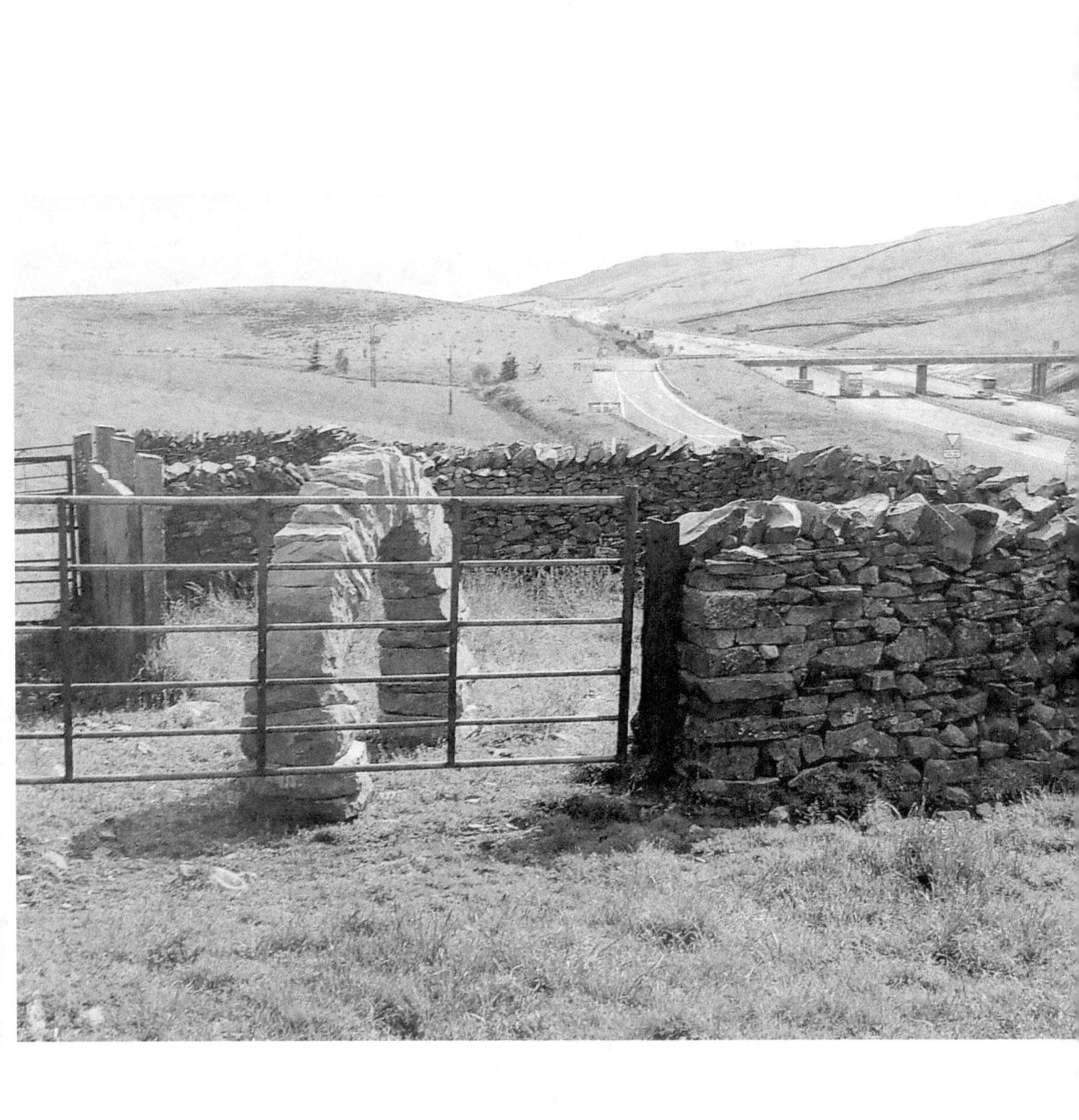

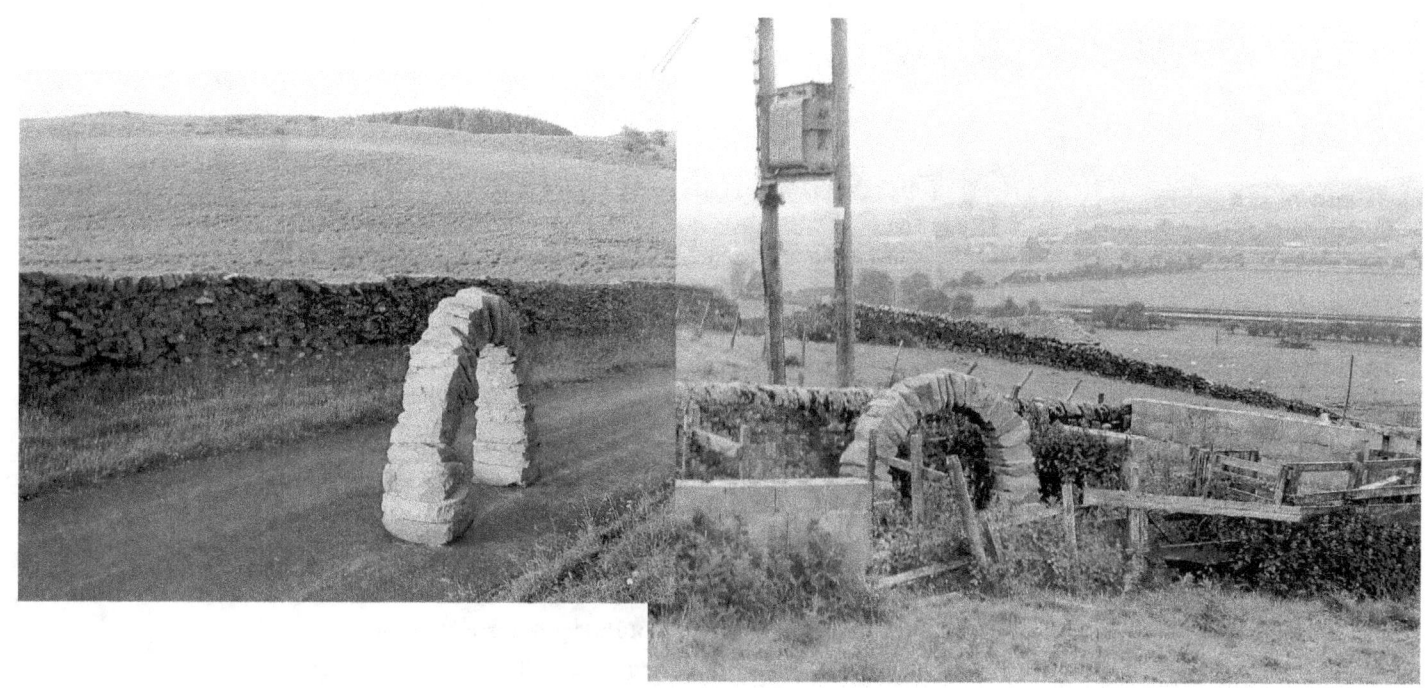

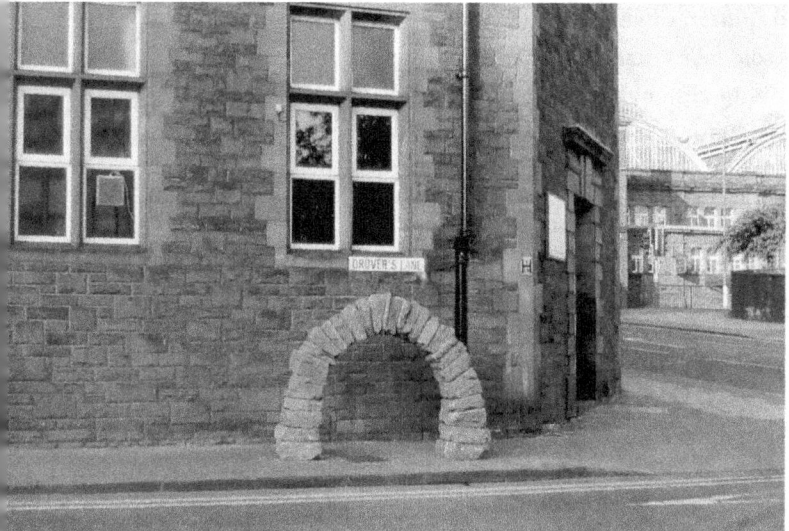

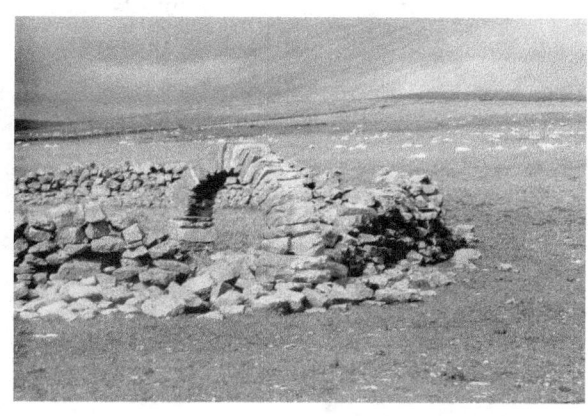

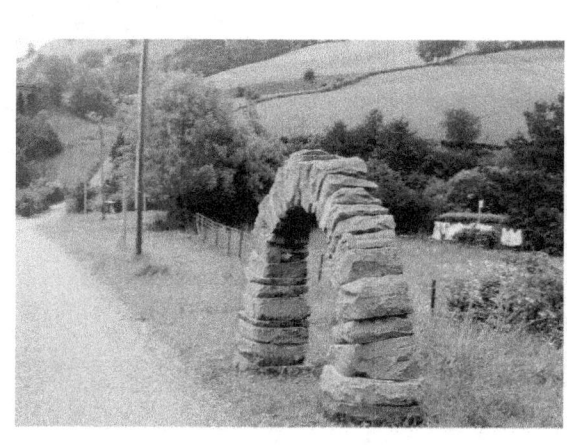

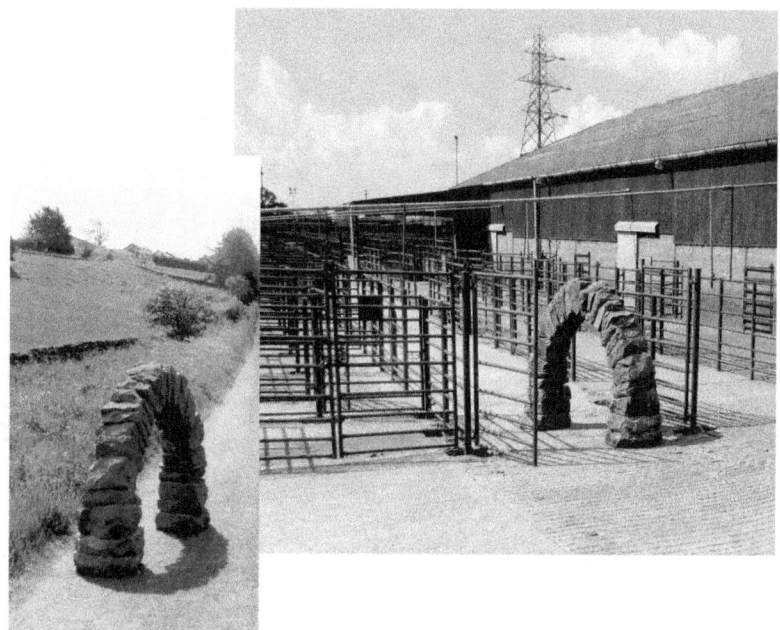

The Storm King Wall (1997)

The *Storm King Wall* was built at the Storm King Art Center sculpture park 55 miles from New York City. It was a longer variation on an earlier wall that Goldsworthy had made at Grizedale, *The wall that went for a walk* (1990). The earlier wall was a 150-yard long stone structure that literally snaked through the forest. The serpentine form of *The wall that went for a walk* relates to *Lambton Earthwork* and *Sidewinders* (the latter another Grizedale sculpture). *The wall that went for a walk* had no 'proper', practical function (unlike the many *Sheepfolds*). It weaved between the trees and followed the lie of the land. Instead of ploughing through trees or rocks, Goldsworthy's curving wall assiduously avoided them. However, the wall didn't need to be there in the first place (a notion that Goldsworthy cannot quite resolve: in *Stone* he relates *The wall that went for a walk* to the old fields that were at Grizedale before the forest, but it's not a convincing argument). 'The wall itself is an expression of movement; a line moving through the landscape' (*Sheepfolds,* 12). Goldsworthy said in *Wall* that he made the larger, serpentine wall in New York State in relation to an old wall that was already there but decayed (2000, 22).

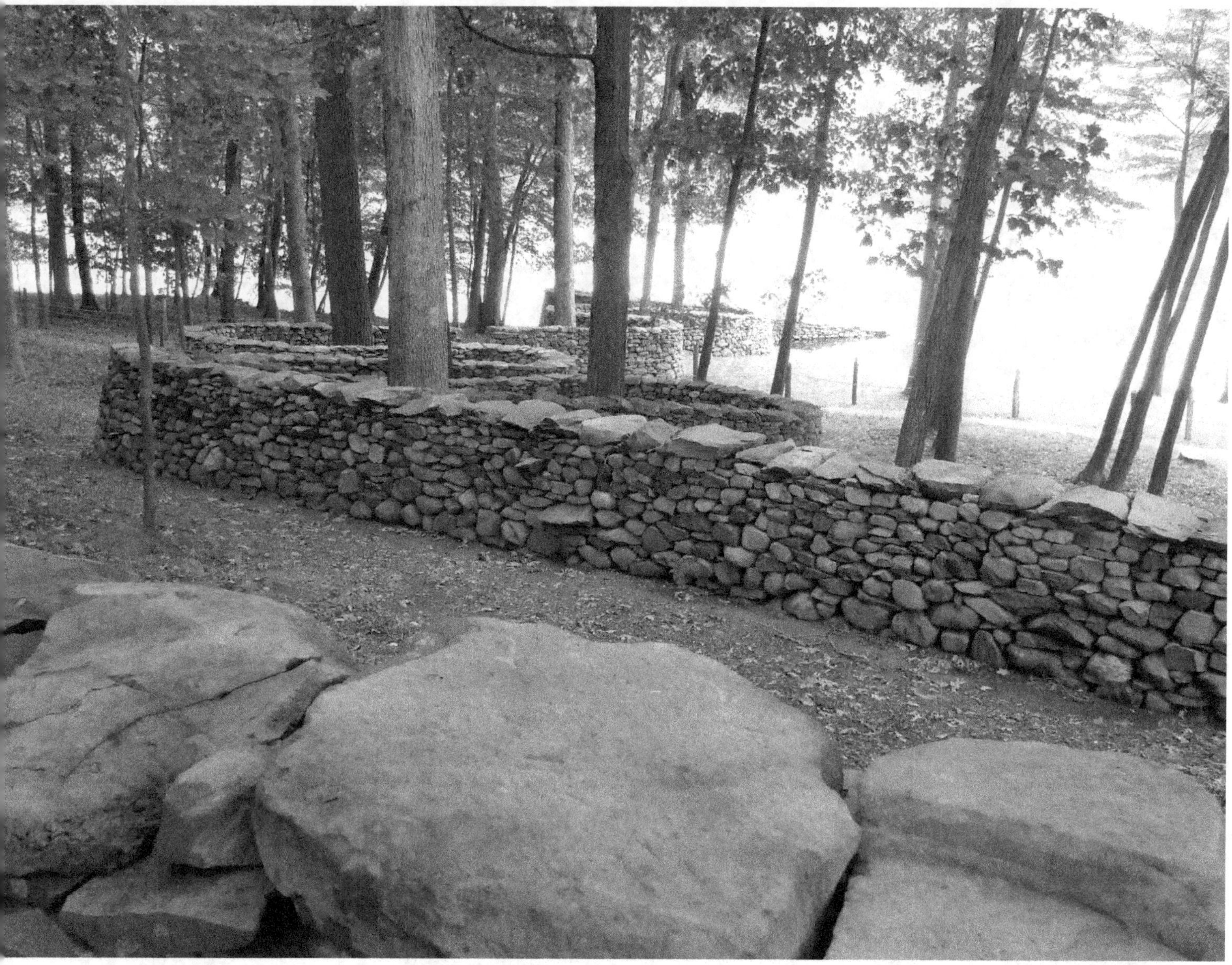

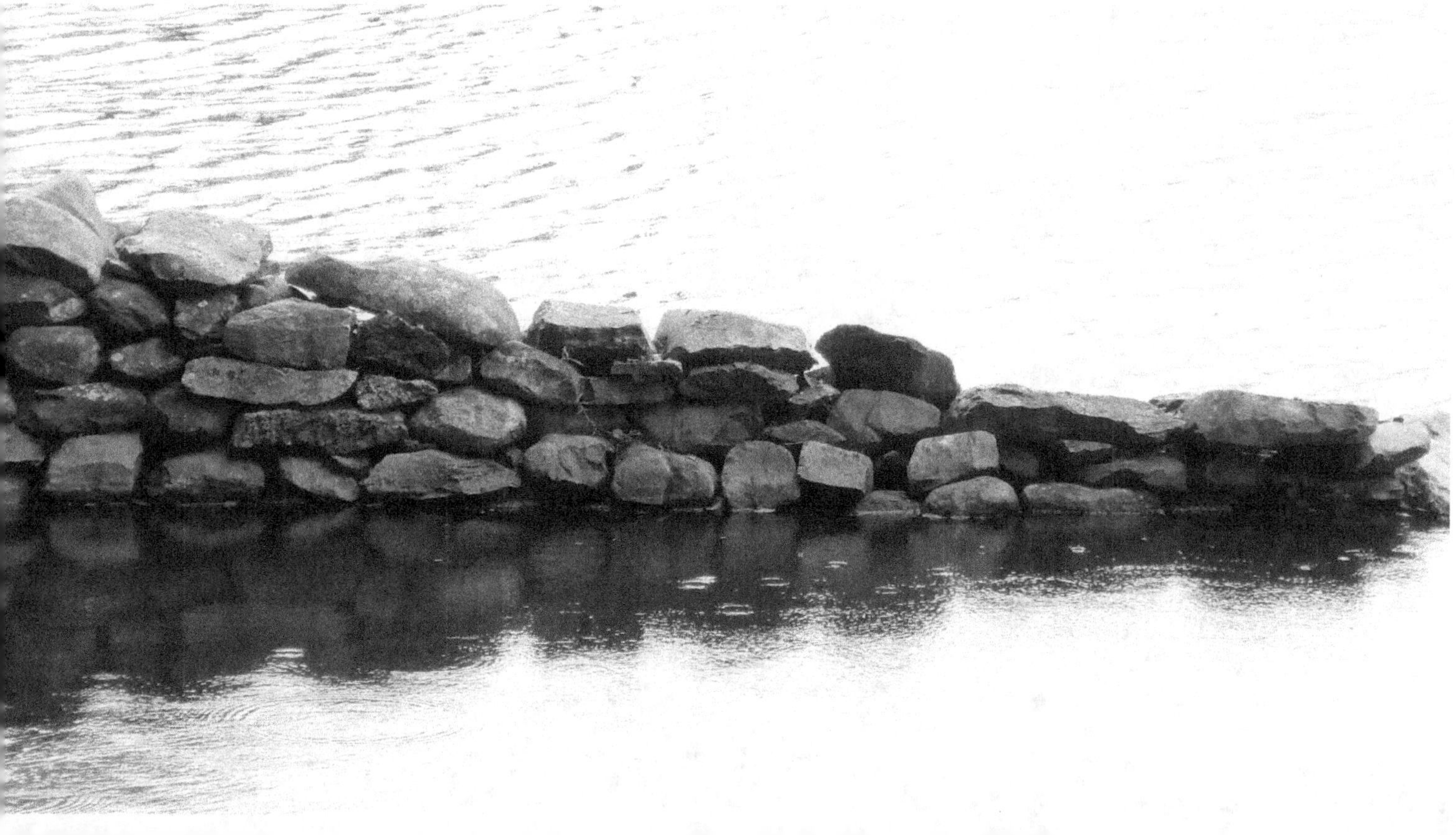

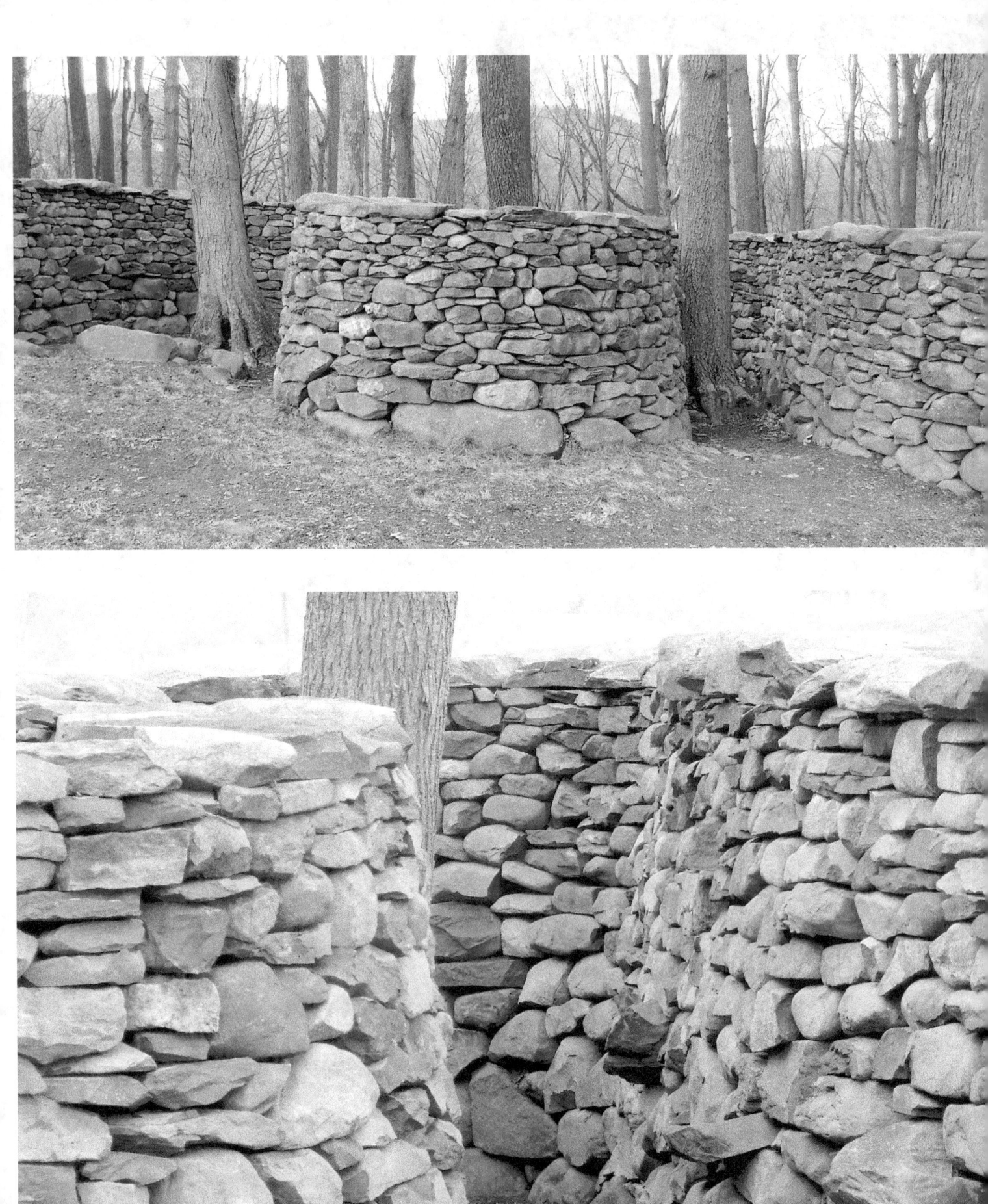

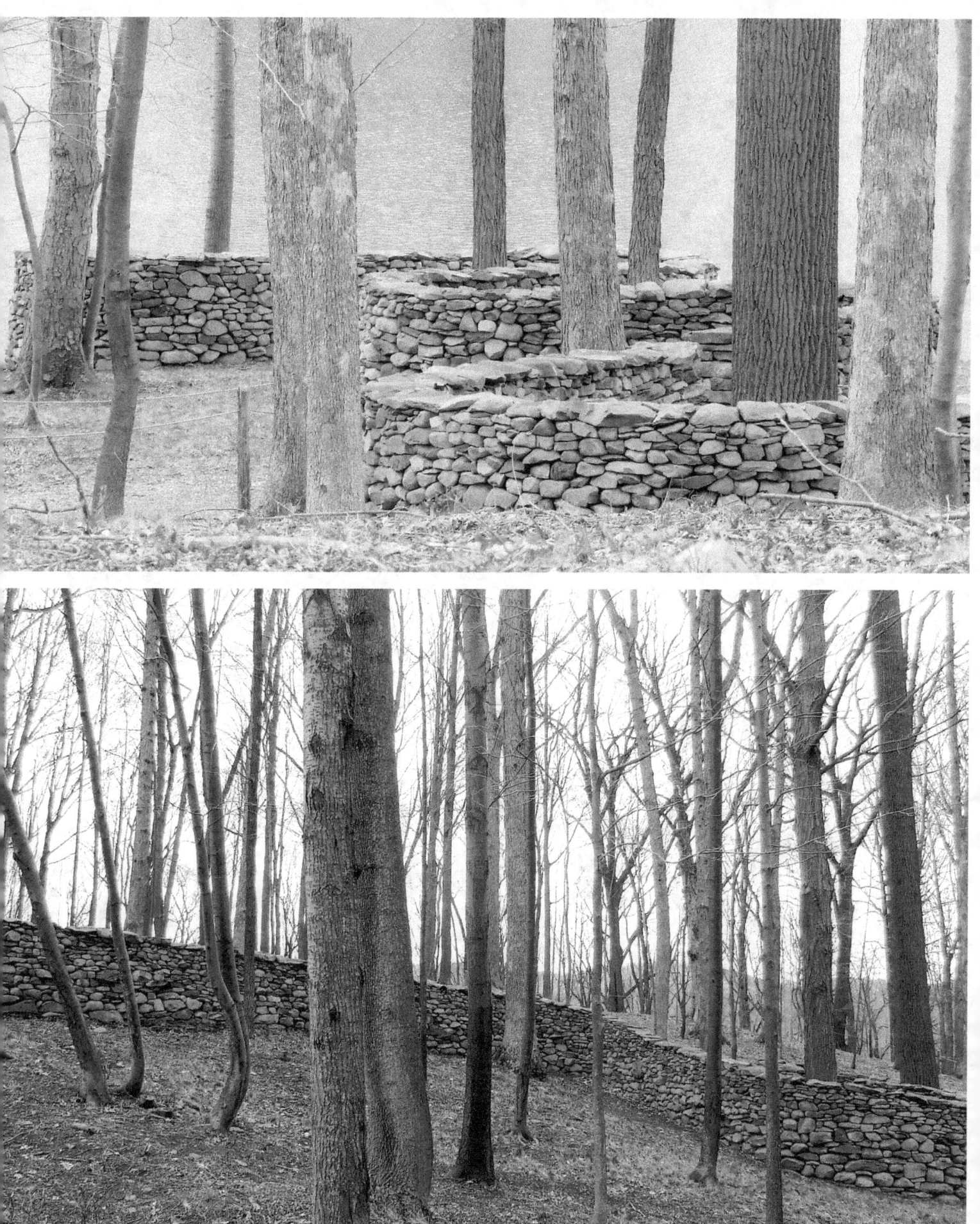

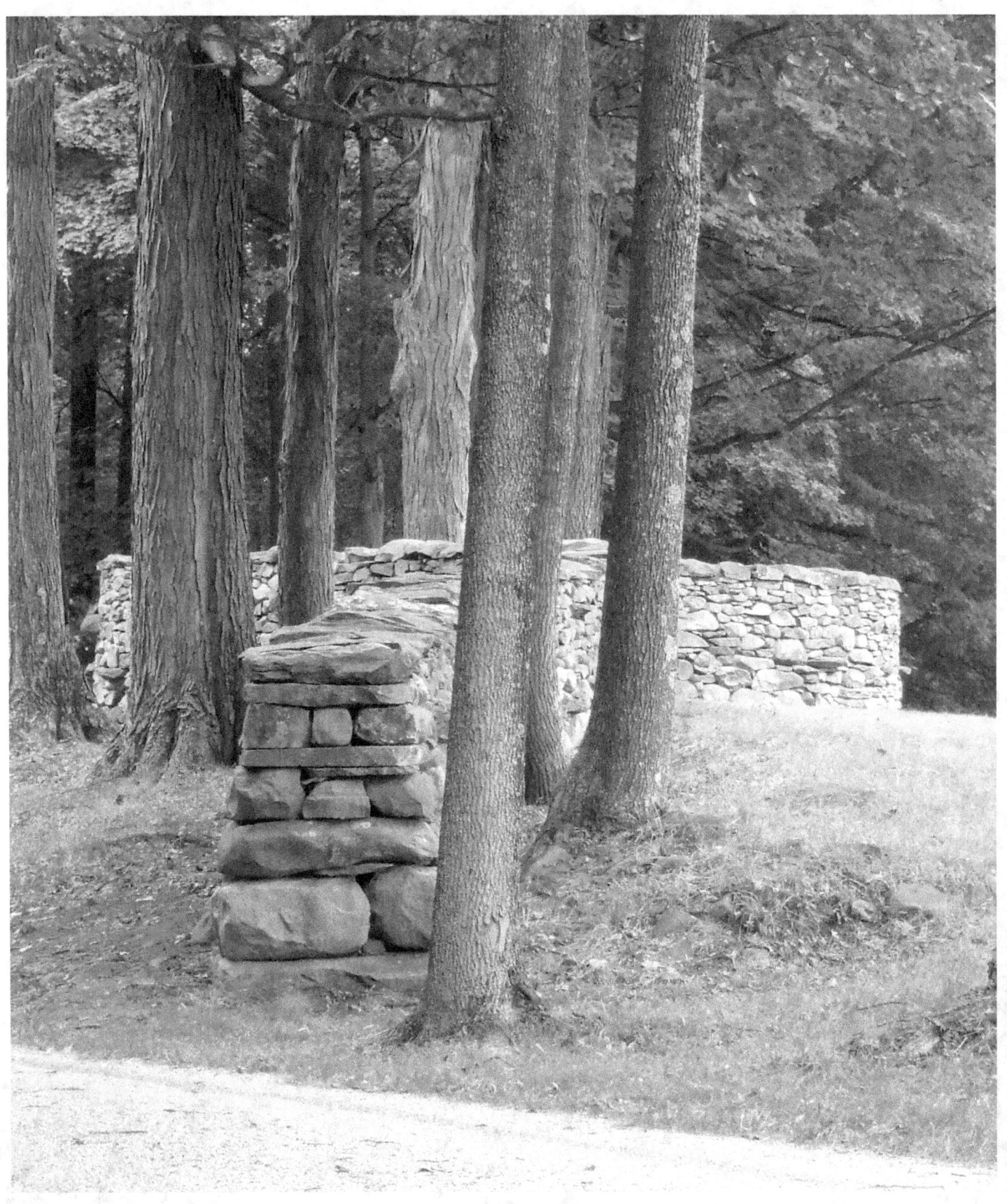

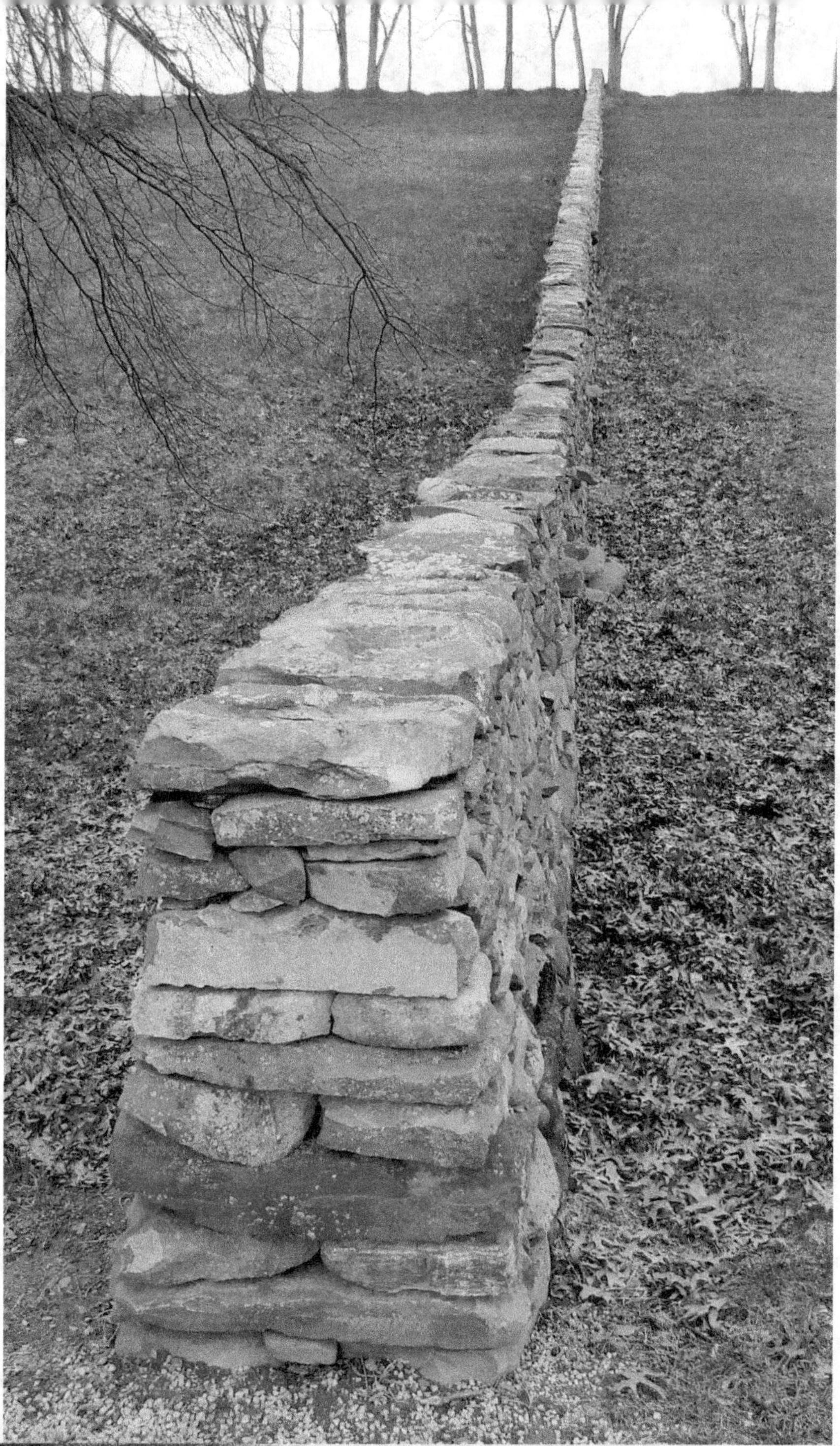

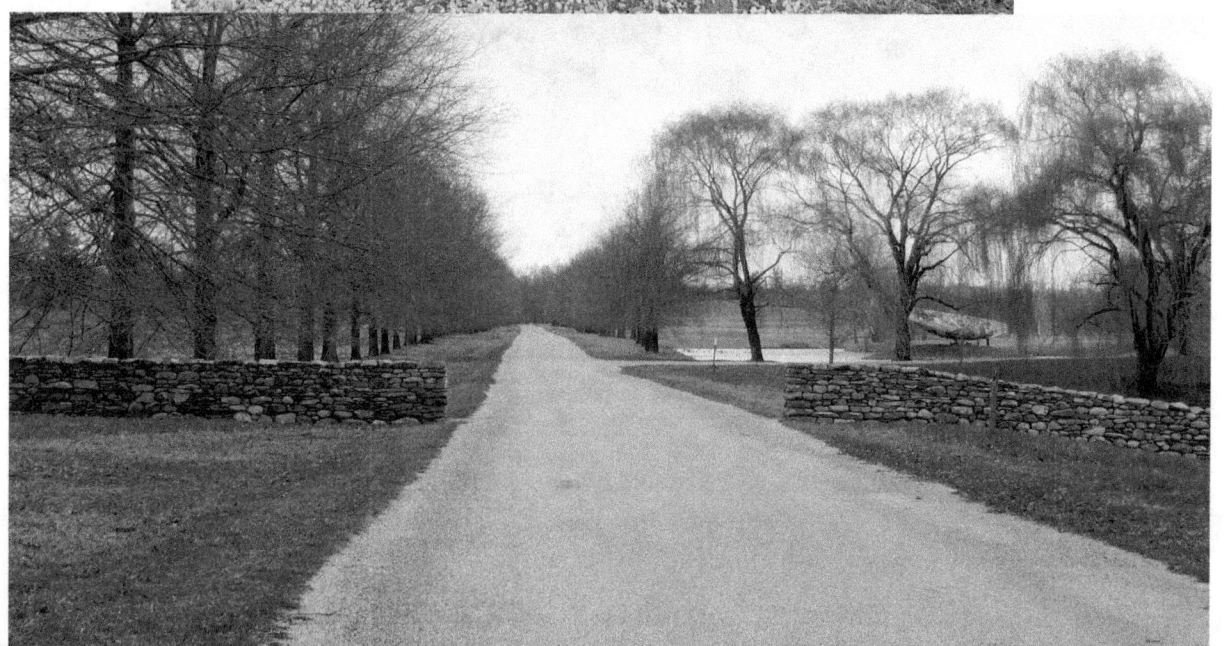

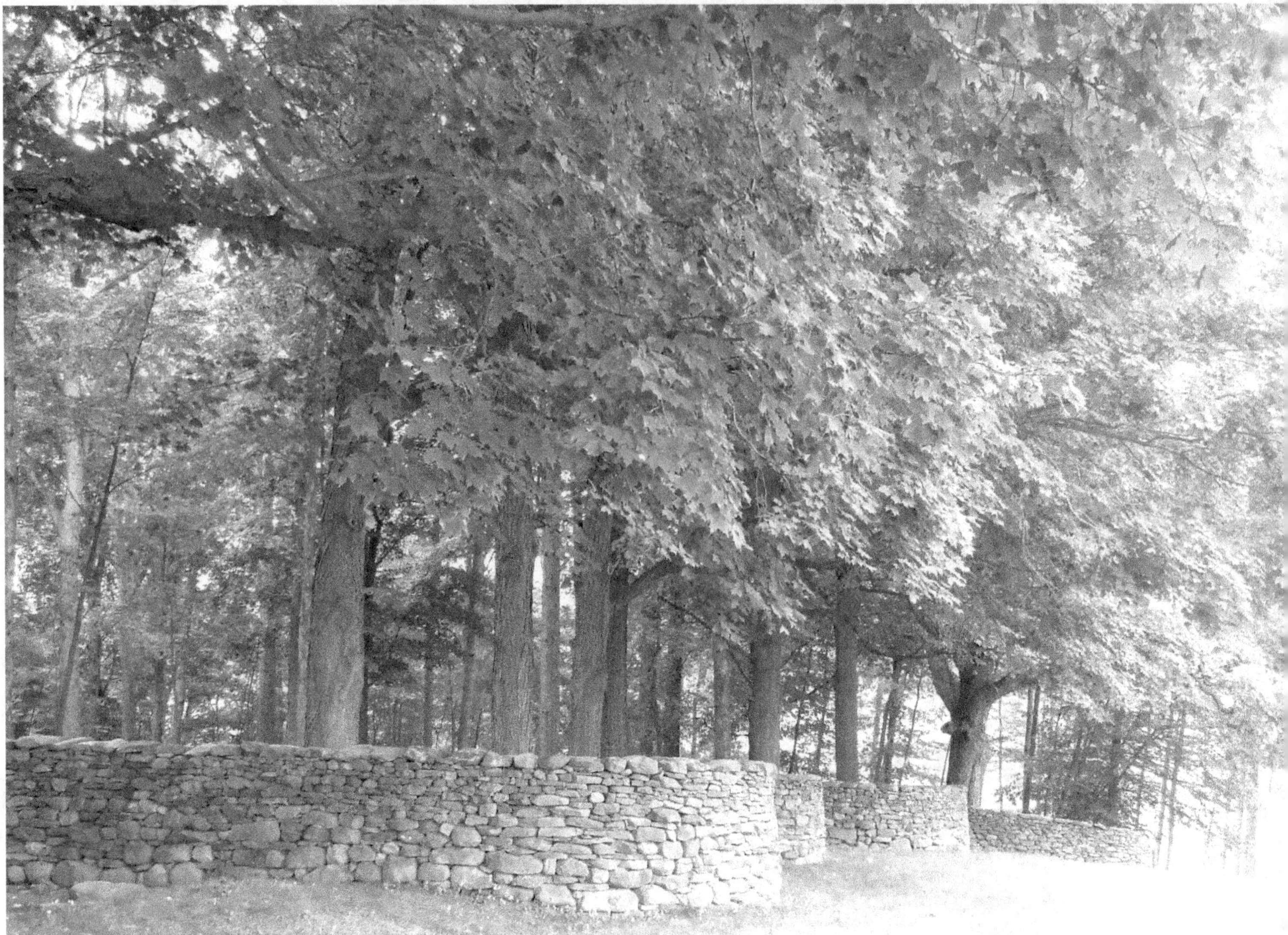

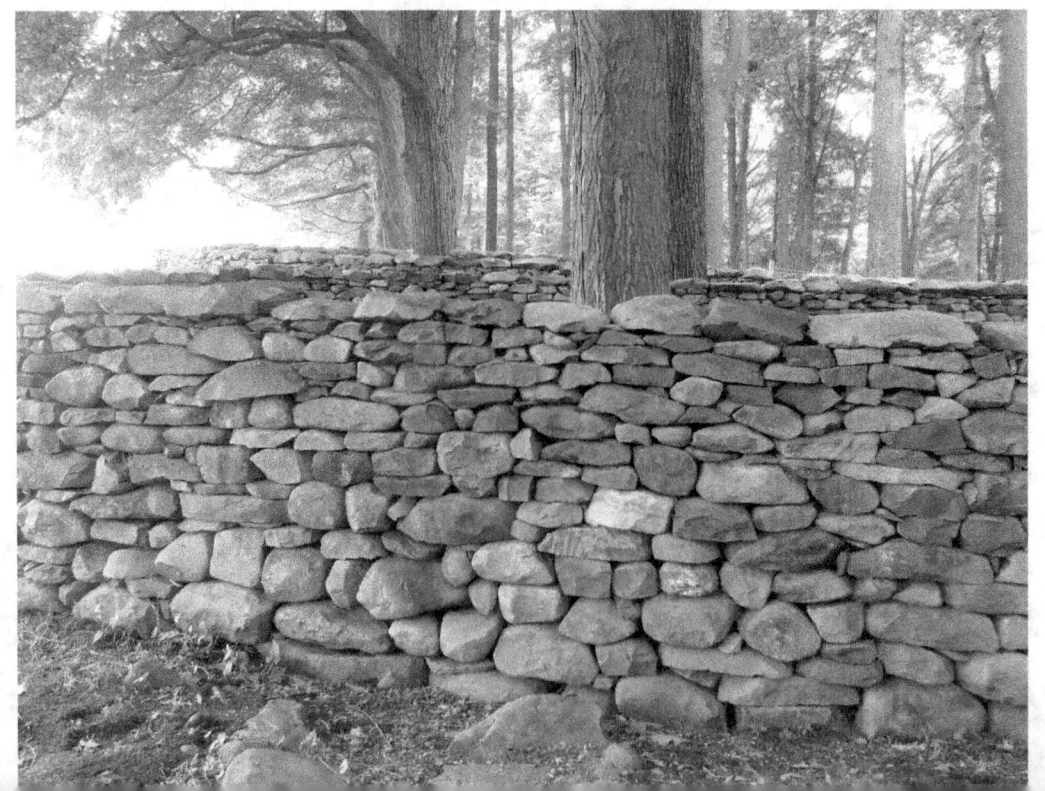

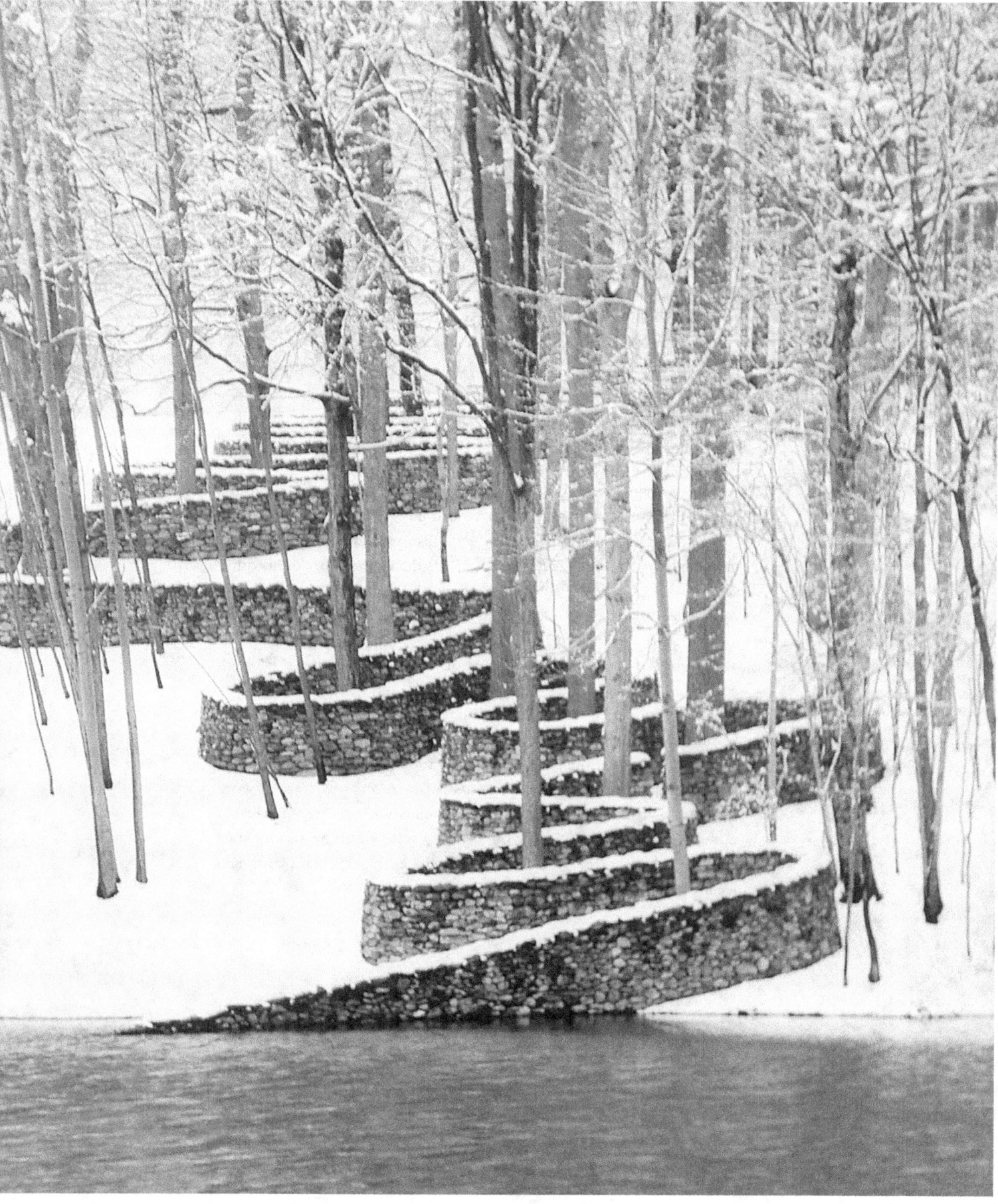

Cairns

As the cairns were being constructed, Goldsworthy explained, all sorts of irregularities would introduce themselves. Like many artists say of their works, Goldsworthy said when he completed a cairn, he only saw the mistakes. But it was precisely the accidents and mistakes which 'give the form a tension and energy' (RA, 101). The perfect artwork was a practical as well as philosophical impossibility. Goldsworthy said he was often surprised by the final result: '[e]ach cairn is a shock, and not what I intended' (ibid.). Getting the belly of the cairn right was critical, Goldsworthy remarked, and the foundation and beginning was usually tricky, but the most important part was the top, the last three feet: '[t]he top draws the energy of the stone to a peak, just as the apex of an arch becomes a focus for its energy' (RA, 103).

Goldsworthy often spoke of searching for the perfect form in his cairns. Every time he built a cairn he said he was looking for the ideal form, and tried to attain it, but always fell short. Goldsworthy seemed more anxious about the shape of his cairns than almost any of his other sculptures. 'I set myself an almost impossible task: to make the perfect form by eye and hand' Goldsworthy said in *Passage* (10). That's it: the artist started out with too high ideals, which could never be accomplished (he didn't begin most other works with the same high goals).

The anxiety perhaps also sprang from the fact that the cairns were built by hand and judged by eye, not from architectural plans. They were intuitive forms, and the shape each cairn took was always being negotiated during construction. Thus, Goldsworthy often talked about work starting slowly at first, about getting the foundation level, about working upwards to the belly, about wondering exactly when he should start working inwards, about putting particular stones in particular places, and feeling anxious again as the cairn approached completion.

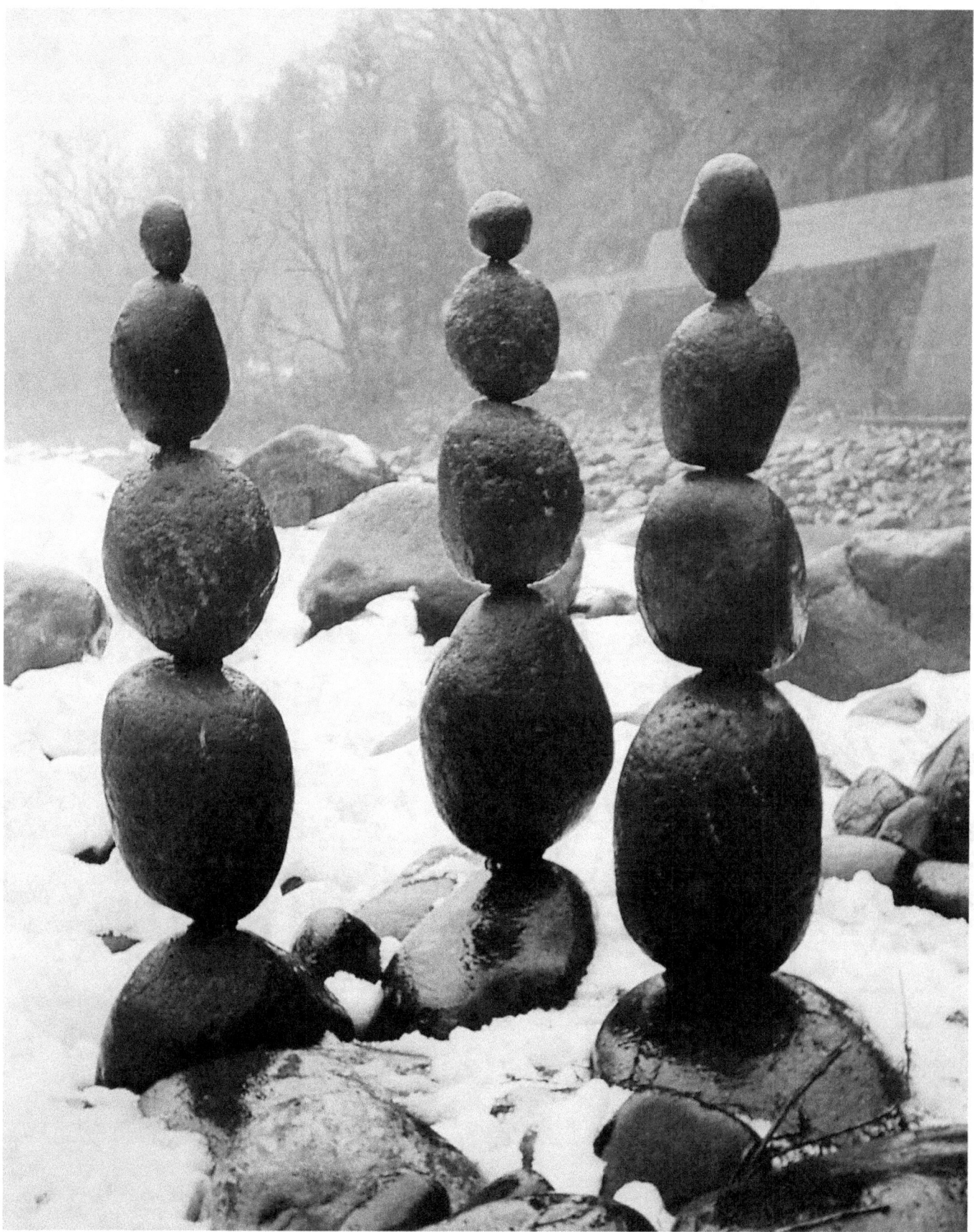

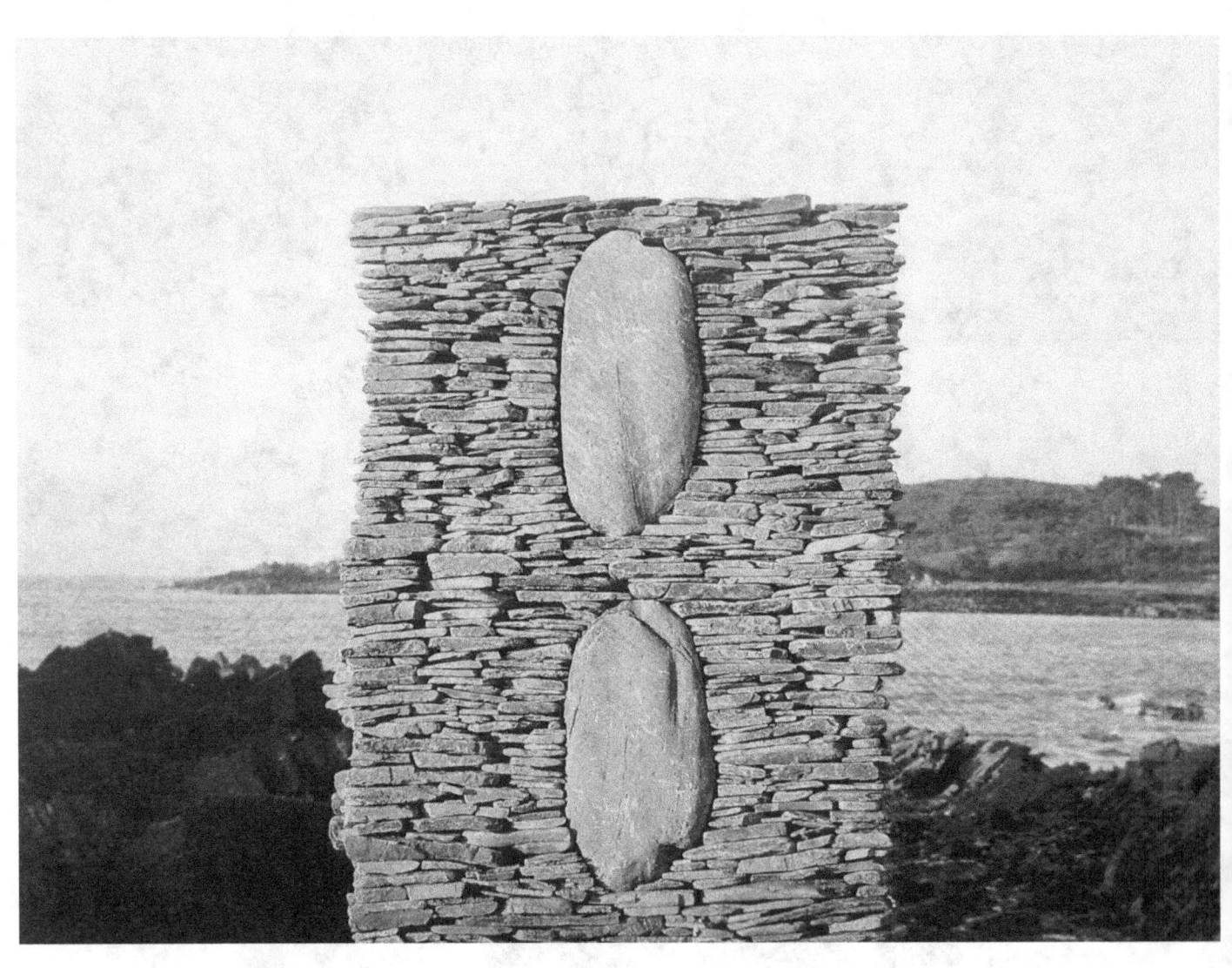

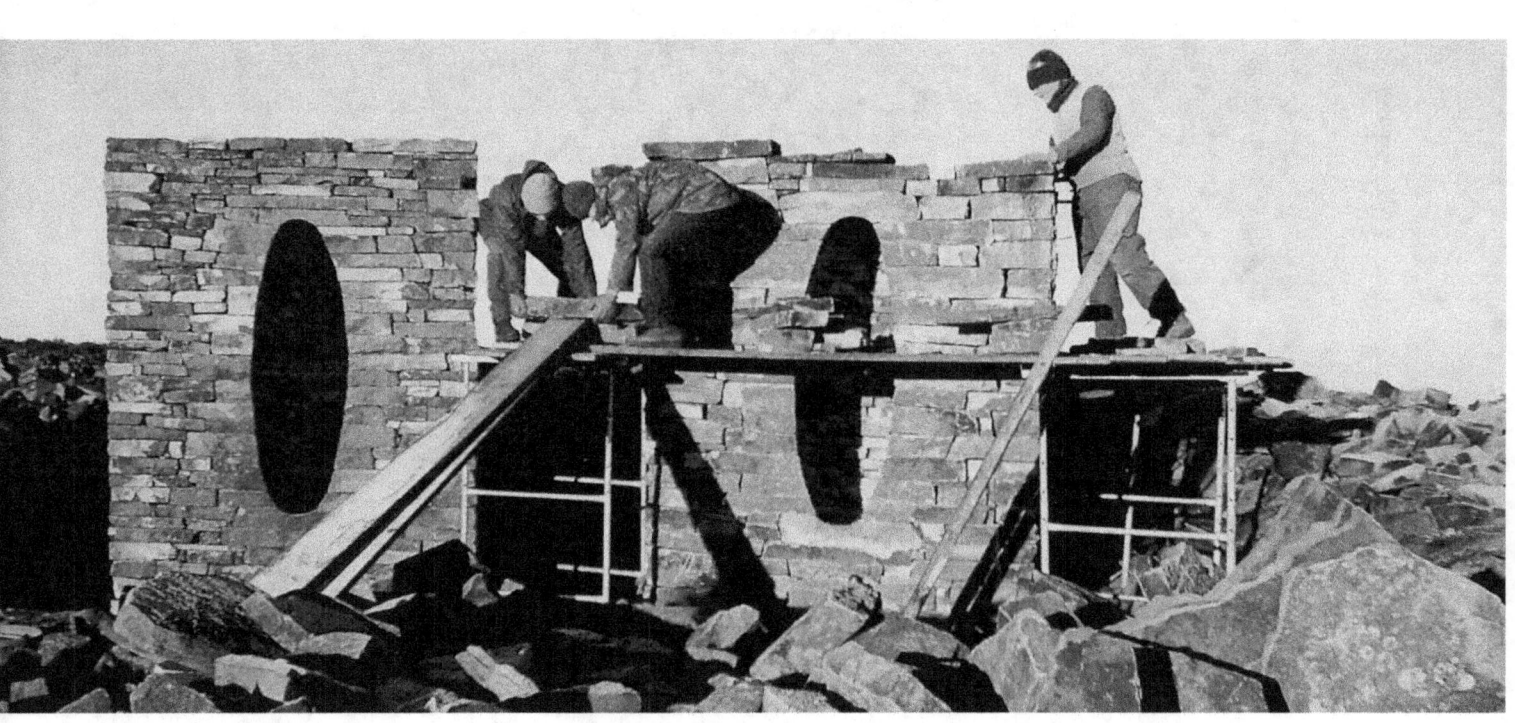

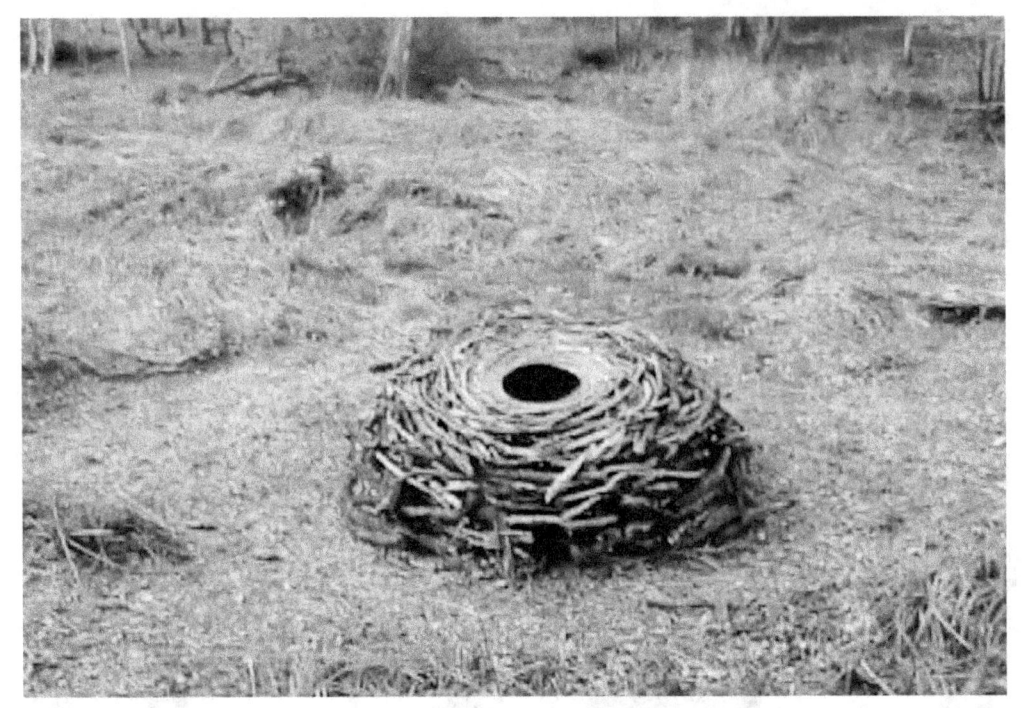

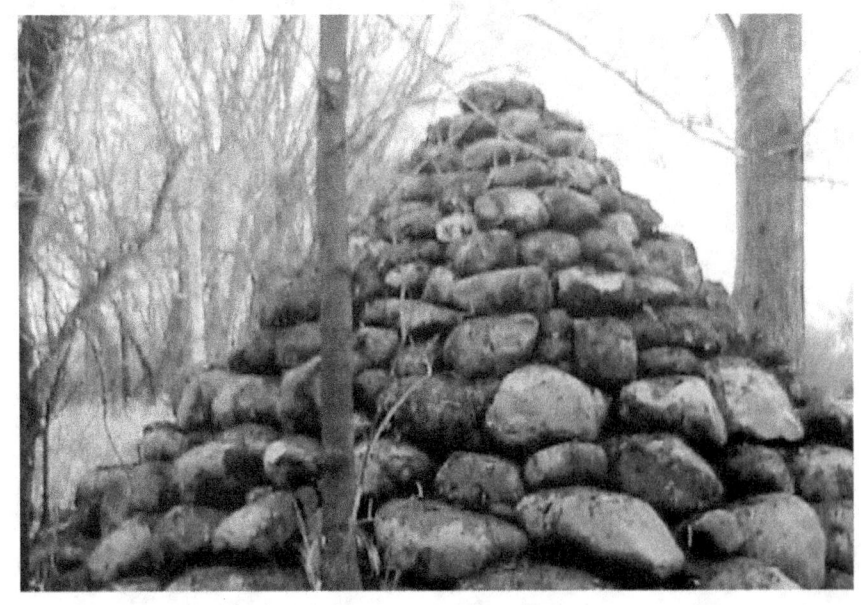

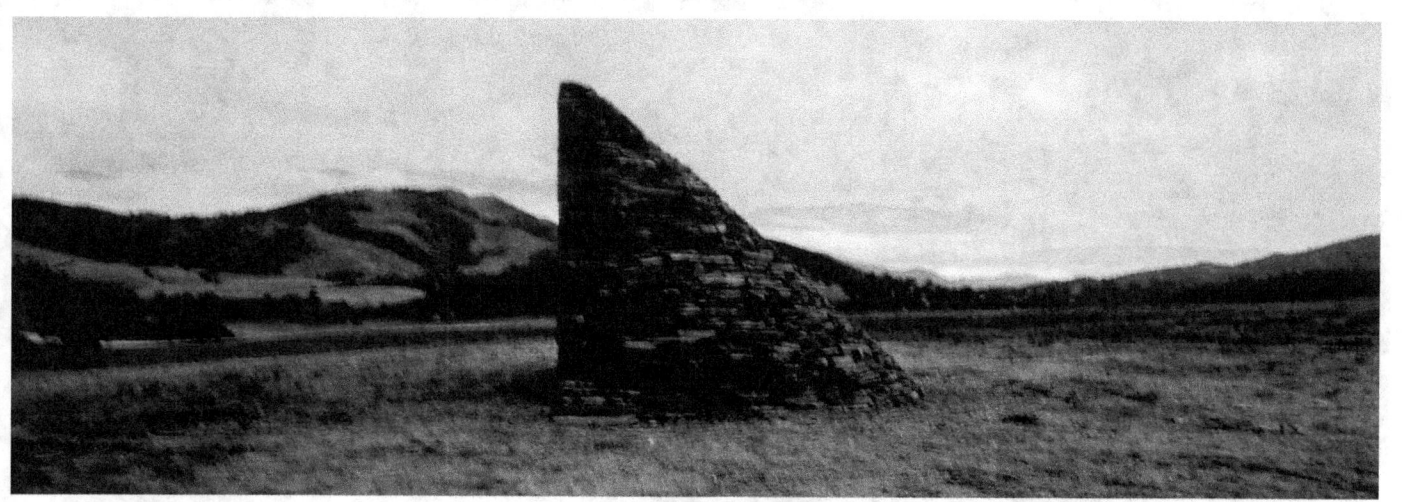

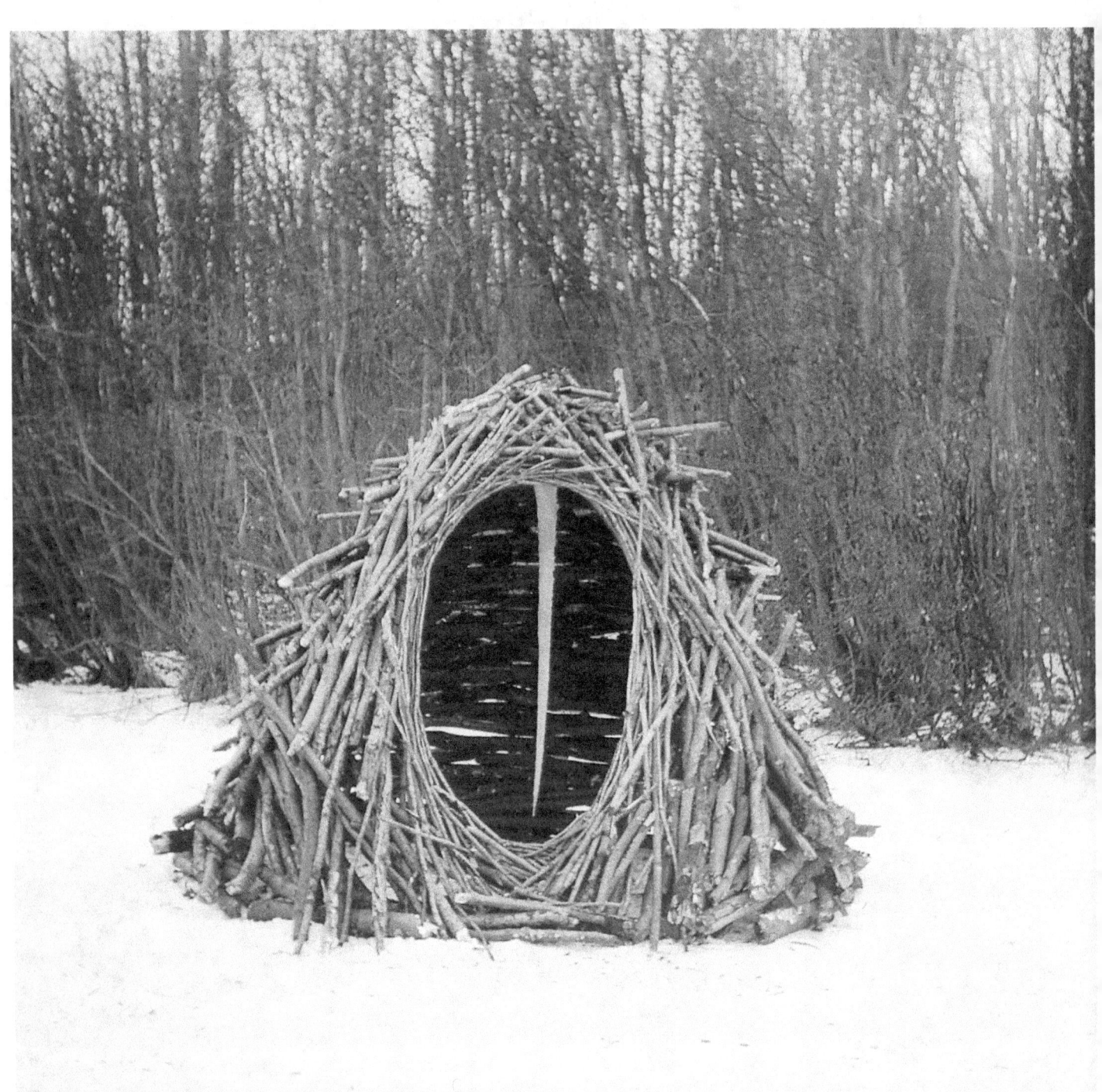

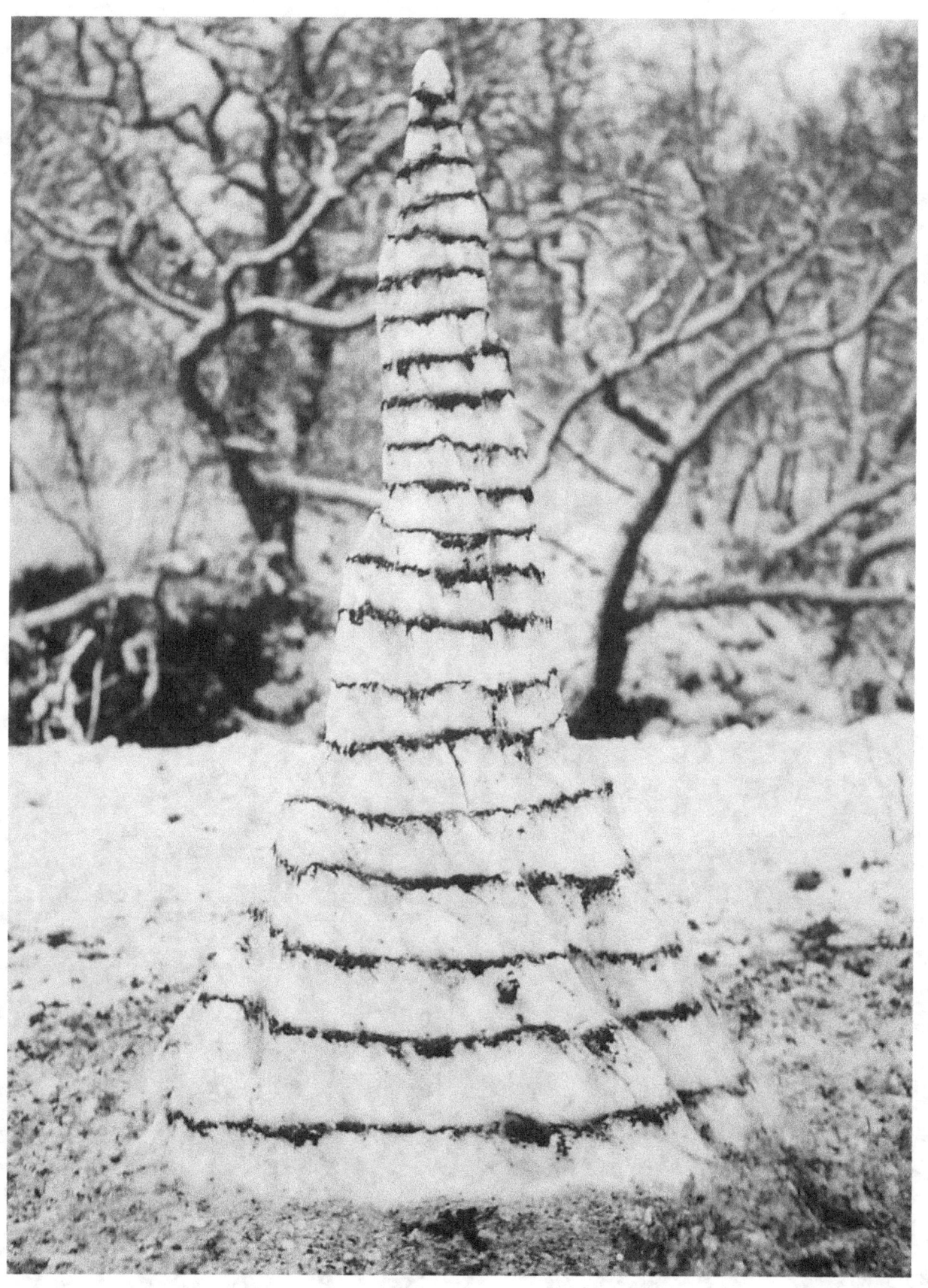

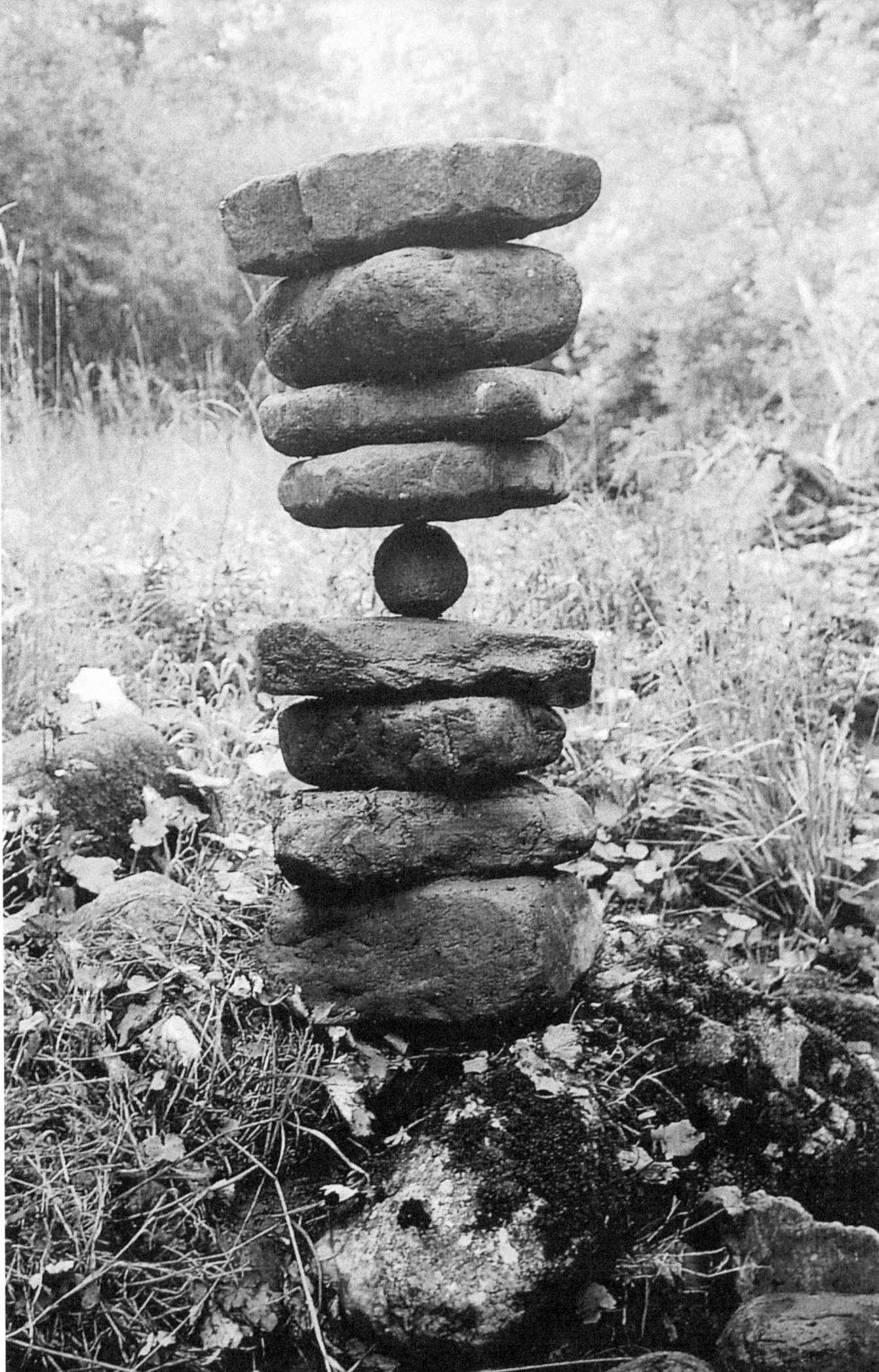

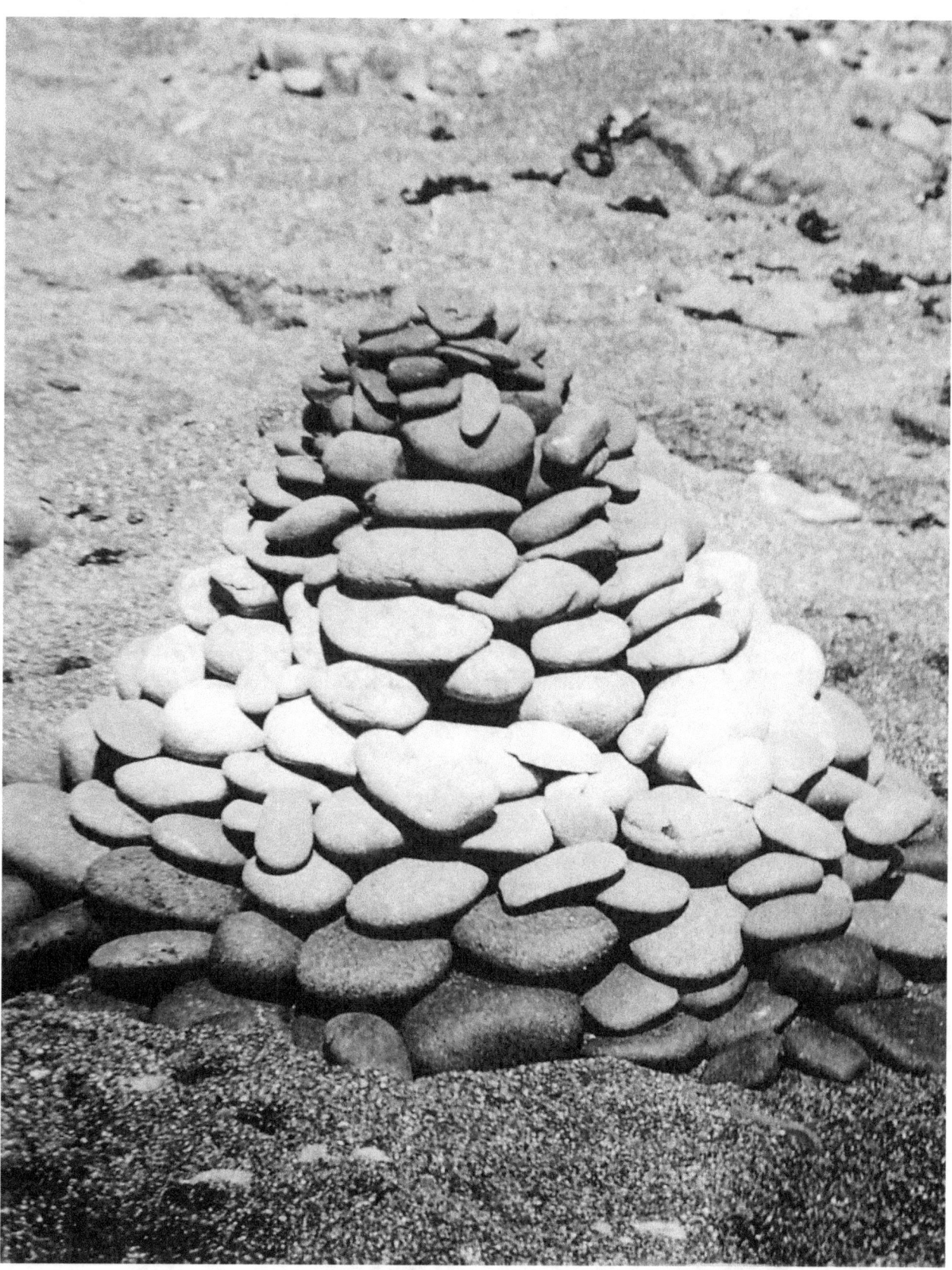

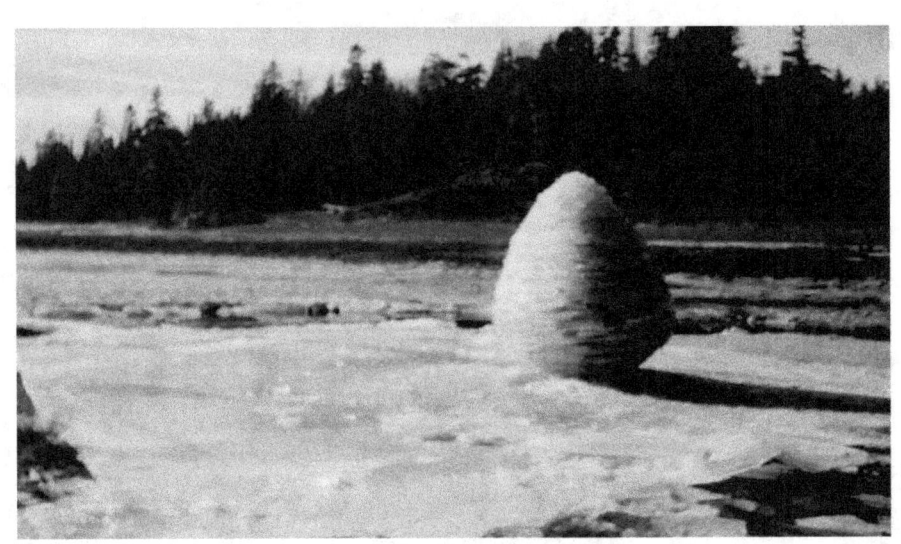

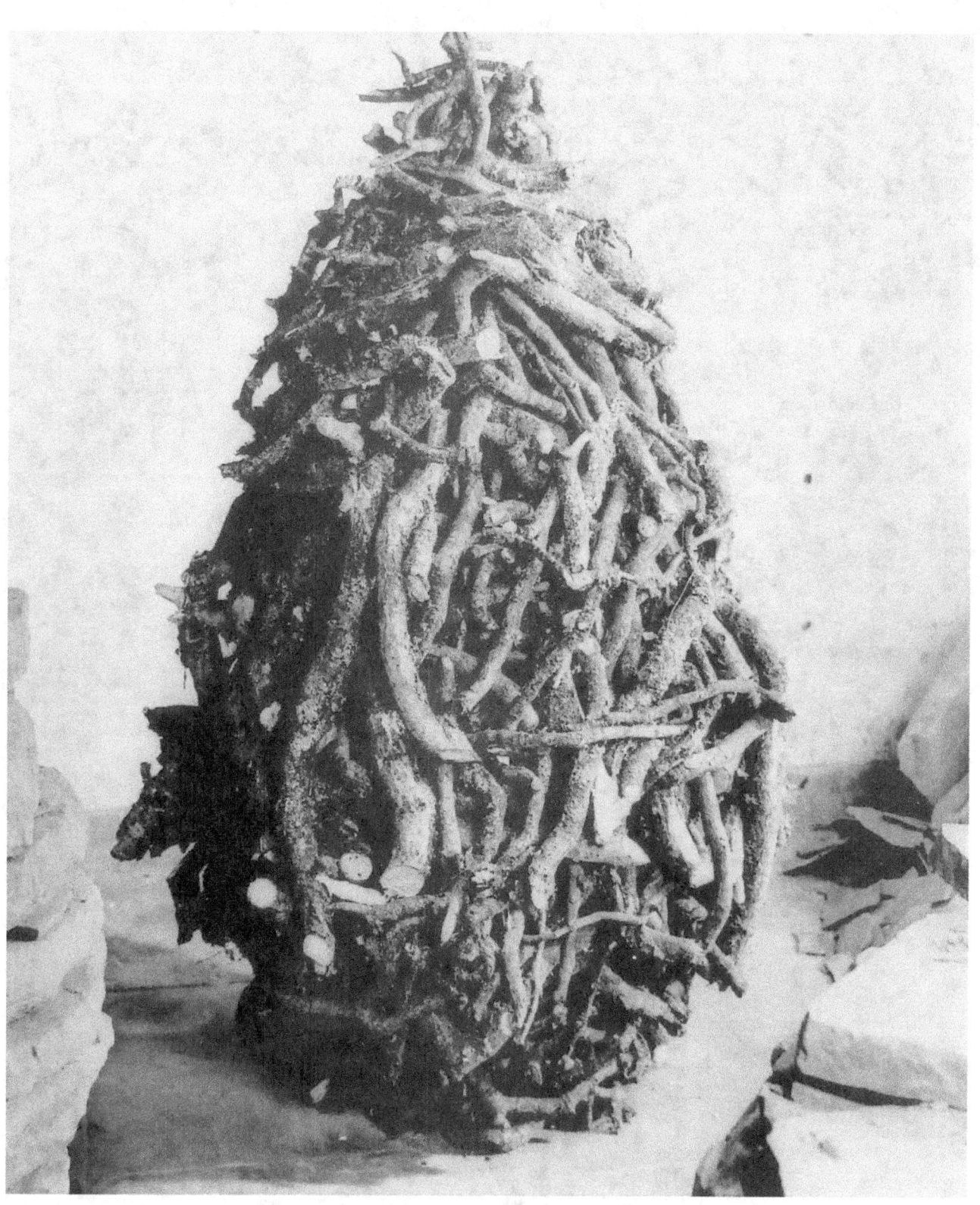

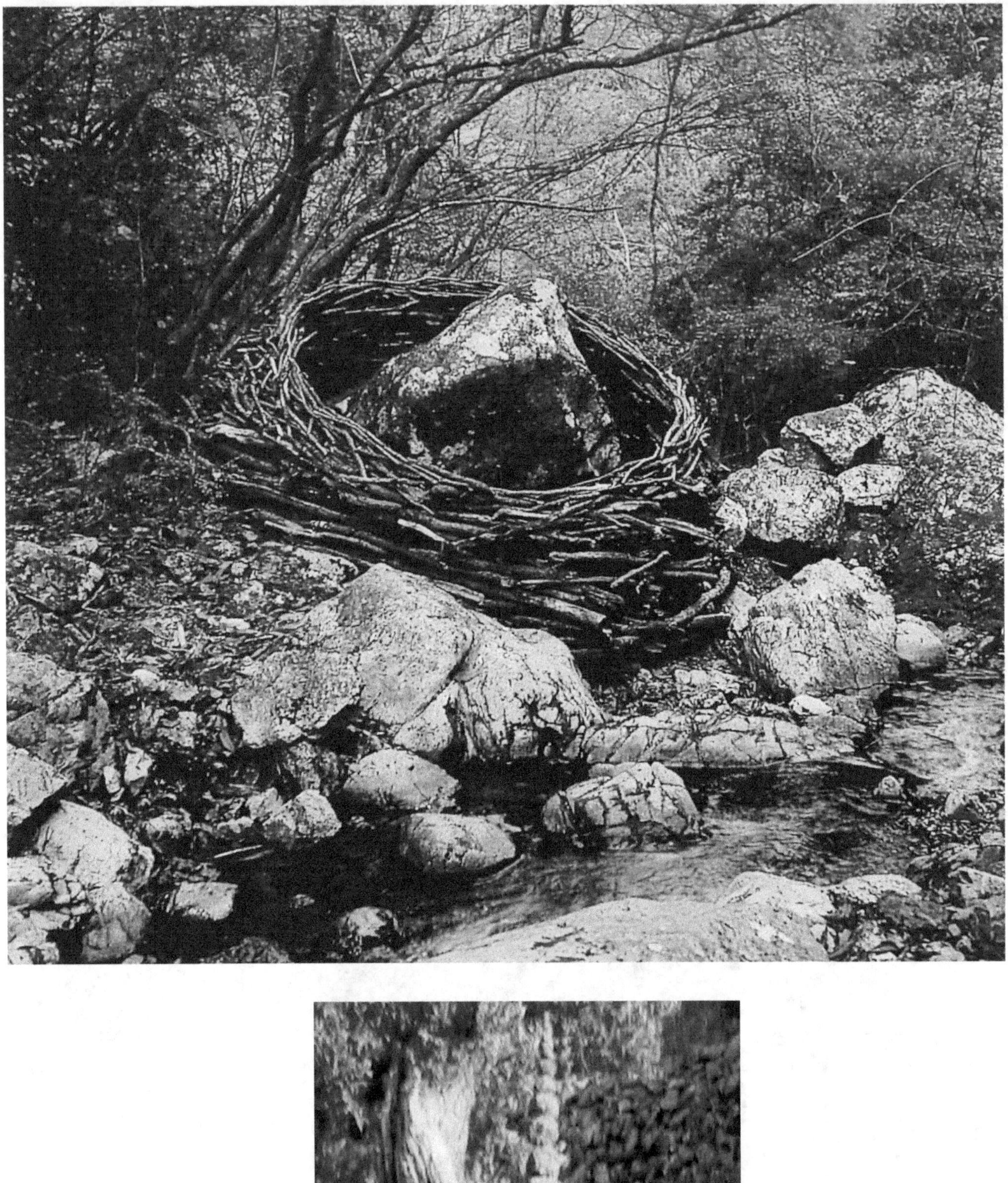

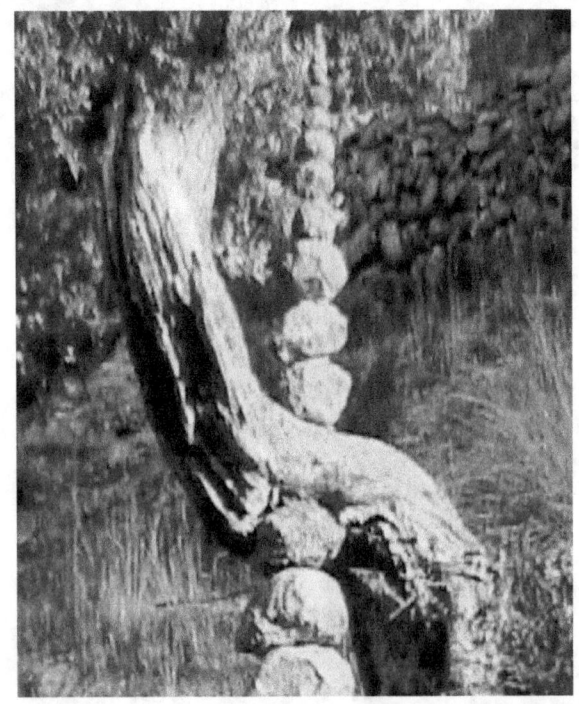

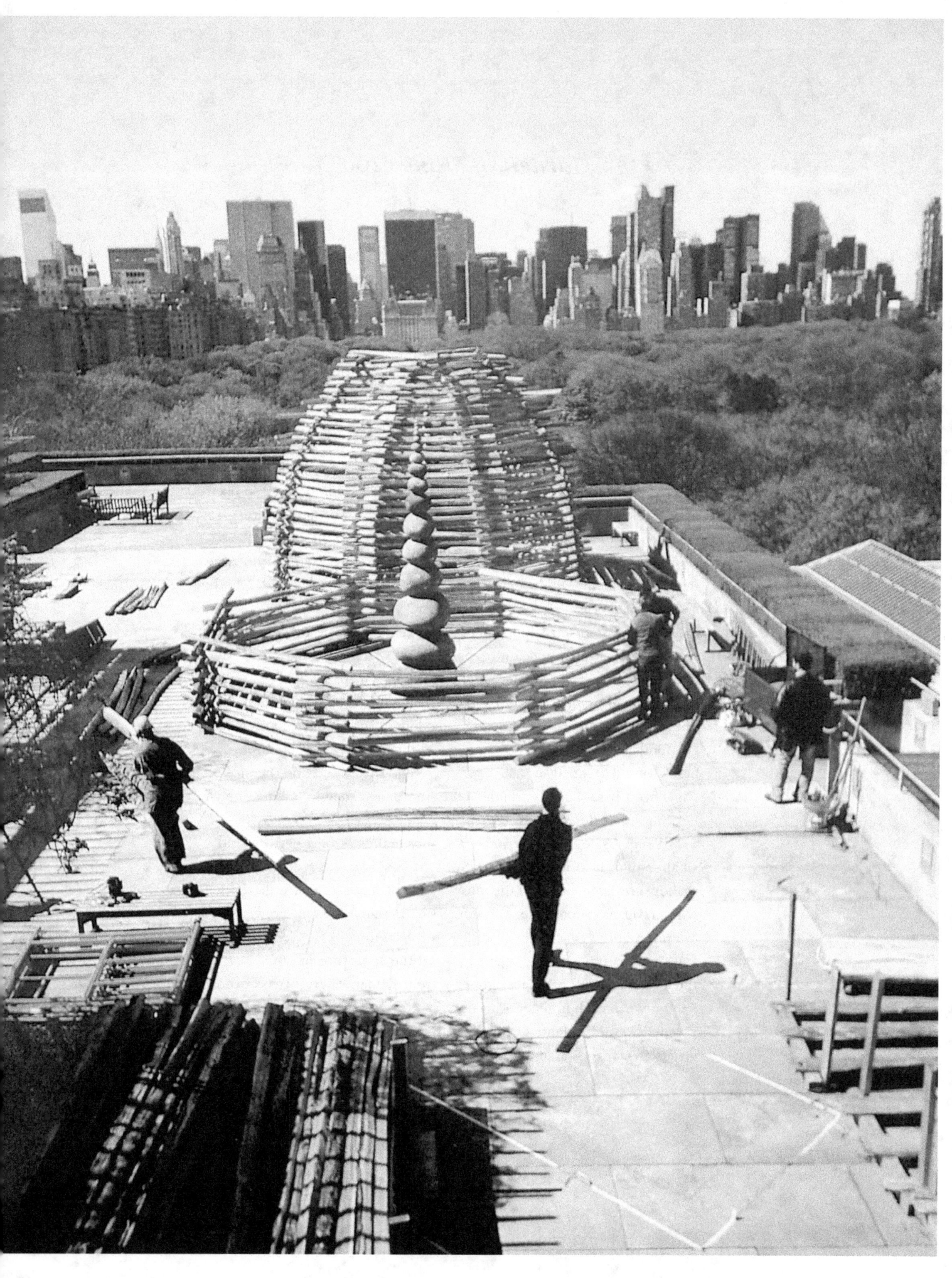

Garden of Stone (2003)

One of the most important of Andy Goldsworthy's later commissions was the installation *Garden of Stone* (2003) at the Museum of Jewish Heritage in Lower Manhattan. *Garden of Stone: A Living Memorial* was a group of 18 hollowed Vermont granite glacial boulders, with an oak tree inside (dwarf oaks, which only grow very slowly, and might take 100 years to reach twelve feet). Goldsworthy explained: 'I've resisted the temptation to put in mature trees... there's something very beautiful and profound about a flick of growth emerging out of a huge boulder, the fragility of that life.' The trees were planted at the top of each stone, with the hollow space below for the roots. The largest boulders weighed 13 tons. The trees will give out acorns in four years, which could be used to plant new trees when the trees in the boulders die. (Why 18? Because 18 corresponds to the Hebrew letter for *chai*, a symbol of life).

Garden of Stone was situated on the second floor garden, overlooking the Hudson River, with socio-political icons such as the Statue of Liberty and Ellis Island easily visible beyond.

Garden of Stone cost a million dollars (the Public Art fund collaborated with the museum), making it easily Goldsworthy's most expensive commission to date. Jacob Ehrenberg was project manager.

The glacial granite boulders were taken from Vermont (near Barre). They were then transported to a Connecticut quarry (Stony Creek) where Ed Monti, a guy in his seventies, hollowed them using a cutting torch. The bases were flattended so that the rocks would sit properly on the ground (Goldsworthy said that in trimming the stones, he aimed to retain as much height to each stone as possible).

The impression that *Garden of Stones* makes is of a garden that's smaller than it looks in photographs. It is set in a gravel space with shallow grey stone steps at the museum end. There's a thick wall, topped with gravel, along one side. The stones vary in size, and some are very big. There's a hole in each stone, with a tree growing out of it. Some of the trees were a few feet tall when I visited the sculpture in 2008 (maybe three or four feet). All of the stones were irregular. There's two or three feet between each boulder. The stones are evenly spaced throughout the garden. No other plants or flowers or trees or bushes are in the garden, giving the impression of a Zen Buddhist or Japanese garden.

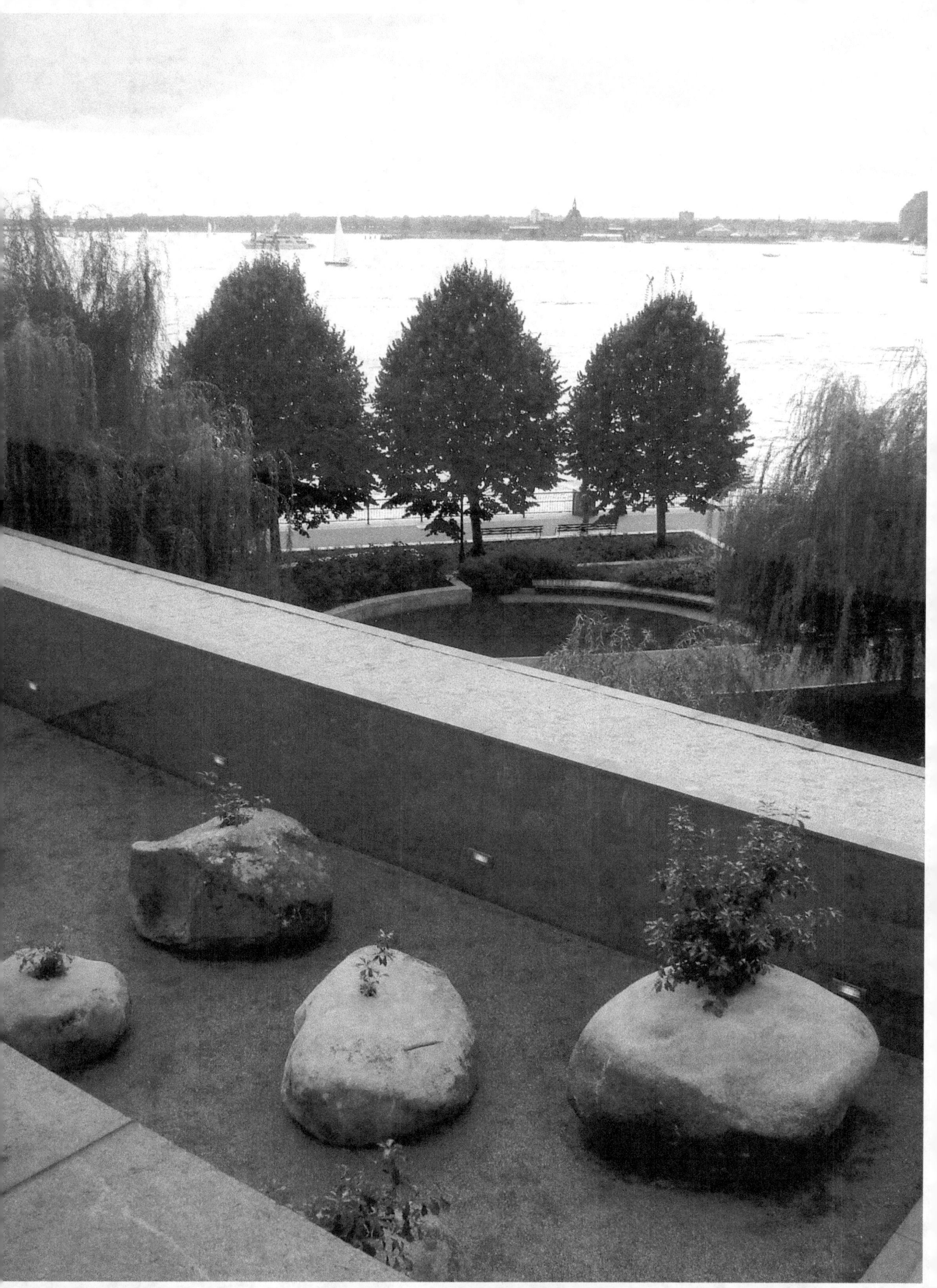

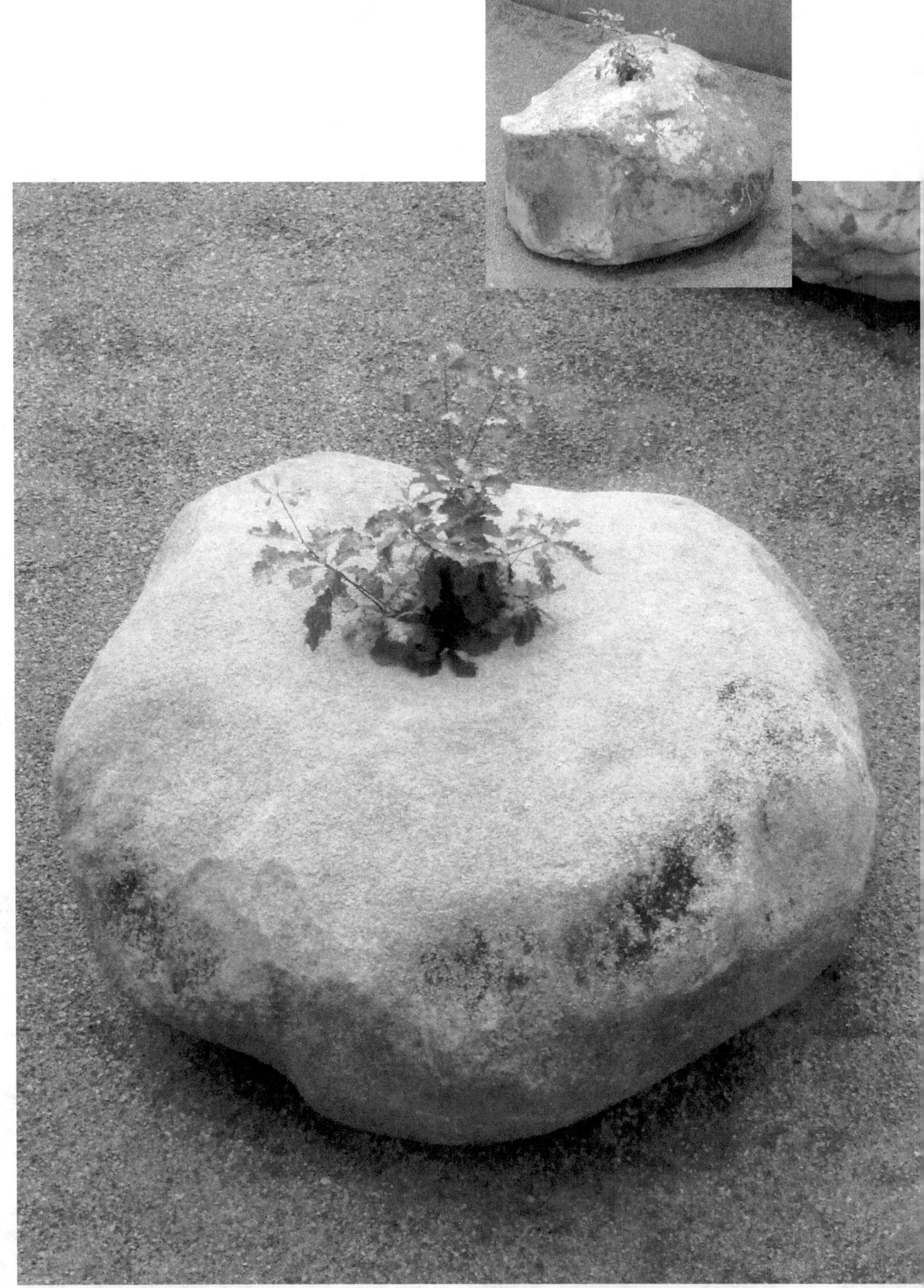

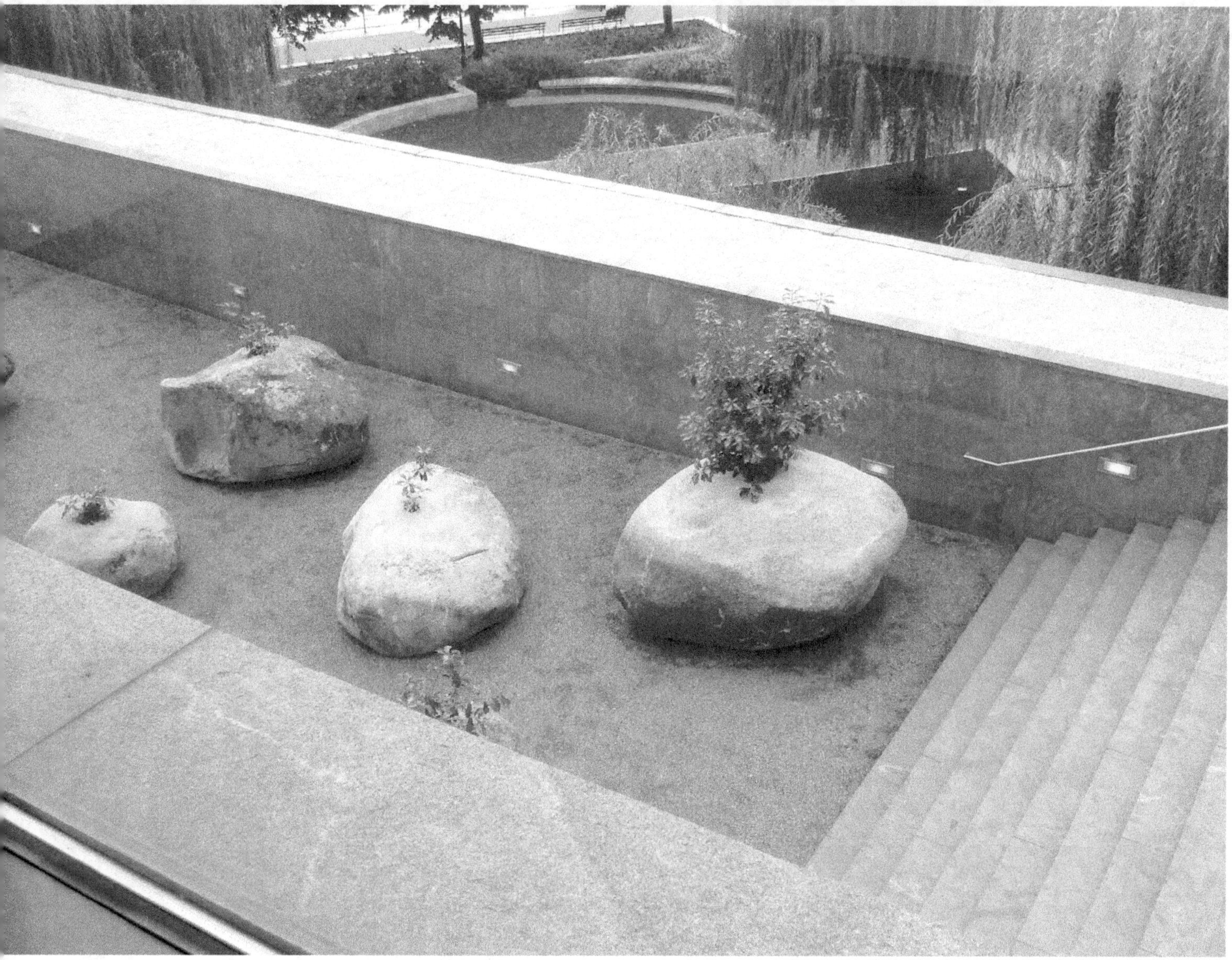

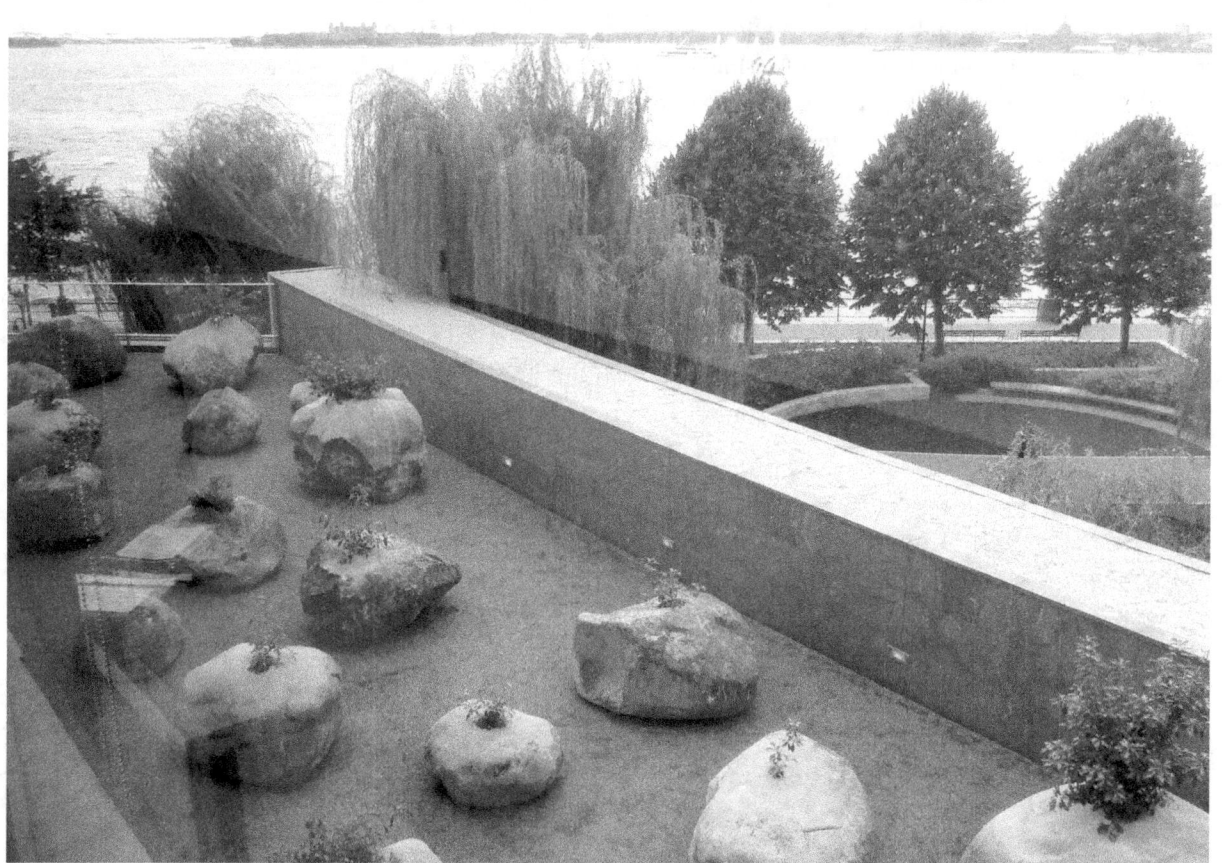

Roof (2005)

Andy Goldsworthy continued his series of prestigious exhibitions in the United States of America with *Roof* (2005), at the National Gallery of Art in the nation's capital. *Roof* consisted of nine slate domes which were basically very large versions of a form Goldsworthy had developed years ago: low, hollow domes of pieces of slate stacked on top of each other, with circular holes at the top. It's a permanent installation – in stone, as most of Goldsworthy's permanent installation tend to be.

Goldsworthy related the dome shape of *Roof* to the famous domes of downtown Washington, including the West Building of the National Gallery, the U.S. Capitol, the National Museum of Natural History and the Jefferson Memorial. For the *Roof* project, Goldsworthy used stone (Buckingham slate) from the same source as the materials for the domes of the Smithsonian Castle and Ford's Theater. That meant that Goldsworthy was using his regular method of choosing source materials that have some link to the site of the installation. In this case, however, Goldsworthy was working in one of the most famous historical centres in the Western world, as well as one of the centres of global political power. So the associations with historical buildings such as Ford's Theater, where President Lincoln was assassinated, or the U.S. Capitol, or the Jefferson Memorial contain far more political punch (or affinities of a different sort) than re-using the old stones from a dry wall in Cumbria for a reworked sheepfold. Sheep on a windswept Cumbrian hillside are one thing, but the buildings where Presidents of America worked and great political events took place is something else.

Roof is set in a terrace or garden behind a very long glass wall (a wall of glass and metal window frames), to the North side of the lobby of the East Building of the National Gallery of Art. Beyond the installation is a high wall, perhaps eight feet tall. The mounds fill up the entire (irregular) space. As it's a roughly rectangular space, and the structures are circular, Goldsworthy has chosen to have the mounds intersect each other, as well as to end abruptly at the walls. Yet he also has two of the mounds extend through the glass wall.

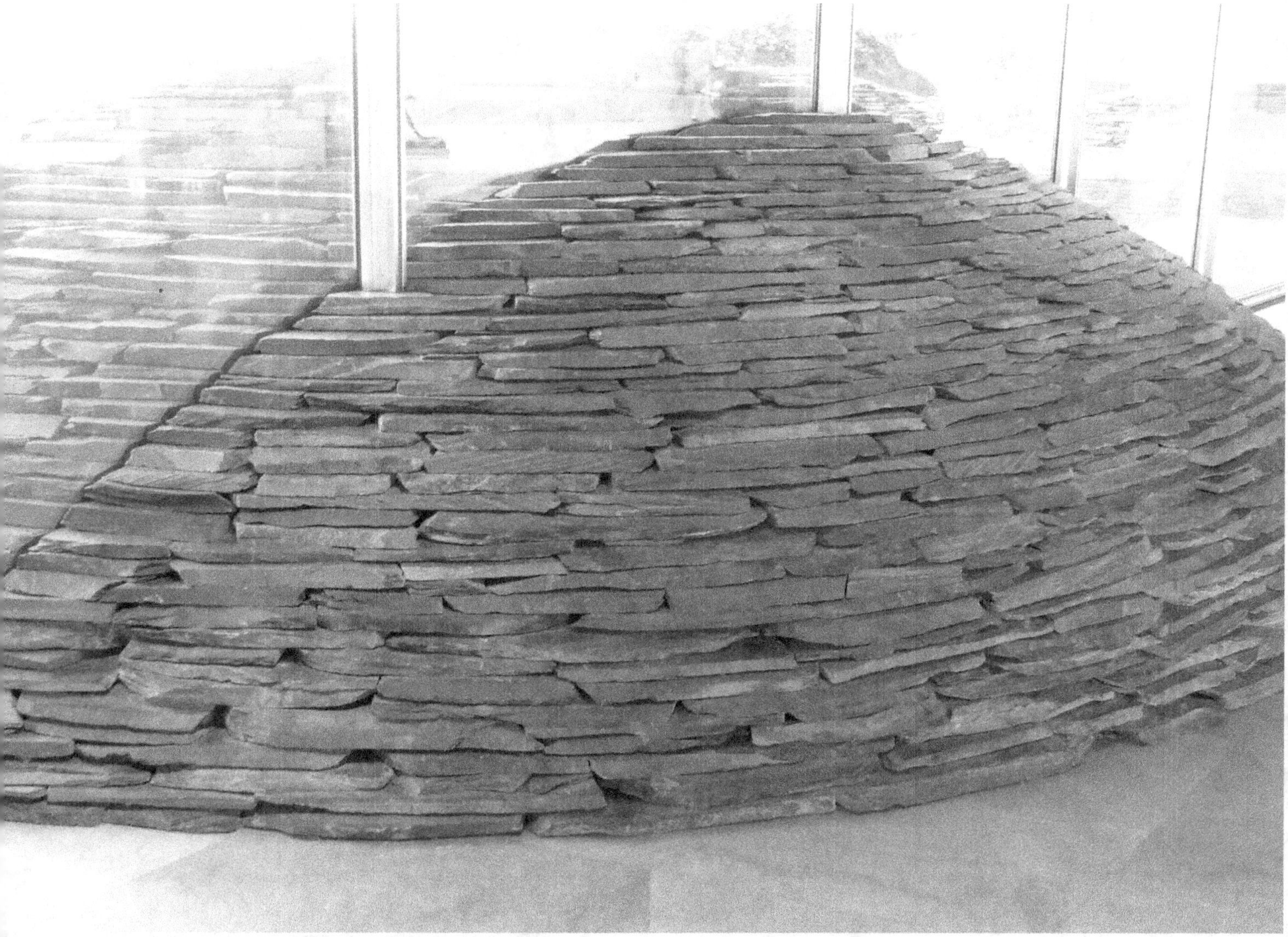

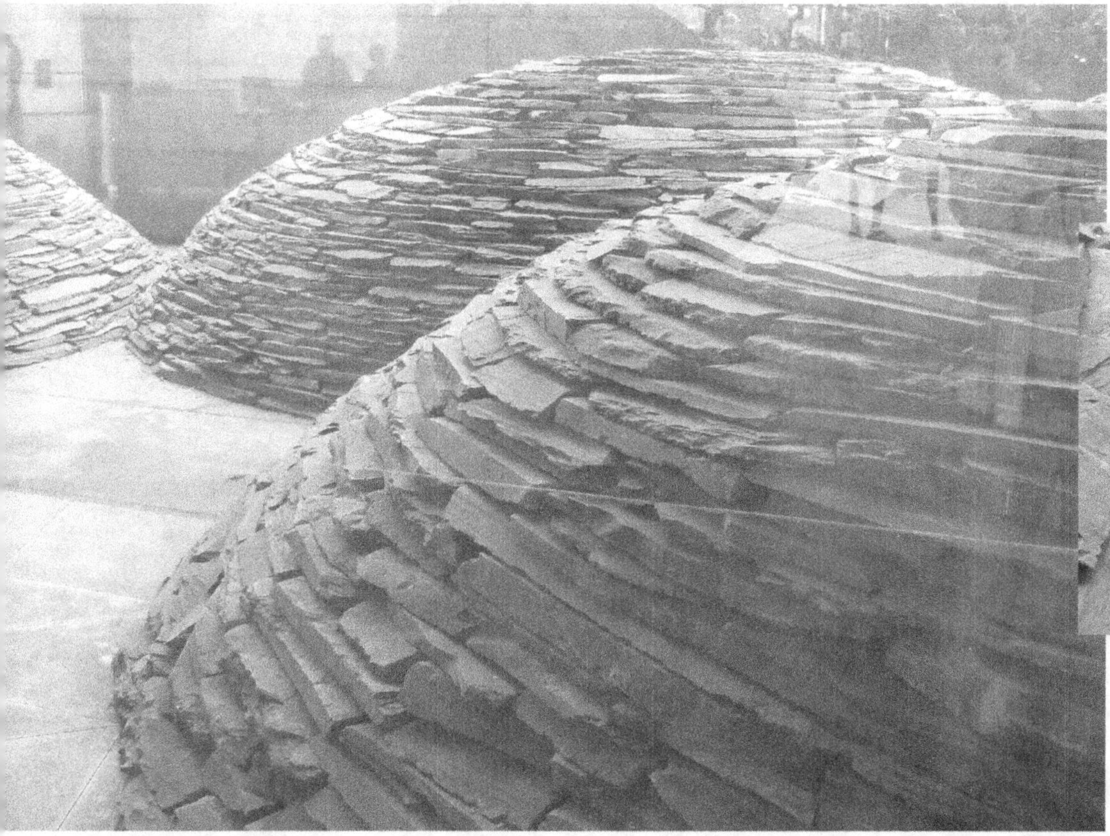

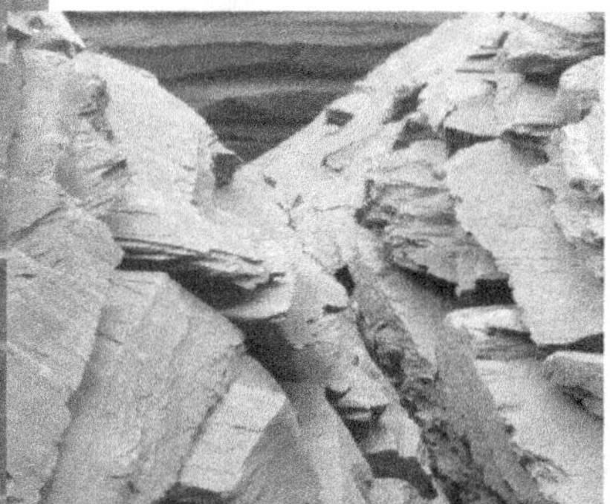

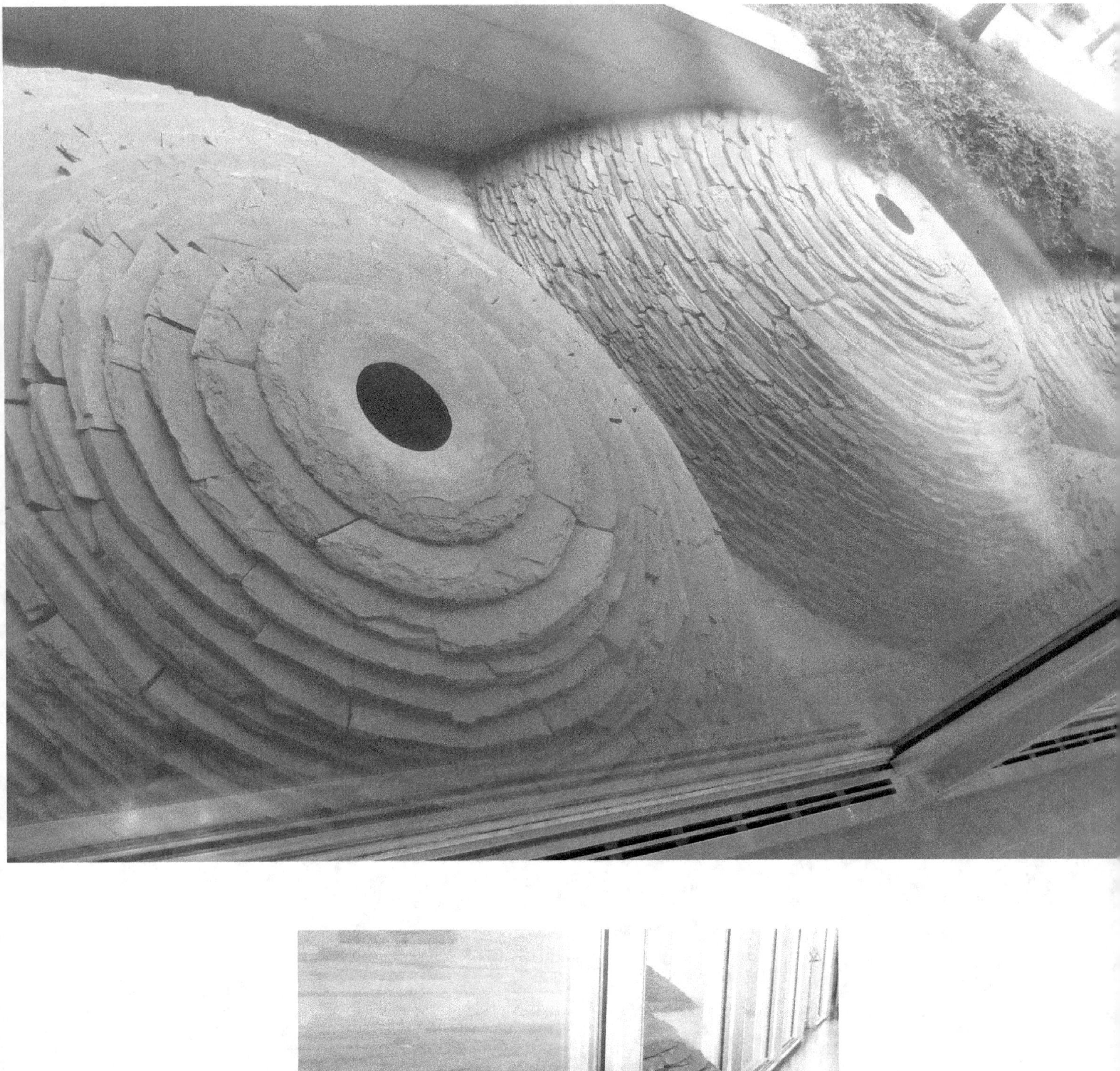

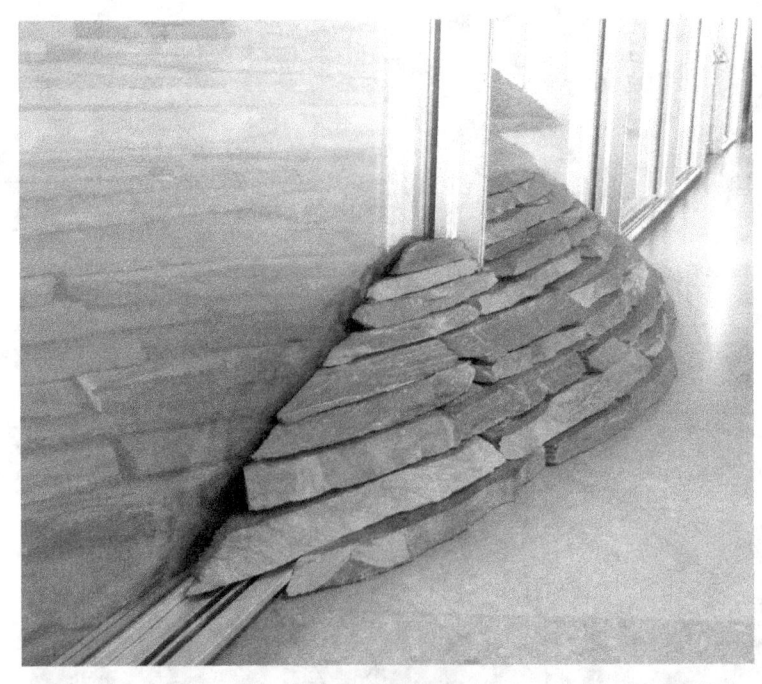

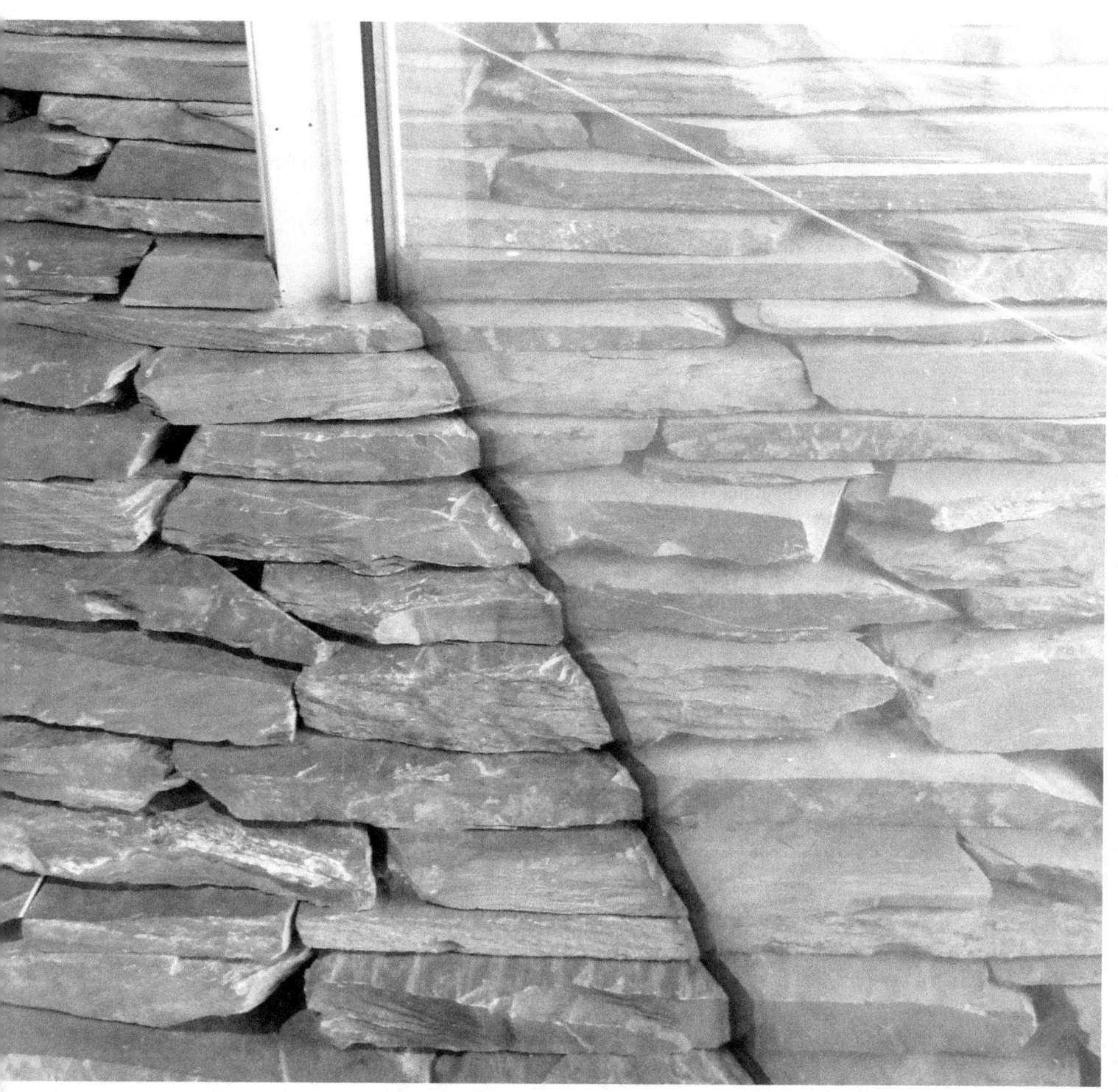

Drawn Stone (2005)

In San Francisco, Andy Goldsworthy was invited to participate in the re-opening of the M.H. de Young Museum (part of the Museum of Fine Arts) in 2005 by creating a site installation. A number of other artists were also asked to contribute to the re-launch of this major museum in San Francisco's Golden Gate Park, including James Turrell.

Goldsworthy designed a series of stones which would have a crack running through them and through the paving stones they stood upon, in the forecourt and outside the entrance to the refurbished museum. Entitled *Drawn Stone* (2005), it is an impressive, large-scale installation. Inevitably, given California's geological situation and the many earthquakes that have occurred there, some viewers the cracked line to tectonic plates.

The boulders (8 Appleton Greenmoore stones from Yorkshire in England) are flattish, and are spaced throughout the irregularly-shaped entrance area. They are about 18 inches to two feet high, and serve as benches for visitors. (That's significant – that this is a Goldsworthy sculpture that the public is invited to touch and sit on).

Placing Goldsworthy's sculpture outside the entrance to the De Young Museum has them act as an intermediary and lead-in to the museum itself: *Drawn Stone* is thus both an indoor and outdoor sculpture, part of the museum but also situated just outside it. It's the same with *Roof* in Washington: those domes are obviously part of the National Gallery of Art, yet they are also placed outside the walls of America's premier museum.

When you visited the de Young Museum, you can follow the crack in the paving and the boulders that Goldsworthy and his team produced, and no doubt people do just that. It begins, actually, outside the museum, and there's a bit of info explaining the work. The crack leads from that spot at the path and leads the visitor into the entrance area and the boulders themselves.

Spire (2008) was not related to the de Young Museum commission: it was a 100-foot tall tower built from trees in the Presidio area of San Francisco. Not the easiest place to find (the Presidio, a former military zone, is a large maze of small streets), it's best to aim for the golf course HQ. The *Spire*'s nearby, along a path. Definitely worth a visit, though.

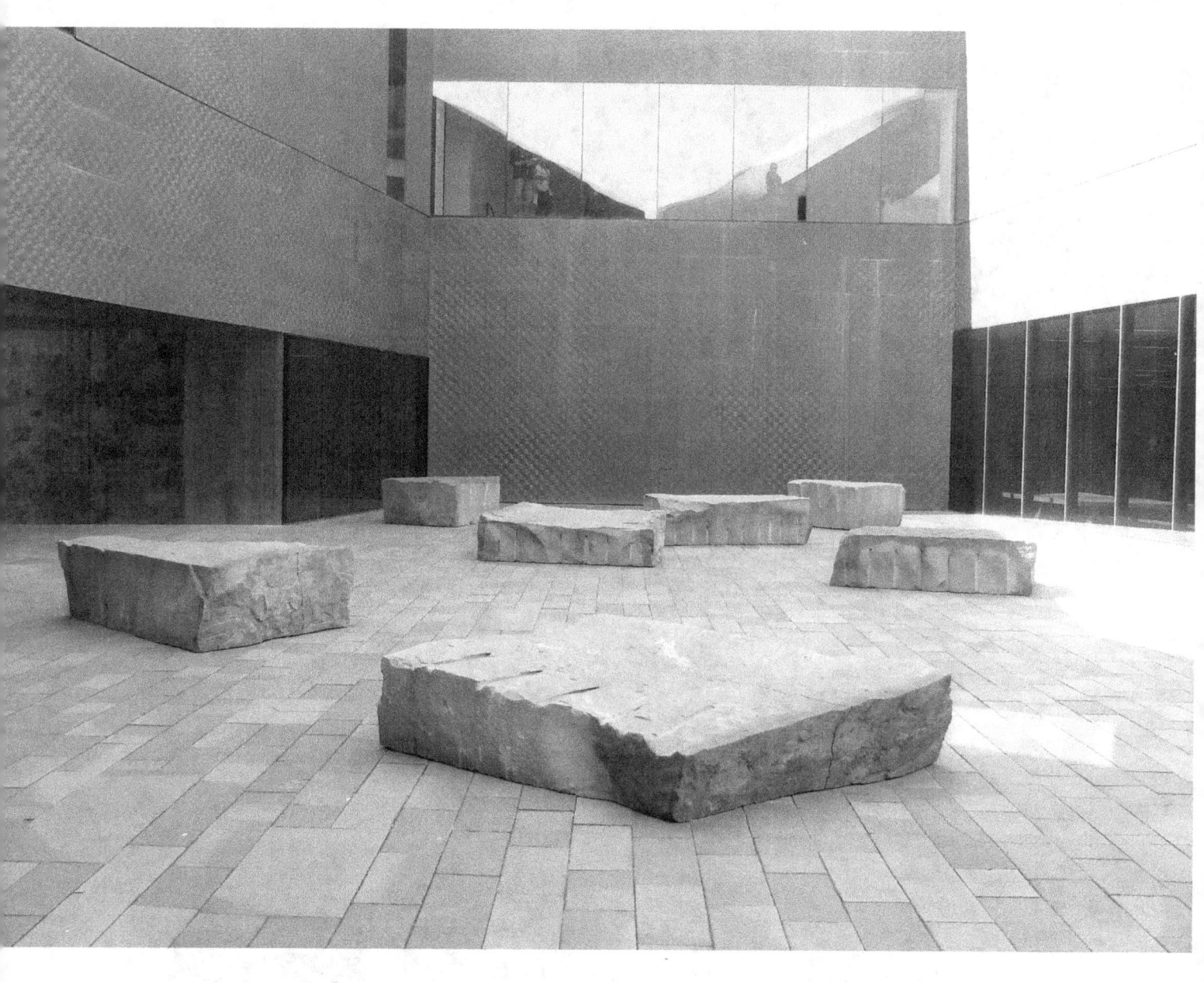

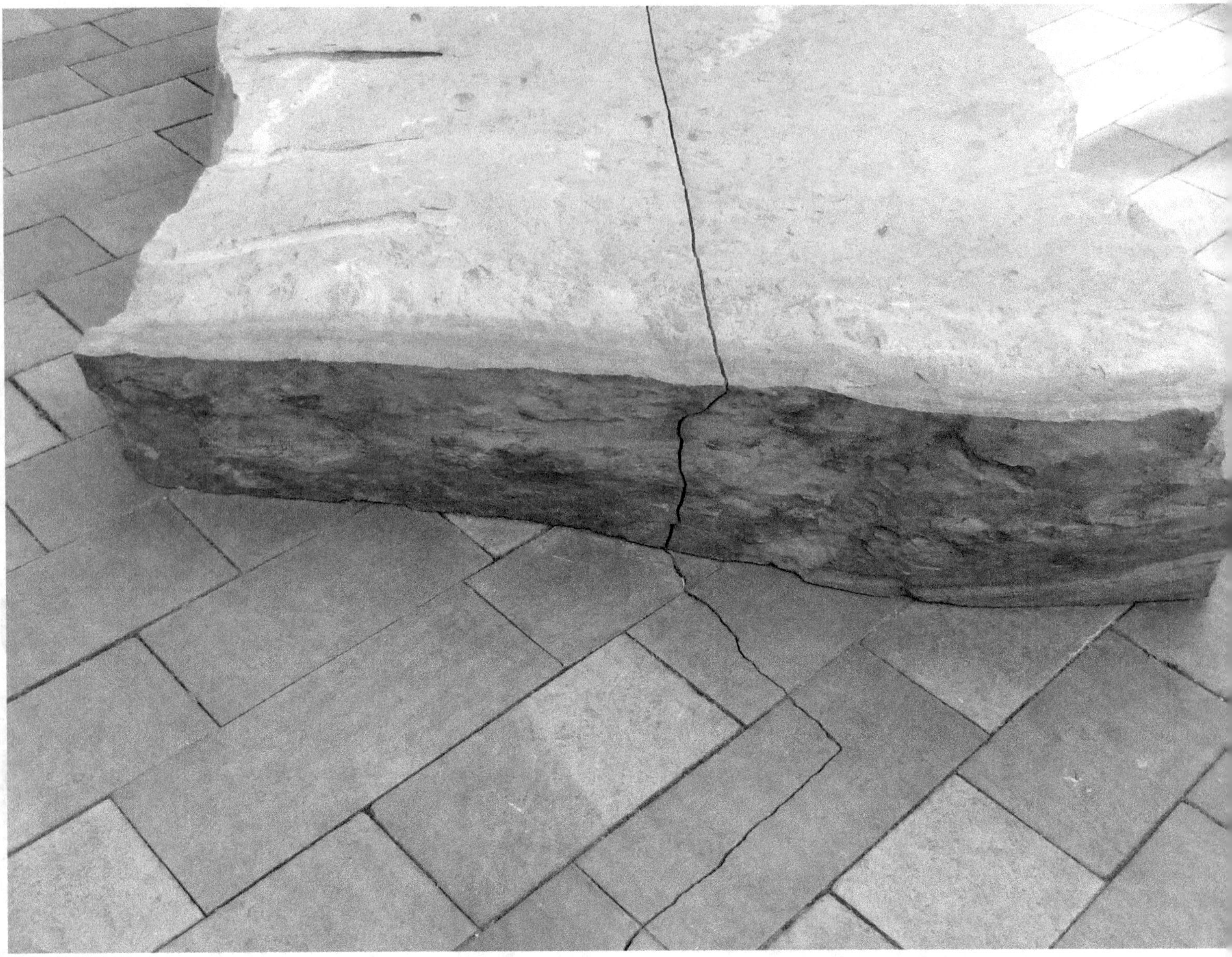

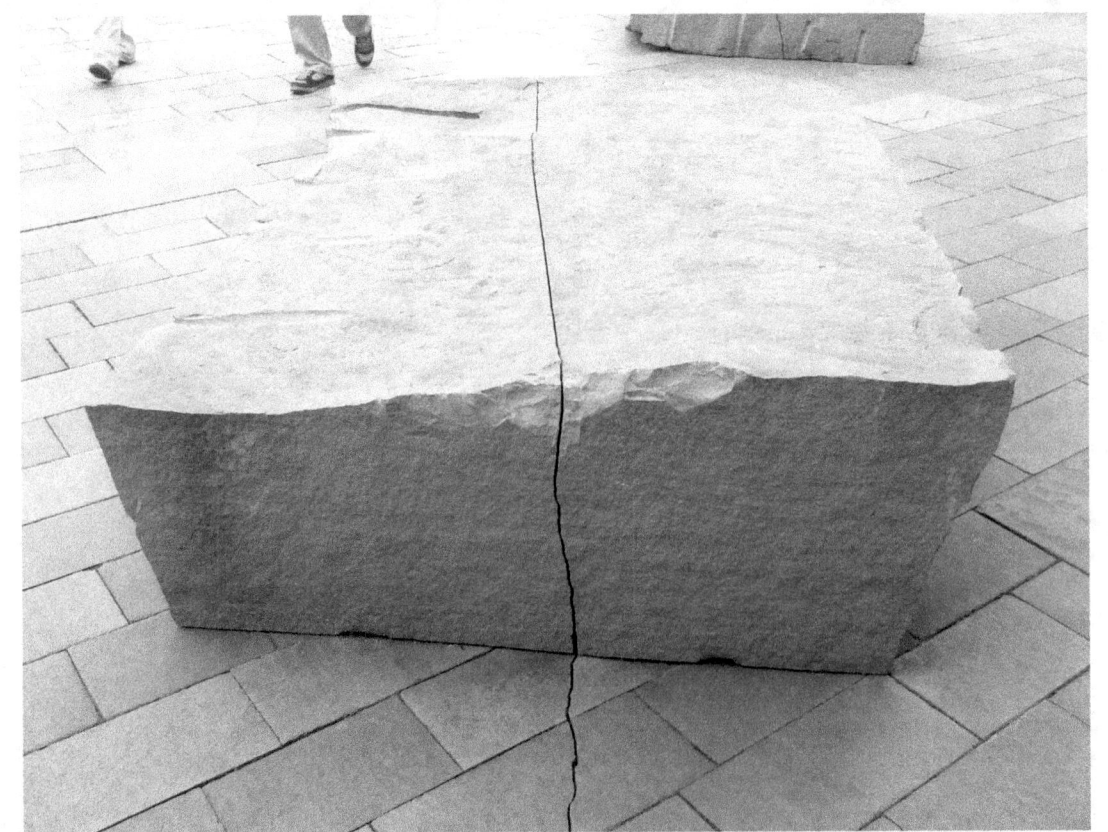

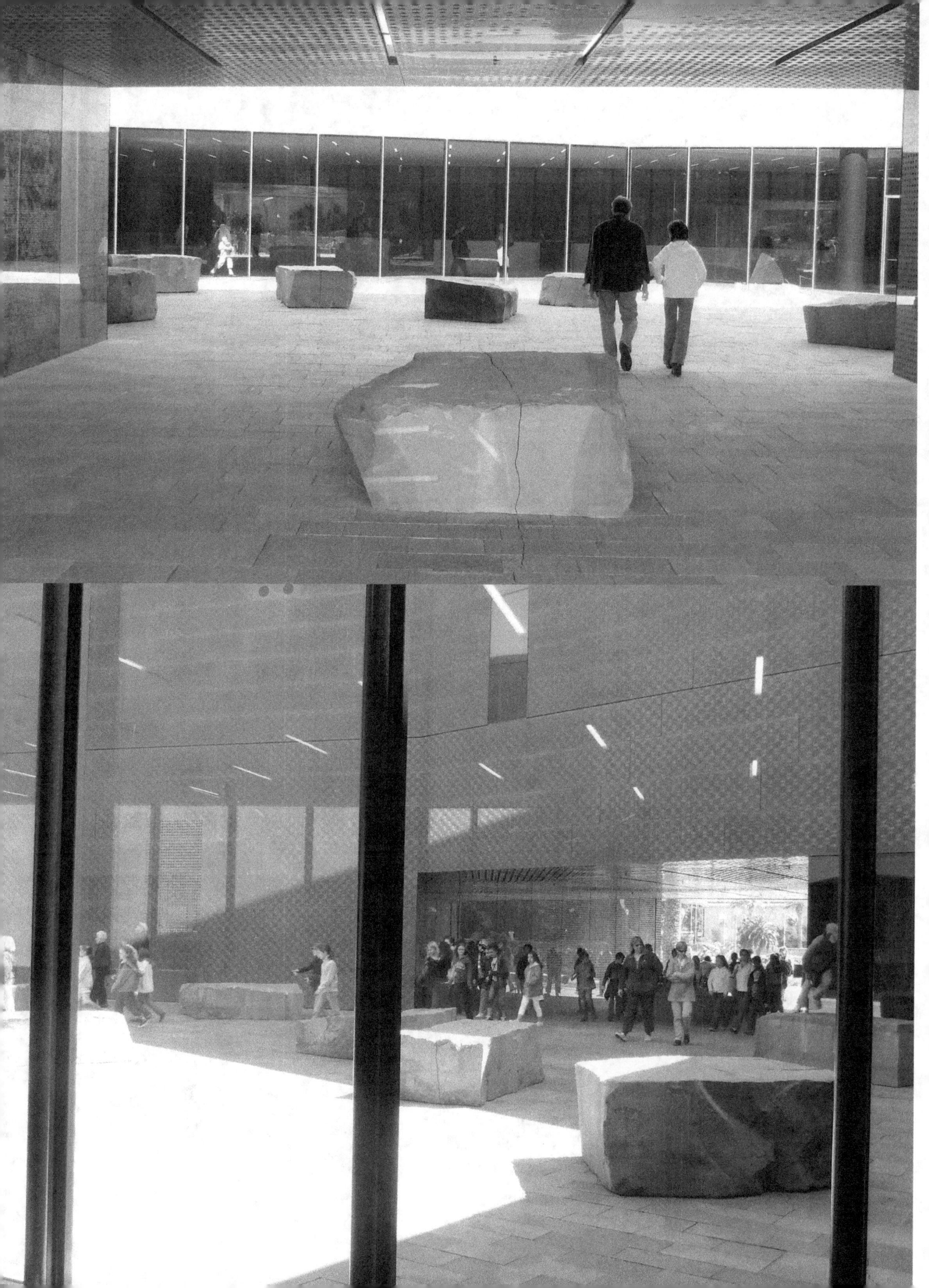

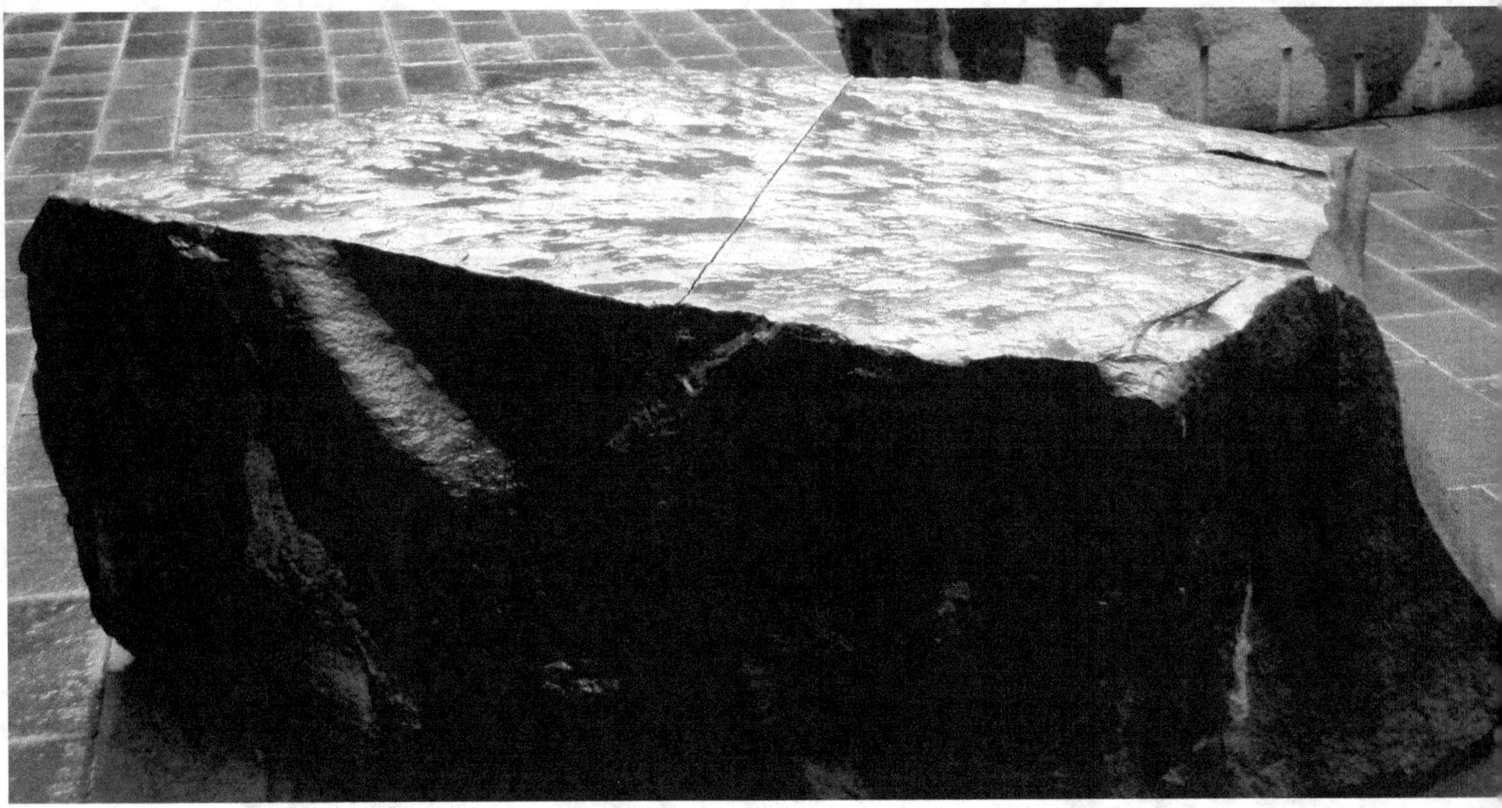

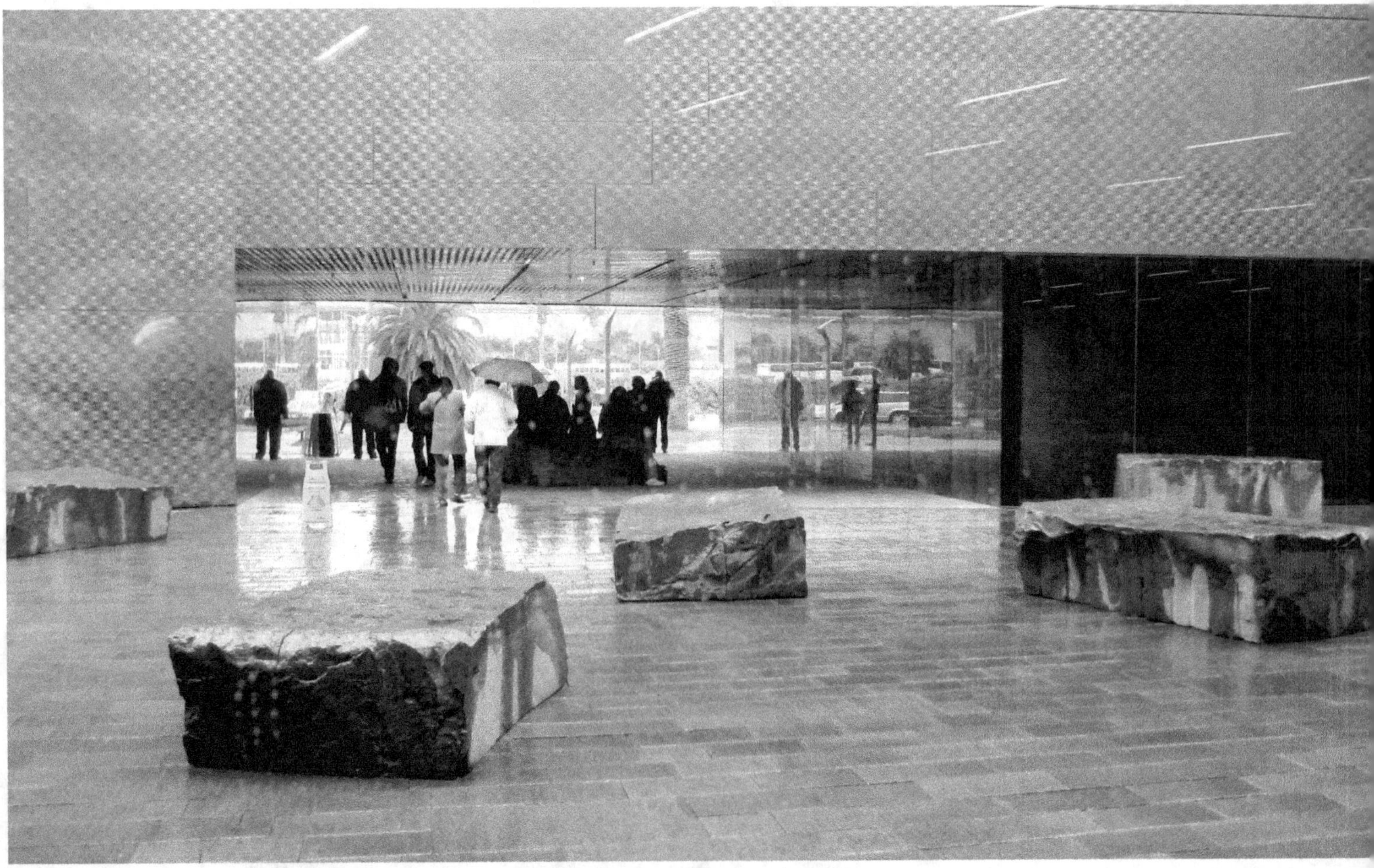

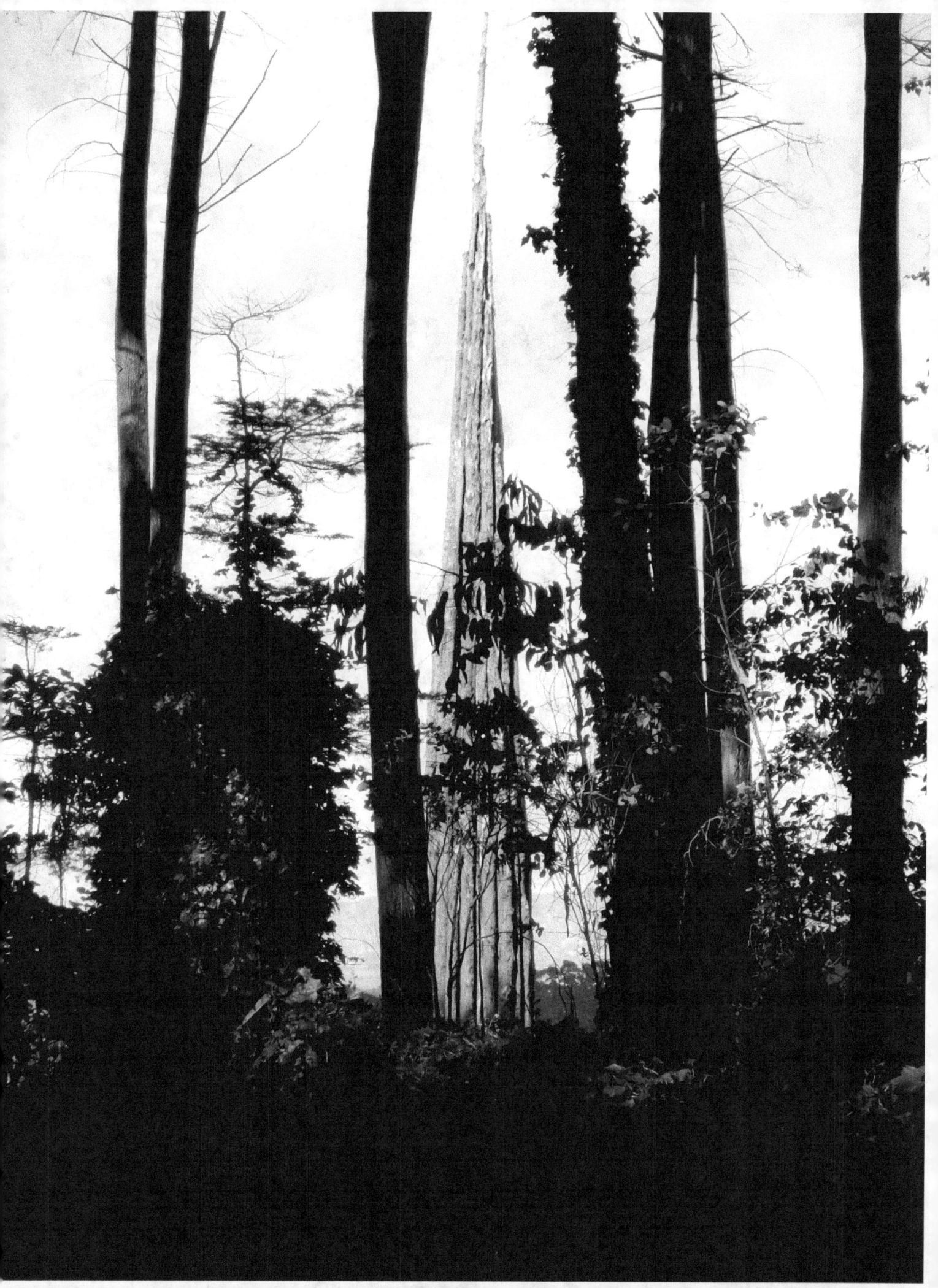

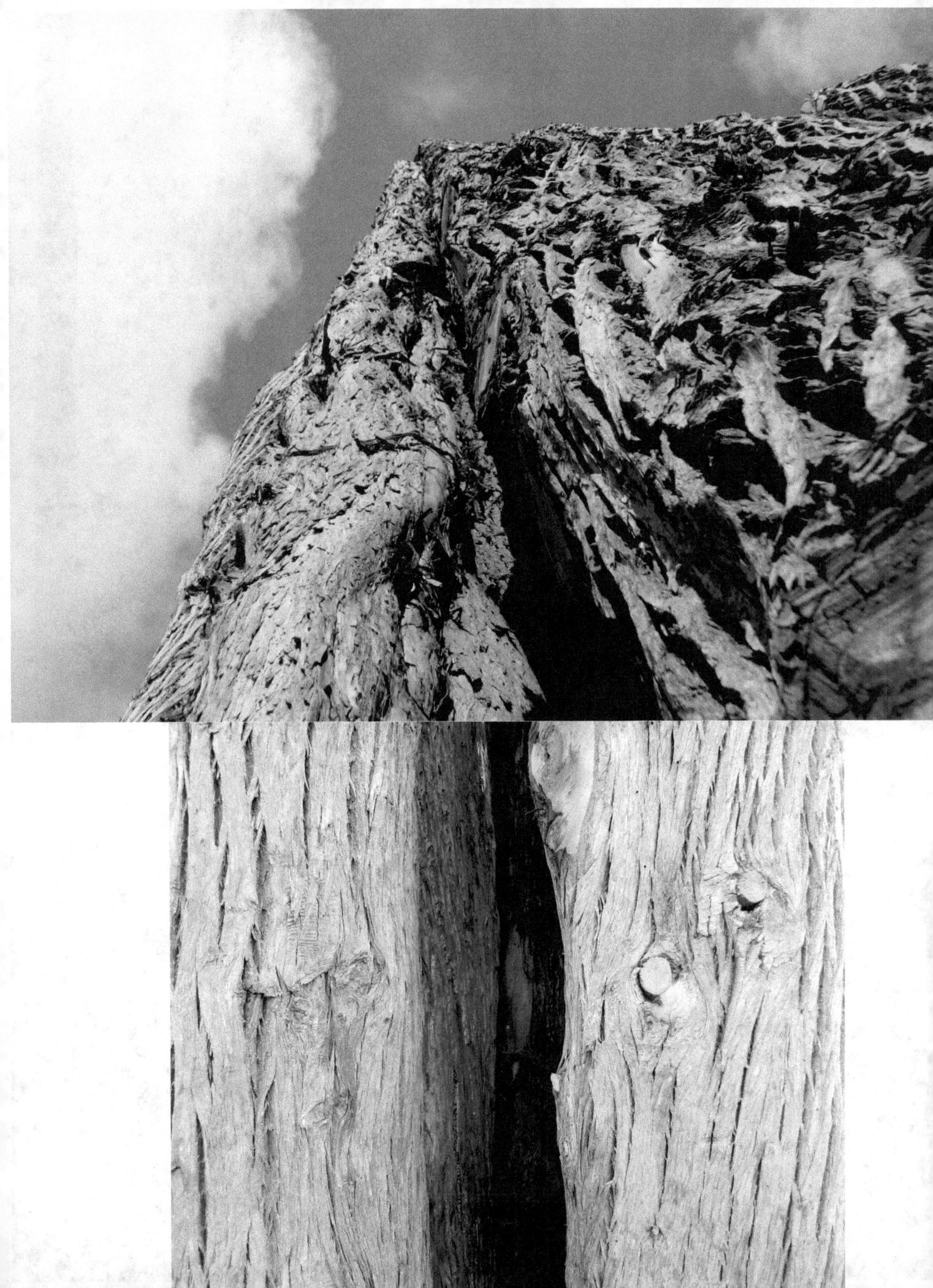

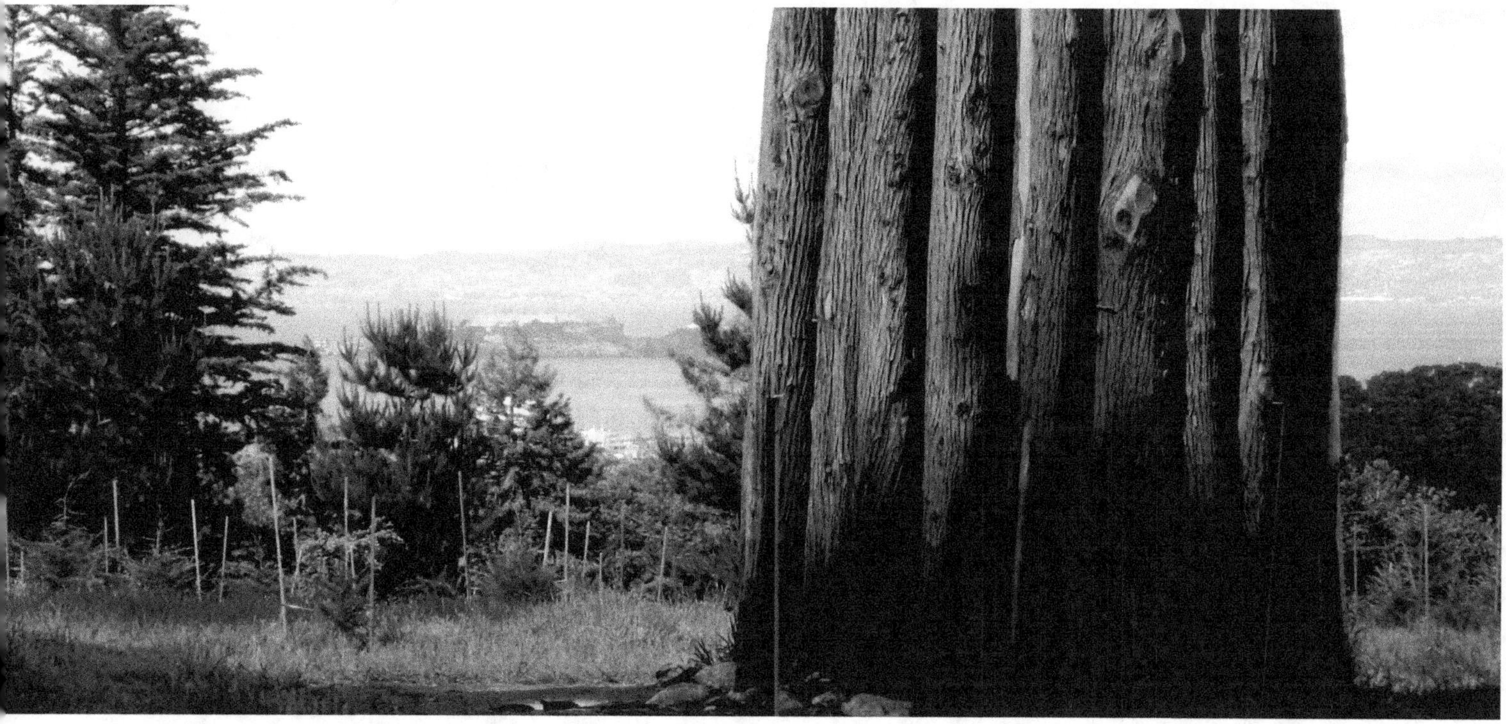

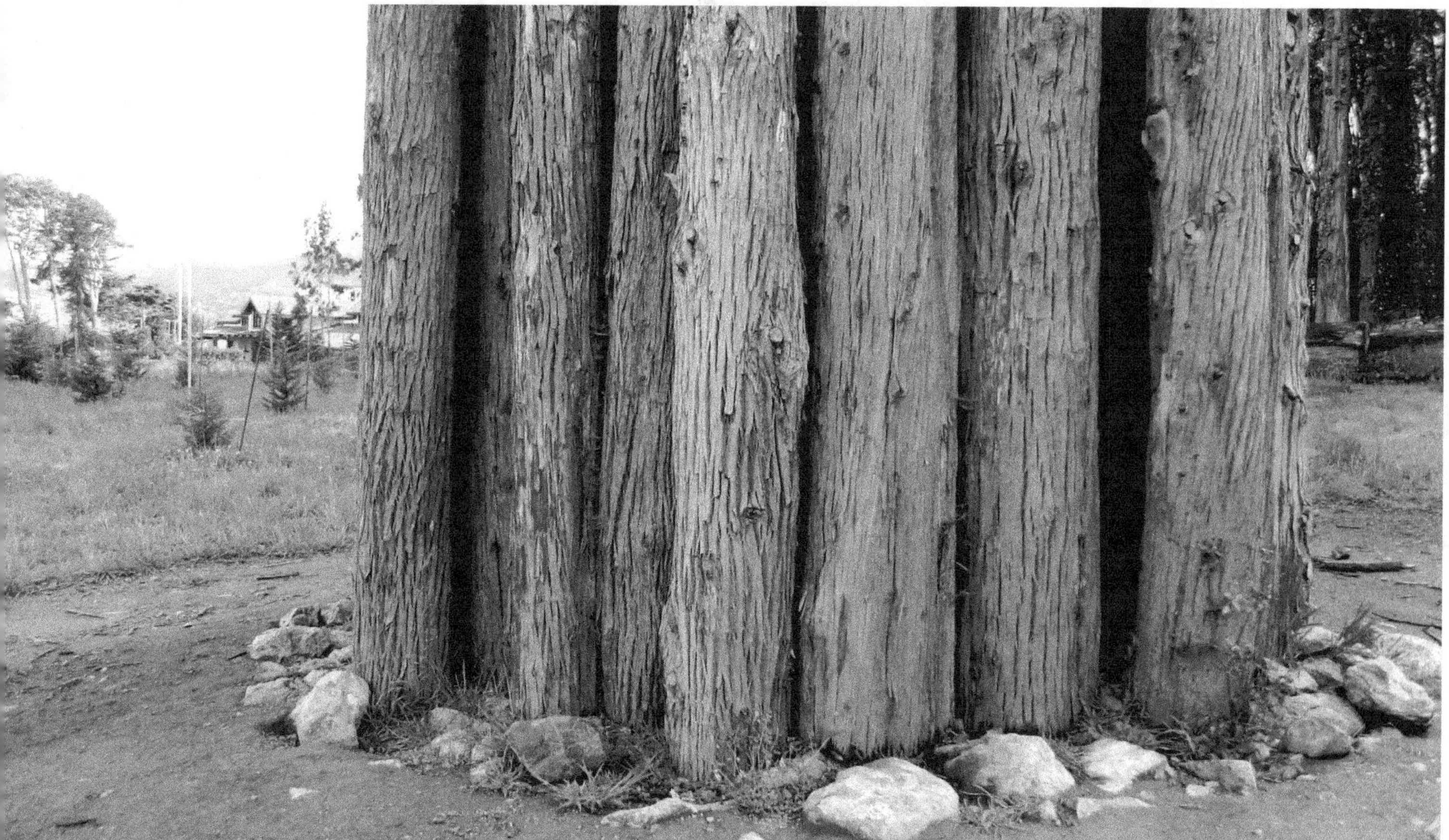

Found Goldsworthy Works

As you study the art of Andy Goldsworthy, you might start to see 'found' Goldsworthy works on your travels. I've discovered some rocks, trees, formations, and situations which remind me of Andy Goldsworthy's art, in places like the deserts of Southwest America and Dartmoor in England. I have included some discoveries here.

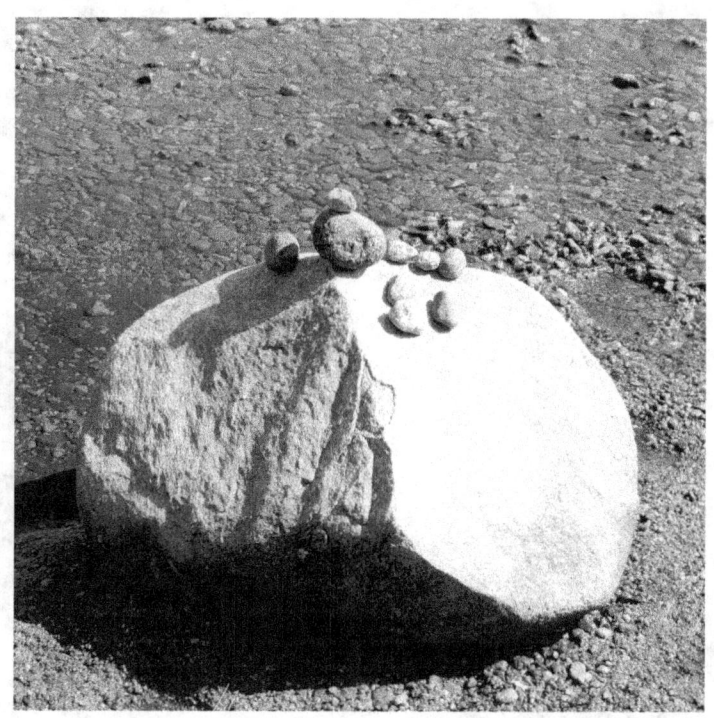

Someone had placed these stones on some boulders in a stream in the Rocky Mountains near Estes Park in Colorado.
Is it me or are these sorts of things becoming more common? Surely the influence of land art and artists such as Andy Goldsworthy is increasing.

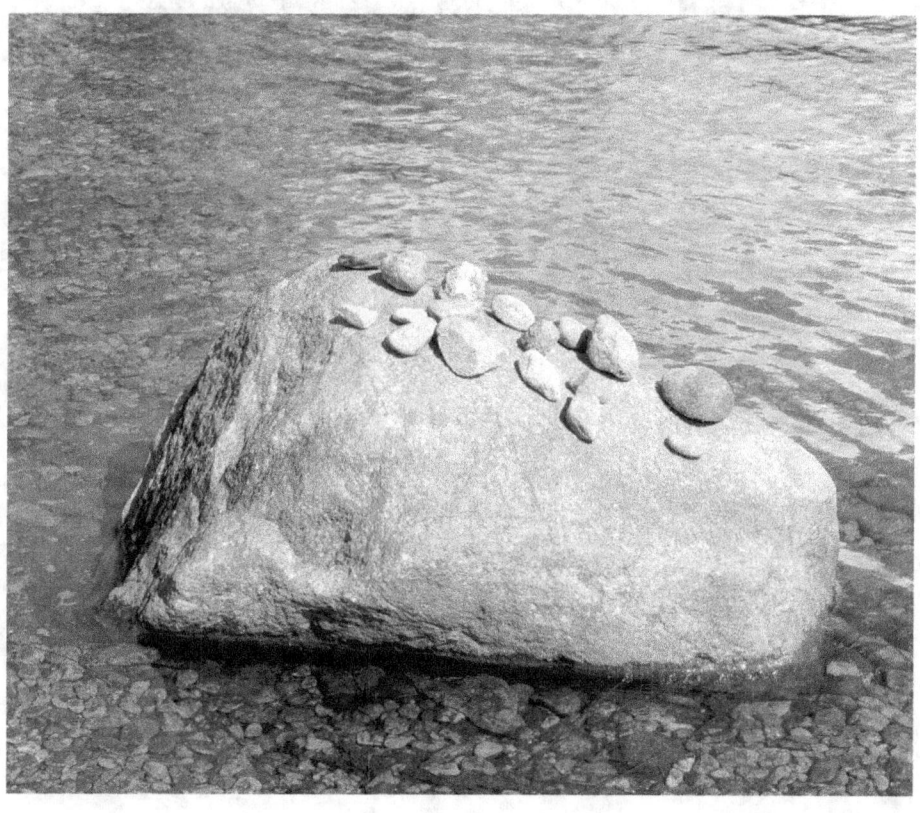

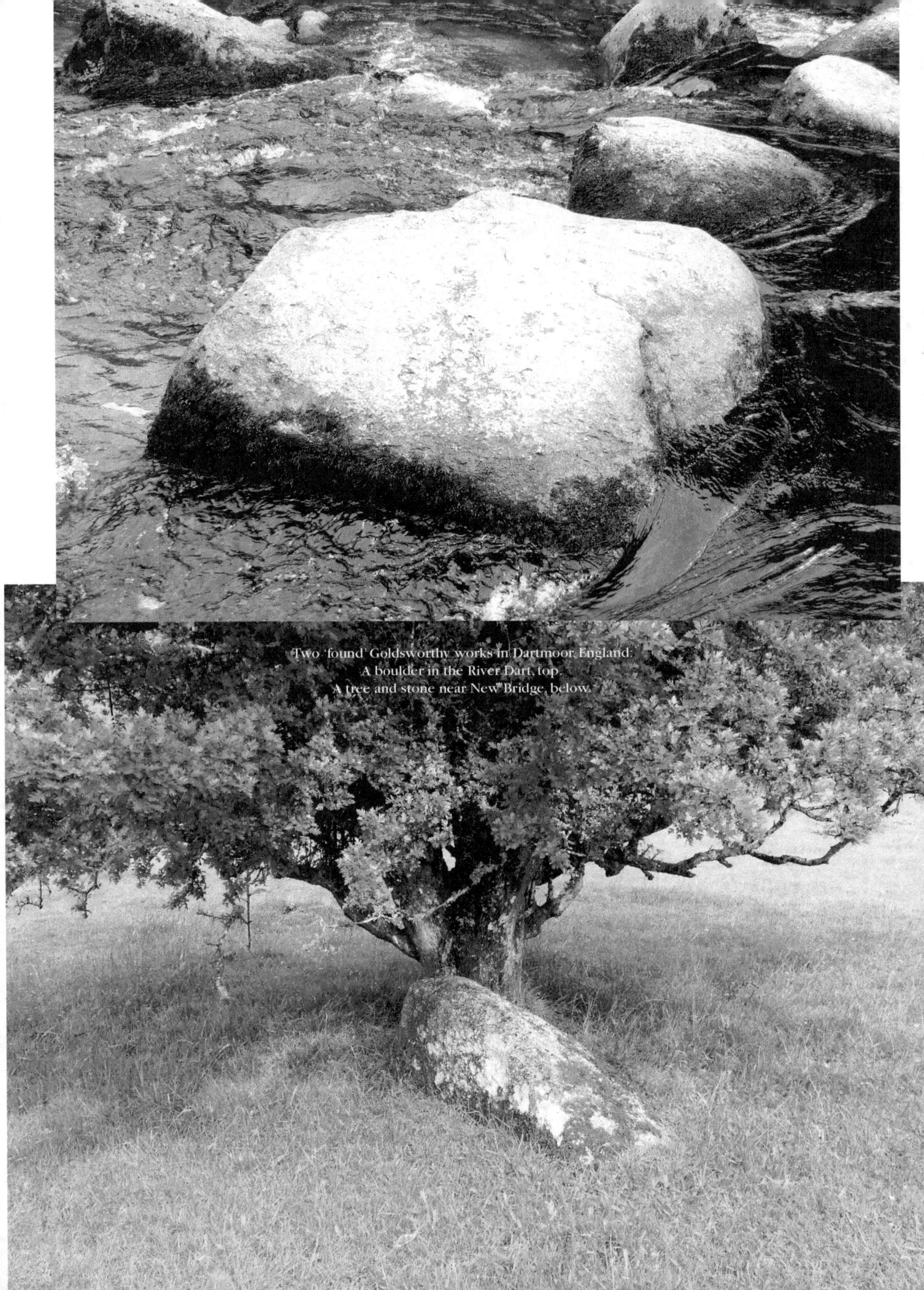

Two 'found' Goldsworthy works in Dartmoor, England:
A boulder in the River Dart, top,
A tree and stone near New Bridge, below.

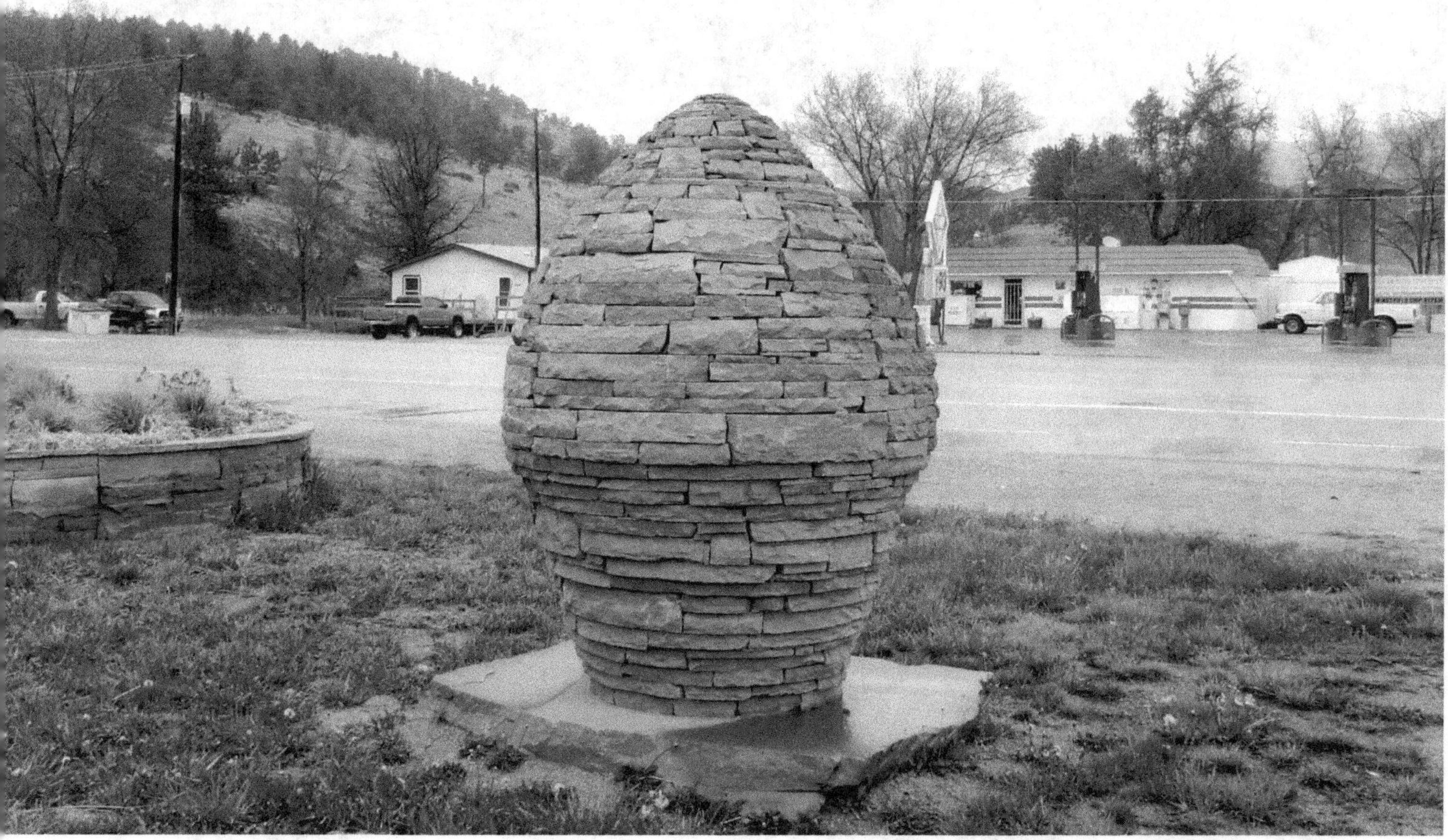

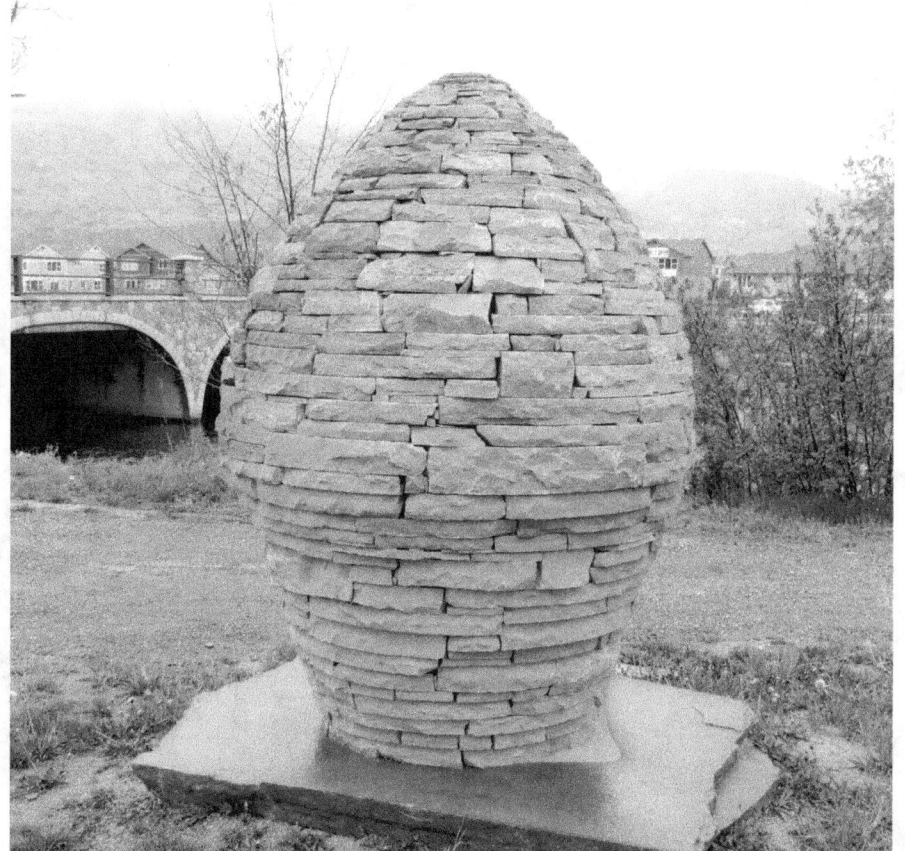

Driving through the Rocky Mountains recently, I passed this stone cone next to the highway in Lyons, Colorado. Surely this has been inspired by Andy Goldsworthy?

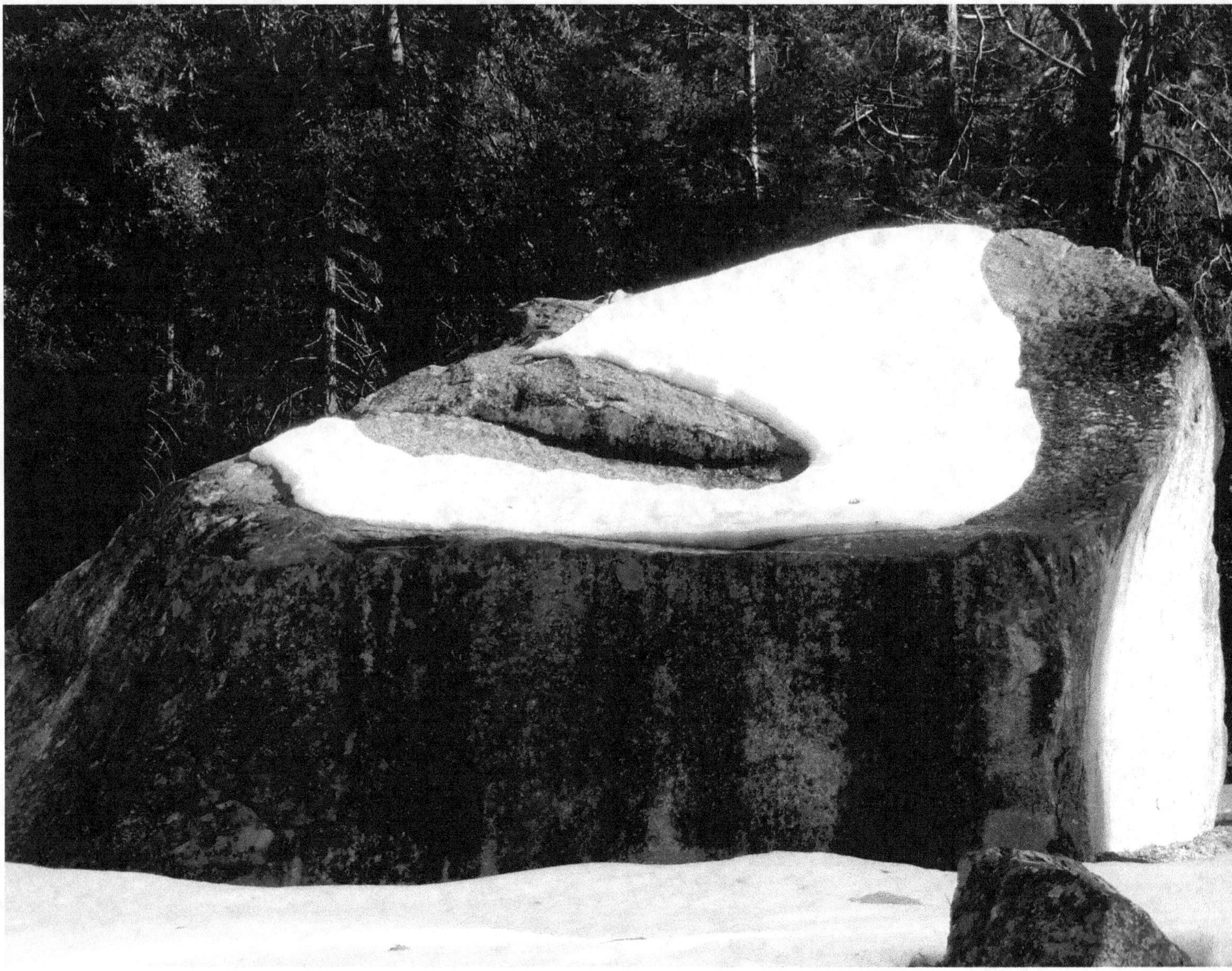

'Found' Goldsworthys:
Boulders in the snow in Yosemite, California,
top and right.
Tree and roots in Kent, England, below.

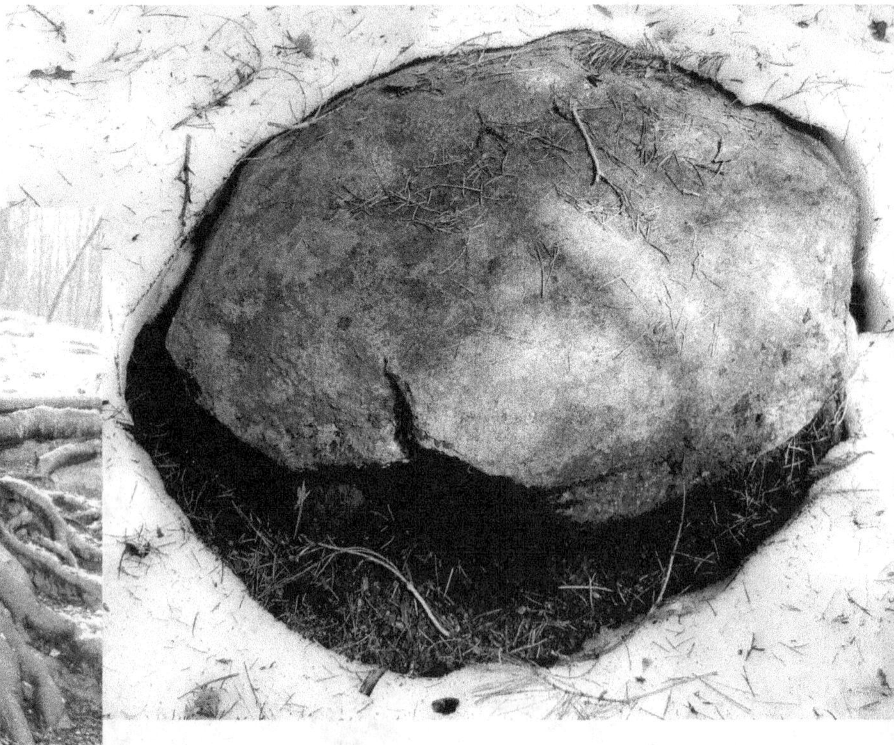

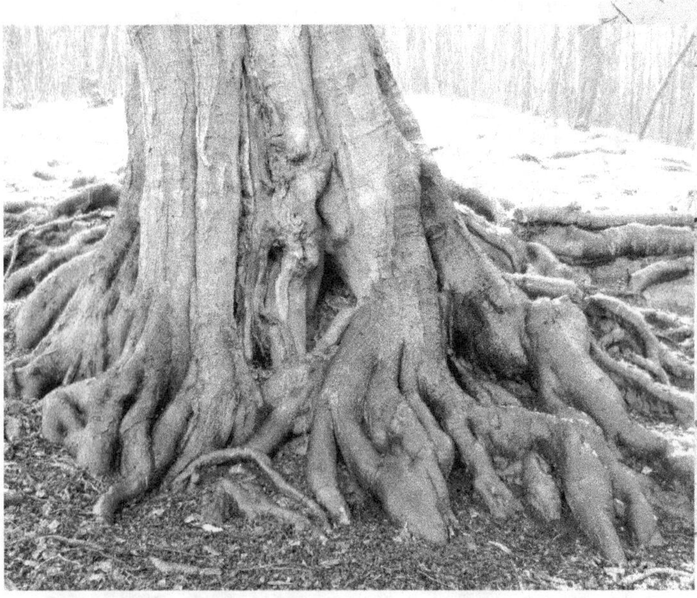

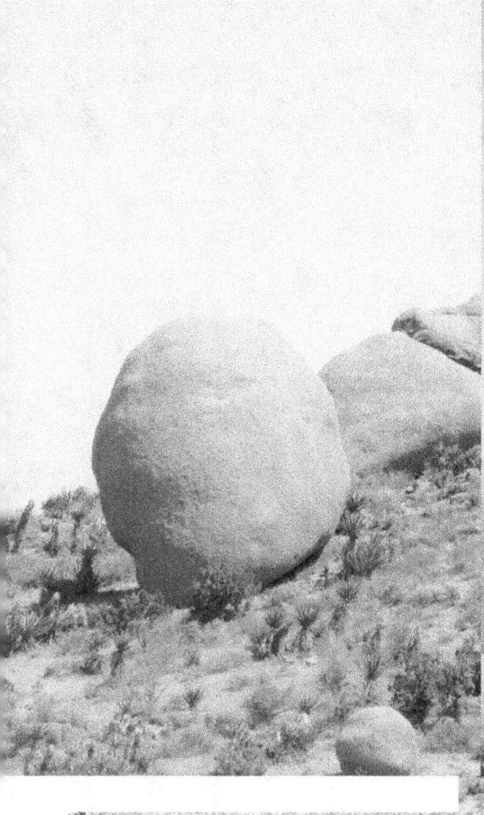

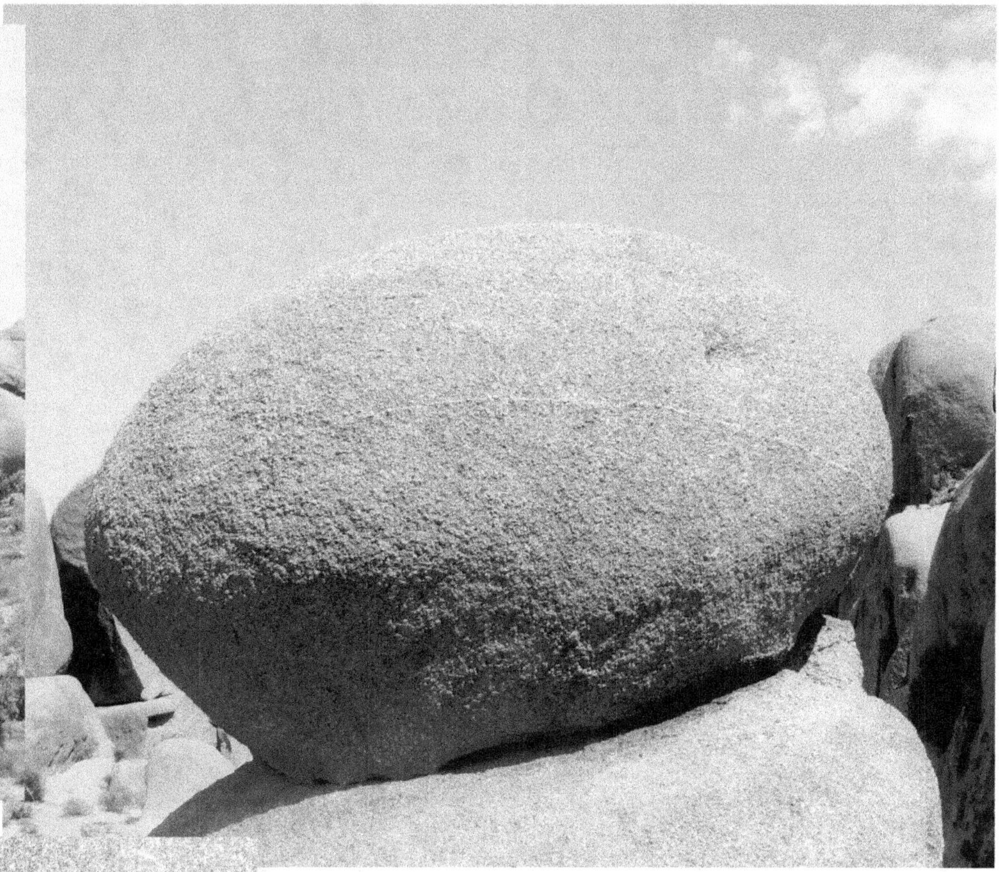

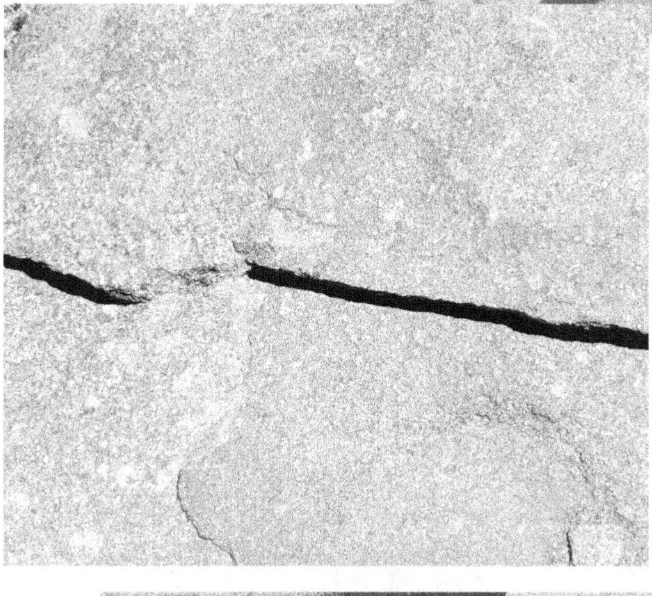

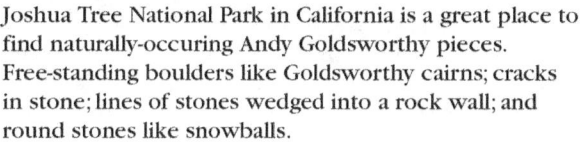

Joshua Tree National Park in California is a great place to find naturally-occuring Andy Goldsworthy pieces. Free-standing boulders like Goldsworthy cairns; cracks in stone; lines of stones wedged into a rock wall; and round stones like snowballs.

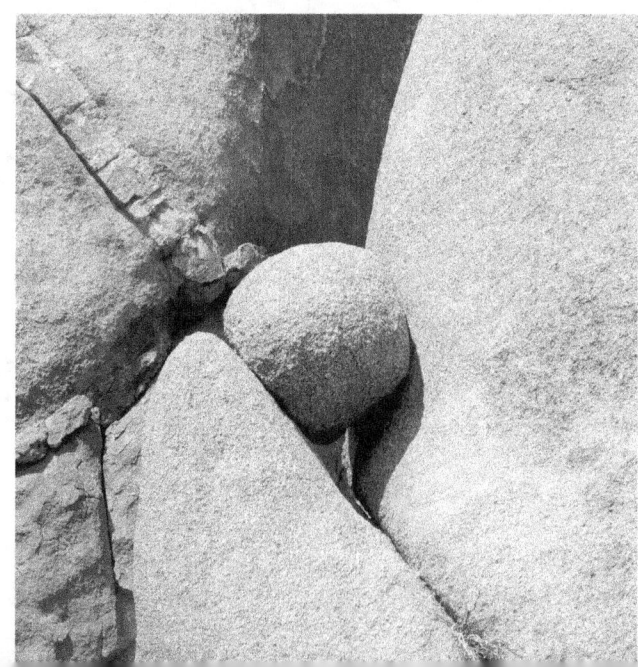

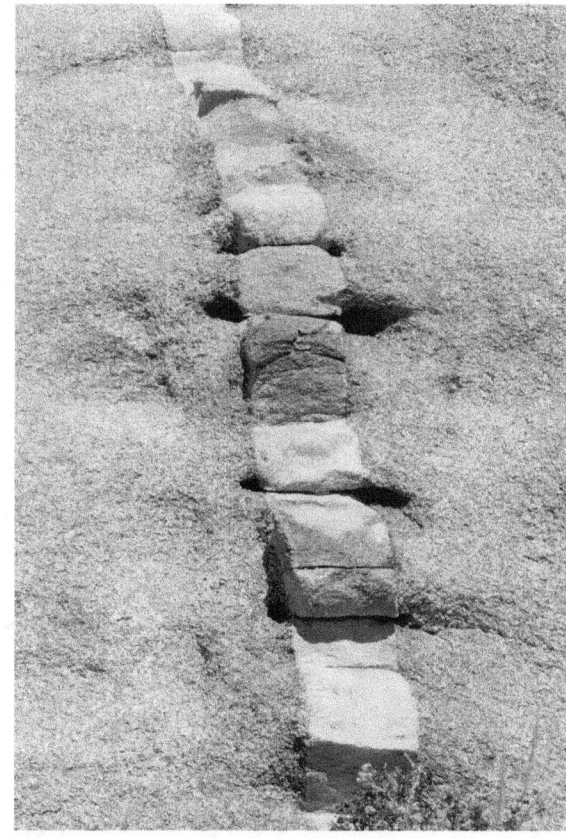

Some of Andy Goldsworthy's Influences

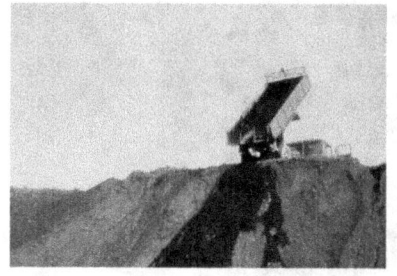
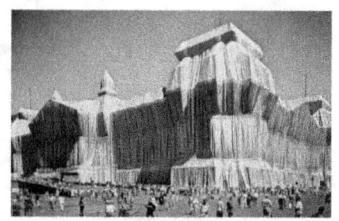
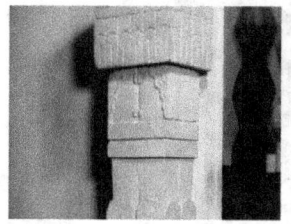

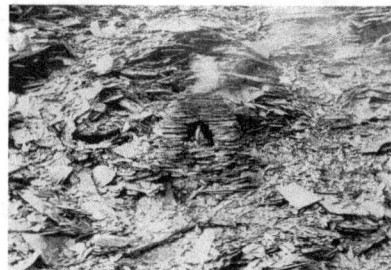
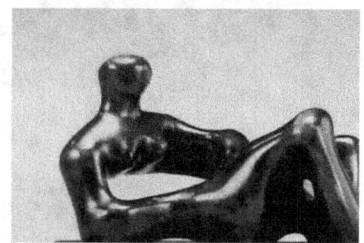
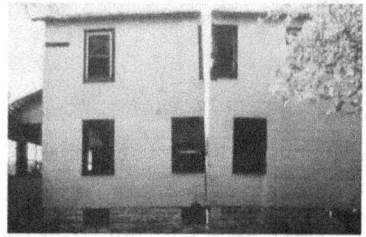

Some of Andy Goldsworthy's artistic influences: clockwise from top:
Robert Smithson, Christo, Yves Klein, Henry Moore, Gordon Matta-
Clark, David Nash and Constantin Brancusi.

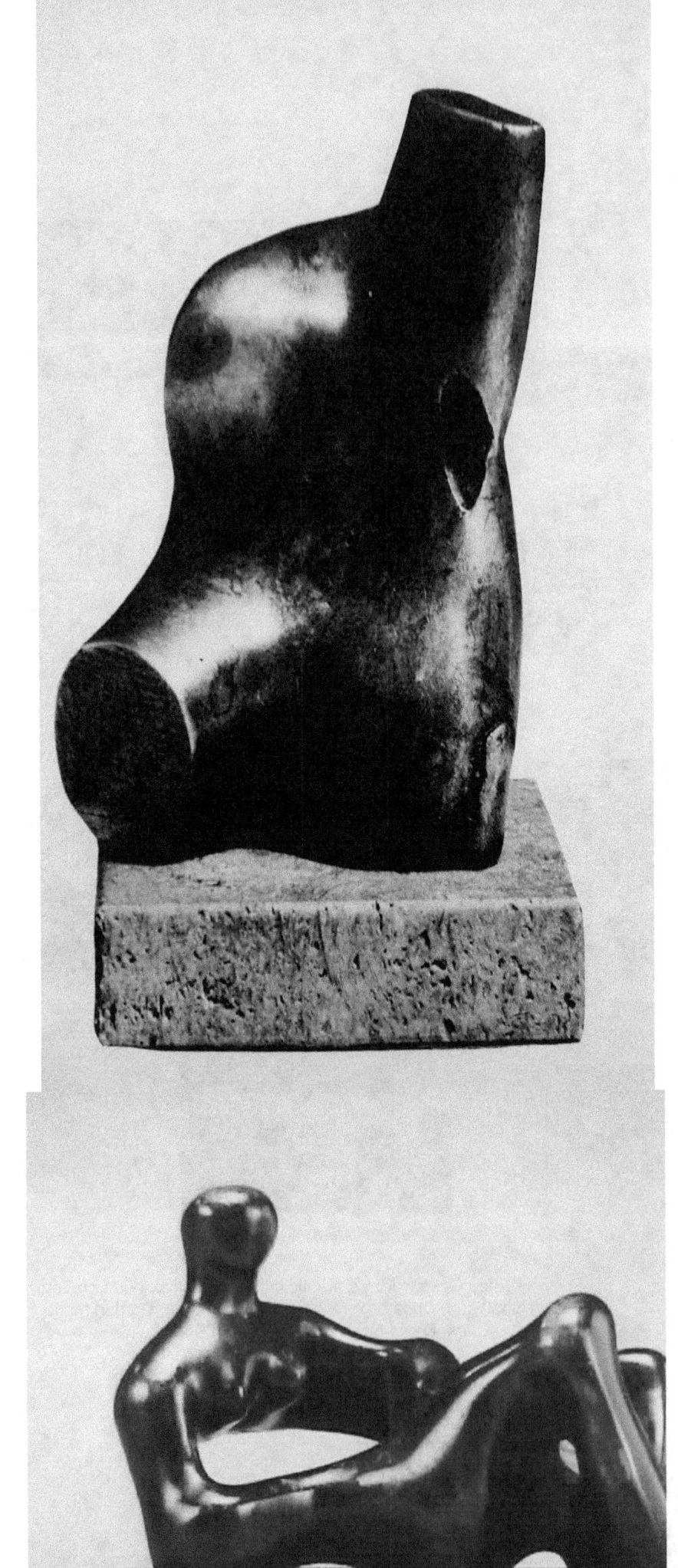

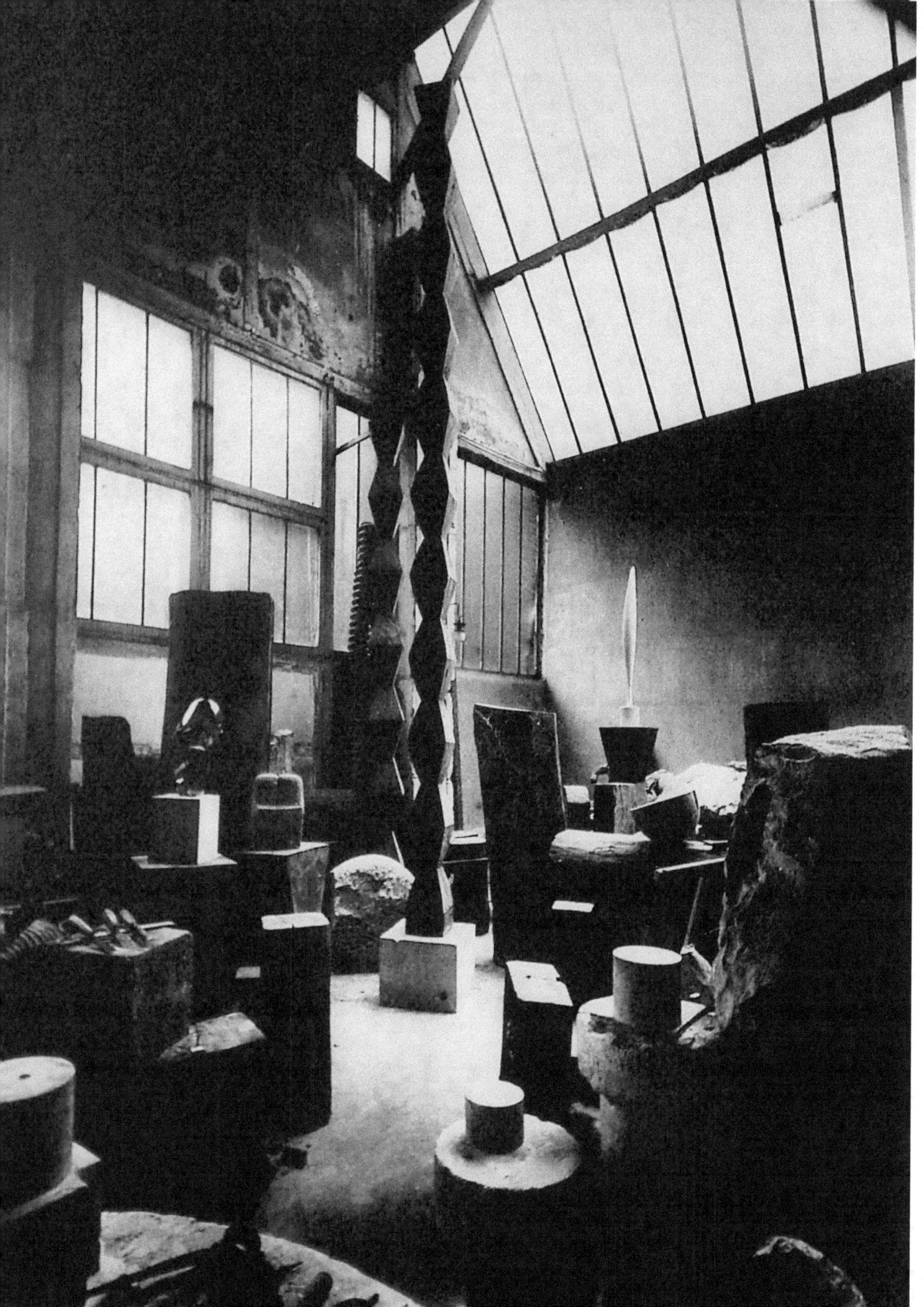

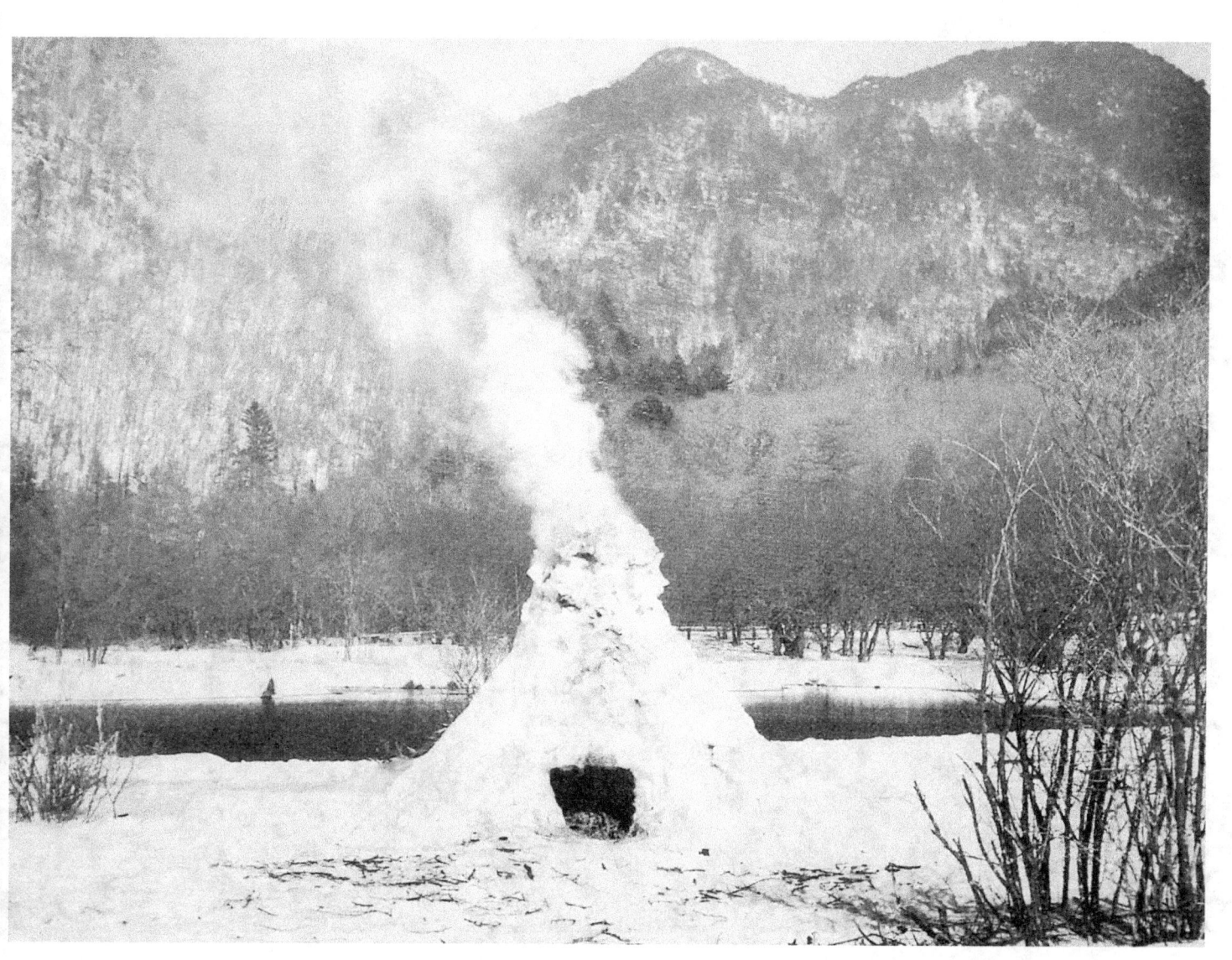

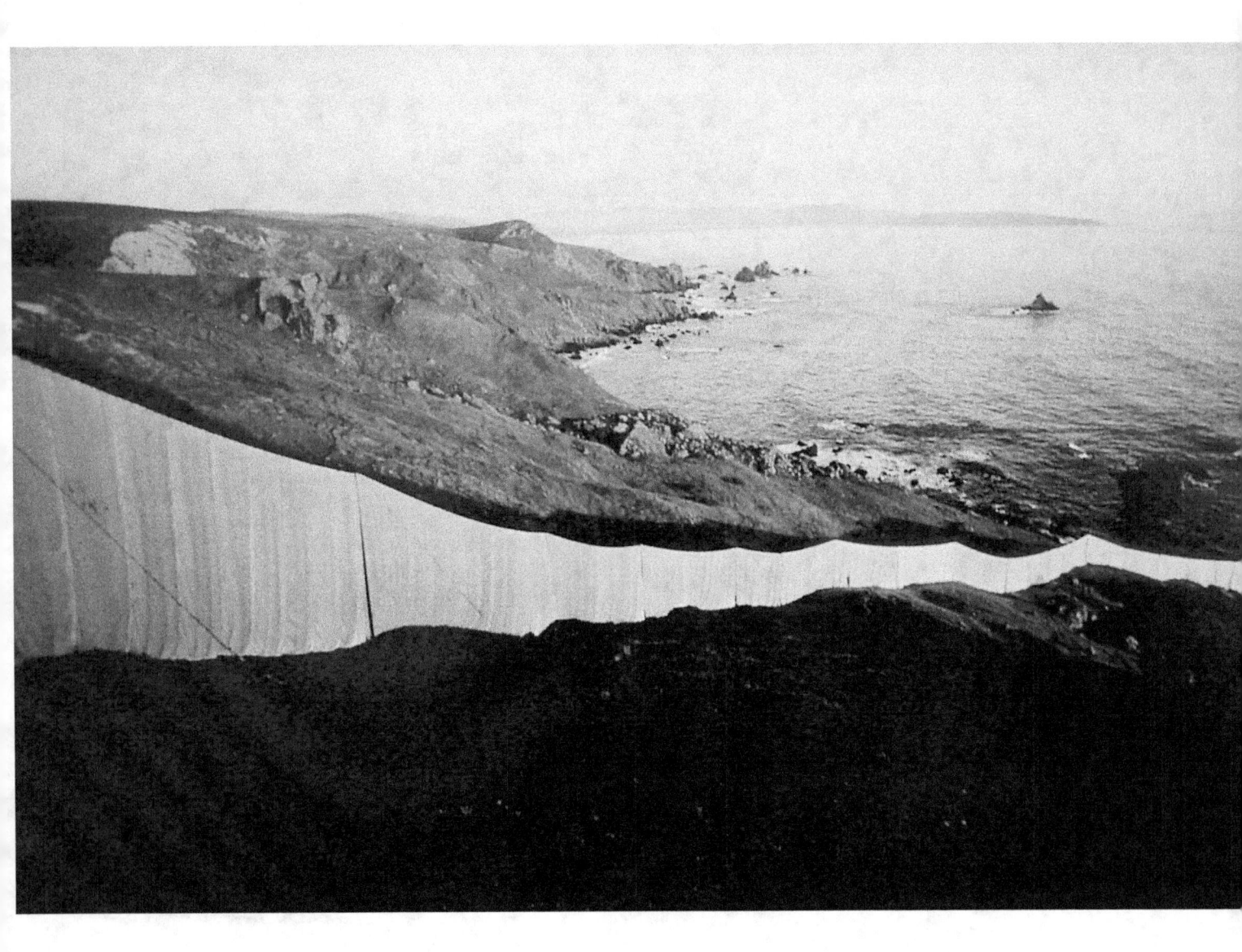

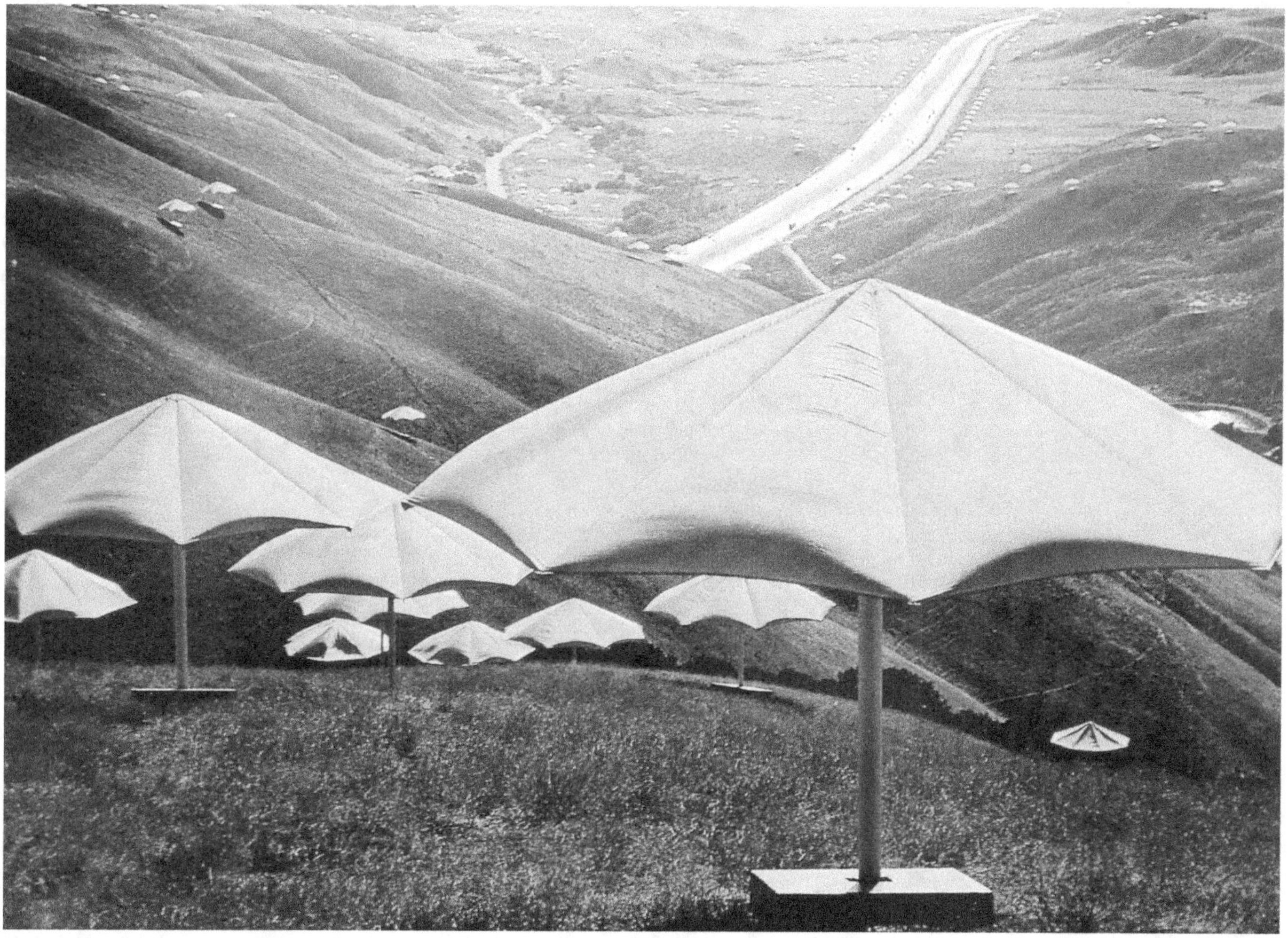

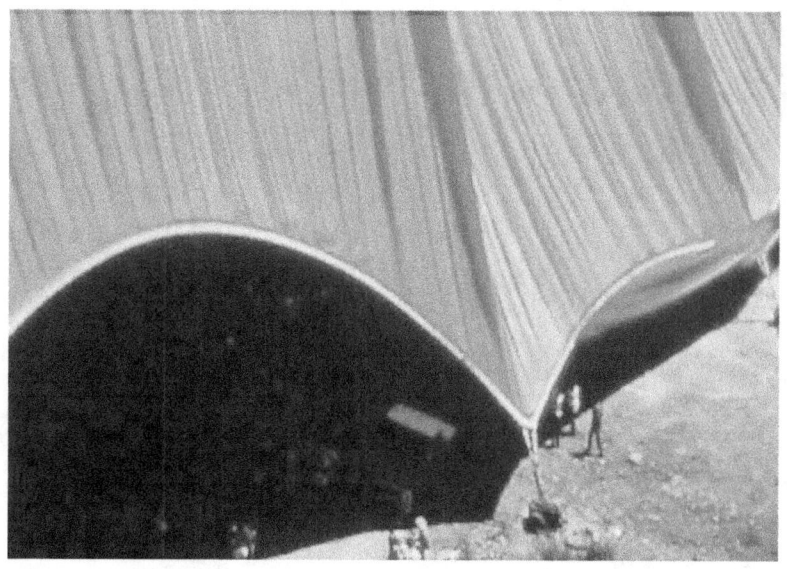

Bibliography

ANDY GOLDSWORTHY

Andy Goldsworthy, Alan Rankle, Nigel Jepson, Brampton Banks, Cumbria, 1982

Rain sun snow hail mist calm: Photoworks by Andy Goldsworthy, Henry Moore Centre for the Study of Sculpture, Leeds, Yorkshire, 1985

Land Matters, Blackfriars Arts Centre, Reed Press, 1986

"Hampstead Heath", *Aspects,* 32, Spring, 1986

& J. Fowles. *Winter Harvest,* Scottish Arts Council, 1987

Mountain and Coast: Autumn Into Winter: Japan 1987, Art Data, 1988

Parkland, Yorkshire Sculpture Park, West Bretton, 1988

Touching North, Fabian Carlsson, London, 1989

Snowballs in Summer Installation, Old Museum of Transport, Glasgow, 1989

Garden Mountain, Centre d'Art Contemporain, Castres, 1989

Leaves, Common Ground, London, 1989

Singular Visions, University of Warwick, 1989

Andy Goldsworthy, Viking, London, 1990

Hand to Earth: Andy Goldsworthy, Sculpture, 1976-1990, Henry Moore Centre for Sculpt-ure, Leeds, Yorkshire, 1990

interview, *Third Ear,* BBC Radio 3, June 30, 1989, in 1990 (HE)

"Geometry and Nature", interview, *Art & Design,* in A. Papadakis, 1991

Sand Leaves, Arts Club of Chicago, IL, 1991

Ice and Snow Drawings, Fruitmarket Gallery, Edinburgh, 1992

Andy Goldsworthy: Breakdown, Rose Art Museum, 1992

Andy Goldsworthy: Futatsu no aki, Tochigi Kenritsu Bijutsukan, Tokyo, 1993

"Andy Goldsworthy: an artist's diary", *Arts Review,* 45, Sept, 1993

"Andy Goldsworthy", *Art & Design,* 9, 5/6, May/ June 1994

Stone, Viking, London, 1994

Black Stones, Red Pools, Pro Arte Foundation, 1995

Wood, Viking, London, 1996

Sheepfolds, with S. Chettle, P. Nesbitt, A. Humphries, Michael Hue-Williams Gallery, London, 1996

Végètal, Ballet Atlantique-Regine Chopinot, La Rochelle, France, 1996

Alaska Works, Anchorage Museum of History and Art, Anchorage, AK, 1996

Andy Goldsworthy: A Collaboration With Nature, Abrams, New York, NY, 1996

Andy Goldsworthy: Jack's Fold, ed. J. Glasman, University of Hertfordshire, St Albans, Hertfordshire, 1996

Hand to Earth: Andy Goldsworthy Sculpture, T. Friedman, Thames and Hudson, London, 1997 & 2004

Cairns, Musée départemental de Digne, Reserve Geologique de haute Provence, 1997

Andy Goldsworthy, Musée d'art contemporain de Montréal, Canada, 1998

Arch, with D. Craig, Thames & Hudson, London, 1999

Andy Goldsworthy, with M. Kuipers & T. Karreman, Province Noord-Holland aan Staats-bosbeheer, 1999

Wall, intr. K. Baker, Thames & Hudson, London, 2000

Time, Thames & Hudson, London, 2000

Midsummer Snowballs, intr. J. Collins, Thames & Hudson, London, 2001

Andy Goldsworthy – Réfuges d'Art, Editions Artha, 2002

Passage, Thames & Hudson, London, 2004

Enclosure, Thames & Hudson, London, 2007

OTHERS

H. Adams. "The Woodman", *Art and Artists*, 13, Apl, 1979
—. "Fabian Carlsson Gallery: London: Exhibit", *New Art Examiner*, 15, May, 1988
C. Adcock. *James Turrell*, University of California Press, Berkeley, CA, 1990
W.C. Agee. *Don Judd*, Whitney Museum of American Art, New York, NY, 1968
—. "Unit, Series, Site: A Judd Lexicon", *Art in America*, May, 1975
—. *The Sculpture of Donald Judd*, Art Museum of South Texas, Corpus Christi, TX, 1977
D. Alberge. "Making an impression with the elements", *The Independent*, Feb 18, 1989
L. Aldrich. *Cool Art: 1967*, Museum of Contemporary Art, 1968
P. Allison *et al. Beyond the Minimal*, Architectural Association Publications, London, 1998
L. Alloway. "The American Sublime", *Living Arts*, 1, 2, June, 1963
—. *Systematic Painting*, New York, NY, 1966
—. *Christo*, Abrams, New York, NY, 1969
—. "Robert Smithson's Development", *Artforum*, Nov, 1972
—. "Residual Sign Systems in Abstract Expressionism", *Artforum*, Nov, 1973
L. Anderson. "Mary Miss", *Artforum*, Nov, 1973
W. Anderson. *American Sculpture in Process, 1930/ 1970*, New York Graphics Society, Boston, MA, 1975
C. Andre. "Frank Stella: Preface to Stripe Painting", in D. Miller, 1959
—. "An Interview with Carl Andre", P. Tuchman, *Artforum*, 8, 10, June, 1970
—. *Carl Andre, Sculpture, 1958-1974*, Kunsthalle, Bern, 1975
—. "Object v Phenomenon", *Sculpture Today*, The International Sculpture Center, Toronto, 1978
—. *Carl Andre: Sculpture*, State University of New York Press, Albany, NY, 1984
—. *Carl Andre: works on land*, Exhibitions International, 2001
C. Andreae. "Art shaped by the weather", *Christian Science Monitor*, Sept 21, 1987
—. "Fire and ice", *Art News*, 89, 7, Sept, 1990
J. Andrews. *The Sculpture of David Nash*, Lund Humphries, London, 1999
M. Andrews. *Landscape and Western Art*, Oxford Paperbacks, Oxford, 1999
E. de Antonio & Mitch Tuchman. *Painters Painting*, Abbeville Press, New York, NY, 1984
"Andy Goldsworthy", *Rambler Magazine*, 16, Summer, 2003
M. Archer. "A Walk In the Endless Summer From Duncansby Head To the Place of the Camel Droppinh", *Art Monthly*, Sept, 1991
—. *Art Since 1960*, Thames & Hudson, London, 1997
D. Archibald. "Art forms fashioned with the help of mother nature", *Dumfries and Galloway Standard*, Nov 18, 1988
—. "Andy's unique view of nature takes him round the world", *Dumfries and Galloway Standard*, Feb 3, 1988
D. Ashton. *American Art Since 1945*, Thames & Hudson, London, 1982
—. *Modern American Sculpture*, Abrams, New York, NY, 1968
M. Auping. *Common Ground*, John and Mable Ringling Museum of Art, Sarasota, 1982
—. "Hamish Fulton", *Art in America*, 71, Feb, 1983
A. Aycock. "Work", "Maze", 1975, in A. Sondheim, 1977
J. Baal-Teshuva, ed. *Christo: The Reichstag and Urban Projects*, Prestel Verlag, Munich, 1993
Y. Baginsky. "Sculptor for whom success snowballs", *Scotland on Sunday*, Jan 15, 1989
M. Bailey. "Carve a name in ice", *The Observer*, June 11, 1989
E. Baker: "Judd the Obscure", *Art News*, 67, 2, 1968
K. Baker. "Andre in Retrospect", *Art in America*, Apl, 1980a

—. "Reckoning with Notation: The Drawings of Pollock, Newman, and Louis", *Artforum*, 18, 10, Summer, 1980b

—. *Minimalism: Art of Circumstance*, Abbeville, New York, NY, 1988

—. "Andy Goldsworthy: Haines", *Art News*, 91, 8, Oct. 1992

—. "Goldsworthy's natural approach", *San Francisco Chronicle*, June 1, 1994

—. "An earthy show", *San Francisco Sunday Examiner*, Feb 19, 1995

—. "Setting the record straight on Yves Klein", *San Francisco Chronicle*, June 11, 1995

—. "Art that knocks and sculpts and rearranges wood", *San Francisco Chronicle*, Oct 20, 1996

—. "A welcome complexity in new shows", *San Francisco Examiner*, Dec 13, 1996

—. "Feat of Clay in the (Un)making: many reverberations in cracking wall at Haines", *San Francisco Chronicle*, Dec 11, 1996

—. "Searching for the window into nature's soul", *Smithsonian*, Feb, 1997

S. Bann & W. Allen, eds. *Interpreting Contemporary Art*, Reaktion Books, London, 1991

—. "Shrines, Gardens, Utopias", *New Literary History*, 24, 4, Autumn, 1994a

—. "The Map As Index of the Real: Land Art and the Authentication of Travel", *Imago Mundi*, 46, British Library, London, 1994b

G. Baro. "Toward Speculation in Pure Form", *Art International*, Summer, 1967

—. "American Sculpture", *Studio International*, 172, 896, 1968

—. "Sculpture made visible: Barry Flanagan in discussion with Gene Baro", *Studio International*, 178, 915, Oct, 1969

M. Bartlett. "A tribe of one: Andy Goldsworthy at Haines Gallery", *ArtWeek*, 23, 19, July 9, 1992

G. Battock, ed. *The New Art*, Dutton, New York, NY, 1966

—. *Idea Art*, Dutton, New York, NY, 1973

—. "Art in America: Confusions", *Domus*, Mch, 1975

—. ed. *New Artists Video*, Dutton, New York, NY, 1978

—. ed. *The Art of Performance*, Dutton, New York, NY, 1984

—. ed. *Minimal Art: A Critical Anthology*, University of California Press, Berkeley, CA, 1995

G. Beal. "Richard Long: "the simplicity of walking, the simplicity of stones"", in T. Neff, 1987

—. ed. *Art In the Landscape*, Chinati Foundation, Texas, 2000

J. Beardsley. *Probing the Earth: Contemporary Land Projects,* Smithsonian Press, Washington, DC, 1977

—. *Art in Public Spaces*, Partners For Liveable Places, Washington, DC, 1981

—. *Earthworks and Beyond: Contemporary Art in the Landscape*, Abbeville Press, New York, NY, 1984/ 1998

M.R. Beaumont. "Romantic Sculpture", in A. Papadakis, 1988

—. "Fabian Carlsson Gallery: London: Exhibit", *Arts Review*, 40, Mch 11, 1988

—. "Andy Goldsworthy", *Arts Review*, 41, July 14, 1989

M. Beeren. *Century in Sculpture*, Stedelijk Museum, Amsterdam, 1992

A. Benjamin, ed. *Installation Art, Art & Design*, 30, 1993

L. Bennett. *The Life and Work of Andy Goldsworthy*, Heinemann, London, 2005

N. Bennett, ed. *The British Art Show: Old Allegiances and New Directions, 1979-1984*, Arts Council/ Orbis, London, 1984

M. Berger. *Labyrinths: Robert Morris, Minimalism and the 1960s,* Harper & Row, New York, NY, 1989

—. *Minimal Politics*, University of Maryland, Fine Arts Gallery

S. Bérubé. "Goldsworthy et Singer: l'art de jouer avec la nature", *La Presse*, Apl 25, 1998

R. Bevan. "A snake in the British Museum", *Art Newspaper*. 5, 43, Dec 1994

L. Biggs: *Between Object and Image*, British Council, London, 1986

W. Bishop. "A corporate collection", *British Journal of Photography*, June 12, 1987

M. Bloem, ed. *Lawrence Weiner*, Stedelijk Museum, Amsterdam, 1989

K.C. Bloomert & C.W. Moore. *Body, Memory and Architecture*, New Haven, CT, 1977

M. Bochner. "Art in Process – Structures", *Arts Magazine*, 40, 9, 1966a
—. "Primary Structures", *Arts*, June, 1966b
—. "Systematic", *Arts Magazine*, 41, 1, Nov, 1966c
—. "Serial Art Systems: Solipsism", *Arts Magazine*, 41, 8, Summer, 1967
S. Boettger. *Earthworks*, University of California Press, Berkeley, CA, 2002
Y. Bois. *Donald Judd*, Galerie Lelong, Paris, 1991
D. Bonetti, David. "Facing Eden: 100 years of landscape art in the Bay Area, is a show that limns a strong tradition", *San Francisco Examiner*, June 25, 1995
A. Bonnano. "Andy Goldsworthy", *Art and Design*, 9, 5/6, May/ June 1994
C. Borland *et al. The Cauldron,* Henry Moore Institute, Leeds, Yorkshire, 1996
D. Bourdon. "Walter de Maria: The Singular Experience", *Art International*, Dec 20, 1968
—. *Christo*, Abrams, New York, NY, 1971
—"The Mini-Conceptual Age", *Village Voice*, Oct 17, 1974
—. "You Can't Tell a Painter By His Colors", *Village Voice*, Mch 24, 1975
—. *Carl Andre: Sculpture, 1959-1977*, Jaap Rietman, New York, NY, 1978
—. *et al: Niki de Sant-Phalle: Fantastic Vision*, Nassau County Museum of Fine Art, Rosyln, New York, NY, 1987
—. "Andy Goldsworthy at Lelong", *Art in America.* 81, 11, Nov, 1993
—. *Designing the Earth*, Abrams, New York, NY, 1995
C. Brown. "Natural arts", *The Magazine,* July, 1987
D. Brown. "New British sculpture in Normandy", *Arts Review*, Feb 10, 1989
I. Brown. "From urban nightmare to primal scream: Chopinot/ Goldsworthy at the Playhouse", *Electronic Telegraph*, 820, Aug, 23, 1997
J. Brown *et al. Michael Heizer: Sculpture in Reverse*, see M. Heizer, 1984
—. ed. *Occluding Front: James Turrell*, Lapis Press, Larkspur Landing, CA, 1985
D. Bruckner. "Earth works", *New York Times Book Review*, Jan, 1996
P. Buchanan. "The Nature of Goldsworthy", *The Architectural Review*, Feb, 1988
J. Burnham. "Hans Haacke: Wind and Water Sculpture", 1967, in A. Sonfist, 1983
—. *Beyond Modern Sculpture*, Braziller, New York, NY, 1968
—. "A Dan Flavin Retrospective in Ottawa", *Artforum*, 8, 4, Dec, 1969
—. "Robert Morris", *Artforum*, 8, 7, 1970
—. "Haacke's Cancelled Show at the Guggenheim", *Artforum*, June, 1971
—. *Great Western Salt Works*, Brazillier, New York, NY, 1974
K. Bussman & F. Matzner, eds. *Hans Haacke*, Cantz, Stuttgart, 1993
J. Butterfield. *The Art of Light and Space*, Abbeville Press, New York, NY, 1993
D. Cameron. "When is a door not a door?", *XLIII esposizione Internazionale d'Arte La Biennale di Venezia*, Edizioni La Biennale, Venice, 1988
—. "Art for the new year: who's worth catching?", *Art & Auction*, Jan, 1994
J. Campbell. *The Power of Myth*, with B. Moyers, ed. B.S. Flowers, Doubleday, New York, NY, 1988
—. *The Hero With a Thousand Faces,* Paladin, London, 1988
—. *An Open Life*, Larson Publications, New York, NY, 1988
—. *The Hero's Journey: Joseph Campbell On his Life and Work,* ed. P. Cousineau, Harper & Row, San Francisco, CA, 1990
P. Carlson. "Donald Judd's Equivocal Objects", *Art in America*, Jan, 1984
K. Carter: "*Stone*", *New Welsh Review*, 27, Winter, 1994-95
T. Castle. "Nancy Holt, Siteseer", *Art in America*, Mch, 1982
A. Causey. *Nature as Material: An Exhibition of Sculpture and Photographs Purchased For the Arts Council Collection,* Arts Council, London, 1980
—. "Environmental Sculptures", in A. Goldsworthy, 1990
—. "Space and Time in British Land Art", *Studio International*, 193, 98, Feb, 1977
G. Celant. "Introduction", *Arte Povera*, Praeger, New York, NY, 1969
—. *Conceptual Art, Arte Povera, Land Art,* Galeria Civica d'Arte Moderna, Turin, 1970
—. "Tony Cragg and Industrial Platonism", *Artforum*, 20, 3, Nov, 1981
—. *Dennis Oppenheim*, Edizioni Charta Srl, 1997
A. Chave: "Minimalism and the Rhetoric of Power", *Arts*, Jan, 1990
H.B. Chipp, ed. *Theories of Modern Art,* University Press of California, Los

Angeles, CA, 1968

A. Christian. "Art of a craftsman: the sculptures of Andy Goldsworthy reflect a deep passion for the natural world", *Resurgence Magazine*, Feb, 1998

B. Christian. "Scottsdale center present "nature oriented" shows", *Scottsdale Life*, Aug 18, 1994

M. Church. "A shower of stones, a flash in the river", *Sunday Telegraph*, Apl 10, 1994

A. Clabburn. "A sanctuary in the city", *The Age*, Oct, 22, 1997

F. Colpitt. *Minimal Art: The Critical Perspective,* University of Washington Press, Seattle, WA, 1990

B. Commoner. *The Closing Circle: Nature, Man and Technology*, Knopf, New York, NY, 1975

M. Compton & D. Sylvester. *Robert Morris*, Tate Gallery, London, 1971

—. *Some Notes on the Work of Richard Long*, British Council, London, 1976

Concept Art, Minimal Art, Land Art, Edition Cantz, Stuttgart, 1990

L. Cooke. "Richard Long replies to a critic", *Art Monthly*, 68, July, 1983

—. *Alison Wilding*, Serpentine Gallery, London, 1985

J. Coplans. "Serial Imagery", *Artforum*, 7, 2, Oct, 1968

—. *Donald Judd*, Pasadena Art Museum, CA, 1971

—. "Robert Smithson", *Artforum*, Apl, 1974

R. Cork. "Paying the price", *Listener Guide*, Dec 9, 1985

—. "Burnished in bush country", *The Times,* May 28, 1993

—. "Andy Goldsworthy", *The Times*, Apl 23, 1994

D. Cosgrove, ed. *Mappings*, London, 1999

T. Cragg. *Writings*, Editions Isy Brachot, Brussels, 1992

—. *Sculptures on the Page*, Henry Moore Institute, Leeds, Yorkshire, 1997

M. Craig-Martin. *Minimalism*, Tate Gallery, Liverpool, 1989

D. Crane. *The Transformation of the Avant Garde: The New York Art World, 1940-1985*, University of Chicago Press, Chicago, IL, 1987

M. Crichton. *Jasper Johns*, Thames & Hudson, London, 1977

P. Crowther, ed. *The Contemporary Sublime, Art & Design*, 40, 1995

P. Curtis. *Modern British Sculpture from the Collection*, Tate Gallery, Liverpool, 1988

C. Dal Canto. "As nature dictates", *Casa Vogue*, 248, Feb, 1993

—. "Stones", *Casa Vogue*, 266, 1994

G. Danto. "A clearing in the woods", *Art News*, 93, 2, Feb, 1994

P. Davey. "Delight", *Architectural Review*, 193, Apl, 1993

A. Davies. "Richard Long and Hamish Fulton", *Art Monthly*, 25, Apl, 1979

R. Davies & T. Knipe, eds. *A Sense of Place: Sculpture in Landscape*, 1984

R. Deakin. "Zen and the art of Andy Goldsworthy", *Modern Painters*, 10, 1, Spring, 1997

W. de Maria. "The Lightning Field", *Artforum*, 18, 8, Apl, 1980

P. de Monchaux, *et al*, eds. *The Sculpture Show*, Arts Council of Great Britain, London, 1983

N. de Oliveira *et al*. *Installation Art*, Thames & Hudson, London, 1994

—. *et al. Installation Art in the New Millennium*, Thames & Hudson, London, 2003

M. Derby. "Fleeting moments: Andy Goldsworthy at Karekare", *Art New Zealand*, 63, Winter 1992

R. Deutsche *et al. Hans Haacke*, MIT Press, Cambridge, MA, 1986

E. Develing. *Carl Andre*, Gemeentemuseum, The Hague, 1969

—. & L. Lippard. *Minimal Art*, Stadtische Kunsthalle, Dusseldorf, 1969

J. Dibbets, in L. Bear & W. Sharp: "DIBBETTS", *Avalanche*, 1, Autumn, 1970.

R. Donnell. *Double Vision: Perspectives On Gender and the Visual Arts*, Farleigh Dickinson University Press, Rutherford, NJ, 1995

M. Dobson. "Breath of fresh air", *The New Statesman*, Jan 10, 1986

—. "Shared sentiments", *BBC Wildlife*, Jan, 1987

L. Dougherty. "Art in nature: a new site for sculpture in Denmark", *Maquette*, Sept, 1994

M. Drabble. "Andy Goldsworthy", *Modern Painters*, 2, 3, Autumn, 1989

C. Drury. *Shelters and Baskets*, Orchard Gallery, 1988

—. *Vessel: Sculpture 1990-95*, Towner Art Gallery, 1995
—. *Stones and Bundles*, Rebecca Hossack Gallery, London, 1995
—. *Silent Spaces*, Thames & Hudson, London, 1998/ 2004
—. *Journeys On Paper*, Stephen Lacey Gallery, London, 2000
—. interview with W. Furlong, in M. Gooding, 2002
—. *Defying Gravity*, North Carolina Museum of Art, NC, 2003
—. *Heart of Stone*, Aberystwyth Art Gallery, Wales, 2003
A. Dumas. "Andy Goldsworthy at Fabian Carlson Gallery", *Art in America*, May, 1988
M. Duncan. "On site: straddling the great divide", *Art in America.* 83, 3, Mch, 1995
—. "Live from the Getty", *Art in America,* 86, 5, May, 1998
R. Durand. "Andy Goldsworthy", *Le printemps de Cahors: catalogue des expositions,* Marval, Paris, 1996
L. Durrell. *Justine*, Faber, London, 1963
—. *Spirit of Place*, Faber, London, 1971
A. Dyson. *Richard Long: Sao Paulo Biennial 1994,* The British Council, 1994
J.C. Eade, ed. *Projecting the Landscape*, Humanities Research Centre, Canberra, 1987
D. Ebony. "Goldsworthy's Living Memorial", *Art in America*, Nov, 2003
M. Eliade. *Patterns in Comparative Religion*, Sheed & Ward, London, 1958
—. *Shamanism: Archaic Techniques of Ecstasy*, Princeton University Press, Princeton, NJ, 1972
—. *Myths, Dreams and Mysteries*, Harper & Row, New York, NY, 1975
—. *From Primitives to Zen: A Sourcebook*, Collins, London, 1977
—. *A History of Religious Ideas*, I, Collins, London, 1979
—. *Ordeal by Labyrinth*, University of Chicago Press, Chicago, IL, 1984
—. *Symbolism, the Sacred and the Arts*, Crossroad, New York, NY, 1988
G. Evans. "Sculpture and Reality", *Studio International*, 177, 908, Feb, 1969
J. Fabricus. *Alchemy: The Medieval Alchemists and Their Royal Art*, Aquarian Press, Northamptonshire, 1989
D. Factor. "Los Angeles", *Artforum*, 4, 9, May, 1966
S. Farr. "Andy Goldsworthy: stone works in America", *Reflex*, 8, 6, Dec, 1995
R. Ferguson *et al*, eds. *Discourses: Conversations in Postmodern Art and Culture*, MIT Press, Cambridge, MA, 1990
S. Field. "Touching the Earth", *Art and Artists*, 8, Apl, 1973
J. Fineberg: "Robert Morris Looking Back", *Arts Magazine*, 55, 1, 1980
—. *Art Since 1940: Strategies of Being*, Laurence King, London, 2000
A. Fisher & J. Saward. *The British Maze Guide*, Minotaur Designs, 1991
—. & D. Kingham. *Mazes,* Shire Publications, 1991
J. Fisher. "Richard Long", *Aspects*, 14, Spring, 1981
S. Foley. *Unitary Forms: Minimal Structures by Carl Andre, Donald Judd, John McCracken, Tony Smith*, Museum of Modern Art, San Francisco, CA, 1970
N. Foote. "Long Walks", *Artforum*, 18, Summer, 1980
W. Forma. *Five British Sculptors*, New York, NY, 1965
P. Frank & M. McKenzie. *New, Used and Improved: Art For the '80s*, Abbeville Press, New York, NY, 1987
D. Frankel. "Andy Goldsworthy", *Artforum*, Oct, 2000
M. Fried. "Shape as Form: Frank Stella's New Paintings", *Artforum*, 5, 3, Nov, 1966
—. "Art and Objecthood", *Artforum*, 5, Summer, 1967
M. Friedman. "Robert Morris: Polemics and Cubes", *Art International*, 10, 10, Dec, 1966
—. *14 Sculptors*, Walker Art Center, Minneapolis, MN, 1969
E. Fry. *Alice Aycock*, University of South Florida Art Galleries, Tampa, FL, 1981
—. "The Poetic Machines of Alice Aycock", *Portfolio*, Nov, 1981
—. *et al. Robert Morris*, Museum of Contemporary Art, Chicago, IL, 1986
R.H. Fuchs. "Memories of Passing: A Note on Richard Long", *Studio International*, 187, 965, Apl, 1974
—. *Carl Andre*, Van Abenmuseum, Eindhoven, 1978
—. *Richard Long*, text, in R. Long, 1986

P. Fuller. *Peter Fuller's Modern Painters: Reflections on British Art*, ed. J. McDonald, Methuen, London, 1993

H. Fulton. *Hamish Fulton: Selected Walks, 1969-89*, Albright-Knox Art Gallery, Buffalo, New York, NY, 1990

—. *Richard Long*, Thames & Hudson, London, 1991

—. *One Hundred Walks*, Haags Gemeetemuseum, The Hague, 1991

—. "Into a Walk Into Nature", *Thirty One Horrors*, Lenbachhaus, Munich, 1995

—. *Walking Artist*, Annely Juda, London, 1998

—. *Wild Life*, Pocketbooks, Edinburgh, 2000

—. *Walking Artist*, Richter Verlag, Düsseldorf, 2001

—. "Specific Places and Particular Events", in B. Tufnell, 2002

S. Gardiner. "Their medium is nature", *Landscape Architecture*, 80, Feb, 1990

M. Garlake. "Andy Goldsworthy", *Art Monthly*, 93, Feb, 1986

J. Gear. "Andy Goldsworthy", *Review*, Dec. 1, 1996

L. Gendron. "Le sculpteur d'éphémère", *L'actualité*, 22, 12, Aug, 1997

J. Gibson. *The Senses Considered as a Perceptual System*, Houghton Mifflin, Boston, MA, 1966

A. Gide. *The Counterfeiters*, tr. D. Bussy, Penguin, London, 1966

J. Giovannini. *Mary Miss*, Architectural Association, London, 1987

P. Giquel. "Andy Goldsworthy: Centre d'art contemporain Midi-Pyrénées", *Art Press*, 158, May, 1991

T. Godfrey. "Richard Wilson's watertable, Andy Goldsworthy", *Burlington Magazine*, 136, 1096, July, 1994

—. *Conceptual Art*, Phaidon, London, 1998

E. Goheen. *Wrapped Walk Ways*, Abrams, New York, NY, 1978

R. Goldberg. *Performance: Live Art Since the 60s*, Thames & Hudson, London, 1998

A. Goldstein, ed. *Reconsidering the Object of Art: 1965-1975*, Museum of Contemporary Art, L.A., CA, 1995

M. Gooding & W. Furlong. *Song of the Earth,* Thames and Hudson, London, 2002

A. Gopnik. "Basic Stuff: Robert Smithson, Myth, Science and Primitivism", *Art Magazine*, Mch, 1983

A. Graham-Dixon. "Turning over an old leaf", *The Independent*, Feb 3, 1988

—. "Cutting Ice", *The Independent*, June, 24, 1989

—. "An artist does the strand", *The Independent*, Aug 5, 1989

—. "Great Britain: neo, no: still faithful to the old guard", *Art News*, 88, 7, Sept, 1989

J. Grande. *Balance: art and nature*, Black Rose Books, Montréal, 1994

—. "Back to nature?", *Sculpture*, 13, 4, July/ Aug, 1994

—. *Art Nature Dialogues*, State University of New York Press, NY, 2004

N. Graydon. "Magic in the field", *Ritz*, 133, 1989

B. Graziani. "Robert Smithson's Picturable Situation", *Critical Inquiry*, 20, 3, Spring, 1994

C. Greenberg. *Art and Culture,* Beacon Press, Boston, MA, 1961

H. Gresty & D. Reason. *Landscape*, Kettle's Yard, Cambridge, 1986

—. *Bare: Alison Wilding: Sculptures, 1982-1993*, Newlyn Art Gallery, Cornwall, 1993

G. Greig. "Circular Tours In the Name of Art", *Sunday Times*, June 16, 1991

C. Grout. "Andy Goldsworthy: une esthétique pragmatique", *Art Press*, 192, May, 1994

H. Haacke. *Framing and Being Framed*, New York University Press, New York, NY, 1975

A. Haden-Guest. "The King of Wrap", *The Sunday Times Magazine*, Jan, 1994

C. Hagen. "Art in review", *New York Times*, Sept 17, 1993

J. Haldane. *A Road From the Past To the Future*, Crawford Arts Centre, St Andrews, 1997

—. "Images After the Fact", *Modern Painters*, 11, 3, Fall, 1998

—. "Back To the Land", *Art Monthly*, June, 1999

O. Hahn & P. Restany. *Christo*, Editioni Apollinaire, Milan, 1966

C. Hall. "Shared earth", *Arts Review*, 43, June 14, 1991

—. "Site lines", *Arts Review*, 46, Oct, 1994

J. Hamlin. "Andy Goldsworthy: artist lets nature take its course", *San Francisco Chronicle*, May 4, 1994

A.M. Hammacher. *The Sculpture of Barbara Hepworth*, Abrams, New York, NY, 1968

C. Harrison. "Barry Flanagan's Sculpture", *Studio International*, 175, 900, May, 1968

—. "Sculpture's Recent Past", in T. Neff, 1987

B. Haskell. *BLAM! The Explosion of Pop, Minimalism, and Performance, 1958-64*, Whit-ney Museum of American Art, New York, NY, 1984

—. *Donald Judd*, Whitney Museum of American Art, New York, NY, 1988

J. Hattam. "Restoration art focussing on nature's power to reclaim [Andy Goldsworthy]", *Sierra*, May-June, 2003

M. Hayde. "Nature is his studio: Great Britain's Andy Goldsworthy, master of the ephemeral "earth sculpture", will give a free lecture at Stanford", *Palo Alto Weekly,* Jan 27, 1995

N. Hedges. "Growth, decay and the movement of change", *World Magazine*, 45, Jan, 1991

M. Heizer, D. Oppenheim & R. Smithson. "Discussion", *Avalanche*, 1, Autumn, 1970

—. *Sculpture in Reverse*, Museum of Contemporary Art, Los Angeles, CA, 1984

A. Henri. *Environments and Happenings*, Thames & Hudson, London, 1974

—. *Total Art*, Praeger, New York, NY, 1974

C. Henry. "Lumps of the Landscape", *The World of Interiors*, Oct, 1987

—. "A style with natural life", *Glasgow Herald*, Aug 21, 1987

—. "Artist in love with nature puts down roots", *Glasgow Herald*, July 19, 1988

—. "Goldsworthy at Work or Paving the Way", *Artline*, 14, 33, Nov, 1988

—. "Royal Botanic Garden: Edinburgh: Exhibit", *Arts Review*, 40, July 15, 1988

—. "Melting moments", *Glasgow Herald*, July 28, 1989

—. "Natural History Museum: London: Exhibit", *Arts Review*, 41, Oct 6, 1989

—. "Andy Goldsworthy: Stone shapes a life", *The Herald*, Apl 22, 1994

—. "Only branching out", *The Herald*, Jan, 18, 1997

A. Hess. "Technology Exposed", *Landscape Architecture*, May, 1992

T. Hess. *Barnett Newman*, Walker, New York, NY, 1969

—. & L. Nochlin. *Woman as Sex Object: Studies in Erotic Art*, Newsweek, New York, NY, 1972

—. & E. Baker. *Art and Sexual Politics*, Art New Series, Macmillan, New York, NY, 1973

Galerie Max Hetzler. *Carl Andre, Gunther Forg, Hubert Kiecol, Richard Long, Meuser, Reinhard Mucha, Bruce Nauman and Ulrich Ruckreim*, Cologne, 1985

P. Hill. "Sjoerd Buisman", *Alba*, 11, Spring 1989

R. Hill. "Ice and snow drawings", *Crafts*, 119, Nov/ Dec, 1992

E. Hilliard. "In tribute to the wild bunch", *The Independent*, June 22, 1988

G. Hilty. *Recent British Sculpture*, Arts Council, London, 1993

—. *Alison Wilding: Immersion/ Exposure,* Tate Gallery, Liverpool, 1991

A. Hindry. "Sculpture anglaise: le clavier de l'imagination", *Art Press*, 214, June, 1996

R.C. Hobbs. *Robert Smithson: Sculpture,* Cornell University Press, Ithaca, NY, 1981

—. "Earthworks", *Art Journal*, 42, Fall, 1982

N. Hodges ed. *Art and the Natural Environment, Art & Design,* 36, 1994

—. ed. *The Contemporary Sublime, Art & Design,* 40, 1995

N. Holt. "Amarillo Ramp", *Avalanche*, Fall, 1973

—. "Hydra's Head", *Arts Magazine,* Jan, 1975

—. "Sun Tunnels", *Artforum*, Apl, 1977

P. Hovdenakk. *Christo: Complete Editions*, Schellman & Klüser, Munich, 1982

S. Howell. "Kingdom of the ice man", *Observer Magazine*, June 28, 1987

—. "Goldsworthy: the ice-man cometh", *World of Interiors*, July/ Aug, 1989

S. Hubbard & R. Sandall. "Peter Gabriel's *US*: the artists' boxes project: artists' statements", *Contemporary Art*, 1, 2, Winter, 1992

—. intr. *Sculpture At Goodwood: A Vision For 21st Century British Sculpture*, Sculpture At Goodwood, Sussex, 2002

S. Huchet. "Un exercice de la terre: le travail d'Andy Goldsworthy", *Ligeia*, 11/12, Dec, 1992

G. Hughes. "Artists in parks", *Arts Review*, 40, July 15, 1988

—. ed. *Arts Review Yearbook, 1989*, Arts Review Magazine, London, 1989

—. *Arts Review Yearbook, 1990*, Arts Review Magazine, London, 1990

R. Hughes. *Nothing If Not Critical: Selected Essays on Art and Artists*, Collins Harvill, London, 1990

—. *The Shock of the New*, Thames & Hudson, London, 1991

—. *American Visions: The Epic History of Art In America*, Knopf, New York, NY, 1997

T. Hughes. *Poetry in the Making*, Faber, London, 1969

—. *New Selected Poems, 1957-1994*, Faber, London, 1995

H.E. Hugo, ed. *The Portable Romantic Reader,* Viking Press, New York, NY, 1957

L. Hull. "In residence: Grizedale Forest sculpture park", *Maquette*, May/June 1993

S. Hunter, ed. *An American Renaissance: Painting and Sculpture Since 1940*, Abbeville Press, New York, NY, 1986

M. Hutchinson. "So follow him, follow him, down to the hollow", *Hampstead and Highate Express*, Dec 13, 1985

L. Iizawa. "Earth work", *Studio Voice*, Mch, 1988

P. Inch. "Andy Goldsworthy", *Arts Review*, 42, July 13, 1990

R. Ingleby. "Visual arts: Andy Goldsworthy", *The Independent*, Nov 8, 1996

In Praise of Trees, Salisbury Festival, Wilts., 2002

D. Isaac. "When leaves turn to gold", *Echoes*, Mch 24, 1992

Y. Ishii. "Creating beauty from nature", *Chubu Yomiuri Shimbun*, 21, Feb 2, 1988

W. Januszczak. "The Heath Robinson", *The Guardian*, Jan, 5, 1986

—. "The magic of icicle works", *The Guardian*, July 7, 1987

G. Jeppson. *Richard Long*, Harvard College, Cambridge, MA, 1980

E.H. Johnson. *Modern Art and the Object*, Harper & Row, New York, NY, 1976

—. ed. *American Artist on Art*, Harper & Row, New York, NY, 1982

W. Johnson. *Riding the Ox Home: A History of Meditation from Shamanism to Science*, Rider, London, 1982

J. Johnston. "Walling into Art", *Art in America,* 75, 4, Apl, 1987

B. Jones. "A New Wave in Sculpture", *Artscribe*, 8, Sept, 1977

C. Joyce. "Walling into History", *Flash Art*, Summer, 1989

D. Judd. "Frank Stella*", Arts Magazine*, 36, Sept, 1962

—. "In the Galleries", *Arts Magazine*, 37, 10, Sept, 1963

—. "Local History", *Arts Yearbook 7*, 1964

—. "Black, White and Gray", *Arts Magazine*, 38, 6, Mch, 1964

—. "Specific Objects", *Arts Yearbook*, 8, Art Digest, New York, NY, 1965

—. "Barnett Newman", *Studio International*, 179, 919, Feb, 1970

—. *Complete Writings, 1959-1975*, Nova Scotia College of Art and Design, Halifax, Canada, 1975

—. *Complete Writings, 1975-1986*, Van Abbemuseum, Netherlands, 1987

E. Juncosa. "Landscape as experience", *Lapiz*, 61 Oct, 1989

D. Karshan. *Conceptual Art and Conceptual Aspects,* Farleigh Dickinson University, 1970

J. Kastner, ed. *Land and Environmental Art*, Phaidon, London, 1998

R. Katz. *Naked By the Window: The Fatal Marriage of Carl Andre and Ana Mendieta*, Atlantic Monthly Press, New York, NY, 1990

B. Kedar & R. Werblowsky, eds. *Sacred Space: Shrine, City, Land,* New York University Press, Albany, NY, 1998

S. Kemal & I. Gaskell, eds. *Landscape, natural beauty and the arts*, Cambridge University Press, Cambridge, 1993

M. Kemp. "Doing what comes naturally: morphogenesis and the limits of the genetic code", *Art Journal,* 55, 1, Spring 1996

G. Kepes, ed. *Arts of the Environment*, Brazillier, New York, NY, 1972

N. Khan. "Beating nature", *Art Express*, 25, Mch, 1986

P. King *et al.* "Colour in Sculpture", *Studio International*, 177, 907, 1969

C. Kino. "Andy Goldsworthy: Galerie Lelong", *Art News*, 95, 10, Nov, 1996

M. Kirby. *Happenings*, Dutton, New York, NY, 1966

C. Knight: *Art of the Sixties and Seventies: The Panza Collection*, Rizzoli, New York, NY, 1987

N. Konstam: *Sculpture: The Art and the Practice*, Collins, London, 1984

D. Kozinska. "Stones in motion: show of Andy Goldsworthy's work gives a preview of colossal rock arch coming here soon across the Atlantic", *The Gazette*, Apl 18, 1998

R. Kostelanetz. *The Theatre of Mixed Means*, Dial, New York, NY, 1968

—. *On Innovative Performance(s)*, McFarland, Jefferson, NC, 1994

R.E. Krauss. "Richard Serra: Sculpture Redrawn", *Artforum*, May, 1972

—. "Sense and Sensibility: Reflection on Post '60s Sculpture", *Artforum*, 12, Nov, 1973

—. *Passages in Modern Sculpture,* Thames & Hudson, London, 1977

—. "Sculpture in the Expanded Field", *October*, 8, Spring, 1979

—. *Eva Hesse*, Whitechapel Art Gallery, London, 1979

—. *et al. Robert Morris*, Abrams, New York, NY, 1994

Z. Kraus, ed. *From Nature to Art, From Art to Nature*, Venice Biennale, Milan, 1978

D. Krug. "Ecological Design: Andy Goldsworthy, Ballet Atlantique", ArtsEdNet, Getty Education Institute for the Arts, 1997

D. Kuspitt. "Sol LeWitt", *Art in America*, 63, 5, 1975

—. "Authoritarian Abstraction", *Journal of Aesthetics and Art Criticism*, 36, 1, Autumn, 1977

—. "Robert Smithson's Drunken Boat", *Arts Magazine*, Oct, 1981

—. "Aycock's Dream Houses", *Art in America*, Sept, 1985

—. "Donald Judd", *Artforum*, 23, 5, Feb, 1985

J. Kutner. "Brice Marden, David Novros, Mark Rothko: The Urge to Communicate through Non-Imagistic Painting", *Arts Magazine*, 50, 1, Sept, 1975

S. Lacey. "Putting yin and yang into the landscape", *Electronic Telegraph*, 549, Nov 23, 1996

I. Lamaitre. "Interview with Tony Cragg", *Artefactum*, 2, Dec, 1985

T. Lang. "News from the imagination", *Issues in Architecture, Art & Design,* 3, 1, 1993

Land Marks, Edith C. Blum Art Institute, Bard College, Annadale-on-Hudson, 1984

D. Laporte. *Christo*, Pantheon Books, New York, NY, 1985

F. Laughlin. "Andy Goldsworthy, the geometrician", *Landscape Architecture,* Dec, 1997

B. Laws. "Where Art and Nature Meet", *The Telegraph Weekly*, Nov 12, 1988

C. Lebowitz. "Andy Goldsworthy", *Art in America*, Oct, 2000

D. Lee. "Serial Rights", *Art News*, 66, 8, Dec, 1967

—. "London Ecology Centre, Exhibit", *Arts Review*, 38, Jan 17, 1986

—. "Great art of the outdoors: bio-degrading sculptures", *Country Life*, 181, 35, Aug 27, 1987

—. "Pure, ephemeral spires", *The Times*, June 26, 1989

—. "Opinion: Richard Long and Hamish Fulton", *Arts Review*, July 26, 1991

—. "In profile: Goldsworthy", *Arts Review*, 47, Feb 1995

A. Legg, ed. *Sol LeWitt*, Museum of Modern Art, New York, NY, 1978

P. Leider. "Literalism and Abstraction: Frank Stella's Retrospective at the Modern", *Artforum*, 8, Apl, 1970

—. "For Robert Smithson", *Art in America*, Nov, 1973

—. *Stella Since 1970*, Fort Worth Art Museum, TX, 1978

B. Le Messurier. *Dartmoor Artists*, Halsgrove, Tiverton, Devon, 2002

K. Levin. "Robert Smithson", *Art News*, Sept, 1982

—. "Reflections on Robert Smithson's *Spiral Jetty*", *Arts Magazine*, May, 1978

G. Lewis. "No sculpture like snow sculpture", *This is London*, 1709, July 7, 1989

F. Licht. *Sculpture, 19th and 20th Centuries*, Michael Joseph, London, 1967

—. "Dan Flavin", *Artscanada*, Dec, 1968

D. Lillington. "Andy Goldsworthy: organic chemistry", *Time Out*, Apl 13, 1994

L. Lippard. "New York Letter: Apl-June, 1965", *Art International*, 9, 6, 1965

—. "New York Letter: Recent Sculpture as Escape", *Art International*, Feb, 1966a

—. "An Impure Situation", *Art International*, May 20, 1966b

—. *Ad Reinhardt*, Jewish Museum, New York, NY, 1966c

—. *Pop Art*, Oxford University Press, New York, NY, 1966d

—. "The Silent Art", *Art in America*, 55, 1, Jan-Feb, 1967a

—. "Sol LeWitt: Non-Visual Structures", *Artforum*, Apl, 1967b

—. "Tony Smith", *Art International*, Summer, 1967c

—. "Rebelliously Romantic?", *New York Times*, June 4, 1967d

—. "Escalataion in Washington", *Art International*, 12, 1, Jan, 1968

—. ed. *Surrealists on Art*, Prentice-Hall, Englewood Cliffs, NJ, 1970

—. *Tony Smith*, Thames & Hudson, London, 1972a

—. *Grids*, Philadelphia Institute of Contemporary Art, PA, 1972b

—. *Six Years: The Dematerialization of the Art Object from 1966 to 1972*, Praeger, New York, NY, 1973

—. *From the Center: feminist essays on women's art*, Dutton, New York, NY, 1976

—. *Eva Hesse*, New York University Press, New York, NY, 1976

—. *et al. Sol LeWitt*, Museum of Modern Art, New York, NY, 1978

—. "Complexities: Architectural Sculpture in Nature", *Art in America*, Feb, 1979

—. "Dinner Party", *Art in America*, Apl, 1980

—. *Ad Reinhardt*, Abrams, New York, NY, 1981

—. *Overlay*, Pantheon, New York, NY, 1983

C. Loeffier, ed. *Performance Anthology*, Contemporary Art Press, San Francisco, CA, 1979

R. Long. *Richard Long: In Conversation*, Parts 1 & 2, MW Press, Noordwijk, Holland, 1985-86

—. *Richard Long*, text by R.H. Fuchs, Thames & Hudson, London, 1986

—. *Old World New World*, Anthony d'Offay, London, 1988

—. *Richard Long: Walking in Circles,* Hayward Gallery/ Thames & Hudson, London, 1992

—. *Kicking Stones,* Anthony d'Offay Gallery, London, 1990

—. *Mountains and Water*, Anthony d'Offay, London, 1992

—. *From Time to Time*, DAP, 1997

—. *Richard Long*, Hatje Cantz, Stuttgart, 1997

—. *A Walk Across England*, Thames & Hudson, London, 1997

—. *Mirage*, Phaidon, London, 1998

—. *Selected Walks, 1979-1996*, Morning Star Press, 1999

—. *Richard Long: a Moving World,* Tate Publishing, London, 2002

—. *Richard Long – Walking the Line*, Thames and Hudson, London, 2002

M. Lothian. "Distant thunder", *Arts Review*, 40, Sept 9, 1988

O. Lowenstein. "Natural Time and Human Experience", *Sculpture*, 22, 5, June, 2003

E. Lucie-Smith. *Sculpture Since 1945*, Phaidon, London, 1987

A. Lund. "Landskab og skultur", *Landskab*, Dec, 1989

R. Lund. "Why Isn't Minimal Art Boring?", *Journal of Aesthetics and Art Criticism*, 45, 2, Winter, 1986

N. Lynton. introduction to *Tony Cragg*, Fifth Triennale India, British Council, 1982

—. *David Nash: Sculpture, 1971-90*, Serpentine Gallery, London, 1990

R. Mabey. "Art and ecology", *Modern Painters*, 3, 4, Winter, 1990

C. Maclay. "Grounds for exploration", *San Jose Mercury News*, Feb 5, 1995

D. Macmillan. "David Nash: Brancusi Joins the Garden Gang", *Art Monthly*, 65, Apl, 1983

L. MacRitchie. "Ancient Egypt", *Financial Times*, Dec 12, 1994

—. "Residency on earth", *Art in America*, 83, 4, Apl, 1995

S. Madoff. "Andy Goldsworthy", *Garden Design*, 13, June, 1994

W. Malpas. *Richard Long: The Art of Walking*, Crescent Moon, 1995/ 1998

—. *Land Art, Earthworks, Installations, Environments, Sculpture*, Crescent Moon,

1996/ 1998/ 2004

A.T. Mann. *Sacred Architecture*, Element Books, Shaftesbury, Dorset, 1993

J. van der Marck. *Wrapped Museum*, Museum of Contemporary Art, Chicago, IL, 1969

—. *Herbert Bayer*, Dartmouth College Museum, Hanover, NH, 1977

M. Marmer. "James Turrell", *Art in America*, 69, May, 1981

R. Martin. "Andy Goldsworthy: Fabian Carlsson, London", *Flash Art*, 140, May/ June, 1988

—. *The Sculpted Forest: Sculpture in the Forest of Dean*, Redcliff, Bristol, 1990

B. Matilsky. *Fragile Economies*, Rizzoli, New York, NY, 1992

D. Matless & G. Revill. "A solo ecology: the erratic art of Andy Goldsworthy", *Ecumene*, 2, 4, 1995

K. Matsui. "Column people", *Asahi Shimbun*, Feb 2, 1988

J. May. "Landscape Fired by Ice", *Landscape*, Dec, 1987

D. Mayhall. *The Minimal Tradition*, The Aldrich Museum of Contemporary Art, Ridgefield, CT, 1979

D. Marzona & E. Carlini. *Minimal Art*, Taschen, Cologne, 2004

B. McAvera. "Public art: site sensitivities", *Art Monthly*, 215, Apl, 1998

A. McGill. "Portrait of the artist as a bent twig", *London Standard*, Jan 22, 1984

D. McKinney. *Yves Klein, Brice Marden, Sigmar Polke*, Hirschl & Alder Modern, New York, NY, 1989

A. McPherson. "David Nash: interviewed by Allan McPherson", *Artscribe*, 12, June, 1978

K. McShine. *Primary Structures*, Jewish Museum, New York, NY, 1966

—. *Information*, Museum of Modern Art, New York, NY, 1970

—. *An International Survey of Recent Painting and Sculpture*, MOMA, New York, NY, 1984

W. Messer. "A tale of two festivals: Printemps de Cahors: Les rencontres d'Arles", *Art World*, 12, Winter, 1997

L. Metrick. "Disjunctions In Nature and Culture: Andy Goldsworthy", *Sculpture*, 22, 5, June, 2003

J. Meyer, ed. *Minimalism*, Phaidon, London, 2000

U. Meyer. *Conceptual Art*, Dutton, New York, NY, 1972

R. Millard. "The sculptor Andy Goldsworthy is turning part of Cumbria into a sculpture park", *The Independent*, Mch 25, 1996

D.C. Miller, ed. *Sixteen Americans*, Museum of Modern Art, New York, NY, 1959

M. Miller. *The Garden as an Art*, State University of New York Press, Albany, NY, 1993

M. Miss. *Mary Miss: Interior Works*, Bell Gallery, University of Rhode Island, Autumn, 1981

T. Mizutani. "Conversation with nature", *Bijutsu Techo,* Mch, 1988

—. "Close relation with nature", *Mainichi Shimbun*, Jan 29, 1988

R.C. Morgan. "Richard Long's Poststructural Encounters", *Arts*, 61, 6, Feb, 1987

—. *Art Into Ideas*, Cambridge, 1996

J. Morland. *New Milestones: Sculpture, Community and the Land*, Common Ground, London, 1988

H. Morphy & M. Boles, eds. *Art from the Land*, University of Washington Press, 2000

R. Morris. "Notes on Sculpture", *Artforum,* Feb, 1966, Oct, 1966, June, 1967, Apl, 1969

—. "Aligned with Nazca", *Artforum*, Oct, 1975

—. *Robert Morris: Mirror Works, 1961-1978*, Leo Castelli Gallery, New York, NY, 1979

—. *et al. Earthworks*, Seattle Art Museum, Seattle, WA, 1979

—. *Selected Works*, Contemporary Arts Museum, Houston, TX, 1981

—. *Continuous Project Altered Daily*, MIT Press, Cambridge, MA, 1993

S. Morris. "A Rhetoric of Silence: Redefinitions of Sculpture in the 1960s and 1970s", in S. Nairne, 1981

J. Morrison. "Landmatters", *British Journal of Photography*, 133, June 6, 1986

A. Morgan. "Maze and labyrinth", *Sculpture*, 14, 4, July/ Aug, 1995

D. Morse. "At Runnymede Farm, the crop is sculptures", *San Francisco*

Examiner, May 2, 1997

G. Müller. "Michael Heizer", *Arts Magazine*, Dec, 1969

—. "The Earth, Subjected To Cataclysms, Is a Cruel Master", *Arts Magazine*, Nov, 1971

A. Murphey. "White magic", *The Observer*, Dec, 1996

S. Nairne & N. Serota. *British Sculpture in the Twentieth Century*, Whitechapel Art Gallery, London, 1981

H. Nakamura. "Andy Goldsworthy and Anthony Green", *Ikebana Ryusei*, 38, Apl, 1988

D. Nash. *Fletched Over Ash*, AIR Gallery, 1978

—. "David Nash", *Aspects*, 10, Spring, 1980

—. *Stoves and Hearths*, Duke Street Gallery, London, 1982

T.A. Neff, ed. *A Quiet Revolution: British Sculpture Since 1965*, Thames & Hudson, London, 1987

B. Nemitz. *Trans Plant: Living Vegetation in Contemporary Art*, Hatje Cantz, Stuttgart, 2000

C. Nemser. "An interview with Eva Hesse", *Artforum*, May, 1970

—. "My Memories of Eva Hesse", *Feminist Art Journal*, Winter, 1973

P. Nesbitt. "At Home with Nature: Andy Goldsworthy in Scotland", *Alba*, Spring, 1989

—. "A Landscape Touched by Gold", in G. Hughes, 1990

E. Newhall. "Andy Goldsworthy", *New York Magazine*, Sept 13, 1993

M. Newman. "New Sculpture in Britain", *Art in America*, Sept, 1982

R. Nilsen. "Show only a nibble of Goldsworthy art", *Arizona Republic*, Sept 25, 1994

M. Nixon. *Eva Hesse*, MIT Press, Cambridge, MA, 2002

P. Noever. *Donald Judd: Architecture*, Hatje Cantz, Stuttgart, 2003

I. Noguchi. *A Sculptor's World*, Harper & Row, New York, NY, 1968

J. Norrie. "Andy Goldsworthy", *Arts Review*, July 3, 1987

B. Oakes, ed. *Sculpting the Environment*, Van Nostrand Reinhold, New York, NY, 1995

P. Oakes. "The Incomparable Andy Goldsworthy", *Country Living*, 48, Dec, 1989

S. Oksenhorn. "Art, naturally", *The Aspen Times*, 116, 50, Dec 9, 1995

W. Oliver. "A natural at work", *Yorkshire Post*, Feb 24, 1986

R. Onoratio. "Illusive Spaces: The Art of Mary Miss", *Artforum*, Dec, 1978

—. *Mary Miss - Perimeters/ Pavilions/ Decoys*, Nassau County Museum, 1979

D. Oppenheim. *Dennis Oppenheim*, Musée d'Art Contemporain, Montréal, 1978

—. *Selected Works, 1967-1990*, Abrams, New York, NY, 1992

E. Osaka. *Andy Goldsworthy: Mountain and Coast: Autumn Into Winter*, Gallery Takagi, Nagoya, 1987

P. Osborne, ed. *Conceptual Art*, Phaidon, London, 2002

W. Packer. "Andy Goldsworthy's Transient Touch", *Sculpture*, July, 1989

—. "Sculpture from the countryside", *Financial Times*, July 7, 1987

T. Padon. "New York, New York", *Sculpture*, 13, 1, Jan/ Feb, 1994

A.C. Papadakis, ed. *British and American Art: The Uneasy Dialectic, Art & Design*, 3, 9/1, Academy Group, London, 1987

—. ed. *Abstract Art and the Rediscovery of the Spiritual, Art & Design*, 3, 5/6, Academy Group, London, 1987

—. ed. *The New Romantics, Art & Design*, 4, 11/12, Academy Group, London, 1988

—. *et al*, eds. *New Art*, Academy Group, London, 1991

R. Parker & G. Pollock. *Old Mistresses: Women, Art an Ideology*, Routledge & Kegan Paul, London, 1981

—. *Framing Feminism*, Pandora Press, London, 1987

D. Parr. "City focus: St. Louis: 'a different kind of energy'", *Art News*, 95, 3, Mch, 1996

J. Partridge. "Forest work", *Craft*, 81, July/ Aug, 1986

T. Passes. "Rain sun snow hail mist calm", *Venue Magazine*, Sept 11, 1986

A. Patrizio. "Cube garden: sculpture at the Edinburgh Festival 1990", *Arts Review*, 42, July 27, 1990

P. Patton. "Robert Morris and the Fire Next Time", *Art News,* 82, 10, Dec, 1983

E. Pavese, ed. *Christo: Surrounded Islands*, Abrams, New York, NY, 1986

N. Pennick. *Mazes and Labyrinths*, Hale, London, 1990

C. Peres. "Arte: collaborare con la natura, *Casa Vogue*, 228, Mch, 1991

J. Perreault. "A Minimal Future? Union-Made: Report on a Phenomenon", *Arts Magazine*, 41, Mch, 1967

J. Perrone. "Seeing Through Boxes", *Artforum*, 15, Nov, 1976

K. Petersen & J.J. Wilson: *Women Artists: Recognition and Reappraisal from the Early Middle Ages to the Twentieth Century*, Women's Press, London, 1978

C. Peterson. "Inside the Goldsworthy installation", *Aspen Times*, Dec 16, 1995

P. Piguet. "Vassivière: une île pour la sculpture: an island for the sculpture", *Cimaise*, 41, 228, Jan, 1994

R. Pincus-Witten. *Postminimalism*, Out of London Press, New York, NY, 1977

—. *Entries: Maximalism*, Out of London Press, London, 1983

—. *Post-Minimalism into Maximalism*, UMI Research Press, Ann Arbor, MI, 1987

J. Poetter. *Donald Judd*, Cantz, Stuttgart, 1989

G. Pollock. *Vision and Difference: femininity, feminism and histories of art*, Routledge, London, 1988

L. Ponti. "Tony Cragg", *Domus*, 611, Nov, 1980

F. Popper. *Art, Action and Participation*, New York University Press, New York, NY, 1975

J.C. Powys. *Maiden Castle*, Cassell, London, 1937

—. *A Glastonbury Romance*, Macdonald, London, 1955

—. *Wolf Solent*, Penguin, London, 1964

—. *Autobiography*, Macdonald, London, 1967

A. Price. "A Conversation With Alice Aycock", *Architectural Design*, Apl, 1980

G. Prince. "With mud on their hands, growth, decay and the movement of change", *World Magazine*, Jan, 1991

J. Prinz. *Art Discourse*, Rutgers University Press, New Brunswick, NJ, 1991

S. Prokopoff: *A Romantic Minimalism*, Institute of Contemporary Art, Philadelphia, PA, 1967

J. Prown *et al*. *Discovered Lands, Invented Pasts*, Yale University Press, New Haven, CT, 1992

E. Rankin. "Popularising public sculpture in Britain: from landscape gardens to forest trails", *de Arte*, 53, Apl, 1996

C. Ratcliff. *In the Realm of the Monochrome*, Renaissance Society, University of Chicago, Chicago, IL, 1979

—. "The Compleat Smithson", *Art in America*, Jan, 1980

—. *Out of the Box*, Allworth Press, London, 2001

B. Redhead. *The Inspiration of Landscape: Artists in National Parks*, Phaidon, London, 1989

M. Regimbald. "L'homme qui plantait des arches [The man who planted arches]", *Espace*, 45, Autumn, 1998

W. Reh & C. Steenbergen. *Architecture and Landscape*, Prestel Publishing, 1996

K.J. Reiger, ed. *The Spiritual Image in Modern Art*, Theosophical Publishing House, Wheaton, IL, 1987

B. Reise. "'Untitled 1969': A Footnote on Art and Minimal Stylehood", *Studio International*, 179, 910, Apl, 1969

T. Rettig. "Contextualizing the work of Reinhard Reitzenstein", *Espace*, 25, Sept, 1993

N. Reynolds. "Lottery aid elevates sheep pens to fine art", *Electronic Telegraph*, 436, July 26, 1996

H. Risatti. "The Sculpture of Alice Aycock", *Woman's Art Journal*, Summer, 1985

A.C. Ritchie: *Sculpture in the Twentieth Century*, MOMA, New York, NY, 1952

J. Roberts. *Postmodernism, Politics and Art*, Manchester University Press, Manchester, 1990

C. Robins. "Object, Structure or Sculpture: Where Are We?", *Arts Magazine*, 40, 9, 1966

—. "Empty Paintings", *SoHo Weekly News*, Apl 22, 1976

—. *The Pluralist Era: American Art, 1968-1981*, Harper & Row, New York, NY, 1984

P. Rodaway. *Sensuous Geographies*, Routledge, London, 1994

B. Rose. "New York Letter", *Art International*, Feb 15, 1964

—. "Looking at American Sculpture", *Artforum*, 3, Feb, 1965a

—. "ABC Art", *Art in America*, 53, 5, Nov, 1965b

—. *A New Aesthetic*, Washington Gallery of Modern Art, Washington, DC, 1967

—. *American Art Since 1900*, Thames & Hudson, London, 1967

—. *American Painting*, Skira/ Rizzoli International, New York, NY, 1986

—. *Robert Morris*, Corcoran Gallery, Washington, DC, 1990

H. Rosenberg. *The De-Definition of Art*, Horizon Press, New York, NY, 1972

R. Rosenblum. "Notes on Sol LeWitt", in A. Legg, 1978

—. *Modern Painting and the Northern Romantic Tradition*, Thames & Hudson, London, 1978

—. "Romanticism and Retrospective: An Interview with Robert Rosenblum", in A. Papadakis, 1988

—. "A postscript: some recent neo-romantic mutations", *Art Journal*, 52, 2, Summer, 1993

C. Ross. *Star Axis*, University of New Mexico Press, Albuqerque, NM, 1992

S. Ross. "Gardens, earthworks, and environmental art", in S. Kemal, 1993

—. *What Gardens Mean*, University of Chicago Press, Chicago, IL, 1998

M. Roth. "Robert Smithson on Duchamp", *Artforum*, Oct, 1969

—. ed. *The Amazing Decade: Women and Performance Art in America 1970-80*, Astro Artz, Los Angeles, CA, 1983

M. Rothko. *Mark Rothko in New York*, Guggenheim Museum, New York, NY, 1994

R. Rubinstein. "Andy Goldsworthy: Galerie Lelong", *Art News*, 92, 10, Dec, 1993

M. Ryan, ed. *Gravity and Grace: The Changing Condition of Sculpture, 1965-1975*, Hay-ward Gallery, London, 1993

A. Saalfield. *Mary Miss*, Fogg Art Museum, Cambridge, MA, 1980

T. Sakurai. "Here comes the gold light'. *Ikebana Ryusei*, 10, Jan, 1988

—. "Goldsworthy with snow", *Ikebana Ryusei*, 10, Feb, 1988

I. Sandler. *American Art of the 1960s,* Harper & Row, New York, NY, 1988

—. *Art of the Postmodern Era: From the 1960s to the Early 1990s*, Harper-Collins, London, 1997

P. Schjeldahl. *Art in Our Time: The Saatchi Collection*, Lund Humphries, London, 1984

P. Schuck. "Interview: Earth, Water, Wind", *Contemporanea*, Apl, 1990

W. Scott. "In the gallery", *New York Post,* Dec 21, 1996

P. Selz. *Directions in Kinetic Sculpture*, University of California Press, Berkeley, CA, 1966

—. *Art in Our Times: A Pictorial History 1890-1980*, Thames & Hudson, London, 1982

A. Seymour. *The New Art*, Hayward Gallery, London, 1972

—. "Walking in Circles", in R. Long, *Walking in Circles*

—. "Old World New World", in R. Long, *Old World New World*

E. Shanes: *Constantin Brancusi*, Abbeville, New York, NY, 1989

G. Shapiro. *Earthworks: Robert Smithson and After Babel*, University of California Press, Berkeley, CA, 1995

W. Sharp *et al. Earth Art*, Andrew Dickson White Museum of Art, Cornell University, Ithaca, NY, 1969

A. Sherman. "Bound to earth", *Metro*, Feb 23, 1995

N. Shulman. "Monday at the North Pole", *Arts Review*, June 2, 1989

N. Sinden. "Interview: Art in Nature: Andy Goldsworthy", *Resurgence*, 129, Aug, 1988

H.J. Smagula. *Currents: Contemporary Directions in the Visual Arts*, Prentice-Hall, Englewood Cliffs, NJ, 1983

B. Smith. *Fluorescent Light, etc, from Dan Flavin*, National Gallery of Canada, Ottawa, 1969

—. *Donald Judd*, National Gallery of Canada, Ottawa, 1975

D. Smith. *Sculpture and Drawings*, ed. J. Merkert, Prestel-Verlag, Munich, 1986

R. Smith. "Sol LeWitt", *Artforum*, Jan, 1975

—. "Review", *Artforum*, Dec, 1975

—. "De Maria: Elements", *Art in America*, May, 1978

—. review, *New York Times*, Sept, 2004

R. Smithson. "Entropy and the New Monuments", *Artforum*, 4, 10, June, 1966

—. "Incidents of Mirror-Travel in the Yucatan", *Artforum*, Sept, 1967

—. The Monuments of Passaic", *Artforum*, Dec, 1967

—. "Toward the Development of an Air Terminal Site", *Artforum*, Summer, 1967

—. "A Museum of Language in the Vicinity of Art", *Art International*, 12, 3, Mch, 1968

—. *The Writings of Robert Smithson*, ed. N. Holt, New York University Press, New York, NY, 1979

—. *Robert Smithson*, ed. J. Flam, University of California Press, Berkeley, CA, 1996

—. *Robert Smithson: A Collection of Writings*, Pierogi Galery New York, NY, 1997

T. Sokolowski *et al. Robert Morris*, New York University Press, New York, NY, 1989

A. Sondheim, ed. *Post-Movement Art in America*, Dutton, New York, NY, 1977

A. Sonfist. *Alan Sonfist*, Neuberger Museum, New York, NY, 1978

—. ed. *Art in the Land: A Critical Anthology of Environmental Art*, Dutton, New York, NY, 1983

W. Spies. *The Running Fence Project, Christo*, Abrams, New York, NY, 1977

N. Stapen. "Bringing nature inside the museum", *Boston Sunday Globe*, Mch 29, 1992

J. Stathatos. "Andy Goldsworthy's Evidences", *Creative Camera*, 255, Mch, 1986

J. Steele. "In a natural mould", *Farmers Weekly*, May 13, 1988

F. Stella. *Working Space*, Harvard University Press, Cambridge, MA, 1986

N. Stewart. "Richard Long, Lines of Thought: A Conversation with Nick Stewart", *Circa*, Nov, 1984

K. Stiles & P. Selz, eds. *Theories & Documents of Contemporary Art: A Sourcebook of Artists' Writings*, University of California Press, Berkeley, CA, 1996

S.L. Stoops. *Andy Goldsworthy: Breakdown*, Rose Art Museum, 1992

W.J. Strachan. *Open Air Sculpture in Britain*, Zwemmer, London, 1984

E. Suderburg, ed. *Space, Site, Intervention*, University of Minnesota Press, Minneapolis, MN, 2000

T. Sultan. *Inability To Endure or Deny the World: Representation and Text In the Work of Robert Morris*, Corcoran Gallery, Washington, DC, 1990

G. Sutton. "Land art", *Landskab*, Dec, 1989

D. Sylvester. *About Modern Art*, Chatto & Windus, London, 1996

L. Talbot. "Fleeting beauty from the elements forger", *Hampstead and Highgate Express*, Feb 12, 1988

H. Teague. "Good as Goldsworthy", *Aspen Magazine*, 1996

M. Thomas. "Monkeys and guerrillas", *Photofile*, 35, May, 1992

J. Thym. "An artist by nature" *Oakland Tribune*, Feb 8, 1995

G. Tiberghien. *Land Art*, Art Data, London, 1995

S. Tillim. "Earthworks and the New Picturesque", *Artforum*, Dec, 1968

C. Tomkins. *Post- to Neo-: The Art World of the 1980s*, Penguin, London, 1989

M. Treib. "Frame, moment and sequence: the photographic book and the designed land-scape", *Journal of Garden History*, 15, 2, Summer, 1995

M. Tromble. "A conversation with Andy Goldsworthy", *ArtWeek*, 23, 19, July 9, 1992

—. "A conversation with Robin Lasser", *ArtWeek*, 24, 20, Oct 21, 1993

E. Tsai. *Robert Smithson Unearthed*, Columbia University Press, New York, NY, 1991

M. Tuchman. *American Sculpture of the Sixties*, Los Angeles County Museum of Art, 1967

P. Tuchman. "Minimalism and Critical Response", *Artforum*, 15, 9, May, 1977

—. "Background of a Minimalist: Carl Andre", *Artforum*, Mch, 1978

—. "Minimalism", *Three Decades: The Oliver-Hoffmann Collection*, Museum of Contemporary Art, Chicago, IL, 1988

M. Tucker. *Robert Morris*, New York, NY, 1970

W. Tucker. *The Language of Sculpture*, Thames & Hudson, London, 1974

B. Tufnell & A. Wilson. *Hamish Fulton: Walking Journey,* Tate Publishing, London, 2002

C. Turnbull. "Beautiful Behaviour: The Photoworks of Andy Goldsworthy", *The Green Book*, 2, 6, 1987

J. Turrell. *Mapping Spaces*, Peter Blum, New York, NY, 1987.

—. interview, in B. Oakes, 1995

G. de Vries, ed. *On Art: Artists' Writings on the Changed Notion of Art After 1965*, Cologne, 1974

A.M. Wagner. *Three Artists (Three Women): Modernism and the Art of Hesse, Krasner and O'Keeffe*, University of California Press, Berkeley, CA, 1996

D. Waldman. *Carl Andre*, Guggenheim Museum, New York, NY, 1970a

—. "Holding the Floor", *Art News*, Oct, 1970b

—. *Robert Ryman*, Guggenheim Museum, New York, NY, 1972

J. Watkins. "In the artist's studio: Andy Goldsworthy: Touching North", *Art International*, 9 Winter, 1989

M. Webster. "Andy Goldsworthy at San Jose Museum of Art", *ArtWeek*, 26, 4, Apl, 1995

S. Webster. "Art in the Woods [Andy Goldsworthy]", *Arts & Activities*, Sept, 2000

U. Weilacher *et al. Between Landscape Architecture and Land Art,* Birkhauser Verlag AG, 1999

L. Weiner. *Lawrence Weiner, Works,* Anatol AV und Filmproduktion Hamburg, 1977

Welsh Sculpture Trust. *Sculpture in a Country Park*, Welsh Sculpture Trust, 1983

C. West. "From genesis to box", *Modern Painters*, 5, 4, Winter, 1992

D. Wheeler. *Art Since Mid-Century: 1945 to the Present*, Thames & Hudson, London, 1991

P. Whitaker. "Andy Goldsworthy", *London Magazine*, 34, 10, Jan, 1995

J. White. *The Birth and Rebirth of Pictorial Space*, Faber, London, 1981

O. Wick *et al. James Turrell*, Turske & Turske Gallery, Zurich, 1990

G. Widdicombe. "Andy Goldsworthy: between a rock and a hard place", *The Independent*, Apl 13, 1994

A. Wildermuth. *Richard Long*, Galerie Buchmann, Basel, 1985

A. Wilding: *Alison Wilding*, with M. Tooby, Tate Gallery, St Ives, Cornwall, 1994

R. Williams. *After Modern Sculpture: Art in the United States and Europe 1965-70,* Manchester University Press, Manchester, 2000

A. Windsor, ed. *British Sculptors of the 20th Century*, Ashgate, Aldershot, Hants., 2003

C. van Winkel. "The Crooked Path, Patterns of Kinetic Energy", *Parkett*, 33, 1992

R. Wishart. "Andy Goldsworthy: art without additives", *Scotsman*, Apl 16, 1994

K. Withers. "Is it art?", *Venue Magazine*, Dec, 1989

G. Woods *et al*, eds. *Art Without Boundaries*, Thames & Hudson, London, 1972

M. Wortz. *Light and Space*, Whitney Museum of American Art, New York, NY, 1980

S. Wrede & W. Adams. *Denatured Visions: Landscape and Culture in the 20th Century*, Abrams, New York, NY, 1991

S. Yard. *Christo: Oceanfront*, Princeton University Press, Princeton, NJ, 1975

—. *Sitings*, La Jolla Museum of Contemporary Art, La Jolla, CA, 1986

M. Yule. "Andy Goldsworthy, a Lake District photowork", *National Art-Collections Fund Review*, 88, 1992

WEBSITES

Andy Goldsworthy, Sheepfolds site: <www.sheepfolds.org>
Andy Goldsworthy, *Rivers and Tides* DVD
    <www.skyline.uk.com/riversandtides>
Robert Smithson <www.robertsmithson.com>
Walter de Maria <www.lightningfield.org>
Christo <www.christojeanneclaude.net>
James Turrell <www.rodencrater.org>
Mary Miss <www.marymiss.com>
Hamish Fulton <www.hamish-fulton.com>
Chris Drury <www.chrisdrury.co.uk>
Donald Judd <www.chinati.org>
Richard Long <www.richardlong.org>
Richard Long Newsletter <therichardlongnewsletter.org>

Earthworks <www.earthworks.org>
The Artists: <www.the-artists.org>
Sculpture at Goodwood, CASS: <www.sculpture.org.uk>
Crescent Moon Publishing: <www.crescentmoon.org.uk>